Get the eBooks FREE!

(PDF, ePub, Kindle, and liveBook all included)

We believe that once you buy a book from us, you should be able to read it in any format we have available. To get electronic versions of this book at no additional cost to you, purchase and then register this book at the Manning website.

Go to https://www.manning.com/freebook and follow the instructions to complete your pBook registration.

That's it!
Thanks from Manning!

Learn Azure
in a Month of Lunches

Learn Azure in a Month of Lunches

IAIN FOULDS

MANNING
SHELTER ISLAND

For online information and ordering of this and other Manning books, please visit www.manning.com. The publisher offers discounts on this book when ordered in quantity. For more information, please contact

Special Sales Department
Manning Publications Co.
20 Baldwin Road
PO Box 761
Shelter Island, NY 11964
Email: orders@manning.com

Manning Publications Co.
20 Baldwin Road
PO Box 761
Shelter Island, NY 11964

Development editor: Kevin Harreld
Technical development editor: Mike Shepard
Technical proofreader: Karsten Strøbaek
Review editor: Aleksandar Dragosavljević
Project editor: Tiffany Taylor
Copy editor: Tiffany Taylor
Proofreader: Elizabeth Martin
Typesetter: Dottie Marsico
Cover designer: Leslie Haimes

ISBN 9781617295171
Printed and bound by CPI Group (UK) Ltd, Croydon, CR0 4YY
1 2 3 4 5 6 7 8 9 10 – DP – 23 22 21 20 19 18

To the ABCs of my life:
Abigail, Bethany, and Charlotte

brief contents

PART 4 THE COOL STUFF 267

contents

preface

When I first started to work with Azure, the number of available services was almost overwhelming. I knew I should pay attention to security, performance, redundancy, and scale, but I didn't know how to apply over a decade of large-scale server administration to the world of cloud computing. Over time, I began to learn about the various Azure services that provide those key components; these services rarely work in isolation, but I didn't know the best way to integrate them or how to decide which service to use for each task. This book is a way to explain to my past self, and many others I've spoken to over the years, how to quickly understand the core services in Azure and make them work together.

This book is over 350 pages long, yet it barely scratches the surface of what you can do in Azure! To help give you a solid understanding of the concepts needed to be successful as you build solutions in Azure, I had to choose which topics to write about. The book doesn't cover all 100 or more Azure services, and it doesn't go into exhaustive detail about the services that are included. Instead, I focus on the core areas in some of the primary services, show examples of how to securely connect everything, and introduce the possibilities of what you can build in Azure.

Cloud computing is constantly changing. There are no three- or four-year release cycles and large update deployments. I think it's a great time to be building solutions and writing code; there's always an opportunity to learn something new and improve yourself. I hope you learn to run great applications in Azure and enjoy exploring all the available services.

acknowledgments

Many people behind the scenes at Manning Publications helped publish this book. A special thanks to Mike Stephens for having the initial vision to get this project started, and to Kevin Harreld for keeping me moving in the right direction. Thank you to publisher Marjan Bace and everyone on the editorial and production teams. My thanks to the technical peer reviewers led by Aleksandar Dragosavljević—Al Pezewski, Andrea Cosentino, Bhaskar V. Karambelkar, Dave Corun, Frank Quintana, Jean-Sebastien Gervais, Joe Justesen, Marco Salafia, Michael Bright, Mike Jensen, Nikander and Margriet Bruggeman, Peter Kreyenhop, Rob Loranger, Robert Walsh, Roman Levchenko, Sushil Sharma, Sven Stumpf, and Thilo Käsemann—and the forum contributors. And finally, on the technical side, thanks to Mike Shepard, who served as the book's technical editor; and Karsten Strøbaek, who served as the book's technical proofreader.

I don't believe in luck or chance; rather, I think you should take an opportunity when it's presented to you. Many thanks to David Tolkov and Tim Teebken, who gave me opportunities to develop into someone capable of writing this book. This was an after-hours project outside of my Microsoft day job, but thanks to Jean-Paul Connock for his support. Go Blues!

Thanks to Rick Claus for supporting the need for strong technical documentation in Azure, and to Marsh Macy and Neil Peterson for their personal support and guidance in writing this book. Maybe now I'll have time to work on that school bus.

about this book

This book is designed to give you a solid foundation to be successful as a developer or IT engineer in Azure. You learn about both Infrastructure as a Service (IaaS) and Platform as a Service (PaaS) solutions, along with when to use each approach. As you work through the chapters, you learn how to plan appropriately for availability and scale, keep security in mind, and consider cost and performance. By the end of the book, you should be able to integrate upcoming technologies such as containers and Kubernetes, artificial intelligence and machine learning (AI + ML), and the Internet of Things (IoT).

When it comes to how you build and run your applications and services, Azure lets you choose the operating system, application tools, and platform you're most comfortable with. This book mostly discusses non-Microsoft technologies such as Linux, Python, and Node.js. Command examples use the Azure CLI, not Azure PowerShell. These were conscious decisions to show you that using Azure doesn't mean you have to use Windows Server, IIS, or ASP.NET.

As you work in the cloud, that often means working across platforms and learning new topics—which is another reason for showing non-Microsoft technologies and platforms. I wanted to introduce you to some of these new areas as you progress through this book, before you encounter them in the real world! Throughout the book, I've tried to teach you the concepts and steps needed to integrate Azure services, so you can switch platforms or languages as you wish and have the same knowledge apply.

Roadmap

The book is organized into 4 parts and 21 chapters:

- Part 1 covers some of the core Azure infrastructure and platform services: virtual machines, web apps, storage, and networking.
- Part 2 dives into how to provide high availability and redundancy: templates, availability sets and zones, load balancers, autoscaling, distributed databases, and traffic routing. By the end of chapter 12, you should have a solid knowledge of how to build high-performance, distributed applications in Azure.
- Part 3 covers security aspects such as backup and recovery, encryption, digital key management, and updates. By the time you've completed chapter 16, you'll be well on the way to secure, stable applications in Azure.
- To finish up the book, in part 4 we have a little fun and explore some new areas of computing such as artificial intelligence and machine learning (AI + ML), containers, Kubernetes, the Internet of Things (IoT), and serverless computing. These chapters introduce areas of Azure that give you a glimpse of what the future of production applications could look like.

Other than part 4, which is aptly named "The Cool Stuff," you should try to work through the book's chapters in order. You don't work on the same project over successive chapters, but each chapter builds on earlier theory and hands-on lab examples.

Chapter 1 guides you through creating a free trial account in Azure, which is enough to complete the hands-on lab exercises in each chapter. I also provide a little more background on Azure and how to find additional help along the way. I mention it a few times in the book (maybe I'm a little biased!), but http://docs.microsoft.com/azure is the best place to go for additional documentation and support in any areas of Azure that interest you.

About the examples and source code

This book contains many examples of source code, both in numbered listings and inline with normal text. In both cases, source code is formatted in a `fixed-width font like this` to separate it from ordinary text.

In many cases, the original source code has been reformatted; we've added line breaks and reworked indentation to accommodate the available page space in the book. Additionally, comments in the source code have often been removed from the listings when the code is described in the text. Code annotations accompany many of the listings, highlighting important concepts.

This book's source code, along with accompanying scripts, templates, and supporting resources, can be found at www.manning.com/books/learn-azure-in-a-month-of-lunches and on the book's GitHub repo at https://github.com/fouldsy/azure-mol-samples.

All the hands-on exercises can be completed in the Azure portal and with the Azure Cloud Shell, a browser-based interactive shell for both the Azure CLI and Azure

PowerShell. There are no tools to install on your machine, and you can use any computer and OS you wish, provided it supports a modern web browser.

The Azure portal often implements minor changes. I've tried to minimize the number of portal screenshots, but don't worry if what you see is a little different than what's shown in the book. The required parameters are usually the same—the layout may just be different. If there are new options in the portal that I don't specifically call out in an exercise or lab, it's usually safe to accept the defaults that are provided.

If you work outside of the Azure Cloud Shell, take care with the command examples. Windows-based shells such as PowerShell and CMD treat line breaks and continuations differently than *nix-based shells such as the Azure Cloud Shell. Many of the command examples run across multiple lines. Commands are shown with a backslash (\) character to indicate the command continues on the next line, as in the following example:

```
az resource group create \
    --name azuremol \
    --location eastus
```

You don't have to type in those backslash characters, but doing so may make long commands more readable on your screen. If you choose to work locally on your computer with a Windows shell, you can use a backtick (`) instead of a backslash. For example, in a PowerShell or CMD shell with Python for Windows installed, change the previous command as follows:

```
az resource group create `
    --name azuremol `
    --location eastus
```

This may seem confusing at first, but I follow this convention in the book because the official documentation at http://docs.microsoft.com/azure uses this format. Azure CLI commands, which are what we mostly use in this book, assume a *nix-based shell and so use a backslash character. Azure PowerShell commands assume a Windows-based shell and so use a backtick. This will quickly make sense, and you'll find it's easy to transition between the two. If you're new to working across platforms, it can be a fun little gotcha!

Book forum

Purchase of *Learn Azure in a Month of Lunches* includes free access to a private web forum run by Manning Publications where you can make comments about the book, ask technical questions, and receive help from the author and from other users. To access the forum, go to https://forums.manning.com/forums/learn-azure-in-a-month-of-lunches. You can also learn more about Manning's forums and the rules of conduct at https://forums.manning.com/forums/about.

Manning's commitment to our readers is to provide a venue where a meaningful dialogue between individual readers and between readers and the author can take place. It is not a commitment to any specific amount of participation on the part of the author, whose contribution to the forum remains voluntary (and unpaid). We suggest you try asking the author some challenging questions, lest his interest stray! The forum and the archives of previous discussions will be accessible from the publisher's website as long as the book is in print.

about the author

IAIN FOULDS is a senior content developer at Microsoft, currently writing technical documentation for Azure container services, virtual machines, and scale sets. Previously, Iain was a premier field engineer with Microsoft for virtualization technologies such as Azure, Hyper-V, and System Center Virtual Machine Manager. With over 15 years of experience in IT, most of it in operations and services, Iain embraced virtualization early with VMware and has helped build and teach others about cloud computing for years.

Iain, originally from England, has lived in the United States for more than a decade and currently resides just outside of Seattle with his wife and two young children, to whom this book is dedicated. He is a fan of football (unfortunately called "soccer" where he lives) and also enjoys ice hockey and almost any form of motor racing. Outside of computing, Iain's interests include performance and classic cars, aviation photography, and claiming to play the guitar. He's also a big model train nerd, regularly attending and volunteering at shows and events throughout the Pacific Northwest.

Part 1

Azure core services

To build the next great application, you need a solid understanding of the basic resources in Azure. Things like storage and networking may not be the coolest things to look at, but they're central to much that you run in Azure. Before you can start to get into redundant, multi-instance virtual machines or Azure web apps, it helps to see the available options and management tasks for a single instance. This approach lets you learn about the differences and similarities between the IaaS approach of VMs and the PaaS approach of web apps. In chapters 1–5, we'll explore VMs and web apps, and core storage and virtual networking features.

1 Before you begin

Azure is one of the largest public cloud computing providers for services such as virtual machines (VMs), containers, server-less computing, and machine learning. We won't dive into all 100 or more Azure services in this book, but you're going to learn about the core services and features that cover most of what you need to start building and running solutions in Azure. We'll look at a common example of how to build and run a web application, and you'll see how to use some of the core infrastructure and platform services that can make your job easier.

With Azure, you don't need a magic wand to predict how many servers or how much storage you need over the next three years. No more delays as you gain budget approval, wait for new hardware to ship, and then rack, install, and configure everything. You don't need to worry about what software versions or libraries are installed as you write your code.

Instead, select a button and create whatever resources are needed. You only pay for each minute those resources are running, or the amount of storage space or network bandwidth used. When you don't need the resources anymore, you can power down or delete them. If you suddenly need to increase the amount of compute power by a factor of 10, select a button, wait a couple of minutes, and it's there. And all of this is managed by someone else, freeing you to focus on your applications and customers.

1.1 Is this book for you?

The IT industry is in a bit of a transition period when it comes to job titles. You may refer to yourself as an IT pro, a software developer, a system administrator, or a DevOps engineer. If you want to learn the core skills needed to build and run secure, highly available applications in the cloud, you're in the right place. In generic terms, you probably fall into the IT operations or development side of things. The truth is, there's a lot of crossover, especially when working in cloud computing. It's important to understand the core infrastructure and platform services to build and run applications that best serve your customers.

This book introduces some of these core concepts in Azure and provides the skills needed to make informed decisions. You should have some prior experience with VMs and know the basics of networking and storage. You should be able to create a basic website, and understand what an SSL certificate or a database is. We'll take a quick look at new and upcoming technologies such as containers, the Internet of Things, machine learning, artificial intelligence, and server-less computing. Both self-described "developers" and "IT pros" should find some neat new areas to learn about!

1.2 How to use this book

I like sandwiches, so lunch is a great time for me to play with cool new technology. You may be a night owl who has some extra time in the evening, or you may be an early-morning person (what's wrong with you?!) who can work through a chapter at breakfast. There's no right or wrong time to learn, but if you can set aside about 45 minutes, you should be able to read a chapter and complete its exercises. Each chapter covers something new, so give yourself time to absorb each day's lesson.

1.2.1 The main chapters

The book is broken into four parts, which is convenient if you believe there are four weeks in a month:

- Part 1 (chapters 1–5) covers some of the core Azure resources. If nothing else, try to follow these chapters in order to have a solid understanding. You can then focus on the other chapters that most excite you.
- Part 2 (chapters 6–12) covers availability and scale. You'll learn how to automatically scale resources in and out, load-balance traffic, and handle maintenance events without downtime. To learn about running highly available applications on a global scale, this section is for you.
- Part 3 (chapters 13–16) is for the security geeks. It covers things like how to encrypt VMs, store SSL certificates in a secure vault, and back up and restore your data.
- Part 4 (chapters 17–21) covers a mix of cool areas to give a taste of what Azure can do for you and your customers. We'll look at automation, containers, the Internet of Things, and server-less computing. Pick something that interests you, and have fun!

1.2.2 *Try it now*

Do you just want to read, or do you want to roll up your sleeves and play with Azure? Throughout the book are little tasks that let you quickly try something new. If you have the time, try them. Most of the hands-on time comes in a lab exercise at the end of the chapter, but there's a lot of value in breaking up the reading by trying new concepts along the way.

1.2.3 *Hands-on labs*

Each chapter wraps up with a hands-on lab exercise. Some chapters, like this one, have a lab exercise in the middle of the chapter. These lab exercises are where you learn how all the pieces of Azure come together and can start to build some mental muscle memory. Grab your keyboard and mouse, and begin building something awesome!

1.2.4 *Source code and supplementary materials*

This book's source code, along with accompanying scripts, templates, and supporting resources, can be found at www.manning.com/books/learn-azure-in-a-month-of-lunches and on the book's GitHub repo at https://github.com/fouldsy/azure-mol-samples. In addition, you can participate in the book's forum at https://forums.manning.com/forums/learn-azure-in-a-month-of-lunches.

1.3 *Creating your lab environment*

This book isn't heavy on concepts and architecture—it's more about hands-on time with the Azure platform. To do this, you need an Azure account.

1.3.1 *Creating a free Azure account*

Azure offers a free trial account that's good for 30 days and provides up to $200 of free credit. This free credit should be enough to make it through all the chapters and exercises, with room to explore a little and have fun along the way! There are also many Azure services and features that remain free, even after your trial period ends.

> **Try it now**
> Follow along with the steps in this section to create your free Azure account.

1. Open your web browser to https://azure.microsoft.com/free, and select the Start Free button, as shown in figure 1.1.
2. When prompted, sign in to your Microsoft account. If you need a Microsoft account or want to create a new one, choose the Create a New Microsoft Account link.

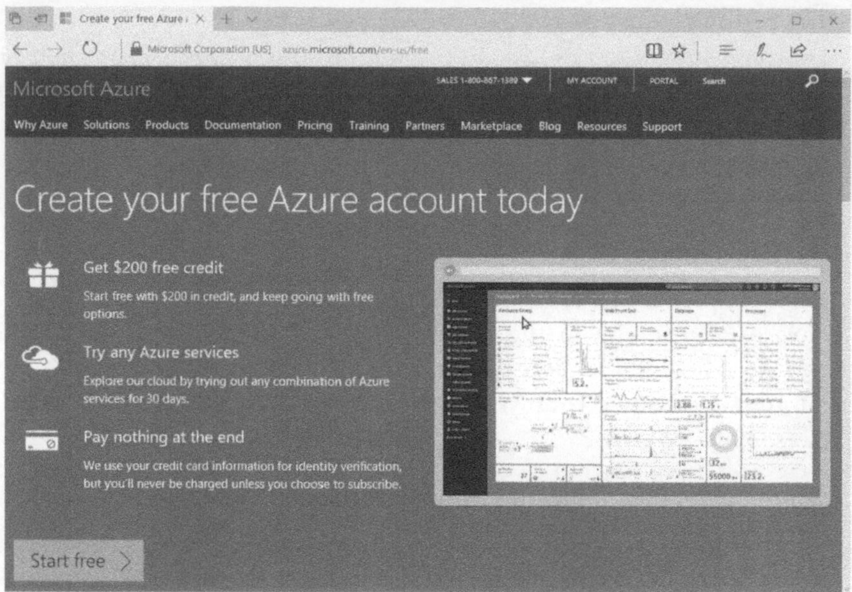

Figure 1.1 To follow along with all the exercises in this book, create a free Azure account if you don't already have one.

3. Once signed in to a Microsoft account, complete the prompts to create a free Azure account, as shown in figure 1.2:
   a. Enter your personal details in the About Me section.
      - To help minimize abuse and fraud, provide a phone number to verify your identity by text message or phone call.
      - A credit card is also required for identity verification, but there's no catch here. Your account doesn't start billing you until after 30 days or when use up your $200 free credit. It won't automatically transition to a pay-as-you-go subscription at the end of your trial.
   b. Review and accept the Azure subscription agreement and privacy policy, and then select Sign Up.
3. It may take a few minutes to get your Azure subscription ready. Once the sign-up process finishes and the Azure portal loads, take the quick tour to learn how to move around.

Your dashboard—the home page of the portal—looks empty right now. But in the next chapter you'll dive into creating your first VM, and it will start to look like figure 1.3!

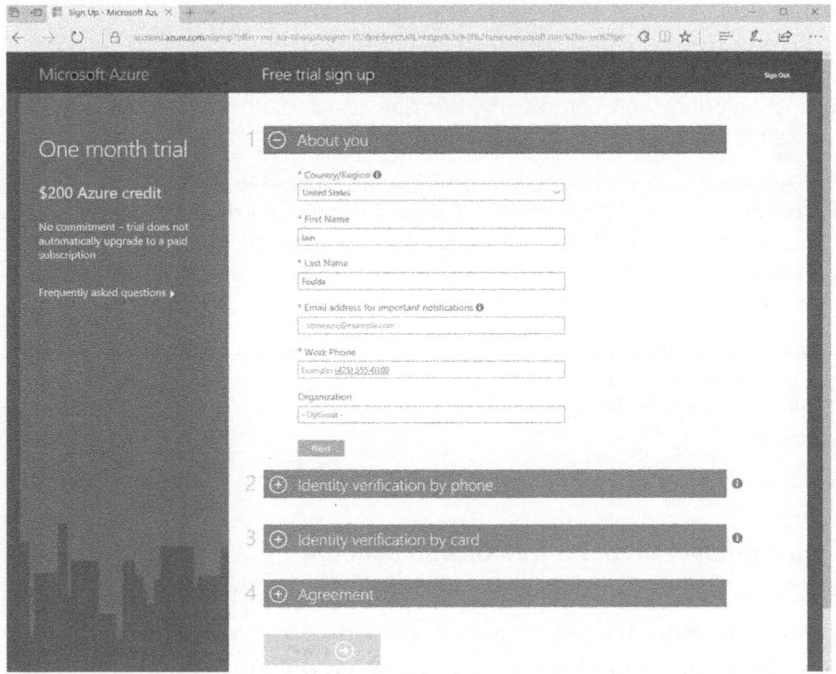

Figure 1.2 Complete Azure account sign-up information

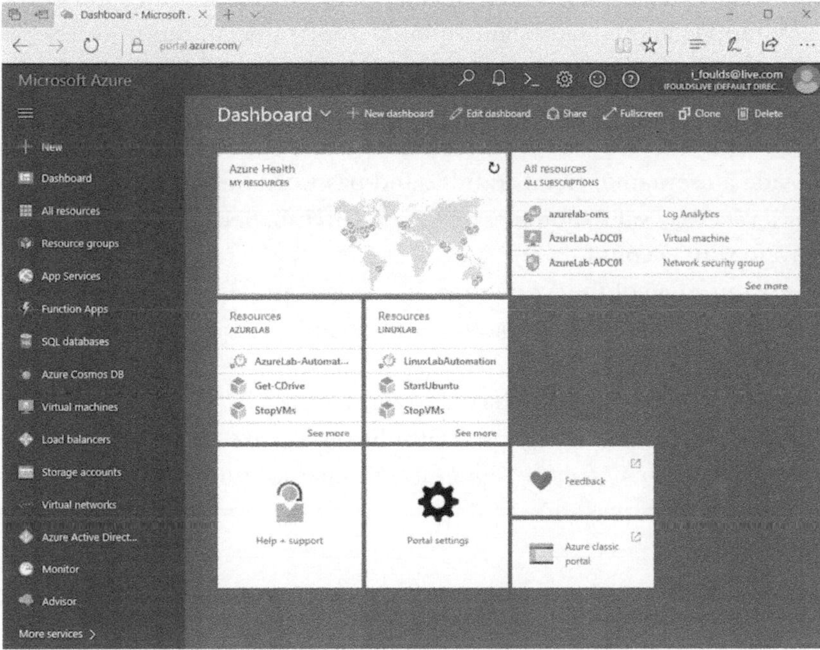

Figure 1.3 The Azure portal, ready for you to create your own applications and solutions

Is free truly free?

Azure has a Marketplace that contains hundreds of prebuilt images (the basis of VMs) and solutions you can deploy. We use some of these Marketplace offerings throughout the book, and it's a great way to quickly deploy an entire application suite.

Not all of these Azure Marketplace offerings are free—some third-party publishers combine licensing or support costs into the solution you deploy. For example, a VM that you deploy from Red Hat may incur an additional fee that covers the Red Hat support agreement and license. These charges aren't covered by your free trial credit; only the base VM usage is covered.

The exercises in this book only use resources that remain within the free trial. But if you go off exploring other cool Marketplace offerings in Azure, pay attention to what you build. Any solution that includes additional fees should clearly spell it out before you deploy!

1.3.2 Bonus lab exercise: Create a free GitHub account

GitHub is a free web service that many organizations and individuals use to manage projects such as code, templates, and documentation. Azure has hundreds of free templates and script examples that you can use and contribute to. This is one of the strengths of the open source community—sharing and giving back to others.

Some of the exercises in this book use resources from GitHub. You don't need a GitHub account to do any of this, but if you don't have an account, you won't be able to save any modifications and begin to build your own collection of templates and scripts. Creating a GitHub account is an optional but highly recommended, part of building your lab environment:

1. Open your web browser to www.github.com. To create a free GitHub account, provide a username, email address, and password.
2. You'll receive a validation message from GitHub. Select the link in the e-mail to activate your account.
3. Check out some of the Azure repositories that provide sample resources:
   a. *Azure Quickstart templates*—https://github.com/Azure/azure-quickstart-templates
   b. *Azure CLI*—https://github.com/Azure/azure-cli
   c. *Azure DevOps utilities*—https://github.com/Azure/azure-devops-utils
   d. *Learn Azure in a Month of Lunches book resources*—https://github.com/fouldsy/azure-mol-samples

1.4 A little helping hand

This book can't cover everything Azure offers. Even if I tried, by the time you read this chapter, I bet there will be something new in Azure! Cloud computing moves quickly, and new services and features are always being released. I may be a little biased, but as you start to explore Azure and want to learn about additional services, the excellent https://docs.microsoft.com/azure site is the best place to start. Every Azure service is documented with quickstart examples, tutorials, code samples, developer references, and architecture guides. You can also access both free and paid support options if you need help along the way.

1.5 Understanding the Azure platform

Before you get into the rest of this book, let's take a step back and understand what Azure is and the services that are available. As I mentioned earlier, Azure is a cloud computing provider on a global scale. At the time of writing, there are 40 active Azure regions, with another 10 planned. Each region contains one or more datacenters. By comparison, the two other major cloud providers operate in 16 regions (AWS) and 15 regions (Google Cloud).

Cloud computing provides more than just compute resources. There are more than 100 services in Azure, grouped in families of related services such as compute, web + mobile, containers, and identity. With all these services, Azure covers many different service models. Let's grab a slice of pizza for lunch to understand what this means: see figure 1.4.

Figure 1.4 Pizza as a Service model. As you move from homemade pizza, where you provide everything, to the restaurant model, where you just show up, the responsibilities and management demands change accordingly.

In the Pizza as a Service model, there are four options to choose from. As you progress through the models, you worry less and less about the process to eat a slice of pizza:

- *Homemade*—You make the dough; add the sauce, toppings, and cheese; bake the pizza in your oven; get drinks; and sit down to eat at your dining table.
- *Take + bake*—You buy a ready-made pizza. You just need to bake it in your oven, get drinks, and sit down to eat at your dining table.
- *Home delivery*—You order a pizza delivered to your home. You just need to get drinks and sit down to eat at your dining table.
- *Restaurant*—You want to go out and eat pizza with minimal effort!

Now that you're hungry, let's look at the more traditional model that involves some compute resources: see figure 1.5. This looks a little more like something you see in Azure. As you progress through the models, you manage fewer of the underlying resources and can focus more of your time and energy on your customers:

- *On-premises*—You configure and manage the entire datacenter, such as the network cables, storage, and servers. You're responsible for all parts of the application environment, support, and redundancy. This approach provides the maximum control, but with a lot of management overhead.
- *Infrastructure as a Service (IaaS)*—You purchase the base compute resources from a vendor that manages the core infrastructure. You create and manage the VMs, data, and applications. The cloud provider is responsible for the physical infrastructure, host management, and resiliency. You may still have an infrastructure team to help support and deploy VMs, but they're free from the time and cost of managing the physical equipment.

  This approach is good when you first start to move applications out of your own on-premises environment. The management and operations are often similar to an on-premises environment, so IaaS provides a natural progression for the business, IT, and application owners to become comfortable with the cloud.
- *Platform as a Service (PaaS)*—You purchase the underlying platform stack from a vendor that manages the OS and patches, and bring your applications and data. Don't worry about VMs or the virtual network, and your operations team can focus more of their time on application reliability and performance.

  This approach is often the beginning of the IT organization and the business becoming comfortable with running applications in the cloud. Your focus is on the applications and your customers, with fewer worries about the infrastructure to run those apps.
- *Software as a Service (SaaS)*—You just need access to software, with a vendor providing everything else. Developers can build against an existing platform to provide customizations or unique features, without having to maintain a large code base.

  This approach is often daunting at first, but you likely already know of and use successful SaaS offerings such as Salesforce, Office 365, or the Google suite of Mail or Docs. You use e-mail, create documents or presentations, or manage customer contact information and sales information. Your focus is on the content that you create and manage, not how to make the application run.

Most of what you create in Azure falls into the IaaS and PaaS areas. The main use cases include VMs and virtual networking (IaaS), or the Azure Web Apps, Functions, and Cosmos DB (PaaS) services. If you're a developer, the PaaS solutions are probably the areas you're most interested in, because Microsoft covers the infrastructure parts to let you focus on your code. IT pros may lean more toward the IaaS solutions to build out and control the Azure infrastructure.

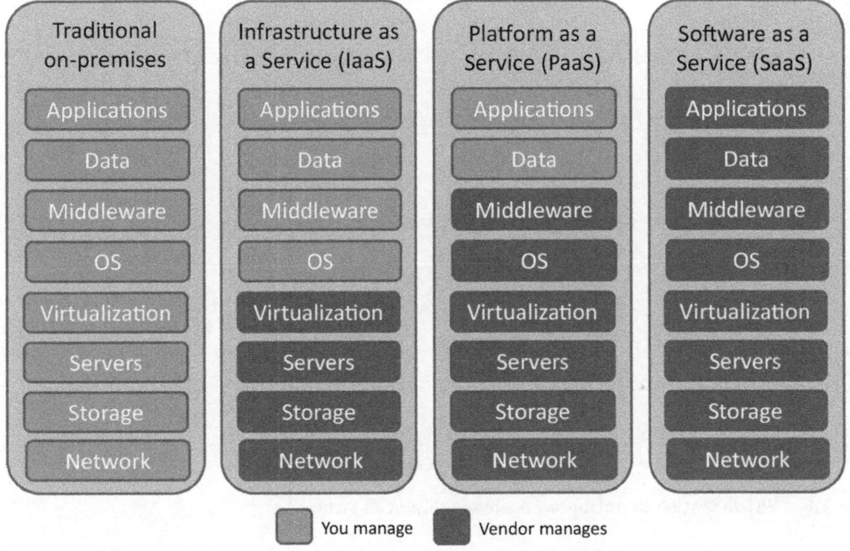

Figure 1.5 Cloud computing service model

> **Never stop learning**
> Don't forget that even as a business moves from IaaS toward the PaaS model, the IT pro remains relevant! It's important to understand what goes on underneath the PaaS layer when you design or troubleshoot a solution. If you're an IT pro, don't skip the chapters on PaaS solutions in Azure—there's a lot you can add to your business and customers if you understand the transition to that deployment model.

1.5.1 *Virtualization in Azure*

Virtualization is the real magic behind Azure. The IaaS, PaaS, and SaaS models use virtualization to power their services. The concepts of virtualization are nothing new, going all the way back to the mainframe days of the 1960s. In the mid-2000s, server virtualization in the datacenter started to gain momentum, and by now only a few workloads are deployed to bare-metal servers rather than being virtualized.

Entire books are dedicated to virtualization, but to give you a quick overview, virtualization logically divides physical resources in a server into virtual resources that can be securely accessed by individual workloads. A VM is one of the most common resources in cloud computing. A VM contains a virtual CPU (vCPU), memory (vRAM), storage (vDisk), and network connectivity (vNIC), as show in figure 1.6.

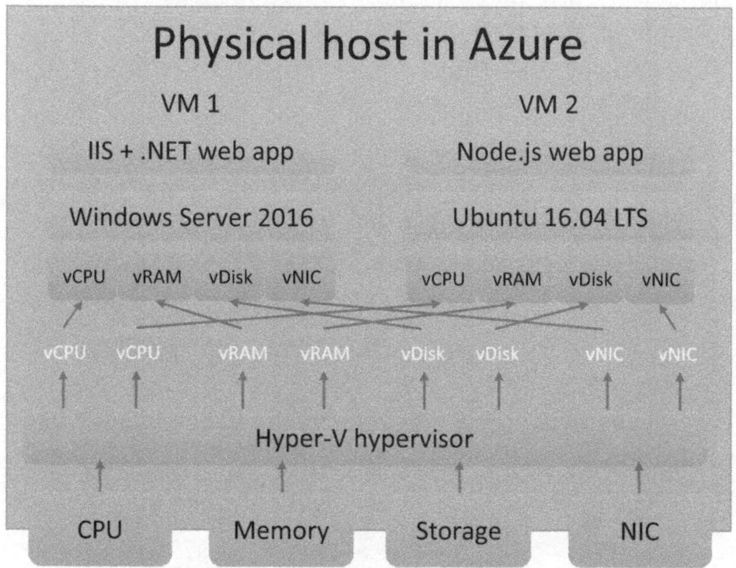

Figure 1.6 Virtualization in action on a physical host in Azure

In addition to physical servers, storage and networking are also now commonly virtualized, which allows the Azure platform to quickly define everything you need in software. No physical interaction or manual configuration of devices is required. You don't have to wait for another team to provide an IP address, open a network port, or add storage for you.

At its core, Azure runs on Windows—sort of. A modified version of the Hyper-V hypervisor powers the compute servers. Hyper-V is a type 1 (bare-metal) hypervisor that has been available in Windows Server for a decade. And don't worry, you can still run Linux as a fully supported, first-class workload! Microsoft is a huge contributor to the Linux community and kernel; some of the core software-defined networking in Azure is powered by a custom-built solution based on Debian Linux—Software for Open Networking in the Cloud (SONiC)—that Microsoft has made open source. You can take a virtual tour of Microsoft's datacenters at www.microsoft.com/cloud-platform/global-datacenters.

1.5.2 *Management tools*

With so many Azure services, how do you use them? Any way you want! If you want to select everything in a web browser, there's an awesome web-based portal. Comfortable with PowerShell? As you'd expect, there's an Azure PowerShell module. There's also a cross-platform command-line interface (CLI) tool that's great if you're on macOS or Linux. And developers can interact with Azure through REST APIs using a variety of common languages such as .NET, Python, and Node.js.

AZURE PORTAL

The Azure portal should work in any modern web browser, and it's a convenient way to use Azure without installing anything on your computer. The portal is also a great way to learn how to create and manage resources by quickly seeing a visual representation of everything.

New features and services are constantly being added to Azure, so the portal may change ever so slightly from what you see in the screenshots in this book or online documentation and blogs. The wording on a button may change a little, or a new option may be added, but the core operations all remain the same. Welcome to the brave new world of cloud computing!

AZURE CLOUD SHELL

If you want to get your hands on the keyboard and type in commands, the portal also includes the Azure Cloud Shell, shown in figure 1.7. This shell is a web-based interactive console that provides a Bash shell, the Azure CLI, and some preinstalled application development tools such as Git and Maven. There's also a PowerShell version of the Cloud Shell that, as the name implies, provides access to the latest Azure PowerShell cmdlets.

You can access the Azure Cloud Shell from a web browser on any computer without needing to install any tools at http://shell.azure.com. Editors like Visual Studio Code (http://code.visualstudio.com) provide Cloud Shell access within the application. There's even an Azure app available for iOS and Android that allows you to use the Azure Cloud Shell straight from your iPhone.

With the Azure Cloud Shell, you always have access to the latest version of the CLI or PowerShell tools. Persistent storage is attached that allows you to create and save scripts, templates, and configuration files.

LOCAL AZURE CLI AND POWERSHELL TOOLS

Although there are advantages to the Azure Cloud Shell, you often need access to your local filesystem and tools. You can install the Azure CLI or Azure PowerShell locally so that you can work with local resources and Azure resources.

In this book, we mostly use the Azure CLI (technically, the Azure CLI 2.0). It may seem odd to choose this over Microsoft's native PowerShell—the advantage is that samples and exercises can work both in the Azure Cloud Shell and locally on your computer, regardless of what OS you use. Although this isn't part of setting up your

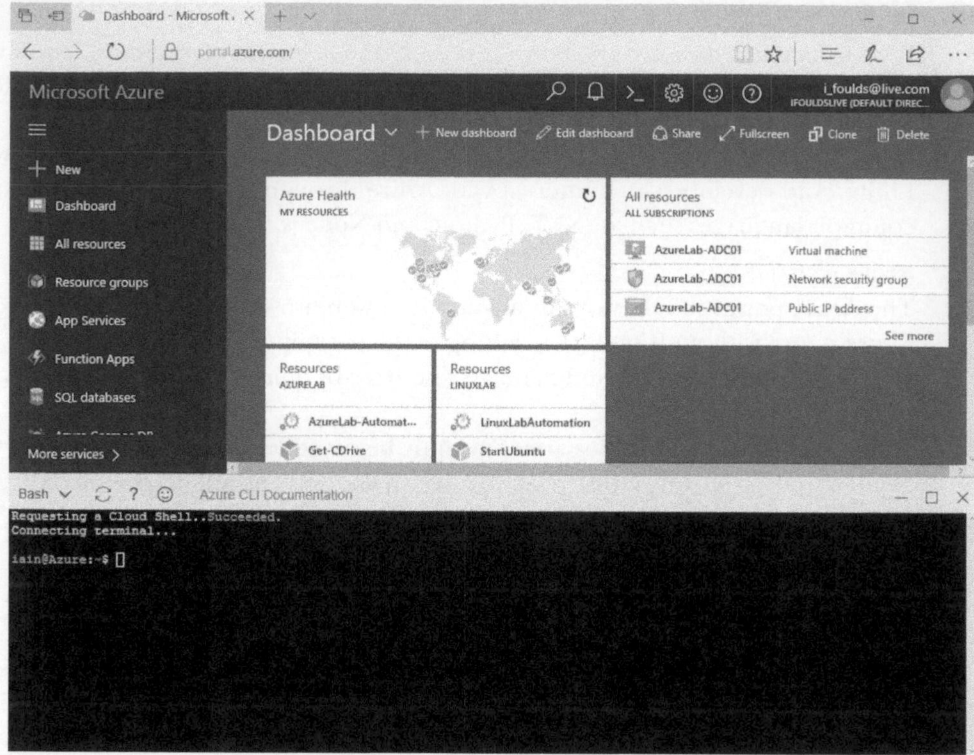

Figure 1.7 The Azure Cloud Shell in the web-based portal

lab environment, the following guides detail how to install the Azure management tools on your computer:

- *Getting Started with Azure PowerShell*—https://docs.microsoft.com/powershell/azure/get-started-azureps
- *Install Azure CLI*—https://docs.microsoft.com/cli/azure/install-azure-cli

2 Creating a virtual machine

Ready to see how quickly you can set up a web server in Azure? In this chapter, we dive straight into one of the most common requests when it comes to VMs: building a basic web server. This workload is a great example of the core Infrastructure as a Service (IaaS) components in Azure. Let's assume that you work for a pizza store that wants to expand its operations and accept online orders for pizza delivery or takeout. To build an online presence, you need a website. In the first couple of parts of this book, we explore the different features and services in Azure that let you build and run both IaaS and PaaS web applications. You can start to make informed decisions as to when to build and run a VM to power a website, and when you might use PaaS to do so.

In this chapter, you create an Ubuntu Linux VM and install a basic webserver. Don't worry about using Linux—you create a Windows VM in the end-of-chapter lab exercise! Ubuntu is a common web server platform, and it's a great way to learn about SSH public-key authentication. You'll then see how to open a network port for customers to access your website on the internet. A high-level overview of this basic environment is shown in figure 2.1.

2.1 Creating a VM from your web browser

The Azure CLI and Azure PowerShell tools are incredibly powerful, but a big strength of Azure is how much time has gone into building a great portal experience. The Azure portal is a web-based graphical tool that lets you see how all the different components come together and do a quick visual check that all is well. The portal includes a couple of unique things that the other tools don't provide, and it's fast to use because you don't have to install anything.

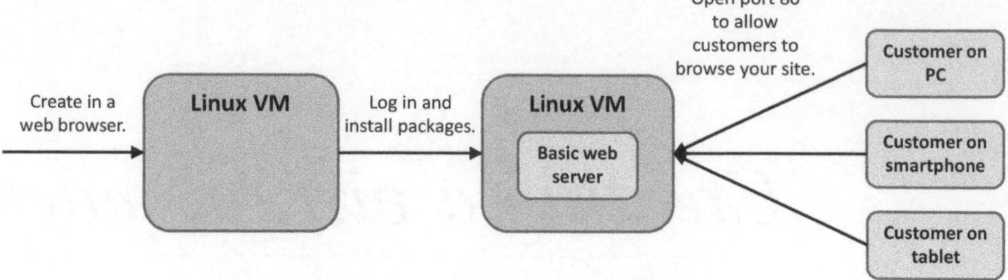

Figure 2.1 In this chapter, you create a basic VM, log in to install a web server, and then open a network port to allow customers to browse to the sample website.

> **Try it now**
> We're not waiting around! Begin creating a VM by working through the following steps.

1. Open a web browser to https://portal.azure.com. Log in with the account you created in the previous chapter to set up your lab environment.
2. Once logged in, select Create a Resource in the upper-left corner of the dashboard.
3. Choose Compute from the list of resources you can create, and then choose See All. There are hundreds of available images, which form the basis of all VMs. Select Ubuntu Server by Canonical, and then choose Ubuntu 18.04 LTS. That's currently the most recent version of Ubuntu, but if there's a newer Long Term Support (LTS) version by the time you're reading this, go ahead and select that.
4. To get started, select Create. In the settings window that opens, type a name for your VM, such as `webvm`.

   Note the drop-down menu for VM disk type. The default option is to use an SSD disk type. The following section looks at disk types in Azure.

2.1.1 Azure storage

Storage for VMs in Azure is straightforward. How many disks do you want, how big, and what type? The first two really aren't Azure-specific. So, what types of storage are available?

- *Premium SSD disks*—Uses low-latency, high-performance SSDs. Perfect for production workloads. This type is what you should mostly use for best performance for your applications.
- *Standard SSD disks*—Uses standard SSDs. Delivers consistent performance compared to HDDs. Great for development and testing workloads, or budget-conscious and low-demand production use.

- *Standard HDD disks*—Uses regular spinning disks. Ideal for infrequent data access such as archive data or backups. Not recommended for running application workloads.

You don't need to dig much deeper into the specifics of storage to create a quick web server. You'll learn more in chapter 4. For now, it's enough to know that when you pick a VM size, that also helps define what type of storage you use.

The virtual disks are Azure *managed disks*. These disks allow you to create a VM and attach additional data disks without worrying about underlying storage accounts, resource limits, or performance quotas. Managed disks are also automatically encrypted at rest—there's nothing you need to configure to secure your data!

2.1.2 Basic settings, continued

Let's move on from storage and complete the Basics settings pane in the portal.

Try it now

Continue with your first VM by completing the steps in this section.

5. The next option in the portal is to enter a username for a user account. This user account is created on your VM and is the name you enter to log in to the VM.
6. The default option is to use an SSH public key as the authentication type. Throughout this book, we're going to use SSH keys. SSH keys may be totally new to you, but they're not that complicated. See the following sidebar if you need a little more help.

   Let's create an SSH public-key pair with the Azure Cloud Shell. Select the Cloud Shell icon at the top of the dashboard, as shown in figure 2.2.

Secure shell (SSH) key pairs

Secure shell (SSH) is a protocol used to communicate securely with remote computers and is the most common way to log in to Linux VMs. It's similar to using a Remote Desktop Protocol (RDP) connection to a Windows VM, except in Linux the SSH session is typically all console-based. With public-key cryptography, you can use a digital key pair to authenticate you with a remote Linux VM.

An SSH key pair has two parts: a public key and a private key. The public key is stored on your Linux VM in Azure. You keep a copy of the private key. When you need to log in to your Linux VM, the public key on the remote VM is matched with the private key you keep locally. If the key pairs match, you're logged in to the VM. There's a little more to it than that, but at its core, public-key cryptography is a great means to verify identity.

> ***(continued)***
> I'd like you to get into the habit of using SSH keys to log in to Linux VMs. SSH keys are a lot more secure than passwords because, among other things, they aren't susceptible to brute-force password attacks. You should always focus on security as a central concept, especially in the cloud.

Figure 2.2 Select and launch the Cloud Shell in the Azure portal by selecting the shell icon.

7 The first time you open the Cloud Shell, it will take a few moments to create persistent storage that's always then connected to your sessions. This storage allows you to save and retrieve scripts, configuration files, and SSH key pairs. Accept any prompts to allow this storage to be created.

8 If needed, select Bash from the drop-down menu in the upper-left corner of the Cloud Shell, as shown in figure 2.3.

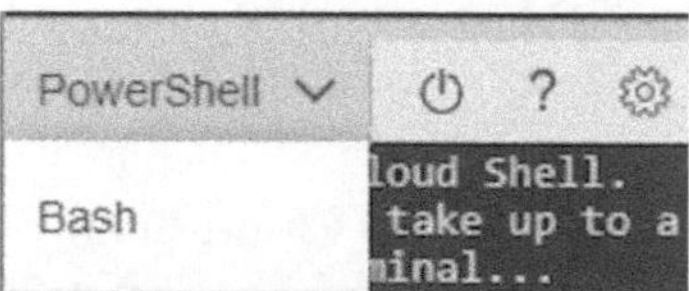

Figure 2.3 The exercises in this book mostly use the Bash version of the Cloud Shell. The first time you access the Cloud Shell, it will probably load the PowerShell shell. Select the Bash version, and then wait a few seconds for Azure to switch the shell. Each time you access the Cloud Shell after this change, the Bash version should load automatically.

9 To create a key pair, enter the following command:

```
ssh-keygen
```

Accept the default prompts by pressing the Enter key. In a couple of seconds, you have an SSH public-key pair that you can use with all your VMs! The `ssh-keygen` command defaults to a 2,048-bit length key and uses the RSA version 2 protocol. This is a good balance of security and is the recommended type for most use cases. Figure 2.4 shows an example of a completed SSH key pair in the Cloud Shell.

10 To view your public key and use it with a VM, enter the following command:

```
cat .ssh/id_rsa.pub
```

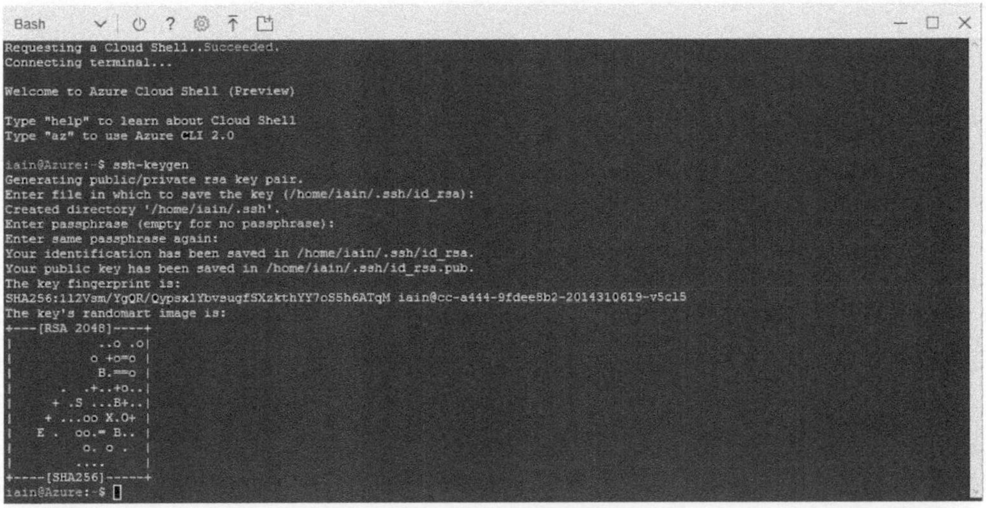

```
Requesting a Cloud Shell..Succeeded.
Connecting terminal...

Welcome to Azure Cloud Shell (Preview)

Type "help" to learn about Cloud Shell
Type "az" to use Azure CLI 2.0

iain@Azure:~$ ssh-keygen
Generating public/private rsa key pair.
Enter file in which to save the key (/home/iain/.ssh/id_rsa):
Created directory '/home/iain/.ssh'.
Enter passphrase (empty for no passphrase):
Enter same passphrase again:
Your identification has been saved in /home/iain/.ssh/id_rsa.
Your public key has been saved in /home/iain/.ssh/id_rsa.pub.
The key fingerprint is:
SHA256:112Vsm/YgQR/QypsxlYbvsugfSXzkthYY7oS5h6ATqM iain@cc-a444-9fdee8b2-2014310619-v5cl5
The key's randomart image is:
+---[RSA 2048]----+
|          ..o .o|
|         o +o=o |
|          B.==o |
|     .  .+..+o..|
|    + .S ...B+..|
|   + ...oo X.O+ |
|  E .  oo.= B.. |
|        o. o .  |
|        ....    |
+----[SHA256]-----+
iain@Azure:~$
```

Figure 2.4 An SSH key pair created in the Azure Cloud Shell with the `ssh-keygen` command

Select the output, and copy it. Be careful when copying the output of the public key, because it's sensitive to additional whitespace or you missing a character. An example of a complete SSH public key is as follows:

```
ssh-rsa AAAAB3NzaC1yc2EAAAADAQABAAABAQDPGaOBsfhJJOHAWAv+RLLR/vdUTzS9HOIj
➥JyzWWLsnu0ESH2M6R+YYPPNXv9X7dmVyM1zCXXEaLucpnyFjevbwPedxTgifyxgCFTgylr1
➥kg7o4EyCTGBGhTA+hSHuhXGXa12KPdKWehsPwHMa6Hs8fbt/in9Z1k2ZAwvbT+LWPcmJgNO
➥FuolIHOsOEeoQQqdXLrGa7NU/3fzSXdT9Y2BT1KLINc4KnwdOuONddLw3iANvK+Gkwax8iK
➥7IicKMoammwvJUCRf+MTEK9pZ84tfsc9qOIAdhrCCLbQhtoWjZpIwYnFk+SNBE8bZZtB8b2
➥vkDFNZlA5jcAd6pUR3tPuL0D iain@cc-a444-9fdee8b2-2014310619-v5cl5
```

TIP The Cloud Shell is browser-based, so the keyboard shortcuts for copy and paste may work a little differently than you're used to. Ctrl-Insert and Shift-Insert should copy and paste, rather than the regular Ctrl-C and Ctrl-V.

11 Paste the contents of your key into the SSH Public Key box. When you do, the portal will prompt you if the key is incorrect.

   Make sure Create New is selected under Resource Group, and then provide a name. I suggest naming resource groups by chapter, to help organize things as you go. For example, name the resource group in this exercise `azuremolchapter2`. Figure 2.5 shows the different windows, or panes, in the Azure portal as you create your first VM.

12 Select the closest location to you from the Location drop-down menu, and select OK. This location is where your VM physically runs. Azure abstracts the exact location, because multiple data centers may exist in each region. In Azure, you provide a region and let the platform place your resources based on availability, capacity, and performance needs.

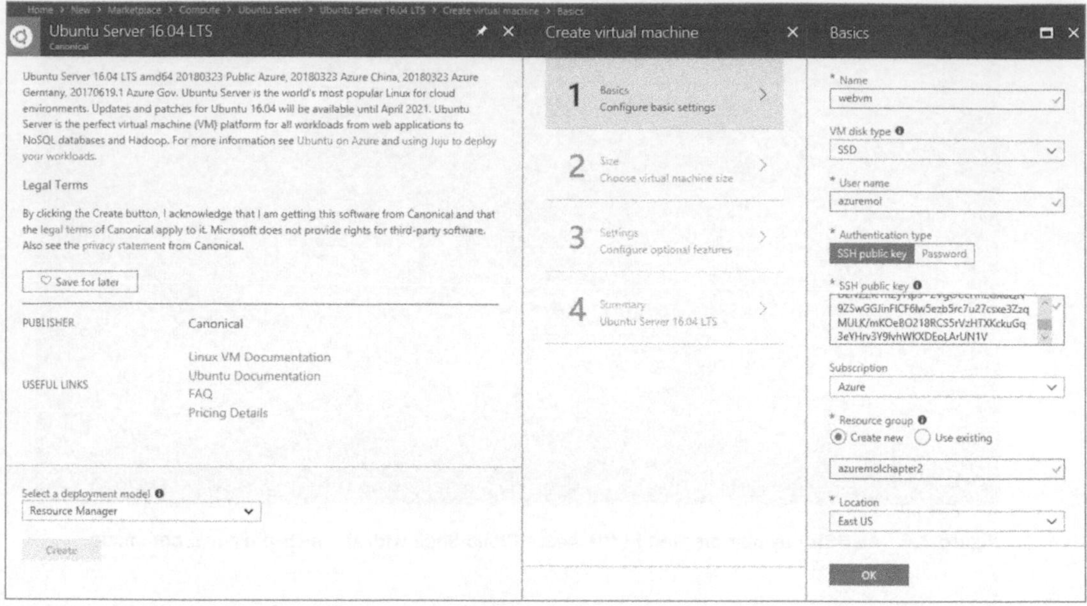

Figure 2.5 Create an Ubuntu Linux VM in the Azure portal. Provide a VM name, and then enter a username and the SSH public key you created. Create a resource group, and select your closest Azure location.

2.1.3 VM sizes

There are various families of VM sizes in Azure. These families contain groups of similar virtual hardware types that are targeted for certain workloads. The sizes are sometimes updated as new hardware and workloads offerings become available, but the core families remain constant. The family types are as follows:

- *General purpose*—Great for development and testing, or low-use production databases or web servers.
- *Compute optimized*—High-performance CPUs, such as for production application servers.
- *Memory optimized*—Larger memory options, such as when you need to run big databases or tasks that require a lot of in-memory data processing.
- *Storage optimized*—Low-latency, high-disk performance for disk-intensive applications.
- *GPU*—Nvidia-based graphics-specialized VMs, if you need graphics rendering or video processing.
- *High-performance computing (HPC)*—Lots of everything! Plenty of CPU, memory, and network throughput for the most demanding of workloads.

Just how big of a VM can you create in Azure? Things are constantly improving, but at the time of writing the largest VM you can create is an M-series (part of the Memory optimized family) with 128 virtual CPUs and 3.8 TB of memory. That should make for a decent Minecraft server, don't you think?!

The key thing to learn here is that the number of VMs and amount of CPU and memory you can request in Azure are limited only by your budget. You'd likely struggle to create VMs of this size in the traditional on-premises world.

Try it now

Continue creating your VM by choosing a size in the following step.

13 In the Sizes pane of the portal, choose one of the recommended VM sizes, such as D2S_v3, and choose the Select button. This is probably way too much power for a basic web server, but it's quick to create the VM and install the required packages!

   If you changed between SSD and HDD on the previous page, the list of available VM sizes may differ. To see a full list of available VM sizes, select See All. You can see size information such as the amount of virtual CPUs and memory assigned, maximum number of data disks that can be attached, and size of local temporary disk.

VM cost savings

The VMs created by default are often overpowered for what you need, but they're quick to deploy and use. This helps cut down on how much time spent installing packages on your lunch break.

In production, pay attention to the memory, CPU, and storage demands of your VMs. Create appropriately sized VMs. This approach is the same as in the on-premises world, where you can end up with VMs that have much more memory or many more virtual CPUs assigned than they need.

There's also a special type of VM in Azure: the *B-series*. These VM sizes use burstable CPU and memory resources, and you can bank credits for unused compute resources. If you want to save your Azure credits, you can choose this series of VMs for the book exercises. They come with a lower price point and are great for scenarios where you don't always need a lot of CPU and memory resources.

With the VM credentials, location, and size selected, now you can configure some of the core VM settings for connectivity, backup, or identity.

2.1.4 Settings

In the Settings pane of the portal, you can review and edit the virtual network settings, as shown in figure 2.6, along with diagnostics, backup, and auto-shutdown settings. Let's take a minute to review some of these concepts.

It sounds obvious, but your VM needs network connectivity if you want to reach your website in a web browser. That means you need both a virtual network and external connectivity.

You can create a VM that's only attached to a virtual network without providing external connectivity, which may be the case for backend database or application servers. To connect to these VMs for administration and maintenance, you can create a virtual private network (VPN) connection, or you can use a private, dedicated connection to Azure from your on-premises networking equipment. In Azure, this dedicated connection is called *ExpressRoute*.

You want to connect your web server to the public internet, so assign a public IP address to the VM. In the real world, you'd probably have more than one web server that runs your application. A load balancer would act as the gateway between your customers on the internet and distribute traffic to the actual web servers. If that starts to sound just like what you do daily, great! Keep reading! We'll dive in to this more robust infrastructure in chapters 8 and 9. For now, we're going to stick with a single VM that connects straight to the internet. (I know, the horror of it all.) By default, Azure creates and assigns a public IP address for you.

A virtual network in Azure is made up of the same core features as a regular physical network:

- An address space and a subnet mask, such as 10.0.0.0/16
- One or more subnets, which you can use to divide external, database, or application traffic, for example

Figure 2.6 When you create a VM, you can change virtual network settings, add extensions, configure backups, and more. For this chapter, there's nothing to change, but for your own deployments, you may want to configure additional settings.

- Virtual network interface cards (NICs) that connect VMs to a given subnet
- Virtual IP addresses that are assigned to resources such as a virtual NIC or load balancer

For your basic web server, you're creating a specific type of virtual IP address: a public IP address. This public IP address is assigned to the virtual NIC and allows external traffic to reach your VM. You control the flow of traffic to your VM with *network security groups*. Think of a regular firewall that you use to open or close various ports and protocols; in Azure, network security groups lock down traffic by default and only allow the specific traffic that you define.

Also in the Settings window are a couple of other areas you can explore, including Availability Zones and Sets, and Extensions. Again, these are cool things (seriously, there's always something new to learn about in Azure!), and I promise we'll dive deeper in later chapters. Note the Auto-Shutdown option, which can automatically turn off VMs at a designated time. This is a great feature to make sure that you don't accidentally leave VMs turned on that cost you money.

> **Try it now**
> Review your VM settings in the Summary window, and then create your first VM!

14 Under the Network Security Group section, open a port for remote management connections. By default, VMs created in the portal are locked down and secured from the internet. From the Select Public Inbound Ports drop-down menu, choose SSH (22). We take a deeper look at network security groups and rules in chapter 5.
15 Choose OK in the Settings pane. Review the information in the Summary window, and select Create. It will take a couple of minutes to create your VM. Once the VM is ready, you can log in and start to install the web server packages.

2.2 Connecting to the VM, and installing the web server

Once your VM is up and running, you can use the SSH key you created a few minutes ago to log in to your VM. You can then begin to install and configure the web server, and you can do it all through the Cloud Shell.

2.2.1 Connecting to the VM with SSH

Let's look at how you can quickly get the connection details for your VM.

> **Try it now**
> If Linux is new to you, don't worry! Follow along with the next few steps to log in to your VM.

16 In the Azure portal, browse to and select Virtual Machines from the navigation bar on the left side of the screen. It takes a couple of minutes to create the VM, so select the Refresh button until the VM status shows Running, and then select your VM and select the Connect button, as shown in figure 2.7.

With a Linux VM, you're shown the SSH command that includes your username and public IP address. Copy this SSH connection command.

On a Windows VM, the Connect button downloads an RDP connection file to your computer that's prepopulated with the public IP address of your VM.

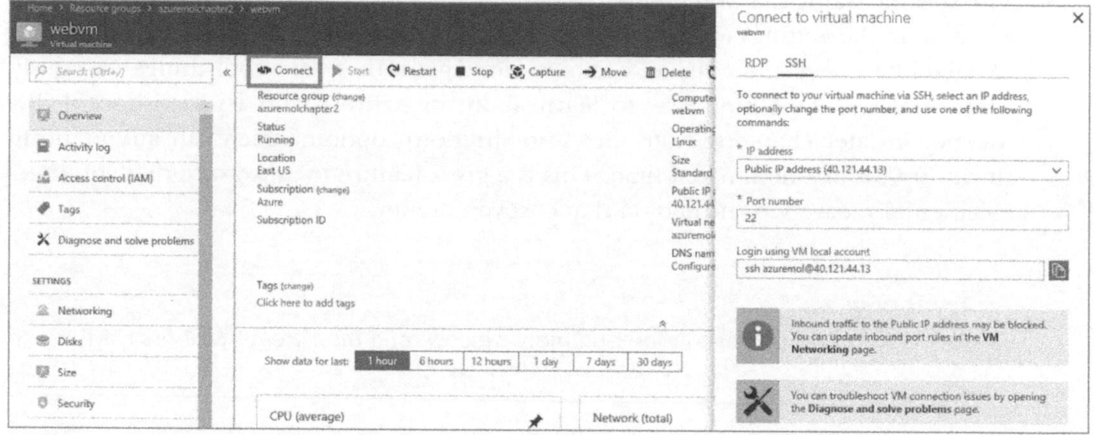

Figure 2.7 Select your VM in the Azure portal, and then select Connect to generate the SSH connection information.

17 If needed, open the Cloud Shell again. If you're going to be switching between the Cloud Shell and the portal, you can minimize the Cloud Shell to keep it available in the background.

18 Paste the SSH command into the Cloud Shell, and then press Enter. The SSH key you created earlier is automatically used to authenticate.

The first time you connect to a VM with SSH, it prompts you to add it to a list of trusted hosts. This is another layer of security that SSH provides—if someone tries to intercept the traffic and direct you to a different remote VM, your local SSH client knows something has changed and warns you before connecting.

Accept the prompt to store the remote VM connection. Figure 2.8 shows the SSH connection process in the Azure Cloud Shell.

At this point, you're either home away from home, or the Linux prompt is totally foreign. Don't worry. You don't need to know a huge number of Linux commands, and every command is explained as we go along. That said, I highly recommend that you learn at least some basic Linux administration skills. A lot of the cloud is based on Linux systems, and there's a big move toward containers and microservices for application development and management. If you're an old-school Windows admin, welcome! There's something lined up for you at the end of the chapter, so bear with me.

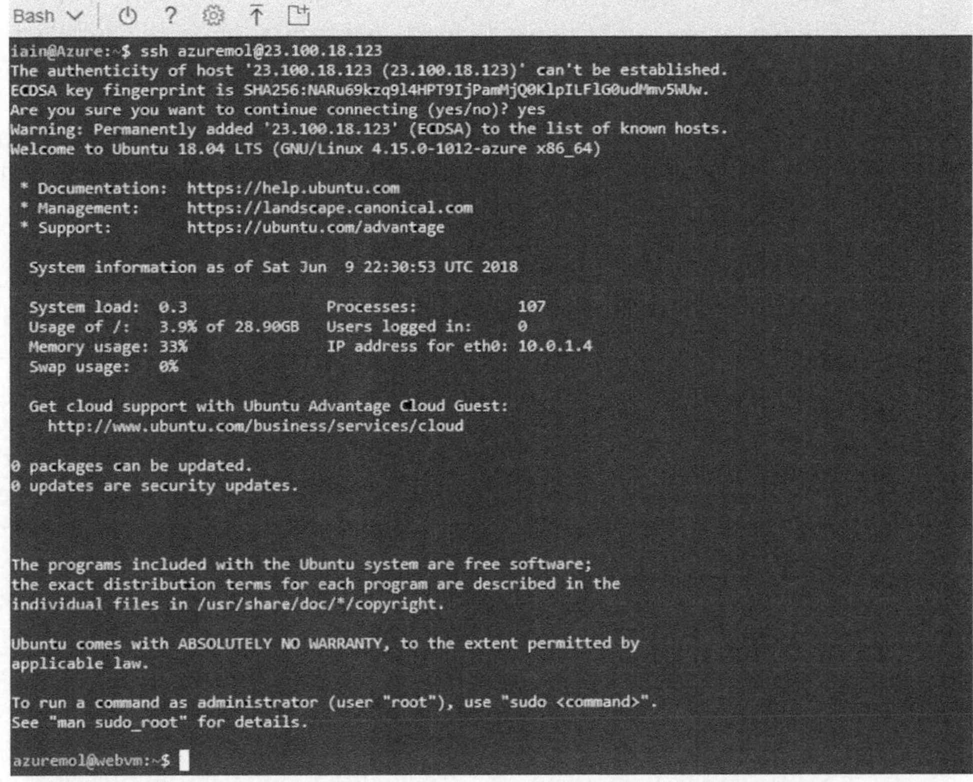

Figure 2.8 Use the connection string shown in the Azure portal to create an SSH connection to your VM from the Cloud Shell.

2.2.2 *Installing the web server*

Create a VM? Check. Connect to the VM with SSH? Check. Now you can install the packages for a web server and get ready to see it in action.

Azure supports many different Linux distributions (distros). Package-management tools and configuration file locations vary a little between each distro. We're going to use Ubuntu in this book because it's one of the most popular and well-documented Linux distros for cloud computing. So, if you get stuck along the way, there should be plenty of documentation to help you out. If you're wanting to use a different distribution that you're already comfortable with, feel free to use that! Otherwise, stick with Ubuntu.

> **Try it now**
>
> From your SSH session to the VM, install the web server packages with APT.

1 In Ubuntu, you install packages with an Advanced Packing Tool (APT). This is a super-powerful package-management tool that automatically installs any additional packages it needs. All you need to do is say "install a web server," and APT installs all the required components.

For this example, install the LAMP web stack. This is probably the most common set of web components: Linux, Apache (a web server), MySQL (a database server), and PHP (a web programming language):

```
sudo apt-get update && sudo apt install -y lamp-server^
```

The first command updates the available packages, which is good practice to make sure you can install the latest and greatest packages. Once that finishes, you run the next command with `&&`. Why not just start a new line for the next command? The `&&` runs the next command only if the preceding command was successful. For example, if there was no network connectivity for `apt` to get the latest packages (humor me, I know you must have network connectivity to connect in the first place!), then there's no point in running the `install` command.

If the `update` command is successful, `apt` then determines what additional packages it needs and begins to install `lamp-server`. Why the caret symbol at the end (`^`)? That tells `apt` to install the entire set of packages that make up the LAMP server, not just a single package named `lamp-server`.

2 The installer may prompt you for a password, or default to using an empty MySQL password. That's not very secure, and for real production use, you need to specify a strong password. In chapter 15, we get really cool and store a strong, secure password in Azure Key Vault that's automatically injected into this MySQL install wizard.

3 It takes a minute or so to install all the packages for your LAMP web stack, and then you're finished. Type `exit` to log out of your VM and return to the Cloud Shell prompt.

That's it! Your web server is up and running, but you won't be able to access it in a web browser just yet. To do that, you need to allow web traffic to reach the VM.

2.3 Allowing web traffic to reach the VM

Your web server is up and running, but if you enter the public IP address of your VM in a web browser, the web page doesn't load. Why? Remember the network security groups we briefly talked about earlier? When you created the VM, a network security group was created for you. A rule was added that allows remote management: in this case, that was SSH. If you create a Windows VM, a rule is added that allows RDP. But that's it. The rest of the VM is locked down. To allow visitors to access your web server over the internet, you need to create a rule in the network security group that allows web traffic. Otherwise, no one can order pizzas!

2.3.1 *Creating a rule to allow web traffic*

Let's mix things up a little and use the Azure CLI to create a rule for web traffic. The Azure CLI is available in the Cloud Shell. There's nothing you need to install. We cover virtual networking and network security groups in more depth in chapter 5; for now, we can check out how quick and powerful the Azure CLI is with just one command.

> **Try it now**
> Open the Azure Cloud Shell, and follow along with these steps to see the Azure CLI in action.

1. If you closed your Cloud Shell window, open it again from the Azure portal. Make sure the Bash shell loads, not PowerShell. If needed, switch to the Bash version.
2. To see the Azure CLI and installed modules, type `az --version`. A list of modules and version numbers is shown. What's great about the Cloud Shell is that it always has the latest and greatest version available.

NOTE If you're observant, you may have noticed that the command output information about the version of Python. Why is this important? Python is a powerful, popular programing language. The Azure CLI is written in Python, which is part of what makes it cross-platform and available for you to install locally on any computer if you don't want to always use the Cloud Shell. To keep up with Microsoft's drive to contribute to the open source community, the Azure CLI is made available on GitHub for anyone to make contributions, suggestions, or report problems (https://github.com/Azure/azure-cli).

3. To open a port, you specify the VM name and its resource group, along with the port number. For web traffic, you need to open port 80. Enter the resource group (`-g`) and VM name (`-n`) you specified when you created your VM:

```
az vm open-port -g azuremolchapter2 -n webvm --port 80
```

2.3.2 *Viewing the web server in action*

Now that you have a port open to your VM, let's see what happens when you try to access it in a web browser:

1. In the Azure portal, select your VM if you navigated away from it.
2. The public IP address is listed in the upper-right corner of the VM overview page, as shown in figure 2.9. Select the address, and copy it.

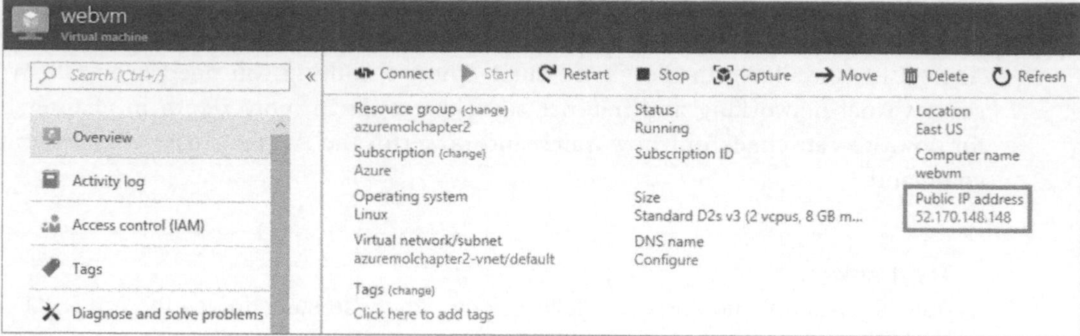

Figure 2.9 Select your VM in the Azure portal to view its information. The public IP address is shown at lower right.

3 In your web browser, open a new tab or window and paste in the public IP address. The default Apache website loads, as shown in figure 2.10! Okay, it doesn't look like a pizza store, but you have the foundation ready to bring in your code and start to build your application!

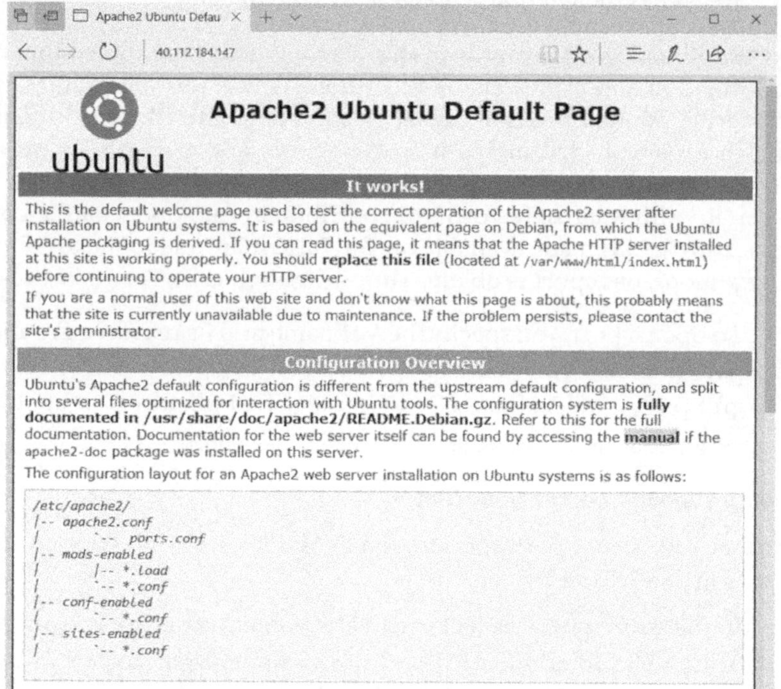

Figure 2.10 To see your web server in action and view the default Apache 2 page, enter the public IP address in a web browser.

2.4 Lab: Creating a Windows VM

We walked step by step through installing the LAMP stack on an Ubuntu Linux VM. This is a common platform for websites, but you may want some love and attention if you have a Windows background! Your development teams or business decision makers may want to use .NET, for example. Even so, you can run .NET Core on Linux VMs, so don't let the language drive your decision.

From what you learned in the step-by-step example, try to create a VM that runs Internet Information Services (IIS). Here are some hints:

- You need a VM that runs Windows Server 2016.
- You use RDP, not SSH, so expect a little different connection experience.
- In Server Manager, look for an option to Add Roles and Features.
- You need to install the web server (IIS).

2.5 Cleaning up resources

As you create resources in Azure, the billing meter starts to spin. You're charged by the minute, so it's wise to form good habits and not leave resources such as VMs running once you're done with them. There are two ways to stop the billing charges for running a VM:

- *Deallocate a VM*—You can select the Stop button from the portal to stop and deallocate a VM, which releases all held compute and network resources.
- *Delete a VM*—This option is rather obvious. If there's nothing left in Azure, there's nothing to pay for. Make sure you're finished with the VM before you delete it. There's no undo button in Azure!

I recommend that you create a resource group for each application deployment as you start to build things in Azure. As you walk through the exercises in this book, that's what you'll do. If you name your resource groups by chapter, such as `azuremolchapter2`, it will be easier to keep track of your resources and what to delete. This makes cleanup a little easier, because you can then delete the entire resource group at the end of each chapter. So, select Resource Groups on the navigation menu at left, open each resource group you've created in this chapter, and then select Delete Resource Group, as shown in figure 2.11. To confirm, you're prompted for the resource group name.

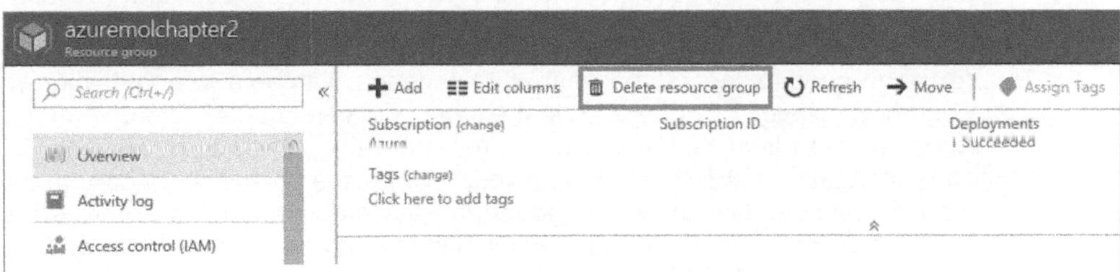

Figure 2.11 To save costs, delete resource groups when you no longer need them.

If you get in the habit of deleting resources once you're done with them, you can comfortably make it through this book on those free Azure credits! At the very least, deallocate your VM at the end of each lesson so you can resume the next day and stop the clock on the billing.

2.6 Houston, we have a problem

Sometimes you'll run into problems in Azure. There, I said it. Usually the Azure platform is good about issues that come up as you create resources:

- The Azure CLI or Azure PowerShell reports back as you run commands, so it should be obvious when something goes wrong. Azure PowerShell typically uses nice, calm red text to get your attention!
- The Azure CLI can be a little more cryptic because it usually includes the actual responses to the underlying REST API calls from the server. If this is all new, it can take a few successes and failures to understand what's going wrong. The helpful part of getting the REST responses is that you can copy and paste the error messages into your favorite search engine and usually get solid results to help you troubleshoot.

Take a REST? We just got started!

When you open a web page in your browser, your computer is communicating with a web server using HTTP. I can almost guarantee you've seen a 404 error message on a website before. That means the web page couldn't be found. Other common errors you may have seen are 403, if you don't have permissions to view the page, and 500, if the server encounters an error.

Even when things go well, under the hood your browser receives code 200 messages when the page loads fine, or code 301 messages if a page has been redirected to a new location. You don't need to understand and keep track of all these codes; it's just a standard way that HTTP facilitates communication between computers.

I talked about how to create and manage Azure resources through the web portal, CLI, or PowerShell. All the Azure services are accessed by Representational State Transfer (REST) application programming interfaces (APIs).

If this is new to you, REST APIs are a (somewhat ...) standardized way of exposing services via HTTP. You use standard HTTP requests such as `GET` and `POST` to request information or make a change, and once the platform accepts and processes the request, you receive a status message. Azure has a well-defined set of REST APIs.

You don't need to understand what all this means. Just be aware that when you see an error message, it's not always in the most human-readable, helpful format. Sometimes you get the raw HTTP response from the REST API that you must decipher by yourself. Again—paste this error into your favorite search engine, and there's a good chance someone has already encountered the problem and has provided a more human-readable reason for what went wrong and what you need to correct!

The most common problems with VMs occur when you connect to your VM. You could be connecting for remote administration with SSH or RDP, or trying to access your applications through a web browser or desktop client. These issues are often network related. I don't get into totally blaming the network folks until later chapters, so here are a couple of quick things to check:

- Can you connect to any other Azure VMs or applications running in Azure? If not, something local to your network is probably preventing access.

  If you can connect to other Azure resources, make sure you've opened the network security group rules I talked about in section 2.3. In chapter 5, we'll dig more into these rules.
- For authentication problems, try the following:
  - Confirm that you have the correct SSH keys. Azure should tell you when you create the VM whether the public key is invalid, but if you have more than one private key, make sure you use the correct one!
  - For RDP issues, try to connect to localhost*<username>* and enter your password. By default, most RDP clients try to present local credentials or network credentials, which your VM won't understand.

3 Azure Web Apps

In the previous chapter, you created a VM and manually installed packages to run a basic web server. You could build an online pizza store with this VM if you were hungry to get started. One of the biggest use cases for Azure VMs is to run web applications, typically at scale. Web applications are a comfortable workload for VMs. Comfortable is nice, if you also like the maintenance that goes with managing all those VMs. You know, fun things like software updates, security patches, centralized logging, and compliance reports. What if you could get all the power of a secure web server to run your web applications, including the ability to automatically scale to meet demands, but without the need to create and manage all those VMs? Let me introduce you to the Azure Web Apps service.

In this chapter, we compare the Infrastructure as a Service (IaaS) approach of VMs and web servers to the Platform as a Service (PaaS) approach. You learn the benefits of Azure Web Apps as you create a web application and see how to work with its development and production releases. You then learn how to deploy your web app automatically from a source control, such as GitHub. This workflow is show in figure 3.1. Azure Web Apps allows you to deploy and run your online pizza store in a matter of minutes, without the need to install and configure a VM and web server packages.

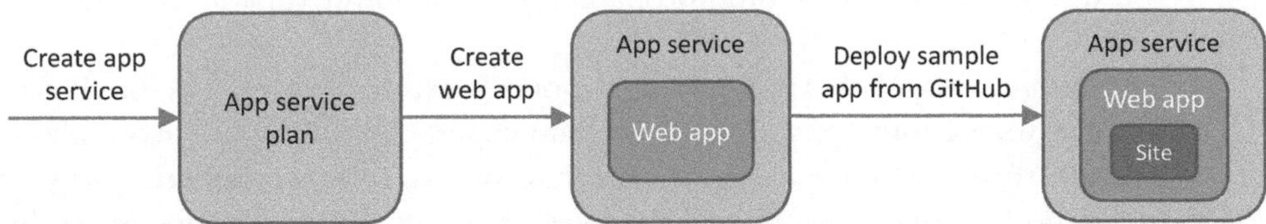

Figure 3.1 In this chapter, you create an app service plan and a basic web app and then deploy a website from GitHub.

3.1 Azure Web Apps overview and concepts

With Azure Web Apps, you start to dip your toes into the wonderful world of PaaS solutions. If you think cloud computing is all about VMs, you should probably reset that idea a little. At the start of this book, I talked about buying computer power and focusing on your applications and customers. As you move from IaaS solutions, such as VMs, and drift toward PaaS solutions, such as web apps, your applications and customers become the focus.

To run web applications on IaaS VMs requires management of the OS, application updates, and security and traffic rules, and configuration of the whole system. With Web Apps, you upload your web application, and all those management tasks are taken care of for you. Now you can focus your time on improving the application experience for your customers, or improving availability with scaling options and traffic management.

Does that mean you should never run VMs to host a web application? Probably not. There are valid reasons to run the entire application stack and configure it yourself. But Web Apps can provide for many of the use cases for running web applications.

3.1.1 Supported languages and environments

What kind of flexibility does Web Apps offer in terms of programming languages you can use to build your web application? Quite a lot! There are two primary platforms for running Web Apps: Windows and Linux. The Windows version of Web Apps has been around for a while and offers many languages beyond the expected ASP.NET and .NET Core. You can run Node.js, Python, Java, and PHP web apps natively. If you run Web Apps on Linux, you can also choose to use .NET Core or Ruby. If you want to be really cool and run your web application in containers, there's also Web Apps for Containers that lets you run native Docker containers for Linux. We dive more into containers and Docker in chapter 19; for now, understand that your options are covered with Web Apps!

When may Web Apps not make sense? Say you really want to torture yourself with a web application written in Perl. In that scenario, you'd likely fall back to running on IaaS VMs that you manage yourself, because there's no support for Perl in Web Apps. But Web Apps arguably supports the most common web programming languages that you'd want to use. You should probably look at a newer version of your app than one written in Perl, too.

Not only does Web Apps provide support for various languages, but it also provides support for various versions of those languages. Take PHP, for example—there are typically three or four versions of PHP that you can select to best support your application. And best of all, you don't have to worry about the dependencies on the underlying web server to support it all, as you would if you managed an IaaS VM yourself. Python is another example of differences between the stable 2.7 and 3.4 (and later) versions, as shown in figure 3.2.

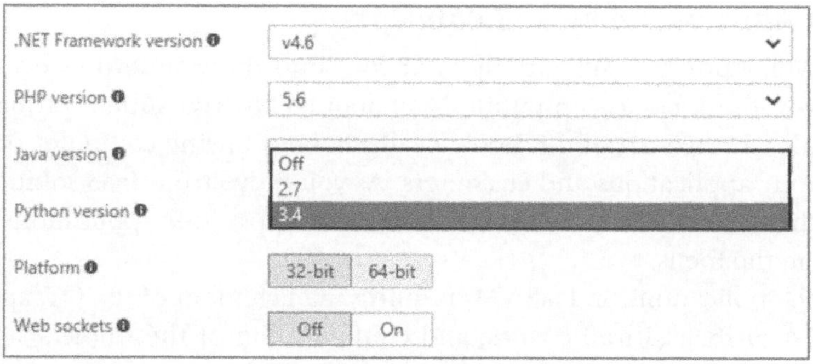

.NET Framework version: v4.6
PHP version: 5.6
Java version: Off / 2.7 / 3.4
Python version
Platform: 32-bit | 64-bit
Web sockets: Off | On

Figure 3.2 Select a specific *version* of a language in the Web Apps application settings.

Web Apps stays up to date on security fixes, too. But don't expect an older version of PHP or Python to continue to be supported indefinitely. There will be a cutoff on supported older versions at a certain point. Again, that may be a time when you fall back to running IaaS VMs yourself if your app needs an older language version. But if you need to run an older version of a given language to support a legacy application, don't get sucked in to a constant maintenance approach. Always look to move those legacy apps to more modern supported platforms.

3.1.2 Staging different versions with deployment slots

Deployment slots provide a staged environment for your web application. You can push new versions of your app to a deployment slot and get them running using environmental variables or database connections, without impacting the live site. When you're happy with how things look and feel in a deployment slot, you can switch this version to the live site in an instant. The previously live site then switches in to a deployment slot of its own, providing an archived version; or, if needed, you can flip the app back to production.

The number of available deployment slots varies based on the tier of web app you select. A larger number of deployment slots enables multiple staged versions to be in use by different developers as they stage and test their own updates.

3.2 Creating a web app

With a little theory under your belt, let's look at a Web App in action. There are a couple of parts to this. First, you create the basic web app and see the default site in your browser. Then you use a sample web page from GitHub and push that to Azure. Maybe your web developers have started to build a frontend for your online pizza store, so you have a basic site ready to upload.

NOTE If you've never used Git before, don't worry. You don't need to understand what Git is doing at this point, and there's room at the end of the chapter to play around and explore a little.

3.2.1 Creating a basic web app

The first step is to create the web app in Azure and make sure the default page loads.

> **PaaS, not IaaS**
> This web app is a new resource and is separate from VMs like that you created in the previous chapter. The VM you created in chapter 2 is an IaaS approach to building and running web applications. The PaaS approach is Web Apps. There's no real relation between the two. In fact, if you followed the advice in the previous chapter and deleted your VM, this web app runs without a VM in your Azure subscription at all!

> **Try it now**
> To create your web app, complete the following steps.

1. Open a web browser to https://portal.azure.com, and log in to your Azure account.
2. In the portal, select Create a Resource in the upper-left corner of the dashboard.
3. Choose Web + Mobile from the list of resources you can create, and then select Web App.
4. Enter a Name for your web app. This name must be globally unique, because it creates the URL to your web app in the form of http://<*name*>.azurewebsite .net. If you're wondering, yes—you can apply a custom domain name here. For now, use the default azurewebsites.net address.
5. By default, a new resource group is created. To help keep things clean and organized as you did in chapter 2, I suggest you name this resource group azuremolchapter3.
6. You can natively use a Linux host for your web apps, but for this exercise, choose Windows as the OS if it isn't already selected.
7. Select App Service Plan/Location, and then choose Create New.

Let's take a minute to go over the available options.

APP SERVICE PLANS

Web Apps is part of the wider App Service family in Azure. App Service also includes Mobile Apps, API Apps, and Logic Apps. All but Logic Apps are available in every region that Azure runs in. A great resource to check out Azure service availability by region is at https://azure.microsoft.com/regions/services. Many services are available globally.

When you need to create an App Service resource, such as a web app, you create or use an existing service plan. The service plan defines the amount of resources available to you, how much automation is available to scale and back up your web app, and how highly available to make your site with staging slots and Traffic Manager. As with anything, you get what you pay for. Each service tier builds on the features of the lower tiers, generally adding more storage and available resources.

The four main service plan tiers are as follows:

- *Free/Shared*—Uses a shared infrastructure, offers minimal storage, and has no options for deploying different staged versions, routing of traffic, or backups. The Shared tier allows you to use a custom domain and incurs a charge for this over the Free tier.
- *Basic*—Provides dedicated compute resources for your web app. Allows you to use SSL and manually scale the number of web app instances you run.
- *Standard*—Adds daily backups, automatic scale of web app instances, and deployment slots, and allows you to route users with Traffic Manager.
- *Premium*—Provides more frequent backups, increased storage, and a greater number of deployment slots and instance scaling options.

The case for isolation

With PaaS solutions like Web Apps, the infrastructure is intentionally abstracted. As the name of some of the service plan tiers implies, web apps run across a shared platform of available resources. That's not at all to say that web apps are insecure and others can view your private data! But compliance or regulatory reasons may require you to run your applications in a controlled, isolated environment. Enter *App Service environments*: isolated environments that let you run App Service instances like web apps in a segmented part of an Azure data center. You control the inbound and outbound network traffic and can implement firewalls and create virtual private network (VPN) connections back on your on-premises resources.

All of these infrastructure components are still largely abstracted with App Service environments, but this approach provides a great balance when you want the flexibility of PaaS solutions but also want to retain some of the more fine-grained controls over the network connections traffic flow.

You can do quite a lot with the Free and Basic tiers, although for production workloads you should probably use the Standard or Premium tier. This chapter's example uses the Standard tier so that you can see all the available features. When you use Web Apps with your own applications, you can decide how many of these features you need and select the most appropriate service plan tier accordingly.

> **Try it now**
> To finish your web app, complete the following steps.

1. Enter an App Service plan name, such as `appservice`. The name doesn't need to be globally unique like your web app name. Choose the most appropriate Azure region for you.
2. Select Pricing Tier, and then choose the S1 Standard Tier if it's not already selected. This tier provides all the core features without providing too many resources for your basic demo website.
3. Choose Select and then OK.
4. Back in the initial Create Web App window, leave Application Insights turned off for now. Application Insights allows you to dive deeper into the performance of your web application and do things like perform live debugging or stream telemetry. If you're a developer, this is cool stuff that you may want to explore when you begin to develop your own web applications in Azure.
5. To create your web app, select Create.
6. It takes a few seconds to create your app service. Browse to and select App Services from the navigation bar on the left side of the screen. It then takes a minute or two for the web app to be created, so click the Refresh button until yours appears, and then select it from the list.
7. From the Overview window of your web app, view and select the web app's URL. Figure 3.3 shows the example of azuremol as the web app name, so the URL is https://azuremol.azurewebsites.net.

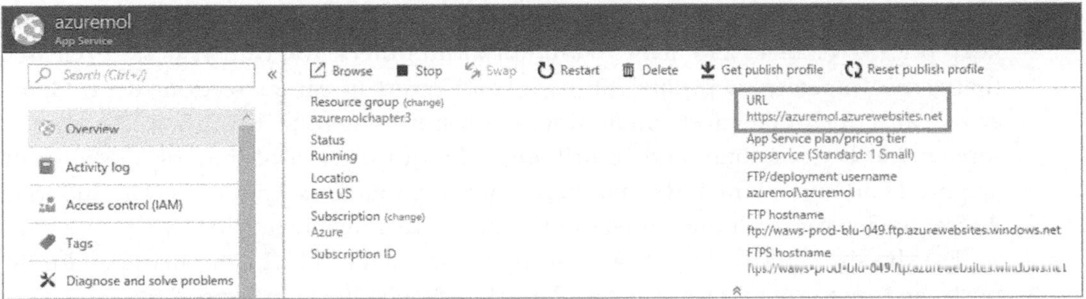

Figure 3.3 Select your web app in the Azure portal. On the right side of the windows is information such as the current state of the web app, the location, and its URL.

8 When you select the URL to your web app, a new browser window or tab opens. The default web app page loads, as shown in figure 3.4! Still doesn't look like pizza …

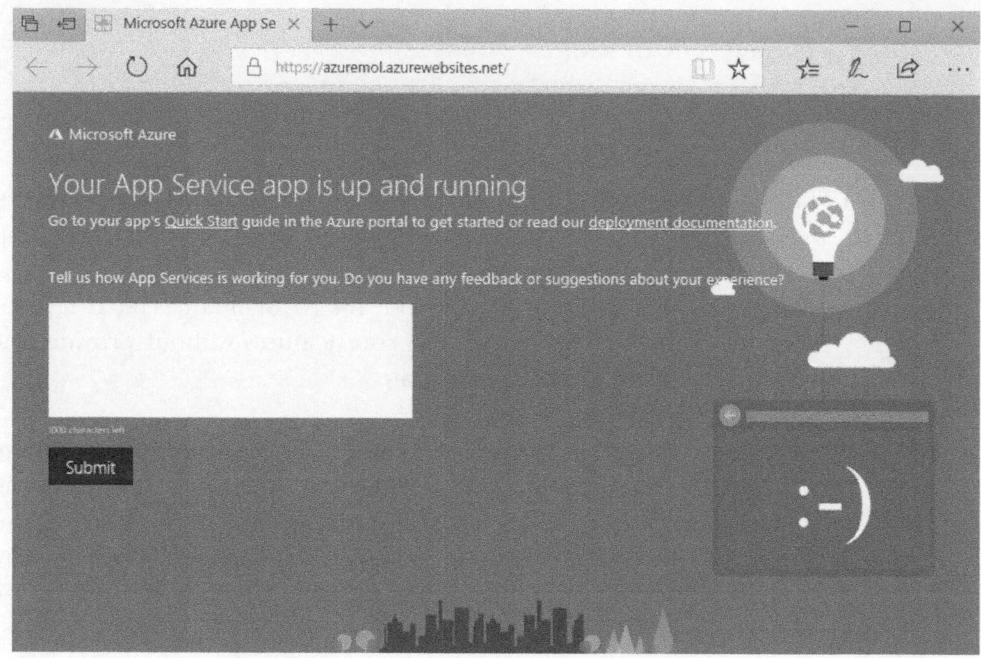

Figure 3.4 To see the default web app page in action, open a web browser to the URL of your site.

3.2.2 *Deploying a sample HTML site*

You have a web app in Azure, but it's the dull, default website. How do you get your own website in Azure? One of the most common cross-platform ways is to use Git.

Most application developers and teams use a source control system. Rather than storing files on your computer and saving changes as you go, source control systems keep track of changes and allow you to work with others. You can create test releases that won't impact your production code, and revert to earlier versions if problems arise. Git is one of the most common source control systems; GitHub is a cloud-based service that lets you share and contribute code with the rest of the world. Microsoft acquired GitHub in June 2018, but there's nothing that forces you to use GitHub with Azure, or vice versa. All the samples in this book are available in GitHub.

For this example, you create a local copy of the static HTML sample site and then push the files to your Azure web app. This workflow is shown in figure 3.5.

Figure 3.5 You create a local copy of the sample files from GitHub with the `git clone` command. To push these local files to your Azure web app, you use `git push`

Try it now

To get a copy of the sample HTML page from GitHub and push it to your web app, complete the following steps.

1 Select your Azure web app in the portal, and then choose Deployment Credentials. These credentials are separate from your Azure login details and let you push your application code from Git to a web app. The same deployment credentials can be used across your Azure subscription, so if you create them now, you can use them throughout the rest of the book.

   To create your own deployment credentials, enter a username and password, and then choose Save.

2 To configure your web app for use with Git, choose Deployment Options > Choose Source > Local Git Repository. Note that there are several other options you can use to store your source code for web apps, including GitHub itself, Dropbox or OneDrive, and Visual Studio Team Services.

3 To confirm and create a local Git repository, select OK.

4 Before you can push to this local Git repository, you need to get the HTML sample site from GitHub.

   Open the Cloud Shell in the Azure portal, and wait a few seconds for your session to connect. To *clone*, or copy, the HTML sample site from GitHub, enter the following command:

```
git clone https://github.com/fouldsy/azure-mol-samples.git
```

   If this is your first time with Git in the Cloud Shell, you need to define a couple of settings for Git to understand who you are. For most of the exercises in this book, it doesn't really matter; but for use with your own projects and applications, it's a great way to track who performs certain actions in a source control system. You only need to define these settings once. Enter your own email address and full name in `git config` as follows:

```
git config --global user.email "iain@azuremol.com"
git config --global user.name "Iain Foulds"
```

5 Change into the azure-mol-samples directory that was created when you cloned the Git repo:

```
cd azure-mol-samples/3/prod
```

6 To get ready to upload this, you must initialize Git and then add and commit your files. Don't worry too much about the Git commands right now! You need to tell Git what files to track and add, and give yourself a way to track those changes later if needed:

```
git init && git add . && git commit -m "Pizza"
```

Now you can push this HTML sample site to your web app. In the Azure portal, the Overview window for your web app listed the Git Clone URL. It looks like the following example:

```
https://azuremol@azuremol.scm.azurewebsites.net:443/azuremol.git
```

Your web app is configured to work with Git repos, so you need to tell the Cloud Shell what that repo is. In Git, you define these locations as *remotes.*

7 Copy your Git clone URL, and then set this URL as a destination for the HTML sample site in the Cloud Shell with the following command:

```
git remote add azure your-git-clone-url
```

To upload or copy files with Git, you *push* them. Where does Git push them to? A *remote* like you configured in the previous step, such as *azure.* The final part of the command is a branch, typically *master.* A branch in Git is how you keep track of different work-in-progress models. A best practice in production environments is to push to release branches that you can name as you wish, such as *dev* or *staging.* These additional branches allow your production code to run as normal; you can then work on new features or updates safely and without impact to real workloads that your customers use.

8 Push the HTML sample site to your web app:

```
git push azure master
```

9 When prompted, enter the password that you created for the deployment credentials.

You can see from the output that the existing default web app site page is removed and the HTML sample site is uploaded and configured to run. Here's some sample output:

```
Counting objects: 6, done.
Compressing objects: 100% (5/5), done.
Writing objects: 100% (6/6), 1.24 KiB | 0 bytes/s, done.
Total 6 (delta 0), reused 0 (delta 0)
remote: Updating branch 'master'.
remote: Updating submodules.
remote: Preparing deployment for commit id 'a3822aa914'.
remote: Generating deployment script.
remote: Generating deployment script for Web Site
remote: Generated deployment script files
remote: Running deployment command...
```

```
remote: Handling Basic Web Site deployment.
remote: KuduSync.NET from: 'D:\home\site\repository' to:
➥ 'D:\home\site\wwwroot'
remote: Deleting file: 'hostingstart.html'
remote: Copying file: 'index.html'
remote: Copying file: 'LICENSE'
remote: Finished successfully.
remote: Running post deployment command(s)...
remote: Deployment successful.
To https://mol-deploy@azuremol.scm.azurewebsites.net:443/azuremol.git
* [new branch]      master -> master
```

To see your updated web app, refresh your site in a web browser or open it again from the Overview window in the Azure portal. It should look like the wonderful example in figure 3.6. Yes, the site is basic, but the workflow for deploying the most basic static HTML site to a complex .NET or Node.js web app is the same!

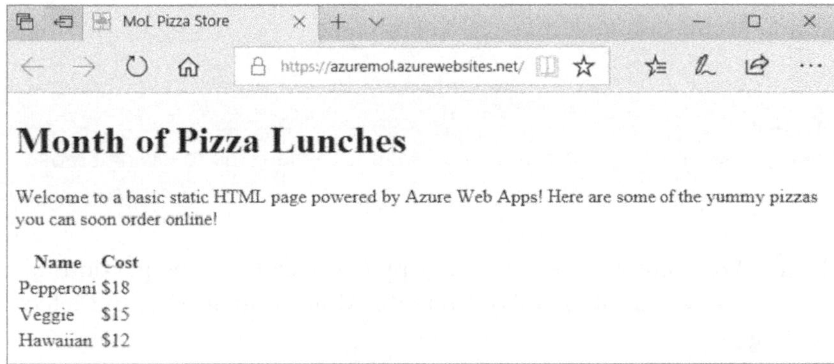

Figure 3.6 Refresh your web browser to see the default web app page replaced with the basic static HTML site from GitHub.

3.3 Managing web apps

Now that you've seen how to create a basic web app and deploy a simple HTML site to it, what about general management? If you run into problems, it would be helpful to see the web server or application logs. To help troubleshoot your apps, you can write output from your app to these log files. Log files can be viewed in real time or written to log files and reviewed later.

3.3.1 Viewing diagnostic logs

Your web app largely runs by itself. There's not a lot you can do from a maintenance perspective on the underlying web host. If your application runs into problems, you may want to look at the logs to see what's going on and troubleshoot the issue. With Azure Web Apps, you configure things like the level of log messages to review, where to store the logs, and how long to keep the logs. Figure 3.7 outlines how you generate and view log files with Web Apps.

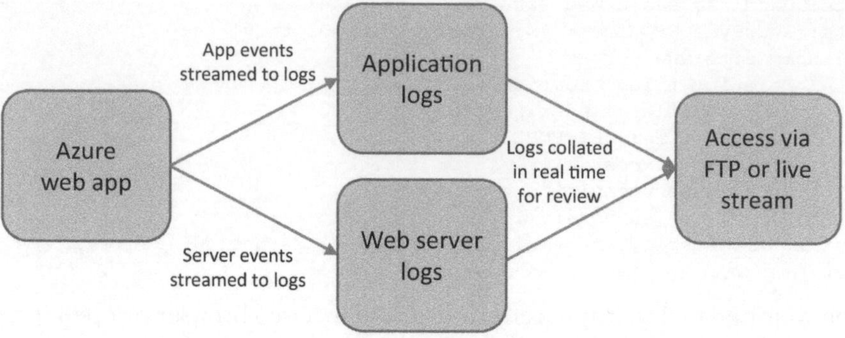

Figure 3.7 Your application can generate application logs and server logs. To help you review or troubleshoot problems, these logs can be downloaded with FTP or viewed in real time.

Try it now

To configure your web app for diagnostic logs, complete the following steps.

1. In the Azure portal, select the web app you created in the previous exercise. In the Overview window, scroll down to the Monitoring section and select Diagnostic Logs.
2. Review the available log options, such as the verbosity and whether you want to enable failed request tracing. If you deal with the infrastructure side of Azure, you may need to work with your application developers to determine what logs they need to help troubleshoot problems. You can then turn on the relevant logging here.
3. Note the FTP username and address to obtain your logs. The password is the same as you created in the previous exercise for the deployment credentials.

   Enter the FTP address shown in the portal blade in a browser or your local File Manager window. At the login prompt, enter the FTP username shown along with the password you previously created.

In the Log Files directory are the various log files, depending on what you enabled for your application. These logs can be cryptic, and usually there's no need to review them unless your web application has problems.

At the root of your FTP session is a directory called site. Inside that directory is wwwroot. This is where your web files are stored. When you pushed your site with Git in the previous example, Git wrote the file to this directory. Instead, you could FTP files straight to here; but Git offers additional features once you get used to it, such as versioning, history, and branches.

You may be thinking, "FTP is a complicated way to get diagnostic logs. Isn't there an easier way?" Why yes, there is! In the Azure portal, right where you configured your diagnostic logs, is a Log Stream option. Can you guess what it does? Let me give you a hint—it has something to do with streaming your log files.

If you select this button in the Azure portal, you can choose between Application Logs and Web Server Logs. These logs read from the same diagnostic logs that are written to file. There's a bit of a delay in the stream, and what's displayed depends on the log levels you specify and whether your web application generates any application events. For the basic HTML site, the stream is rather boring, but it's a great feature to have in the web browser. Figure 3.8 shows example streaming web server logs in the Azure portal.

Try it now

View the streaming log files in the Azure portal. You may need to refresh the page in your web browser a couple of times to generate activity in the logs.

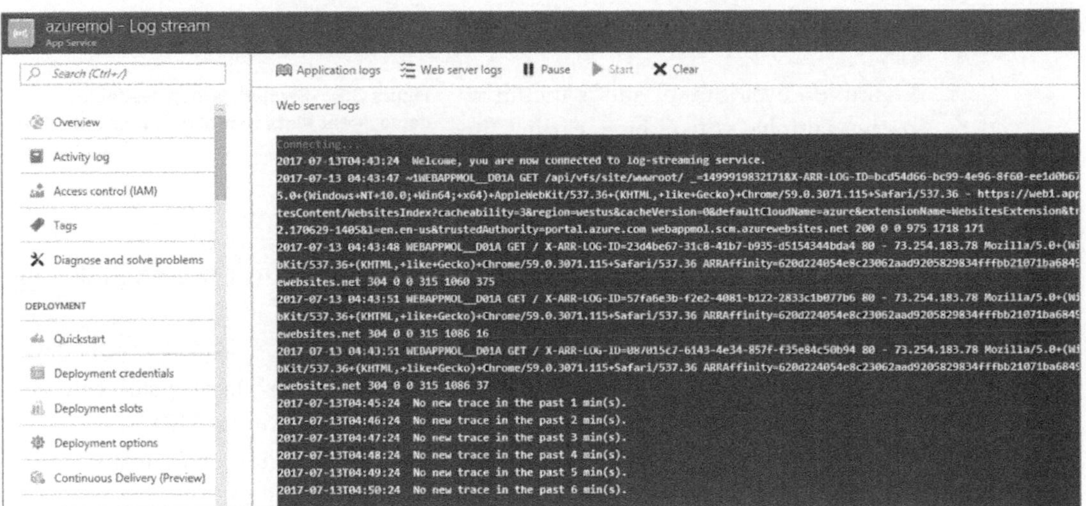

Figure 3.8 You can view the Web Apps web server log streams of live logs from your application to help verify and debug application performance. The console box at the right side on the screen shows the real-time streaming logs from your web app.

As you get more comfortable with Azure and use the Azure CLI or Azure PowerShell module, you can also stream logs with these tools. For developers, you can also enable remote debugging with Visual Studio under the Application Settings area or configure Application Insights to allow your web application to provide telemetry to additional services for monitoring and diagnostics. The key takeaway here is that as you move toward PaaS solutions like web apps, you can still obtain crucial diagnostics logs and application data to troubleshoot and monitor the performance of your web application.

3.4 Lab: Creating and using a deployment slot

We walked through how to create a simple HTML site and push the page to Azure Web Apps with Git. What if you now want to add some new pizza styles and view those before you make the site live for customers to order? Let's use a deployment slot to provide somewhere to upload your changes, review them, and then swap them to production:

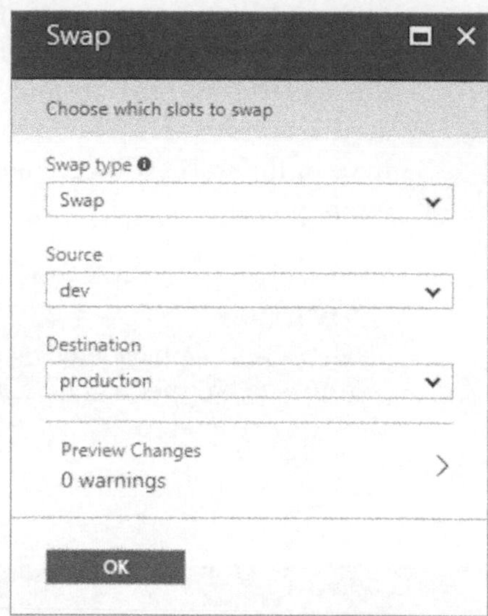

Figure 3.9 Swap between available deployment slots to make your dev site live in production.

1. In your web app, choose Add a Deployment Slot. Leave the default options so you don't clone from an existing deployment slot.
2. Select your deployment slot, and then follow the same procedure to Create a Deployment Source (local Git repository).
3. A sample development site is included in the samples you cloned earlier. In the Azure Cloud Shell, change to the development directory as follows:

```
cd ~/azure-mol-samples/3/dev
```

4. As before, initialize, add, and commit your changes in Git with the following commands:

```
git init && git add . && git commit -m "Pizza"
```

5. Create a link again to the new Git repository in your staging slot with `git remote add dev` followed by your staging slot Git deployment URL.
6. Use `git push dev master` to push your changes to the deployment slot.
7. Select the URL to your staging slot from the Azure portal Overview window.
8. What do you think happens if you select the Swap button? Figure 3.9 shows how you can pick Source and Destination deployment slots to swap. Try it, and see how easy it is to make your development site live as a replacement for the production site!

Deployment slots, behind the scenes

When you swap slots, what was live in the *production* slot is now in the *dev* slot, and what was in *dev* is now live in *production*. Not all settings can swap, such as SSL settings and custom domains; but for the most part, deployment slots are a great way to stage and validate content before it goes live to your customers. You can also perform a *swap with preview*, which gives you the opportunity to be sure the swapped content works correctly before it's publicly live in production.

For production use in DevOps workflows, you can also configure Auto Swap. Here, when a code commit is noted in source control such as GitHub, it can trigger a build to an Azure Web Apps deployment slot. Once that build is complete and the app is ready to serve content, the deployment slots automatically swap to make the code live in production. This workflow is typically used with a test environment to review the code changes first, not to publish live straight to production!

4 Introduction to Azure Storage

There are two things in the IT world that we can be certain of: when things go wrong, storage and networking are inevitably to blame. I say this as someone who's worn the hat of a SAN admin in one of my past lives! I was best friends with the networking team. I'm mostly joking (about being best friends), but it doesn't matter how well an application is designed and written: the foundational infrastructure pieces must be in place to support it. Bear with me in the next couple of chapters as we explore Azure Storage and Azure Networking. These services may be things that you're tempted to brush over and get to the cool stuff in the later chapters, but there's a lot of value in spending some time exploring and learning these core services. It won't make your food taste any better, but it may help your customers as they order their yummy pizza for delivery!

In this chapter, we look at the different types of storage in Azure and when to use them. We also discuss redundancy and replication options for the Azure Storage service, and how to get the best performance for your applications.

4.1 What's so special about storage?

Storage may not seem the obvious topic to examine to build and run applications, but it's a broad service that covers a lot more than you may expect. In Azure, there's much more available than just somewhere to store files or virtual disks for your VMs.

Let's look at what your fictional pizza company needs to build an app that processes orders from customers for takeout or delivery. The app needs a data store that holds the available pizzas, list of toppings, and prices. As orders are received and processed, the app needs a way to send messages between the different application components. The frontend website then needs mouth-watering images to show customers what the pizzas look like. Azure Storage can cover all three of these needs:

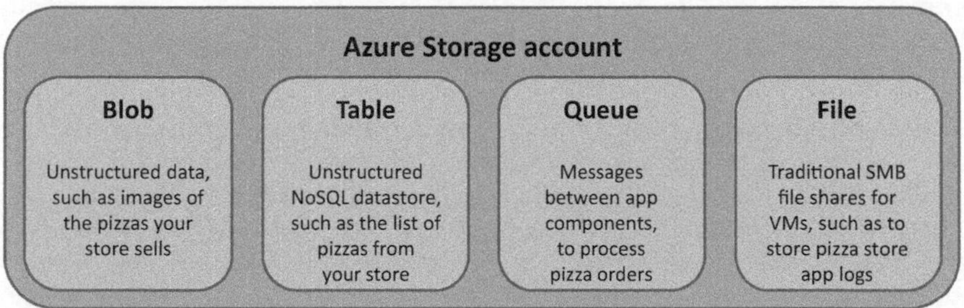

Figure 4.1 An Azure Storage account allows you to create and use a wide variety of storage features, way beyond just somewhere to store files.

- *Blob storage*—For unstructured data such as media files and documents. Applications can store data in blob storage, such as images, and then render them. You could store images of your pizzas in blob storage.
- *Table storage*—For unstructured data in a NoSQL data store. As with any debate on SQL versus NoSQL data stores, plan your application and estimate the performance requirements when it comes to processing large amounts of data. You could store the list of pizzas on your menu in table storage. We explore NoSQL more in the next section.
- *Queue storage*—For cloud applications to communicate between various tiers and components in a reliable and consistent manner. You can create, read, and delete messages that pass between application components. You could use queue storage to pass messages between the web frontend when a customer makes an order and the backend to process and bake the pizzas.
- *File storage*—For a good old-fashioned Server Message Block (SMB) file share, accessible by both Windows and Linux/macOS platforms. Often used to centralize log collection from VMs.

Azure Storage for VMs is straightforward. You create and use Azure managed disks, a type of virtual hard disk (VHD) that abstracts away a lot of design considerations around performance and distributing the virtual disks across the platform. You create a VM, attach any managed data disks, and let the Azure platform figure out redundancy and availability.

Life before managed disks

The Azure Managed Disks service launched in early 2017 with the goal of making VM storage easier. Before managed disks, you had to create a uniquely named storage account, limit the number of virtual disks you create in each, and manually move around custom disk images to create VMs in different regions. The Managed Disks service removes the need for a storage account, limits you to "only" 10,000 disks per subscription, and lets you create VMs from a custom image across regions. You also gain the ability to create and use snapshots of disks, automatically encrypt data at rest, and use disks up to 4 TB in size.

Why is this important? If you run across old documentation or blog posts, they may have you create a storage account for your VMs. Stop right there! Yes, you can convert VMs from unmanaged disks to managed disks, but if you have a clean slate, look to begin each project with managed disks from the start. The use case for unmanaged disks is more to maintain backward compatibility with existing deployments, although I'd argue you should look to convert those workloads to managed disks!

4.1.1 Table storage

Let's discuss a couple of different types of storage. First is *table storage*. Most people are probably familiar with a traditional SQL database such as Microsoft SQL Server, MySQL, or PostgreSQL. These are relational databases, made up of one or more tables that contain one or more rows of data. Relational databases are common for application development and can be designed, visualized, and queried in a structured manner—the *S* in *SQL* (for Structured Query Language).

NoSQL databases are a little different. They don't follow the same structured approach, and data isn't stored in tables where each row contains the same fields. There are different implementations of NoSQL databases: examples include MongoDB, Cassandra, SAP HANA, CouchDB, and Redis. The touted advantages of NoSQL databases are that they scale horizontally (meaning you can add more servers rather than adding more memory or CPU), can handle larger amounts of data, and are more efficient at processing those large data sets.

How the data is stored in a NoSQL database can be defined in a few categories:

- *Key-value*, such as Redis
- *Column*, such as Cassandra
- *Document*, such as MongoDB

Each approach has pros and cons from a performance, flexibility, or complexity viewpoint. An Azure storage table uses a key-value store and is a good introduction to NoSQL databases when you're used to an SQL database such as Microsoft SQL or MySQL. Figure 4.2 shows an example of what data stored in a table looks like.

You can download and install the Microsoft Azure Storage Explorer from www.storageexplorer.com if you like to visualize the data. You don't need to do this

PartitionKey	RowKey	Timestamp	cost	description
pizzamenu	001	2018-06-12T03:49:39.148Z	18	Pepperoni
pizzamenu	002	2018-06-12T03:49:39.198Z	15	Veggie
pizzamenu	003	2018-06-12T03:49:39.207Z	12	Hawaiian

Figure 4.2 Unstructured data stored in a table: a key-value pair made up of the `PartitionKey` and `RowKey`. The data is shown in the `cost` and `description` fields.

right now. The Storage Explorer is a great tool to learn what tables and queues look like in action. In this chapter, I don't want to take you too far down the rabbit hole of NoSQL databases—in chapter 10, we explore some cool NoSQL databases in depth with Azure Cosmos DB. In fact, in the following exercise, you use the Cosmos DB API to connect to Azure Storage and create a table. The use of Azure tables is more an introduction to NoSQL databases than a solid example of production use.

For now, let's run a quick sample app to see how you can add and query data, just as you'd do with an actual application. These samples are basic but show how you can store the types of pizzas you sell and how much each pizza costs. Rather than use something large like Microsoft SQL Server or MySQL, let's use a NoSQL database with Azure table storage.

> **Try it now**
> To see Azure tables in action, complete the following steps.

1 Open the Azure portal in a web browser, and then open the Cloud Shell.
2 In chapter 3, you obtained a copy of the Azure samples from GitHub. If you didn't, grab a copy as follows:

```
git clone https://github.com/fouldsy/azure-mol-samples.git
```

3 Change into the directory that contains the Azure Storage samples:

```
cd ~/azure-mol-samples/4
```

4 Install a couple of Python dependencies, if they aren't already installed. Here you install the `azurerm` package, which handles communication that allows you to create and manage Azure resources, and two `azure` packages, which are the underlying Python SDKs for Azure CosmosDB and Storage:

```
pip2 install --user azurerm azure-cosmosdb-table azure-storage-queue
```

What does `--user` mean when you install the packages? If you use the Azure Cloud Shell, you can't install packages in the core system. You don't have permissions. Instead, the packages are installed in your user's environment. These package installs persist across sessions and let you use all the neat Azure SDKs in these samples.

5 Run the sample Python application for tables. Follow the prompts to enjoy some pizza:

```
python2.7 storage_table_demo.py
```

Snakes on a plane

Python is a widely used programming language that's often used in "Intro to Computer Science" classes. If you mainly work in the IT operations or administration side of things, think of Python as a powerful scripting language that works across OSs. Python isn't just for scripting—it can also be used to build complex applications. As an example, the Azure CLI that you've been using is written in Python.

I use Python for some of the samples in this book because they should work outside of the Azure Cloud Shell without modification. macOS and Linux distros include Python natively. Windows users can download and quickly install Python and run these scripts locally. Python is great for those with little-to-no programming experience, as well as more seasoned developers in other languages. The Azure documentation for Azure Storage and many other services provides support for a range of languages including .NET, Java, and Node.js. You're not limited to using Python as you build your own applications that use tables.

Note that these samples use Python 2.7. There's a more modern Python 3.x, but there can be inconsistencies across OSs with the various Azure SDKs. To minimize problems, I kept the samples basic and compatible with the older Python version; but again, you're not limited to this when you build your own applications.

4.1.2 Queue storage

Azure tables are cool when you start to dip your toes into the world of cloud application development. As you begin to build and manage applications natively in the cloud, you typically break an application into smaller components that can each scale and process data on their own. To allow these different components to communicate and pass data back and forth, some form of message queue is typically used. Enter Azure Queues.

Queues allow you to create, read, and then delete messages that carry small chunks of data. These messages are created and retrieved by different application components as they pass data back and forth. Azure Queues won't delete a message until an application component confirms it has finished acting on it when read.

Try it now

To see Azure Queues in action, run the following Python script from the same azure-samples/4 directory. Follow the prompts to see messages written, read, and deleted from the queue:

```
python2.7 storage_queue_demo.py
```

Let's continue the example application that handles pizza orders. You may have a frontend application component that customers interact with to order their pizza, and then a message queue that transmits messages to a backend application component for you to process those orders. As orders are received, messages on the queue can be visualized as shown in figure 4.3.

ID	Message Text	Insertion Time (UTC)	Expiration Time (UTC)	Dequeue Count	Size
887b45dd-5c2f-4bdf-ab08-5c22838b5410	Veggie pizza ordered.	Tue, 12 Jun 2018 03:52:42 GMT	Tue, 19 Jun 2018 03:52:42 GMT	0	21 B
08a1b854-0b18-4e5b-9c48-5b0d0b22b641	Pepperoni pizza ordered.	Tue, 12 Jun 2018 03:52:42 GMT	Tue, 19 Jun 2018 03:52:42 GMT	0	24 B
f4f8c430-9fb7-4454-a884-e8abe3f7ec8a	Hawiian pizza ordered.	Tue, 12 Jun 2018 03:52:42 GMT	Tue, 19 Jun 2018 03:52:42 GMT	0	22 B
69bc8bed-6eac-45c8-af69-866ef9ef2325	Pepperoni pizza ordered.	Tue, 12 Jun 2018 03:52:42 GMT	Tue, 19 Jun 2018 03:52:42 GMT	0	24 B
e6b86b37-5496-4a84-b214-1a5313016834	Pepperoni pizza ordered.	Tue, 12 Jun 2018 03:52:42 GMT	Tue, 19 Jun 2018 03:52:42 GMT	0	24 B

Figure 4.3 Messages are received from the frontend application component that details what pizza each customer ordered in the `Message Text` property.

As the backend application component processes each yummy pizza order, the messages are removed from the queue. Figure 4.4 shows what the queue looks like once you have a veggie pizza in the oven and that first message is removed.

ID	Message Text	Insertion Time (UTC)	Expiration Time (UTC)	Dequeue Count	Size
08a1b854-0b18-4e5b-9c48-5b0d0b22b641	Pepperoni pizza ordered.	Tue, 12 Jun 2018 03:52:42 GMT	Tue, 19 Jun 2018 03:52:42 GMT	0	24 B
f4f8c430-9fb7-4454-a884-e8abe3f7ec8a	Hawiian pizza ordered.	Tue, 12 Jun 2018 03:52:42 GMT	Tue, 19 Jun 2018 03:52:42 GMT	0	22 B
69bc8bed-6eac-45c8-af69-866ef9ef2325	Pepperoni pizza ordered.	Tue, 12 Jun 2018 03:52:42 GMT	Tue, 19 Jun 2018 03:52:42 GMT	0	24 B
e6b86b37-5496-4a84-b214-1a5313016834	Pepperoni pizza ordered.	Tue, 12 Jun 2018 03:52:42 GMT	Tue, 19 Jun 2018 03:52:42 GMT	0	24 B

Figure 4.4 As each message is processed, it's removed from the queue. The first message shown in figure 4.3 was removed once it was processed by the backend application component.

4.1.3 Storage availability and redundancy

Azure datacenters are designed to be fault-tolerant with redundant internet connections, power generators, multiple network paths, storage arrays, and so on. You still need to do your part when you design and run applications. With Azure Storage, you choose what level of storage redundancy you need. This level varies for each application and how critical the data is. Let's examine the available storage-redundancy options:

- *Locally redundant storage (LRS)*—Your data is replicated three times inside the single datacenter in which your storage account was created. This option provides for redundancy in the event of a single hardware failure, but if the entire datacenter goes down (rare, but possible), your data goes down with it.
- *Zone redundant storage (ZRS)*—The next level up from LRS is to replicate your data three times across two or three datacenters in a region (where multiple datacenters exist in a region), or across regions. ZRS is also available across availability zones, which we explore more in chapter 7.

- *Geo-redundant storage (GRS)*—With GRS, your data is replicated three times in the primary region in which your storage is created and then replicated three times in a paired region. The paired region is usually hundreds or more miles away. For example, West US is paired with East US, North Europe is paired with West Europe, and Southeast Asia is paired with East Asia. GRS provides a great redundancy option for production applications.
- *Read-access geo-redundant storage (RA-GRS)*—This is the premium data-redundancy option. Your data is replicated across paired regions like GRS, but you can also then have read-access to the data in that secondary zone.

4.2 VM storage

Years ago, server storage was expensive, slow, and overly complicated. It wasn't uncommon for a storage vendor to sell you hardware that cost hundreds of thousands of dollars and took days, or even weeks, for an army of their consultants and engineers to configure. As virtualization began to take root in the datacenter and VMware and Hyper-V became more accepted, storage often became the bottleneck. And that's to say nothing of firmware mismatches between storage adapters in the server and on the storage array, redundant network paths failing back and forth, and SSDs being considered the only way to gain performance.

Has Azure magically fixed all these storage problems? Of course not! But it abstracts away 95% of these worries and leaves you to focus on how to build and create awesome experiences for your customers. Let's spend some time on the final 5% that you need to be aware of.

4.2.1 Standard vs. premium storage

Remember that line earlier about how if you wanted the best performance, you had to buy SSDs? There's no magic fix to get around that in Azure—sorry. The truth is that SSDs greatly outperform regular spinning disks. There are physical limits to how fast those spinning disks can, well, spin. The engineers at Microsoft haven't been able to bend the laws of physics just yet! There are still use cases for regular spinning disks, and just as in regular storage arrays, the latest technologies can provide good performance from a pool of spinning disks.

The first, and main, choice you need to make for an Azure VM is what type of storage to use:

- *Premium SSD disks*—Use high-performance SSD disks for optimal performance, greater IOPS, and low-latency. Recommended storage type for most production workloads.
- *Standard SSD disks*—Use standard SSDs. Delivers consistent performance compared to HDDs. Great for development and testing workloads, or budget-conscious and low-demand production use.
- *Standard HDD disks*—Use regular spinning disks for more infrequent data access such as archives or backups.

The VM size you choose helps determine what type of storage you can select. Back in chapter 2, when you created a VM, you picked a size to quickly give you a VM. You happened to pick a D2S_v3 series VM, which gave you access to premium SSD disks. How can you tell which VMs can access premium SSD disks? Look for an *s* in the VM size, for *S*SD. For example:

- D2S_v3, F*s*, GS, and L*s* series VMs can access premium SSD disks.
- D, A, F, and M series VMs can only access standard SSD or HDD disks.

If you select a VM size that can use premium SSD disks, there's no obligation to do so. You could create and use standard SSD or HDD disks. By choosing premium SSD disks, you future-proof the application and give yourself the option to use high-performance SSDs as you need them without the need to resize your VMs and incur a little downtime in the process. All VM sizes can use standard SSD disks.

Try it now

How can you tell what VM sizes are available to you? In the Azure portal, open the Cloud Shell. Enter the following command (feel free to use your own region):

```
az vm list-sizes --location eastus --output table
```

Remember, any size with an s gives you access to premium SSD disks.

4.2.2 Temporary disks and data disks

Now that you've figured out what level of performance you need for your applications, let's discuss another couple of puzzle pieces. Disks are connected two different ways:

- *Temporary disks*—Every VM automatically has local SSD storage attached from the underlying host that offers a small amount of high-performance storage. Take great care in how you use this temporary disk! As the name implies, this disk may not persist with the VM. If the VM moves to a new host in a maintenance event, a new temporary disk will be attached. Any data you stored there will be lost. The temporary disk is designed as a scratch space or application cache.
- *Data disks*—Any disks you specifically create and attach to the VM act as you'd expect in terms of partitions, filesystems, and persistent mount points. Data disks are reattached as the VM moves around the Azure datacenter, and they're where the bulk of your applications and data should be stored. You can still use storage spaces or software RAID to pool data disks at the VM level for even greater performance.

4.2.3 Disk-caching options

It's also important to consider the OS disk that comes with the VM. When you create a VM, you always get at least one disk. That's the disk where the OS itself is installed, and it's tempting to use that disk to install your applications or write log files to it. Unless you run a small proof-of-concept deployment, don't run your applications on the OS disk! There's a good chance you won't get the performance you desire.

Disks in Azure can have a caching policy set on them. By default, the OS disk has *read/write* caching applied. This type of caching typically isn't ideal for application workloads that write log files or databases, for example. Data disks, by contrast, have a default cache policy of *none*. This is a good policy for workloads that perform a lot of writes. You can also apply a *read-only* cache policy, which is better suited for application workloads that primarily read data off the disks.

In general, always attach and use data disks to install and run your applications. Even the default cache policy of none likely offers better performance than the read/write cache policy of the OS disk.

4.3 Adding disks to a VM

Let see how you can add disks to a VM as you create it. In chapter 2, you created a VM with the Azure portal. This time, let's use the Azure CLI to create a VM. The Azure CLI provides a quick way to create a VM and attach a data disk at the same time.

> **Try it now**
>
> To create a VM and see data disks in action, complete the following steps.

1 In the Azure Cloud Shell, create a resource group with `az group create`. Provide a name for the resource group, along with a location:

```
az group create --name azuremolchapter4 --location eastus
```

> **How to slash-dot yourself**
>
> In the following examples and later chapters, the backslash (\) means the command continues on the next line. It's a way to wrap long lines, and this approach is used in a lot of online samples where you can copy and paste the commands. You don't have to type out the backslashes in this book's examples if you don't want to! Just continue typing the additional parameters as part of one big line.
>
> If you're using the Windows command prompt rather than a Bash shell, don't include the backslashes. If you do, you *really* won't get the outcome you desire!

2 Create a VM with the `az vm create` command. The final parameter, `--data-disk-sizes-gb`, lets you create a data disk along with the VM. In the end-of-chapter lab, you can connect to this VM and initialize the disks.

   You create a Linux or Windows VM for this exercise. If you're comfortable with Linux or want to learn how to initialize and prepare a disk for Linux, use the following command to create an Ubuntu LTS VM:

```
az vm create \
  --resource-group azuremolchapter4 \
  --name storagevm \
  --image UbuntuLTS \
  --size Standard_B1ms \
  --admin-username azuremol \
  --generate-ssh-keys \
  --data-disk-sizes-gb 64
```

   If you're more comfortable with Windows, use the following command to create a Windows Server 2016 VM. You can then RDP to the VM to configure the disks later:

```
az vm create \
  --resource-group azuremolchapter4 \
  --name storagevm \
  --image Win2016Datacenter \
  --size Standard_B1ms \
  --admin-username azuremol \
  --admin-password P@ssw0rd! \
  --data-disk-sizes-gb 64
```

   It takes a few minutes to create the VM. The VM already has one data disk attached and ready for use.

What if you want to add another data disk after a few weeks or months? Let's use the Azure CLI again to see how to quickly add a disk. The process is the same for a Linux or Windows VM. All you do is tell Azure to create a new disk and attach it to your VM.

Try it now

Add an additional data disk to your VM as shown next.

Create a new disk with the `az vm disk attach` command. Provide a name and size for the disk. Remember the earlier discussion on standard and premium disks? In the following example, you create a premium SSD disk:

```
az vm disk attach \
    --resource-group azuremolchapter4 \
    --vm-name storagevm \
    --disk datadisk \
    --size-gb 64 \
    --sku Premium_LRS \
    --new
```

Do you recognize the last part of that storage type? LRS means locally redundant storage.

In two commands, you created a VM with the Azure CLI that included a data disk and then simulated how to attach an additional data disk later. Just because you attached these disks, doesn't mean you can immediately write data to them. As with any disk, be it a physical disk attached to an on-premises server, or a virtual disk attached to a VM, you need to initialize the disk and create a partition and filesystem. That's your exercise in the end-of-chapter lab.

4.4 Lab: Exploring Azure Storage

Here's a chance to test your skills. Pick one of the following tasks to complete for your lab exercise.

4.4.1 Developer-focused

If you're more of a developer and don't want to figure out initializing data disks on a VM, go back to the Cloud Shell and explore the two Python demos that use tables and queues. Even if you're new to Python, you should be able to follow along with what's going on:

- Think of some scenarios where you could implement tables or queues in your own applications. What would it take to build cloud-native applications with individual application components that could use queues, for example?
- Modify one of the samples that interests you, to create an additional pizza menu item (if a table) or creates a new pizza order message (if a queue).

4.4.2 VM-focused

If you want to log in to a VM and see that the process to initialize a disk and create a filesystem is the same as any other VM you've worked with, try one of these exercises:

1. Log in to the VM you created in section 4.2. Depending on your choice, you'll connect with SSH or RDP.
2. Initialize the disk, and create a partition:
   a. On Linux, the flow is `fdisk`, `mkfs`, and then `mount`.
   b. On Windows, use whatever sequence you're comfortable with—probably Disk Management > Initialize > Create Volume > Format.

5 Azure Networking basics

In the previous chapter, we explored the Azure Storage service. One of the other core services for cloud applications is Azure Networking. There are a lot of powerful network features in Azure to secure and route your traffic on a truly global scale. These features are designed to help focus on how to build and maintain your apps, so you don't have to worry about details like IP addresses and route tables. If you build and run an online store to handle pizza orders, it must securely transmit the customer data and process payment transactions.

In this chapter, we examine Azure virtual networks and subnets, and how to create virtual network interfaces. To secure and control the flow of traffic, you create network security groups and rules.

5.1 Virtual network components

Think of how many cables are behind your computer desk or in your entertainment center. Now think of all the cables required to connect the computers on a given floor of an office building. What about the entire office building? Ever been in a datacenter or seen photos of one? Try to imagine how large the Azure datacenters are. What about dozens of Azure datacenters, all around the world? Math isn't my strong point, so I can't calculate how many miles and miles of network cables are used to carry all the traffic in Azure!

Network connectivity is a crucial part of modern life. In Azure, the network is central to how everything communicates. For all the thousands of physical network devices and miles of network cables that connect everything in an Azure datacenter, you work with *virtual* network resources. How? Software-defined networks. When you create a VM or a web app, a technician doesn't have to run around the Azure datacenter to physically connect cables for you and assign IP addresses (although that would be funny to watch!). Instead, all of your network resources that define your entire network environment are logically handled by the Azure platform. As you work through this chapter, figure 5.1 shows the virtual network components you'll build.

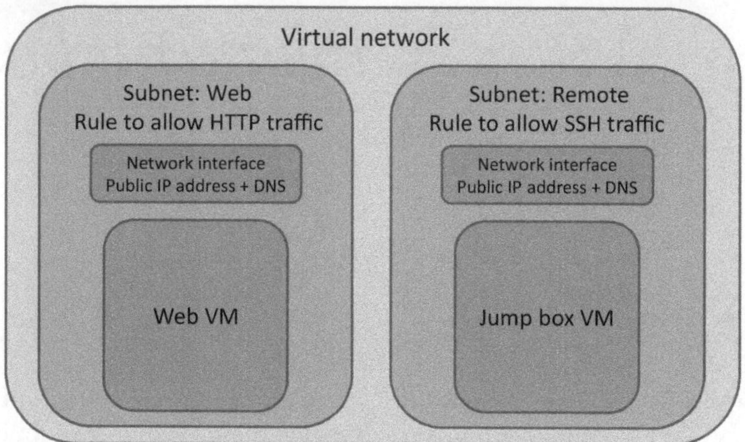

Figure 5.1 Software-defined network connections in Azure

Some of the network components are abstracted if you use PaaS resources. The main components that you use for VMs are as follows:

- Virtual networks and subnets (including IP address pools)
- Virtual network interface cards
- One or more public IP addresses
- Internal DNS name and optional public DNS names for external name resolution
- Network security groups and rules, which secure and control the flow of network traffic like a regular firewall does

5.1.1 *Creating and using virtual networks and subnets*

When you created a VM in chapter 2, you didn't have to adjust any network parameters. The Azure platform can create these resources for you with default names and IP address scopes. Let's create the network resources ahead of time and see how they come together for a VM.

> **Try it now**
> Networking is often easier to visualize when you see it in action. Don't worry too much about how to use your own address spaces or custom DNS names right now. To build out your virtual network and subnet as shown in figure 5.2, complete the following steps.

1. Open the Azure portal, and select Create a Resource in the upper-left corner of the dashboard.
2. Select Networking from the list of marketplace services, and then choose Virtual Network.
3. The menu that opens looks similar to what you saw in chapter 2. Enter a name for the virtual network, such as `vnetmol`.
4. To give yourself a little more room to play with, change the address space to `10.0.0.0/16`.

* Name
vnetmol
* Address space
10.0.0.0/16
10.0.0.0 - 10.0.255.255 (65536 addresses)
* Subscription
Azure
* Resource group
Create new Use existing
azuremolchapter5
* Location
East US
Subnet
* Name
websubnet
* Address range
10.0.1.0/24
10.0.1.0 - 10.0.1.255 (256 addresses)
DDoS protection
Basic Standard
Service endpoints
Disabled Enabled

Figure 5.2 The virtual network and subnet you create in the Azure portal forms the basis for the infrastructure in this chapter.

IP address ranges

Virtual networks span a certain range of IPs—an address space. If you've ever seen an IP address, you may have noticed the subnet mask: often something like 255.255.255.0. This subnet mask is often used in a short form that specifies how big that range is, such as /24.

The Azure portal defaults to a /24 address space. You want to increase the number of additional IP ranges here without too much network knowledge, so you increase the address space to /16. You don't give this type of IP address straight to a VM—in the next step, you create a subnet that covers a smaller section of this address space.

If network address spaces are totally foreign to you, don't worry. For the most part, they aren't something you'll deal with on a daily basis. Sensible Azure governance may work the same way it does in your existing on-premises IT world—one group of folks may manage the Azure virtual networks, and you drop your applications into a precreated space.

5. Choose Create New Resource Group. Enter a name, such as `azuremolchapter5`, and then select an Azure region close to you.
6. Provide a subnet name, such as a `websubnet`, and enter the Subnet Address Range `10.0.1.0/24`. This address range is part of the wider virtual network specified earlier. Later, you'll add another subnet.
7. To create the virtual network, select Create.

5.1.2 Virtual network interface cards

Now that you've created a virtual network and subnet, you need to connect a VM. Just as you do with a regular desktop PC, laptop, or tablet, you use a network interface card (NIC) to connect to the virtual network. And no, there's no free Wi-Fi! But there are VM sizes in Azure that currently provide up to eight NICs with speeds up of up 25 Gbps. Even if I were good at math, that adds up to some serious bandwidth!

You may wonder why you'd create each of these resources ahead of time. You can do all this when you create a VM. That's true, but take a step back and think about network resources as long-lived resources.

Network resources exist separately from VM resources and can persist beyond the lifecycle of a given VM. This concept allows you to create the fixed network resources and create, delete, and create again a VM that maintains the same network resources, such as IP addresses and DNS names. Think of a lab VM, or a development and test environment. You can quickly reproduce the exact same environment, because only the VM changes.

> **Try it now**
> To create a NIC as shown in figure 5.3, complete the following steps.

1. In the Azure portal, select Create a Resource in the upper-left corner of the dashboard.
2. Search for and select Network Interface, and then select Create.
3. Provide a name for your network interface, such as `webvnic`. The virtual network and subnet you created earlier should automatically be selected.
4. I talked about long-lived resources, so let's see how that works. Choose Static for Private IP Address Assignment. Enter the address `10.0.1.4` to create a static IP address for this network interface.

TIP Why .4? What about the first three addresses in the address space? Azure reserves the first three IP addresses in each range for its own management and routing. The first usable address you can use in each range is .4.

5 Leave Network Security Group as None for now; we'll come back to this in a few minutes. If you're one of the cool kids and know all about IPv6, you can check the Private IP Address (IPv6) box and provide a name.
6 Select Use Existing Resource Group, and then select the one you created in the previous section for your virtual network.
7 To create your network interface, select Create.

Figure 5.3 Create a virtual network interface card in the Azure portal.

> **Role separation in Azure**
>
> You don't have to create other compute resources within the same resource group as your virtual network. Think back to the concept of Azure governance we discussed earlier. You may have a group of network engineers who manage all the virtual network resources in Azure. When you create resources for your applications, such as VMs, you create and manage them in your own resource groups.
>
> We discuss in later chapters some of the security and policy features in Azure that allow you to define who can access and edit certain resources. The idea is that if you don't know, or don't want to know, a great deal about the network resources, you can connect to what's given to you, and that's it. The same applies to other engineers or developers—they may be able to see your application resources but not edit or delete them.
>
> This kind of governance model in Azure is nice, but take care to avoid the trap of working in siloes. In large enterprises, it may be inevitable that you're constrained along department lines; but one of the big advantages of cloud computing providers like Azure is speeding up time to deployment of applications, because you don't have to wait for physical network resources to be cabled up and configured. Plan to have the Azure network resources created and configured, and you should then be able to create and manage your application resources seamlessly.

5.1.3 *Public IP address and DNS resolution*

No one can access your resources yet, because no public IP addresses or DNS names are associated with them. Again, let's follow the principal of long-lived resources to create a public IP address and public DNS name, and then assign them to your network interface.

> **Try it now**
>
> To create a public IP address and DNS entry for your network interface as shown in figure 5.4, complete the following steps.

1. In the Azure portal, select Create a Resource in the upper-left corner of the dashboard.
2. Search for and select Public IP Address, and then select Create.
3. Enter a name, such as `webpublicip`. Leave the SKU as Basic and IP Version as IPv4. Standard SKUs and IPv6 addresses are for use with load balancers, which we look at in chapter 8.
4. For IP Address Assignment, you can choose between Dynamic and Static.

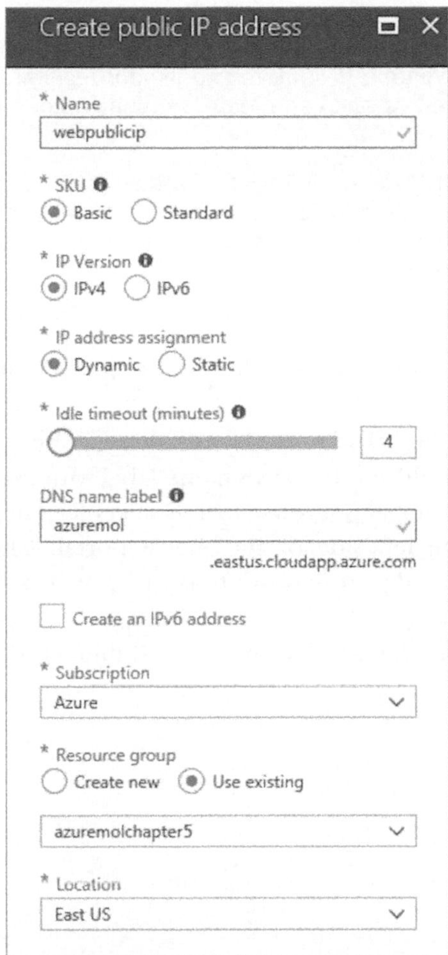

Figure 5.4 Create a public IP address and DNS name label in the Azure portal.

> **IP address assignment types**
>
> A *dynamic* assignment allocates a public IP address when the VM is started. When the VM is stopped, the public IP address is deallocated. There are a couple of important points here:
>
> - You won't have a public IP address until you assign it to a VM and start it.
> - The public IP address may change if you stop, deallocate, and start the VM.
>
> A *static* assignment means you have a public IP address allocated without an associated VM, and that address won't change:
>
> - This is useful for scenarios where you're using an SSL certificate mapped to an IP address, or a custom DNS name and record that points to the IP address.
> - Right now, you're using a single VM. For production use, you'll ideally run your application on multiple VMs with a load balancer in front of them. In that scenario, the public IP address is assigned to the load balancer and typically creates a static assignment at that point.

5 For DNS Name Label, enter a unique name. This name forms the fully qualified domain name (FQDN) for your resource that's based on the Azure region you create it in. In the example shown in figure 5.4, I created a DNS name label for azuremol in the East US region, so my FQDN became azuremol.eastus.cloudapp.azure.com.

> **DNS entries**
>
> What about a custom DNS name? The default FQDN isn't exactly user friendly! Use a static public IP address, and then create a CNAME record in your registered DNS zone. You retain control of the DNS record and can create as many entries as you wish for your applications.
>
> As an example, in the manning.com DNS zone, you might create a CNAME for azuremol that points to a static public IP address in Azure. A user would access azuremol.manning.com to get your application. This address is a lot more user friendly than webmol.eastus.cloudapp.azure.com!

6 Select Use Existing Resource Group, and then choose the group that you created in the earlier section.
7 To create your public IP address and DNS name label, select Create.
8 Now let's associate the public IP address and DNS name label with the network interface you created in the previous step. Browse to and select Resource Group from the navigation bar on the left side of the Azure portal. Choose the resource group in which you created your network resources, such as azuremolchapter5.
9 Select your public IP address from the list of resources, and then choose Associate, as shown in figure 5.5.

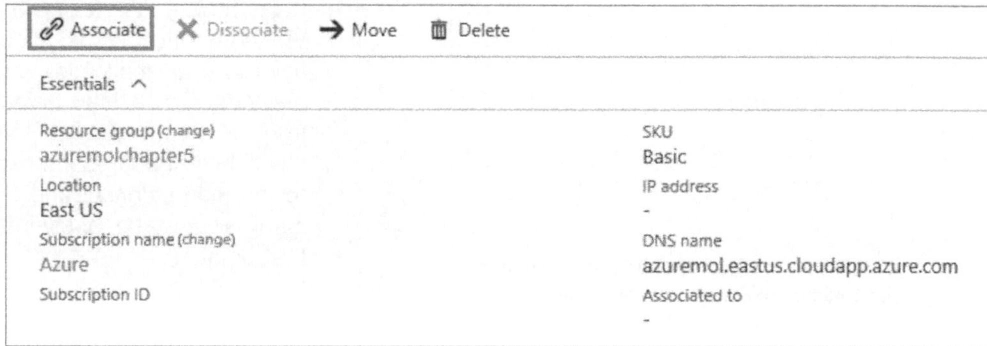

Figure 5.5 To attach the public IP address to your network interface, select Associate at the top of the overview window.

10 Select Network Interface from the Resource Type drop-down menu. Choose your network interface, such as webvnic, and then select OK.

After a few seconds, the public IP address window updates to show the IP address is now associated with your network interface. If you selected Dynamic as the assignment type, the IP address is still blank, as shown in figure 5.6. Remember, a public IP address is allocated once an associated VM is powered on.

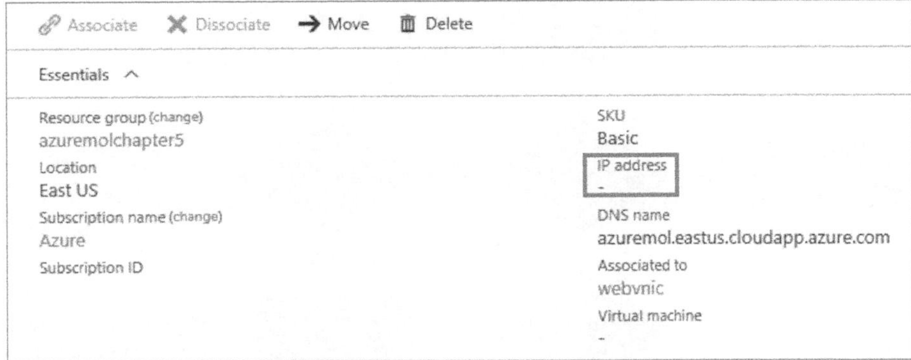

Figure 5.6 The public IP address is now associated with a network interface. With a dynamic assignment, no public IP address is shown until a VM is created and powered on.

5.2 Securing and controlling traffic with network security groups

Pop quiz time: should you connect a VM to the internet without a firewall to control and restrict the flow of traffic? If you answered, "Sure, why not?" then maybe take the rest of your lunch break to read a little about network security on the wild wide web!

I hope your answer was a resounding, "*No!*" Unfortunately, there's too much potential for your VM to come under an automated cyberattack soon after you turn it on. You should always follow best practices to keep the OS and application software up to date, but you don't even want the network traffic to hit your VM if it's not necessary. A regular macOS or Windows computer has a built-in software firewall, and every (competent) on-premises network I've seen has a network firewall between the internet and the internal network. In Azure, firewall and traffic rules are provided by network security groups.

5.2.1 Creating a network security group

In Azure, a *network security group* (NSG) logically applies a set of rules to network resources. These rules define what traffic can flow in and out of your VM. You define what ports, protocols, and IP addresses are permitted, and in which direction. These groups of rules can be applied to a single network interface or an entire network subnet. This flexibility allows you to finely control how and when the rules are applied to meet the security needs of your application.

Figure 5.7 shows the logic flow of an inbound network packet as it passes through an NSG. The same process would apply for outbound packets. The Azure host doesn't differentiate between traffic from the internet and traffic from elsewhere within your Azure environment, such as another subnet or virtual network. Any inbound network packet has the inbound NSG rules applied, and any outbound network packet has the outbound NSG rules applied.

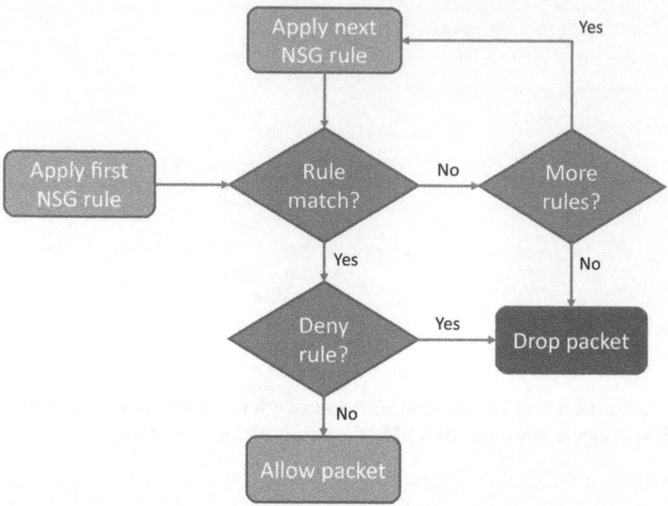

Figure 5.7 Inbound packets are examined, and each NSG rule is applied in order of priority. If an Allow or Deny rule match is made, the packet is either forwarded to the VM or dropped.

Here's what happens to each network packet:

1. The first NSG rule is applied.
2. If the rule doesn't match the packet, the next rule is loaded until there are no more rules. The default rule to drop the packet is then applied.
3. If a rule matches, check whether the action is to deny the packet. If so, the packet is dropped.
4. Otherwise, if the rule is to allow the packet, the packet is passed to the VM.

Let's create an NSG so this starts to make sense.

Try it now

To create a network security group as shown in figure 5.8, complete the following steps.

1. In the Azure portal, select Create a Resource in the upper-left corner of the dashboard.
2. Search for and select Network Security Group, and then select Create.
3. Enter a name, such as `webnsg`.
4. Select Use Existing Resource Group, and then select the one you created earlier. Select Create to create your NSG.

That's it! The bulk of the configuration for an NSG comes when you create the filtering rules. Let's move on and discuss how you do that and put your NSG to work.

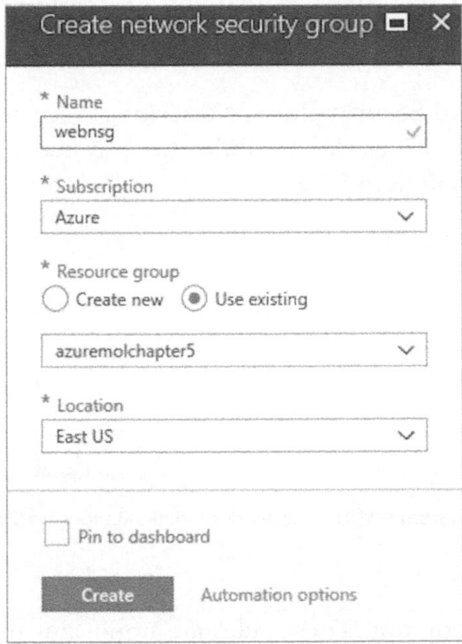

Figure 5.8 Create an NSG in your resource group.

5.2.2 Associating a network security group with a subnet

The NSG doesn't do much to protect your VMs without any rules. You also need to associate it with a subnet, the same way you associated your public IP address with a network interface earlier. Let's associate your NSG with a subnet first.

> **Try it now**
> To associate your virtual network subnet with your network security group, complete the following steps.

1. Browse to and select Resource Group from the navigation bar at left in the Azure portal. Choose the resource group you created your network resources in, such as azuremolchapter5.
2. Select your NSG, such as webnsg.
3. At left, under Settings, are Network Interfaces and Subnets options. Choose Subnets.
4. Select the Associate button, and then select your virtual network and network subnet created in previous steps. Select OK to associate your NSG with the subnet.

The flexibility of NSGs means you can associate multiple subnets, across various virtual networks, with a single NSG. It's a one-to-many mapping, which allows you to define core network security rules that apply to a wide range of resources and applications. Let's see what your NSG looks like and what default rules are applied.

5 At left in your NSG, select Inbound Security Rules. No security rules are listed, at least none that you've created. Select Default Rules to see what the Azure platform creates for you, as shown in figure 5.9.

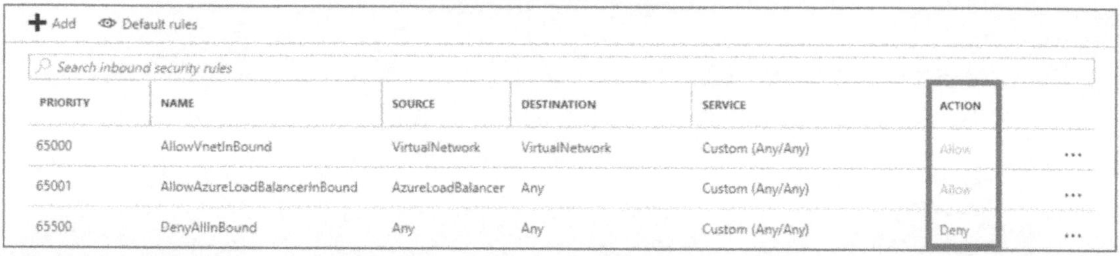

+ Add   Default rules

Search inbound security rules

PRIORITY	NAME	SOURCE	DESTINATION	SERVICE	ACTION	
65000	AllowVnetInBound	VirtualNetwork	VirtualNetwork	Custom (Any/Any)	Allow	...
65001	AllowAzureLoadBalancerInBound	AzureLoadBalancer	Any	Custom (Any/Any)	Allow	...
65500	DenyAllInBound	Any	Any	Custom (Any/Any)	Deny	...

Figure 5.9 Default security rules are created that permit internal virtual network or load-balancer traffic but deny all other traffic.

Three default rules have been created for you. These rules are important to understand:

- *AllowVnetInBound*—Allows any traffic that's internal to the virtual network. If you have multiple subnets in your virtual network, the traffic isn't filtered by default and is allowed.
- *AllowAzureLoadBalancerInBound*—Allows any traffic from an Azure load balancer to reach your VM. If you place a load balancer between your VMs and the internet, this rule ensures the traffic from the load balancer can reach your VMs, such as to monitor a heartbeat.
- *DenyAllInBound*—The final rule that's applied. Drops any inbound packets that make it this far. If there are no prior Allow rules, this rule by default drops all traffic. This means all you need to do is allow any specific traffic you want. The rest is dropped.

The priority of an NSG rule is important. If an Allow or Deny rule is applied, no additional rules are applied. Rules are applied in ascending numerical priority order; a rule with a priority of 100 is applied before a rule of priority 200, for example.

As with previous discussions on the governance of Azure resources, these NSG rules may already be created for you and applied to a given subnet. You create your VMs and run your applications, and someone else manages the NSGs. It's important to understand how the traffic flows in case something goes wrong. A couple of tools in Azure can help you determine why traffic may not reach your application when you think it should!

5.2.3 Creating network security group filtering rules

Now that you have your NSG associated with the network subnet and we've reviewed the default rules, let's create a basic NSG rule that allows HTTP traffic.

> **Try it now**
> To create your own rules with the network security group, as shown in figure 5.10, complete the following steps.

Figure 5.10 Create an NSG rule to allow HTTP traffic.

1. To create an NSG rule, select Add in the Inbound Security Rules section.
2. There are two ways to create rules: *Basic* and *Advanced.* To quickly create prebuilt rules, select Basic at the top of the window.
3. Select HTTP from the Service drop-down menu. Many default services are provided, such as SSH, RDP, and MySQL. When you select a service, the appropriate port range is applied: in this case, port 80.
4. A Priority value is assigned to each rule. The lower the number, the higher the priority. Leave the default low priority, such as 100.
5. You can accept the default Name or provide your own. Then, select OK.

5.3 Building a sample web application with secure traffic

So far, you've created a virtual network and subnet. Then you created a network interface and associated a public IP address and DNS name label. An NSG was created and applied to the entire subnet, and an NSG rule was created to allow HTTP traffic. You're missing one thing: the VM.

5.3.1 Creating remote access network connections

In production, you shouldn't open remote access, such as SSH or RDP, to VMs that run your applications. You typically have a separate jump-box VM that you connect to from the internet, and then you access additional VMs over the internal connection. So far, you've created all the virtual network resources in the Azure portal; let's switch over to the Azure CLI to see how quickly you can create these resources from the command line.

> **Try it now**
> The first NSG was created in the Azure portal. To create another NSG with the Azure CLI, complete the following steps.

1 Select the Cloud Shell icon at the top of the Azure portal dashboard. Make sure the Bash shell opens, not PowerShell.

2 Create an additional NSG in the existing resource group. As in previous chapters, the backslashes (\) in the following command examples are to help with line breaks—you don't have to type these in if you don't want to.

Provide a name, such as remotensg:

```
az network nsg create \
  --resource-group azuremolchapter5 \
  --name remotensg
```

3 Create an NSG rule in the new NSG that *allows* port 22. Provide the resource group and NSG you created in the previous step, along with a name, such as allowssh:

```
az network nsg rule create \
  --resource-group azuremolchapter5 \
  --nsg-name remotensg \
  --name allowssh \
  --protocol tcp \
  --priority 100 \
  --destination-port-range 22 \
  --access allow
```

4 The final step is to create a network subnet for your remote VM. Provide a subnet name, such as remotesubnet, along with an address prefix inside the range of the virtual network, such as 10.0.2.0/24. You also attach the NSG you created in the previous step to the subnet, such as remotensg:

```
az network vnet subnet create \
  --resource-group azuremolchapter5 \
  --vnet-name vnetmol \
  --name remotesubnet \
  --address-prefix 10.0.2.0/24 \
  --network-security-group remotensg
```

Three commands: that's all it takes to create a subnet, create an NSG, and create a rule. Can you start to see the power of the Azure CLI? The Azure PowerShell is equally as powerful, so don't feel like you must create all resources in the Azure portal. As we move forward in the book, we'll use the Azure CLI rather the portal in most cases.

5.3.2 Creating VMs

With all the network components in place, let's create two VMs. One VM is created in the subnet that allows HTTP traffic so you can install a web server. The other VM is created in the subnet that allows SSH so you have a jump box to further secure your application environment and begin to replicate a production deployment. Figure 5.11 reminds you what you're building.

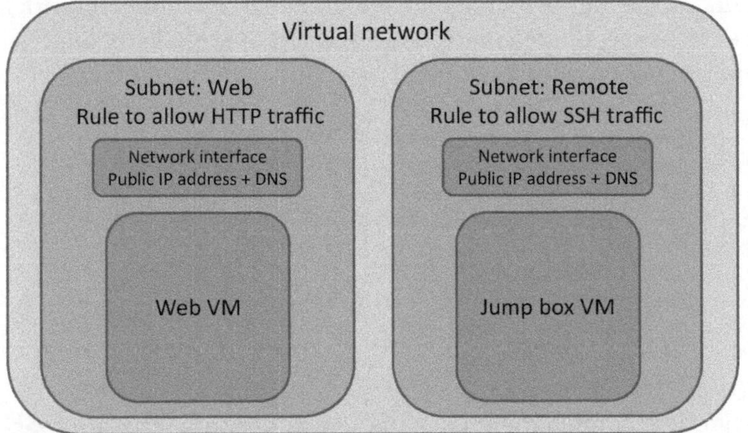

Figure 5.11 (Figure 5.1, repeated.) You're bringing together two subnets, NSGs, rules, network interfaces, and VMs. This is close to a production-ready deployment where one VM runs the web server and is open to public traffic, and another VM in a separate subnet is used for remote connections to the rest of the application environment.

When you create a VM, you can provide the virtual network interface that you created in the previous steps. If you didn't specify this network resource, the Azure CLI will create a virtual network, subnet, and NIC for you using built-in defaults. To quickly create a VM, that's great; but you want to follow the principal of long-lived network resources that another team may manage and into which you'll create your VMs.

Try it now

To use the Azure CLI to create your jump box VM, complete the following steps.

1 Create the first VM for your web server, and provide a name, such as webvm. Attach the network interface, such as webvnic, and enter an image, such as UbuntuLTS. Provide a username, such as azuremol. The final step, `--generate-ssh-keys`, adds to the VM the SSH keys you created in chapter 2:

```
az vm create \
  --resource-group azuremolchapter5 \
  --name webvm \
  --nics webvnic \
  --image UbuntuLTS \
  --size Standard_B1ms \
  --admin-username azuremol \
  --generate-ssh-keys
```

2 Create the second VM for the jump box. This example shows how you can use an existing subnet and NSG, and let the Azure CLI create the network interface and make the appropriate connections. You create a public IP address, such as remotepublicip, as part of this command:

```
az vm create \
  --resource-group azuremolchapter5 \
  --name remotevm \
  --vnet-name vnetmol \
  --subnet remotesubnet \
  --nsg remotensg \
  --public-ip-address remotepublicip \
  --image UbuntuLTS \
  --size Standard_B1ms \
  --admin-username azuremol \
  --generate-ssh-keys
```

The output from both commands shows public IP address. If you try to SSH to your first VM, it fails, because you only created an NSG rule to allow HTTP traffic.

5.3.3 Using the SSH agent to connect to your VMs

I need to introduce one piece of magic with SSH that allows you to use your jump box correctly and connect to the web VM over the Azure virtual network: it's called the *SSH agent.* This only applies to Linux VMs, so if you mainly work with Windows VMs and remote desktop (RDP) connections, don't worry if the SSH talk is new. You can create RDP connections from your jump box with the local remote credentials, or with domain credentials if you configure the server appropriately.

An SSH agent can store your SSH keys and forward them as needed. Back in chapter 2, when you created an SSH public key pair, I talked about the public and private key. The private key is something that stays on your computer. Only the public key is copied to the remote VMs. Although the public key was added to both VMs you created, you can't just SSH to your jump box and then SSH to the web VM. Why? Because that jump box doesn't have a copy of your private key. When you try to make the SSH connection from the jump box, it has no private key to pair up with the public key on the web VM for you to successfully authenticate.

The private key is something to safeguard, so you shouldn't take the easy way out and copy the private key to the jump box. Any other users who access the jump box could potentially get a copy of your private key and then impersonate you anywhere that key is used. Here's where the SSH agent comes into play.

If you run the SSH agent in your Cloud Shell session, you can add your SSH keys to it. To create your SSH connection to the jump box, you specify the use of this agent to tunnel your session. This allows you to effectively pass through your private key for use from the jump box, without ever copying the private key. When you SSH from the jump box to the web VM, the SSH agent tunnels your private key through the jump box and allows you to successfully authenticate.

Try it now

To use SSH with your jump-box VM, complete the following steps.

1. In the Cloud Shell, start the SSH agent as follows:

```
eval $(ssh-agent)
```

2. Add the SSH key you created in chapter 2 to the agent as follows:

```
ssh-add
```

3. SSH to your jump box VM. Specify the use of the SSH agent with the `-A` parameter. Enter your own public IP address that was shown in the output when you created the jump-box VM:

```
ssh -A azuremol@<publicIpAddress>
```

4. This is the first time you've created an SSH connection to the jump-box VM, so accept the prompt to connect with the SSH keys.
5. Remember how you created a static private IP address assignment for the web VM in section 5.1.2? This static address makes it a lot easier to now SSH to it! SSH to the web VM as follows:

```
ssh 10.0.1.4
```

6. Accept the prompt to continue the SSH connection. The SSH agent tunneled your private SSH key through the jump box and allows you to successfully connect to the web VM. Now what? Well, you have a lab to see this work!

5.4 Lab: Installing and testing the LAMP web server

You've already done the hard work throughout the chapter. This quick lab reinforces how to install a web server and lets you see the NSG rule on your VM in action:

1. *Install a basic Linux web server.* Think back to chapter 2 when you created an SSH connection to the VM and then installed the LAMP web server package with `apt`. From the SSH connection to your web VM created in section 5.3.2, install and configure the default LAMP web stack.
2. *Browse to the default website.* Once the LAMP web stack is installed, open your web browser to the DNS name label you entered when you created a public IP address in section 5.1.3. In my example, that was azuremol.eastus.cloudapp .azure.com. You can also use the public IP address that was output when you created the web VM. Remember, though: that public IP address is different than the jump box VM you SSH'd to!

Part 2

High availability and scale

Okay, let's start to have some fun! Now that you understand the core resources in Azure, we can dive into areas like redundancy, load balancing, and geographically distributing applications. This is where things get exciting, and the topics you learn about hopefully start to show solutions and best practices that you can use in real-world deployments. There are some awesome features in Azure to replicate data globally, distribute customer traffic to the closest instance of your application, and automatically scale based on demand. These features are the power of cloud computing and where you bring true value to your work.

6 Azure Resource Manager

Most days, you want to spend as little time as possible on how you deploy an application environment, and get on with the actual deployment. In many IT environments, there's a move toward development and operations teams that collaborate and work closely together, with the DevOps buzzword thrown around a lot at conferences and in blogs.

There's nothing inherently new or groundbreaking about the DevOps culture, but often different teams didn't work together as they should. Modern tools have spurred the DevOps movement, with continuous integration and continuous delivery (CI/CD) solutions that can automate the entire deployment of application environments based on a single code check-in by a developer. The operations team is usually the one that builds and maintains these CI/CD pipelines, which allows much quicker tests and deployments of application updates for developers.

The Azure Resource Manager deployment model is central to how you build and run resources, even though you probably haven't realized it yet. Resource Manager is an approach to how to build and deploy resources, as much as the automation processes and templates that drive those deployments. In this chapter, you learn how to use Resource Manager features such as access controls and locks, consistent template deployments, and automated multi-tier roll-outs.

6.1 The Azure Resource Manager approach

When you created a VM or web app in previous chapters, a resource group was first created as the core construct to hold all of your resources. A resource group is central to all resources: a VM, web app, virtual network, or storage table can't exist outside of a resource group. But the resource group is more than just a place to organize your resources—a lot more. Let's look at what the underlying Azure Resource Manager model is and why it's important as you build and run applications.

6.1.1 Designing around the application lifecycle

Hopefully, you won't build an application and then never maintain it. There are usually updates to develop and deploy, new packages to install, new VMs to add, and additional web app deployment slots to create. You may need to make changes to the virtual network settings and IP addresses. Remember how I mentioned in previous chapters that your virtual networks in Azure may be managed by a different team? You need to start to think about how you run on a large, global scale, and in terms of the application lifecycle and management.

There are a couple of main approaches for grouping resources in Azure:

- *All resources for a given application in the same resource group*—As shown in figure 6.1, this approach works well for smaller applications or development and test environments. If you don't need to share large networking spaces and can individually manage storage, you can create all the resources in one place, and then manage updates and configuration changes in one operation.

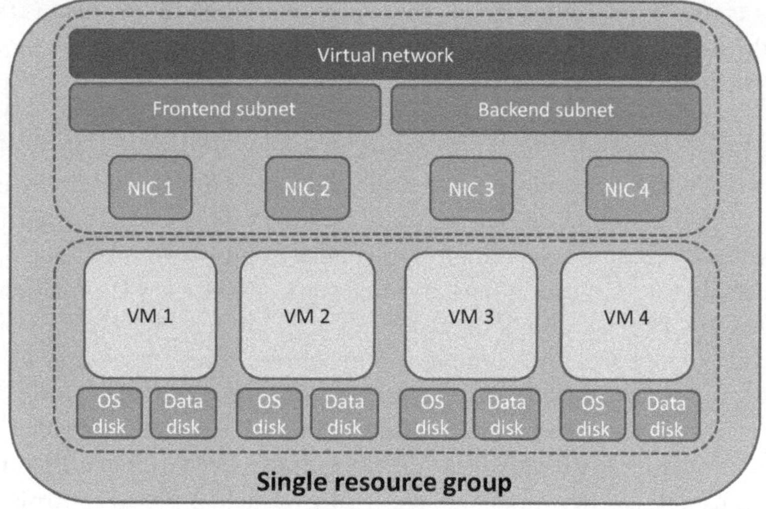

Figure 6.1 One way to build an application in Azure is for all the resources related to that application deployment to be created in the same resource group and managed as one entity.

- *Like-minded resources grouped by function in the same resource group.* As shown in figure 6.2, this approach is often more common in larger applications and environments. Your application may exist in a resource group with only the VMs and supporting application components. Virtual network resources and IP addresses may exist in a different resource group, secured and managed by a different group of engineers.

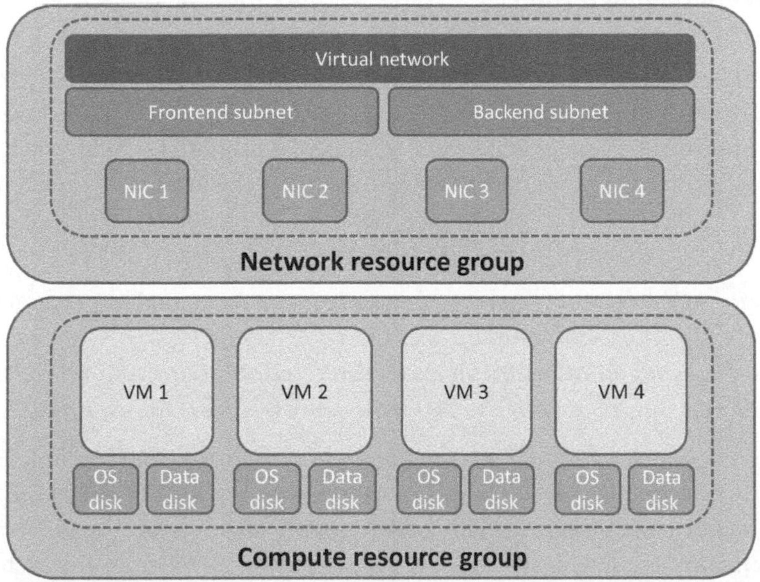

Figure 6.2 An alternate approach is to create and group resources based on their role. A common example is that all core network resources are in a separate resource group than the core application compute resources. The VMs in the compute resource group can access the network resources in the separate group, but the two sets of resources can be managed and secured independently.

Why the different approaches? The answer isn't all down to job security and those lovely silos some teams like to work in. It's more about how you need to manage the underlying resources. In smaller environments and applications where all the resources exist in the same resource group, you're responsible for everything in that environment. This approach is also well-suited to development and test environments where everything is packaged together. Any changes you make to the virtual network only impact your application and resource group.

The reality is that networks don't change often. The address ranges are often well defined and planned so they can coexist across Azure and office locations around the world. Logically, it often makes sense to place the network components in their own resource group. The network is managed separately from the application. Storage may be managed and updated separately in the same way. There's nothing inherently wrong with the division of resources like this, as long as the IT staff doesn't get stuck in a silo mentality, resulting in a lack of cooperation.

For your applications, the division of resources can also be a benefit in that you're largely free to make the changes and updates as you wish. Precisely because you don't have the network components in your resource group, you don't need to worry about them when you make application updates.

6.1.2 Securing and controlling resources

Each resource can have different security permissions applied to it. These policies define who can do what. Think about it—do you want an intern restarting your web app or deleting the VM data disks? And do you think your good buddies over in the network team want you to create a new virtual network subnet? Probably not.

In Azure, there are four core roles you can assign to resources, much like file permissions:

- *Owner*—Complete control. Basically, an administrator.
- *Contributor*—Able to fully manage the resource, except making changes to the security and role assignments.
- *Reader*—Can view all information about the resource, but make no changes.
- *User access administrator*—Able to assign or remove access to resources.

Role-based access control (RBAC) is a core feature of Azure resources and automatically integrates with the user accounts across your subscriptions. Think of file permissions on your normal computer. The basic file permissions are read, write, and execute. When combined, you can create different sets of permissions for each user or group on your computer. As you work with network file shares, permissions are a common occurrence to control access. RBAC in Azure works along the same lines to control access to resources, just like file permissions on your local computer or network share; see figure 6.3.

Try it now

Open the Azure portal in a web browser, and then select any resource you have, such as cloud-shell-storage. Choose the Access Control (IAM) button, as shown in figure 6.3. Review the current assignments. Choose the Roles button, and explore all the available role assignments. The information icon for each role shows what permissions are assigned.

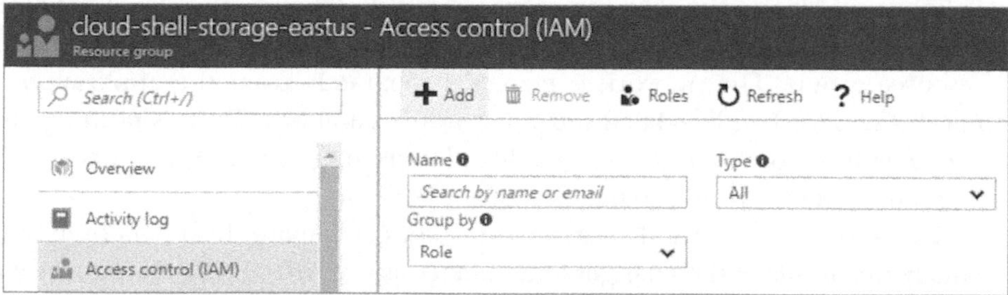

Figure 6.3 The access control for each Azure resource lists what the current assignments are. You can add assignments, or select Roles to see information about what permission sets are available.

As you explore the available roles, you may notice several resource-specific roles. These include the following:

- Virtual Machine Contributor
- Website Contributor
- Network Contributor

Can you guess what those roles mean? They take the core platform Contributor role and apply it to a specific resource type. The use case here goes back to that concept of how you manage like-minded resources. You might be assigned the Virtual Machine Contributor or Website Contributor role. Any VMs or web apps created in that resource group would then be available for you to manage. But you couldn't manage network resources, which may be in a different resource group entirely.

6.1.3 Protecting resources with locks

The permissions-based approach of RBAC is great to limit who can access what. But mistakes can still happen. There's a reason you typically don't log on to a server as a user with administrative, or root, permissions. One wrong keystroke or mouse click, and you could mistakenly delete resources. Even if you have backups (you do have backups, right? And you test them regularly?), it's a time-consuming process that may mean lost productivity or revenue to the business. In chapter 13, you'll learn more about the ways the Azure Backup, Recovery, and Replication services protect your data.

Another feature built in to the Resource Manager model is resource locks. Each resource can have a lock applied that limits it to read-only access or prevents delete operations. The delete lock is particularly helpful, because it can be all too easy to delete the wrong resource group. Once you start a delete operation, there's no going back or canceling the operation after the Azure platform has accepted your request.

For production workloads, I suggest you implement locks on your core resources to prevent deletes. This is only at the Azure resource and platform levels, not for the data within your resources. For example, you could delete files within a VM or drop a table in a database. The Azure resource locks would apply only if you tried to delete the entire VM or Azure SQL database. The first time a lock kicks in and prevents the wrong resource group from being deleted, you'll thank me!

Try it now

To see Azure resource locks in action, as shown in figure 6.4, complete the following steps.

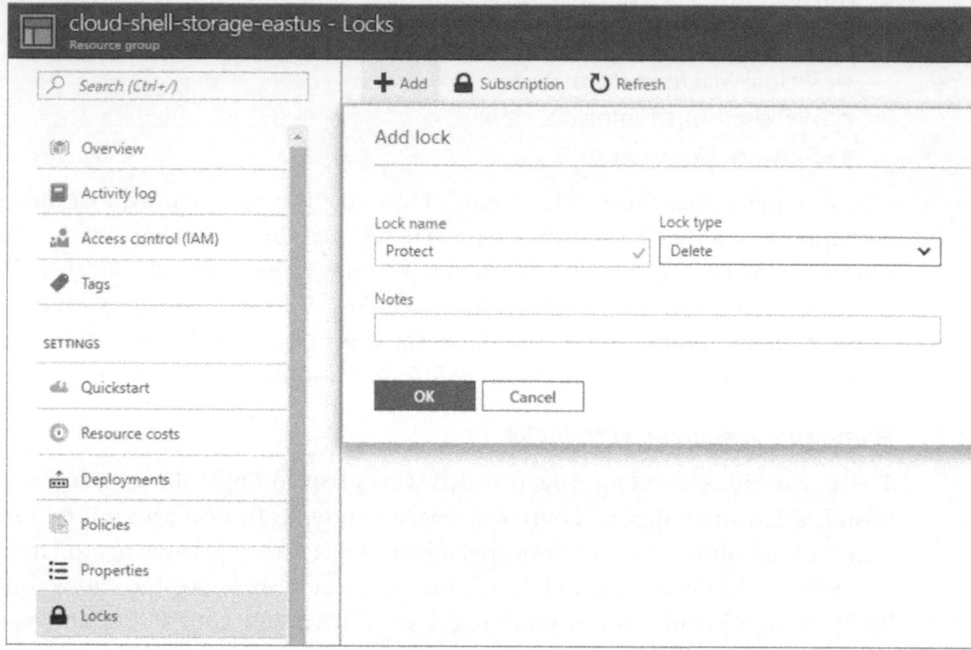

Figure 6.4 Create a resource lock in the Azure portal.

1. Open the Azure portal in a web browser, and then select any resource group you have, such as cloud-shell-storage. Choose Locks at left in the portal.
2. Enter a Lock Name, such as Protect, and then select Delete from the Lock Type drop-down menu. Choose OK, and your new lock appears in the list.
3. Select Overview for the resource group, and then try to delete the resource group. You need to enter the resource group name to confirm that you wish to delete it (which is also a good mental prompt to make sure you have the right resource to delete!).
4. When you choose the Delete button, review the error message that's displayed to see how your lock prevented Azure from deleting the resource.

6.1.4 Managing and grouping resources with tags

One final feature in the Azure Resource Manager model that I want to bring up are *tags*. There's nothing new or special about how you tag resources in Azure, but this is often an overlooked management concept. You can apply tags to a resource in Azure that describes properties such as the application it's part of, the department responsible for it, or whether it's a development or production resource.

You can then target resources based on tags to apply locks or RBAC roles, or report on resource costs and consumption. Tags aren't unique to a resource group and can be reused across your subscription. Up to 15 tags can be applied to a single resource, so there's a lot of flexibility in how you tag and then filter tagged resources.

> **Try it now**
> To see Azure resource tags in action, complete the following steps.

1. Open the Azure portal in a web browser, and then select any resource, such as cloud-shell-storage. Choose the Tags button, as shown in figure 6.5.
2. Enter a Name, such as `workload`, and a Value, such as `development`.
3. Select Save, and then open the Cloud Shell.
4. To filter resources based on tags, use `az resource list` with the `--tag` parameter. Use your own name and value as follows:

```
az resource list --tag workload=development
```

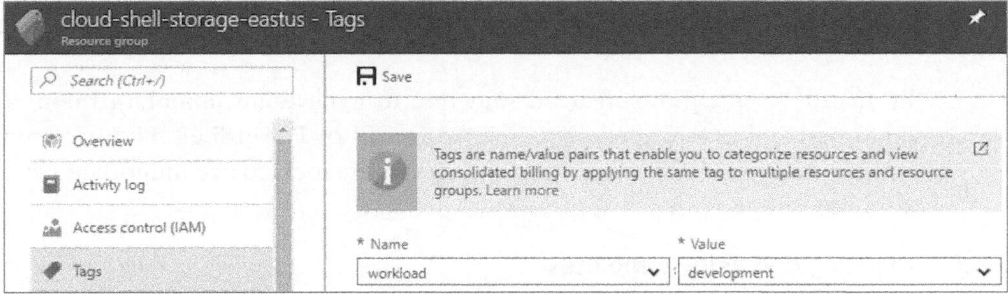

Figure 6.5 You can create up to 15 name:value tags for each Azure resource.

6.2 Azure Resource Manager templates

So far, you've created a small number of Azure resources at a time. To do this, you've used the Azure portal or Azure CLI. Although I haven't shown you Azure PowerShell, I did talk about it in the first chapter, and it's available in the Cloud Shell. Maybe you've tried it without me. That's okay, I don't feel left out! As I mentioned in chapter 1, Azure has tools that let you choose what's most comfortable for you and the environment you work in.

The downside of using the portal or CLI or PowerShell commands is that you must click a bunch of buttons in the web browser or type out lines of commands to build your application environment. You could create scripts to do all this, but you then must build logic to handle how to create multiple resources at the same time, or what order to create resources in.

A script that wraps Azure CLI or PowerShell commands starts to move in the right direction in terms of how you should build and deploy application environments—not just in Azure, but across any platform. There's a move toward infrastructure as code (IaC), which is nothing new if you've been around IT for a while. All it means is that you don't rely on a human to type commands and follow a set of steps; rather, you programmatically create your infrastructure from a set of instructions. Manual deployments introduce a human element that can often lead to minor misconfigurations and differences in the final VMs, as shown in figure 6.6.

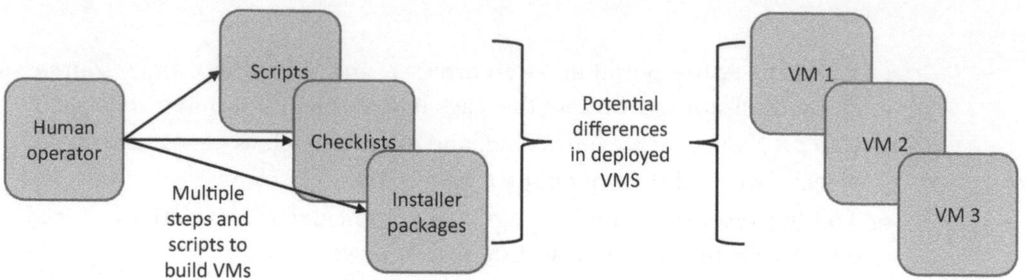

Figure 6.6 Humans make mistakes, such as mistyping a command or skipping a step in a deployment. You can end up with slightly different VMs at the end of the output. Automation is often used to remove the human operator from the equation and instead create consistent, identical deployments every time.

Even with scripts, you still need someone to write them, maintain them, and keep them updated as new versions of the Azure CLI or PowerShell modules are released. Yes, there are sometimes breaking changes in the tools to accommodate new features, although they're rare.

6.2.1 *Creating and using templates*

Resource Manager templates can help reduce human error and reliance on manually written scripts. Templates are written in JSON, an open and cross-platform approach that allows editing them in a basic text editor. With templates, you can create consistent, reproducible deployments that minimize errors. Another built-in feature of templates is that the platform understands dependencies and can create resources in parallel where possible to speed up deployment time. For example, if you create three VMs, there's no need to wait for the first VM to finish deploying before you create the second. Resource Manager can create all three VMs as the same time.

As an example of dependencies, if you create a virtual NIC, you need to connect it to a subnet. Logically, the subnet must exist before you can create the virtual NIC. And the subnet must be part of a virtual network, so that network must be created before the subnet. Figure 6.7 shows the chain of dependencies in action. If you try to write a script yourself, you must carefully plan the order in which resources are created, and even then, you must build in logic to know when the parent resources are ready and you can move on to the dependent resources.

Want to know something cool? You've already used Resource Manager templates, all the way back in chapter 2 and the very first VM you created. As you create a VM in the portal or the Azure CLI, under the hood a template is programmatically created and deployed. Why? Well, why reinvent the wheel and go through the process of building all that logic for the deployments? Let Azure Resource Manager do it for you!

Figure 6.7 Azure Resource Manager handles dependencies for you. The platform knows the order in which to create resources and has awareness of the state of each resource without the use of handwritten logic and loops like those you must use in your own scripts.

Let's see what a section of a Resource Manager template looks like. The following listing shows the section that creates a public IP address, just as you did in earlier examples when you created a VM.

Listing 6.1 Creating a public IP address in a Resource Manager template

```
{
    "apiVersion": "2017-04-01",
    "type": "Microsoft.Network/publicIPAddresses",
    "name": "publicip",
    "location": "eastus",
    "properties": {
      "publicIPAllocationMethod": "dynamic",
      "dnsSettings": {
        "domainNameLabel": "azuremol"
    }
  }
},
```

Even if JSON is new to you, it's written in a (somewhat) human-readable format. You define a resource type—in this example, `Microsoft.Network/publicIPAddresses`. You then provide a name, such as `publicip`, and a location, such as `eastus`. Finally, you define the allocation method, `dynamic` in this example, and a DNS name label, like `azuremol`. These are the same parameters you provided when you used the Azure portal or CLI. If you use PowerShell, guess what? You're prompted for the same parameters.

The difference with the template is that you didn't have to enter any information. It was all included in the code. "Great," you might be thinking, "but what if I want to use different names each time?" Same as with a script, you can dynamically assign them using parameters and variables:

- *Parameters* are values that you're prompted for. They're often used for user credentials, the VM name, and the DNS name label.
- *Variables* can be preassigned a value, but they're also adjusted each time you deploy the template, such as the VM size or virtual network name.

Try it now

To see a complete Resource Manager template, open a web browser to the GitHub repo at http://mng.bz/8jr1. You should recognize all the different resources and values used in the template: it's the basic VM you created in chapter 2.

6.2.2 Creating multiples of a resource type

As you build your templates, try to think ahead about how you may need to grow your applications in the future. You may only need a single VM when you first deploy your application, but as demand for the application grows, you may need to create additional instances.

In a traditional scripted deployment, you create a `for` or `while` loop to create multiple resource types. Resource Manager has this functionality built in! There are more than 50 types of functions in Resource Manager, just like in most programming and scripting languages. Common Resource Manager functions include `length`, `equals`, `or`, and `trim`. You control the number of instances to create with the `copy` function.

When you use the `copy` function, Resource Manager creates the number of resources you specify. Each time Resource Manager iterates over the create operation, a numerical value is available for you to name resources in a sequential fashion. You access this value with the `copyIndex()` function. Let's discuss the previous example to create a public IP address, only this time, let's create two addresses. You use `copy` to define how many addresses you want to create and `copyIndex()` to name the addresses sequentially.

Listing 6.2 Creating multiple public IP addresses with `copy`

```
{
      "apiVersion": "2017-04-01",
      "type": "Microsoft.Network/publicIPAddresses",
      "name": "[concat('publicip', copyIndex())]",
      "copy": {
        "count": 2
      }
      "location": "eastus",
      "properties": {
        "publicIPAllocationMethod": "dynamic",
      }
},
```

You also use the `concat` function to combine the public IP address name and the numerical value of each instance you create. After this template is deployed, your two public IP addresses will be called `publicip0` and `publicip1`. Not super descriptive, but this basic example shows the concept of how you can use a numbering convention as you create multiple resources with the `copy` function.

6.2.3 Tools to build your own templates

So, I'll confess. As much as Resource Manager templates are neat and one of the main ways I suggest you build and deploy applications in Azure, you still need to write the templates. There are a couple of different tools that simplify this for you, and hundreds of sample templates are available from Microsoft and third parties. In fact, one of the best ways to learn how to create and use templates is to examine the quickstart templates Microsoft makes available in its samples repo at https://github.com/Azure/azure-quickstart-templates.

If you want to roll up your sleeves and start to write you own templates, there are two main tools I recommend. The first is Visual Studio Code, a free, open source, multiplatform editor (https://code.visualstudio.com). Along with some built-in functionality such as source control and GitHub integration, extensions are available that can automatically build the different sections, or providers, for the resources to build up a template as shown in figure 6.8. If you download and install VS Code, go to View > Extensions, and then search for *Azure*.

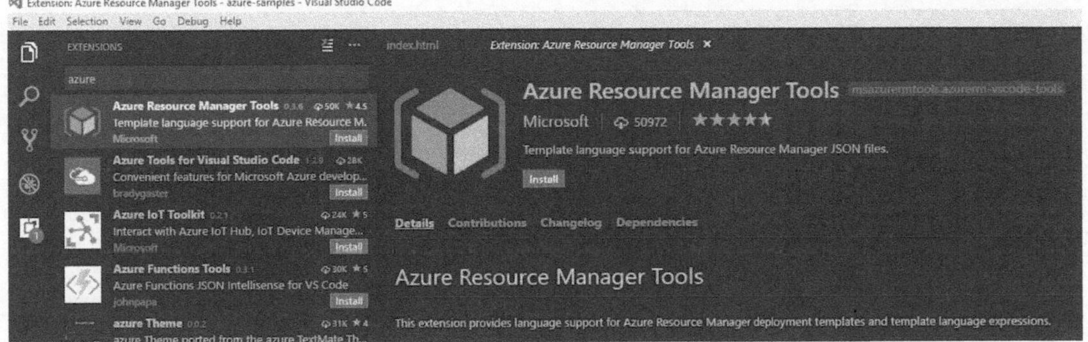

Figure 6.8 Many extensions are available in Visual Studio Code to improve and streamline how you create and use Azure Resource Manager templates.

A more graphical way to build Azure Resource Manager templates is to use the full Visual Studio editor, as shown in figure 6.9. There are versions for both Windows and macOS, but you need a separate license to use it. A Community Edition is available, but take care if you build templates within your company. You typically need a more licensed version, so consult your license experts, because Visual Studio is targeted at application developers.

You can, of course, use a basic text editor. Part of the reason Azure Resource Manager templates are written in JSON is that it removes the need for any special tools. There's a learning curve to working with JSON, which is why I recommend that you explore the quickstart templates on the Azure samples repo. Take care with indentation, trailing commas, and the use of parenthesis, brackets, and braces!

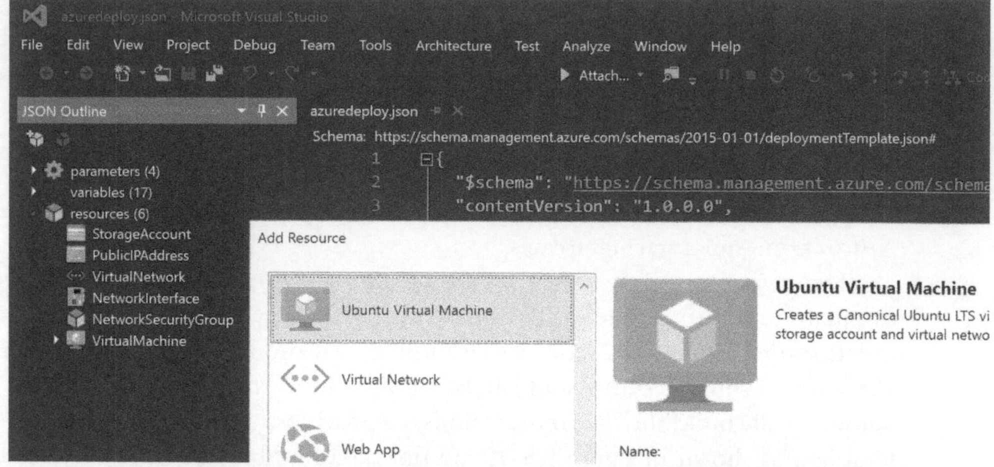

Figure 6.9 With Visual Studio, you can graphically build templates and explore JSON resources.

Life on Mars

There are third-party tools and other ways to use templates in Azure. Hashicorp provides many open source tools and solutions around cloud computing, one of which is Terraform. With Terraform, you define all the resources you want to build in much the same way that you do a native Azure Resource Manager template. You can define dependencies and use variables, too. The difference is that Terraform is technically a cross-provider. The same constructs and template approach can be used across Azure, Google Cloud, AWS, and vSphere, for example. The difference is the provisioners that you use for each resource.

Is it truly a "one template for any provider" approach? No, not at all. Terraform is also an application that parses your template and then communicates with the relevant cloud provider, such as Azure. You get zero editing capabilities, let alone graphical tools, to build your template. You pick an editor and write the template by hand. Again, the best way to learn Terraform is to explore its documentation and example templates.

The reason I bring this is up is back to the concept of choice in Azure. If you find Azure Resource Manager templates written in JSON a little too cumbersome, explore a product like Terraform instead. Don't give up on template-driven Resource Manager deployments. To achieve those reproducible, consistent deployments at scale, templates are the best approach, so find a good template-driven approach that works for you.

6.2.4 Storing and using templates

So, you love the idea of Azure Resource Manager templates, and you've installed Visual Studio or Code to write your own templates. How do you store and deploy them? In the end-of-chapter lab, you deploy a template from the Azure samples repository on GitHub. This is a public repository, and you may not want to make your application templates available to the entire world.

There are a couple of common scenarios to store Resource Manager templates privately:

- Use a private repository or network file share within your organization.
- Use Azure Storage to centrally store and secure templates for deployment.

There's no right or wrong way to store and deploy templates. You have flexibility to use whatever processes and tools are already in place. The advantage of using a repository is that you typically have some form of version control so you can ensure consistent deployments and review the history of your templates if needed. The only limitation is that when you deploy the template, you need to provide the appropriate credentials to access the shared location. This authentication process can vary, such as providing a username or access token as part of the URL to a template in a repository, or providing a shared access signature (SAS) token if you use Azure Storage.

Public repositories such as GitHub can also be a great way to learn and share. I do suggest that you keep your production templates stored privately, but if you create a neat template for a lab environment or to try out some new features, sharing it on GitHub gives a little something back to the IT community and may help others who want to do the same deployments that you do. And as you begin to build your own templates, be sure to check out what templates already exist so that you don't start from scratch and reinvent the wheel every time!

6.3 Lab: Deploying Azure resources from a template

All this theory around deployment models and approaches is great, but you'll (hopefully!) start to see the benefits and efficiency when you use templates for real:

1. Go to the Azure quickstart samples on GitHub (https://github.com/Azure/azure-quickstart-templates), and find one that interests you. A good place to start is a simple Linux or Windows VM.
2. Built into the GitHub samples are buttons to deploy straight to Azure. Once you find a template you like, select Deploy to Azure, as shown in figure 6.10, and follow the steps in the portal. It's much the same as when you created a VM earlier in the book, but there are only a few prompts to complete the required parameters. All the other resources are created for you and abstracted away.
3. The final step to deploy your template is to accept the license agreement shown, and then choose Purchase. You're creating Azure resources when you deploy a template, so Purchase means you agree to pay for the costs of those Azure resources.

One of the basic templates, such as a simple Linux or Windows VM, costs about the same as any other VM you've created so far. Make sure you delete the resource group after your deployment has finished, just like cleaning up after any other exercise.

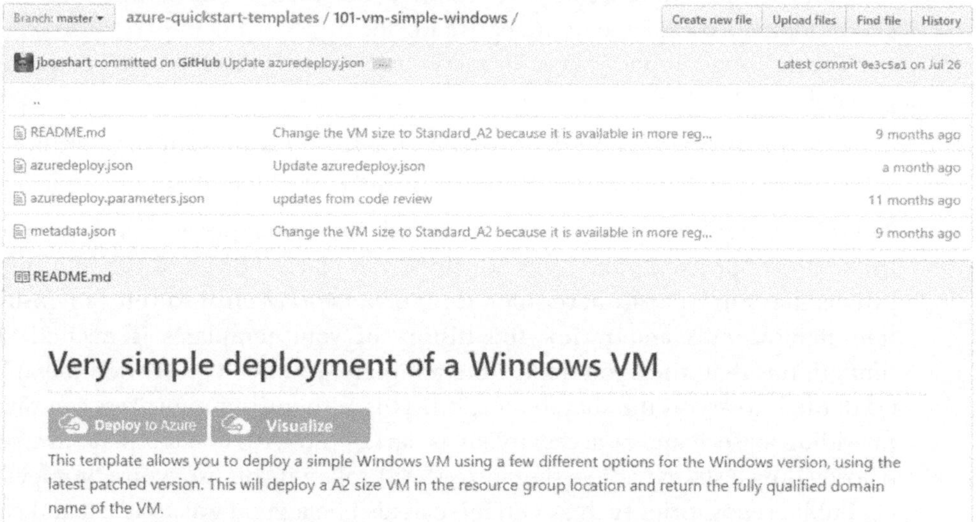

Figure 6.10 For each Resource Manager template in the GitHub sample repo, there's a Deploy to Azure button. If you select this button, the Azure portal loads, and the template is loaded. You're prompted for some basic parameters, and the rest of the deployment is handled by the template.

> **Parameters in templates**
>
> As discussed in section 6.2.1, you can use parameters and variables in your templates. Remember, parameters are values that you're prompted for, and variables are dynamic values that can be applied throughout a template. The values you're prompted for (parameters) vary from template to template. So, depending on which quickstart template you select, you may be prompted for one or two values, or you may have to provide seven or eight.
>
> As you design your templates, try to anticipate how you and other users may want to reuse the template as you deploy applications. You can provide a default value and limit what values are allowed. Take care with these default and allowable values, or you may constrain users too much and force them to create their own templates. Where possible, try to build reusable core templates that have enough flexibility.

4. Once your template has deployed, go back to GitHub and examine the azuredeploy.json file. This file is the Azure Resource Manager template that was used to create and deploy the sample. See if you can understand the different resource types and configurations that are applied. As you work with more Azure resource types and templates, the JSON format will become easier to understand, honest!

7 High availability and redundancy

I can't count the number of times that something in IT has failed me. I've had a laptop hard drive crash the day before a conference, a smoking power supply in an email server, and failed network interfaces on a core router. And don't even get me started on OS, driver, and firmware updates! I'm sure that anyone who works in IT would love to share horror stories of situations they've had to deal with—usually problems the happened late at night or at a critical time for the business. Is there ever such a thing as a good failure, and at a nice time?

If you anticipate failures in IT, you learn to plan and design your applications to accommodate problems. In this chapter, you'll learn how to use Azure high availability and redundancy features to minimize disruptions caused by maintenance updates and outages. This chapter builds a foundation for the next two or three chapters as you start to move from an application that runs on a single VM or web app, to one that can scale and be globally distributed.

7.1 The need for redundancy

If you want customers to trust you for their important pizza business, they expect that the applications you provide will be accessible whenever they need them. Most customers won't look for "hours of operation" on a website, especially if you work in a global environment and customers could be from all over the world. When they're hungry, they want to eat! Figure 7.1 shows a basic example of an application that runs on a single VM. Unfortunately, this application creates a single point of failure. If that one VM is unavailable, the application is unavailable, which leads to customer unhappiness and hunger.

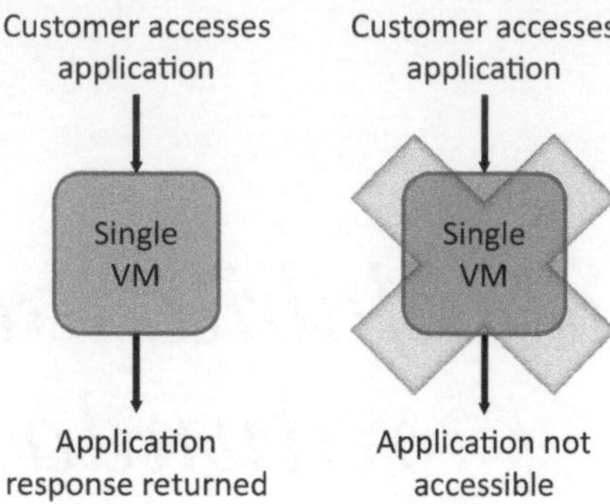

Figure 7.1 If your application runs on a single VM, any outage on that VM causes the application to be inaccessible. This could mean customers take their business elsewhere or, at the least, aren't satisfied with the service you provide.

If you drive a car, there's a good chance there's a spare tire in case you have a puncture. If you a use a laptop or tablet, there's a good chance you plug the device into a charger in case the battery runs out in the middle of work. At home or your apartment, do you have spare lightbulbs in case one of the lights goes out? What about a flashlight or candles in case there's a power outage?

Most people like to have some form of redundancy or backup plan, both in day–to-day life and, especially, in IT. If you're ready to switch over to a spare car tire or lightbulb, you can handle outages and failures with minimal interruption. If you design and build your applications for redundancy, you provide a high level of availability to your customers that minimizes or even hides any interruptions the application encounters.

All Azure datacenters are built for high availability. Backup power supplies, multiple network connections, and storage arrays with spare disks are just some of the core redundancy concepts that Azure provides and manages for you. All the redundancy Azure provides may not help if you run your application on a single VM. To give you flexibility and control over how to make your application highly available, two main features for IaaS workloads are available:

- *Availability Set*—Lets you logically group VMs to distribute them across a single Azure datacenter and minimize disruption from outages or maintenance updates.
- *Availability Zone*—Lets you distribute VMs across physically isolated segments of an Azure region to further maximize your application redundancy. Zones can also provide high availability to network resources such as public IP addresses and load balancers.

For most new application deployments in Azure, I suggest you plan to use availability zones. This approach offers flexibility in how to distribute your application and provides redundancy to the network resources that are often central to how customers ultimately access the underlying VMs. To see how each of these approaches works, let's discuss them in more depth.

> **Like previews at the movie theater**
>
> Azure often provides access to features and services as a *preview*. The technology that runs in these preview programs is designed to let customers try out new and upcoming features for performance and usability purposes.
>
> Support is usually provided for preview features, although that doesn't mean you should throw in all your production workloads. Feel free to use preview features for development and test workloads, or lower-priority production workloads, but know that you may occasionally run into unexpected results.
>
> Preview programs are a great way to get a head start on what's new in Azure. If you participate in a preview feature, try to take some time to provide feedback that can help improve the product's readiness for general release.
>
> Depending on when you're reading this, the limitations of availability zones and the list of supported resources may have changed. You can view the latest information on supported services and regions at http://mng.bz/6k72. Even though a region may be in preview, availability zones offer many benefits that provide redundancy to your entire application, not just VMs. Availability sets won't go away any time soon, but as you deploy workloads in Azure, I'd suggest you go with availability zones to future-proof yourself and protect a larger amount of your application environment.

7.2 VM redundancy with availability sets

If you only want to provide redundancy for VMs, availability sets have you covered. They're proven, reliable, and available across all regions. Availability sets contain a logical group of VMs that indicate to the Azure platform the underlying hardware those VMs run on needs to be carefully selected. If you create two VMs that run on the same physical server, and that one server fails, both of those VMs go down. With potentially tens of thousands or more physical servers in an Azure datacenter, it's highly unlikely you'd have both of those VMs on the same server, but it's possible! It may be not a failure, but a maintenance update that causes the physical server to be briefly unavailable.

What if your VMs run in the same rack, attached to the same storage or networking equipment? You're back to the single point of failure discussed at the start of the chapter.

Availability sets allow the Azure platform to create your VMs across logical groups called *fault domains* and *update domains*. These logical domains let the Azure platform understand the physical boundaries of hardware groups to make sure your VMs are evenly distributed across them. If one piece of hardware has a problem, only a few VMs in your availability set are affected. Or if there are maintenance updates to be applied to the physical hardware, the maintenance affects only a few of your VMs. The relationship of physical hardware to logical fault domains and update domains inside an availability set is shown in figure 7.2.

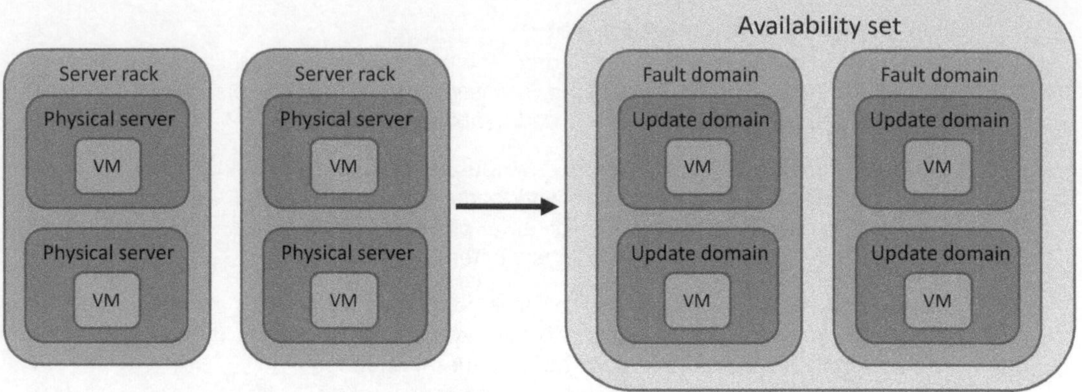

Figure 7.2 Hardware in an Azure datacenter is logically divided into update domains and fault domains. These logical domains allow the Azure platform to understand how to distribute your VMs across the underlying hardware to meet your redundancy requirements. This is a basic example—an update domain likely contains more than one physical server.

7.2.1 Fault domains

A *fault domain* is a logical group of hardware in an Azure datacenter. It contains hardware that shares common power or network equipment. You don't control what these fault domains are, and there's nothing for you to configure at the VM level. The Azure platform tracks what fault domains your VMs are placed in and distributes new VMs across these fault domains so that you always have VMs available if power or a network switch fails.

VMs that use managed disks (remember, *all* of your VMs should use managed disks!) also respect logical fault-domain boundaries and distribution. The Azure platform logically assigns storage clusters to fault domains to ensure that as your VMs are distributed across hardware groups, the managed disks are also distributed across storage hardware. There would be no point in VM redundancy across server hardware if there was a potential for all the managed disks to end up in the one storage cluster!

7.2.2 Update domains

Whereas fault domains create a logical group of hardware to protect against hardware failures, update domains protect against routine maintenance. To do this, a fault domain is further logically divided into update domains. Again, there's nothing for you to configure here. Update domains are a way for the Azure platform to understand how it must distribute VMs across your availability set.

Azure engineers perform (mostly automated) maintenance and apply updates across all the physical hardware in one update domain, and then perform the same maintenance across all hardware in the next update domain. This maintenance work is staggered across update domains to make sure VMs in an availability set aren't all running on hardware that undergoes maintenance at the same time.

There's no relationship between domains across multiple availability sets. The physical resources that make up the fault and update domains in one availability set may not be the same for a second availability set. This awareness means if you create multiple availability sets and distribute your VMs across them, fault domain 1, for example, doesn't always contain the same physical hardware.

7.2.3 Distributing VMs across an availability set

Let's go step by step and see how VMs are distributed across the logical fault and update domains that make up an availability set. This way, you have multiple VMs that can run your pizza store, and customers won't go hungry!

> **Try it now**
> To see availability sets in action, complete the following steps to deploy a Resource Manager template as shown in figure 7.3.

1. Open a web browser to a Resource Manager template from the GitHub samples repo at http://mng.bz/o92f, and then select the Deploy to Azure button. You use a template in this exercise so that you can quickly deploy VMs and let you explore how those VMs are distributed across the availability set.
2. The Azure portal opens and prompts for a few parameters. Choose Create New Resource Group, and then provide a name such as `azuremolchapter7`. Select a region, and then provide your SSH Key Data (you can obtain in this Cloud Shell with `cat ~/.ssh/id_rsa.pub`).

   The template creates an availability set that contains three VMs. These VMs are distributed across the logical fault and update domains. From the previous chapter on Resource Manager, the template uses the `copyIndex()` function to create multiple VMs and NICs.
3. To acknowledge that you wish to create the resources detailed in the template, check the box for "I agree to the terms and conditions stated above" and then select Purchase.

It takes a few minutes to create all three VMs in the availability set. Let the deployment continue in the portal while you read the rest of this section.

When the template starts to deploy, an availability set is created, and the number of update and fault domains you requested are assigned. The following properties were defined in the sample template:

```
"properties": {
    "platformFaultDomainCount": "2",
    "platformUpdateDomainCount": "5",
    "managed": "true"
}
```

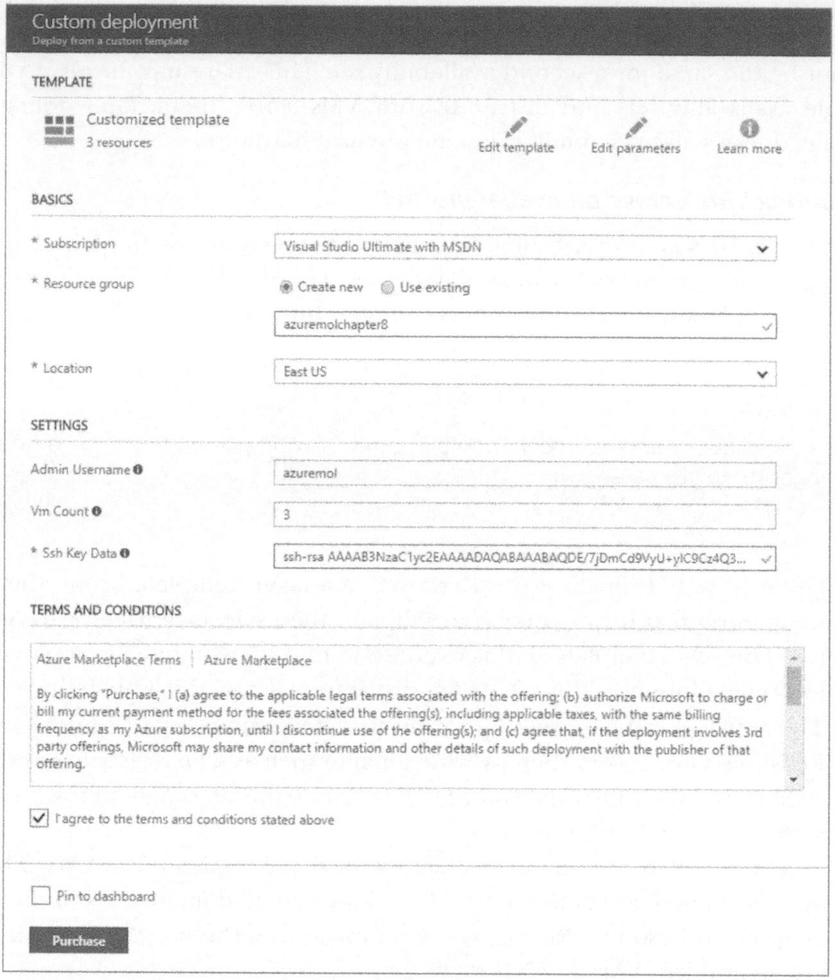

Custom deployment
Deploy from a custom template

TEMPLATE

Customized template
3 resources
Edit template
Edit parameters
Learn more

BASICS

* Subscription: Visual Studio Ultimate with MSDN
* Resource group: Create new / Use existing
azuremolchapter8
* Location: East US

SETTINGS

Admin Username: azuremol
Vm Count: 3
* Ssh Key Data: ssh-rsa AAAAB3NzaC1yc2EAAAADAQABAAABAQDE/7jDmCd9VyU+ylC9Cz4Q3...

TERMS AND CONDITIONS

Azure Marketplace Terms | Azure Marketplace

By clicking "Purchase," I (a) agree to the applicable legal terms associated with the offering; (b) authorize Microsoft to charge or bill my current payment method for the fees associated the offering(s), including applicable taxes, with the same billing frequency as my Azure subscription, until I discontinue use of the offering(s); and (c) agree that, if the deployment involves 3rd party offerings, Microsoft may share my contact information and other details of such deployment with the publisher of that offering.

I agree to the terms and conditions stated above

Pin to dashboard

Purchase

Figure 7.3 The template in GitHub for this exercise loads in the Azure portal and prompts for a few parameters. Provide a resource group name, location, and SSH key, and then deploy the template to create your resources.

These properties create an availability set with two fault domains and five update domains, as shown in figure 7.4, and indicate that the VMs are to use managed disks, so honor the disk distribution accordingly. The region you select for the availability set determines the maximum number of fault and update domains. Regions support either 2 or 3 fault domains, and up to 20 update domains.

As you create more VMs in an availability set, you need to consider how many update domains to use. For example, five update domains mean that up to 20% of your VMs may be unavailable due to maintenance:

- Let's say that you have 10 VMs in your availability set. This means two of those VMs may undergo maintenance at the same time. If you wanted to allow only one VM at a time to undergo maintenance, you'd need to create 10 update domains.

- The more update domains you create, the longer the period when your application is potentially in a maintenance state.

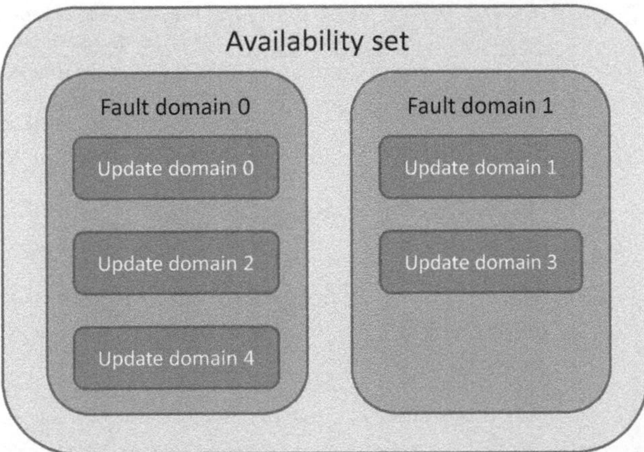

Figure 7.4 The availability set that your sample template deploys contains two fault domains and five update domains. The numbering system is zero-based. The update domains are created sequentially across the fault domains.

When the first VM is created, the Azure platform looks to see where the first available deployment position would be. This is fault domain 0 and update domain 0, as shown in figure 7.5.

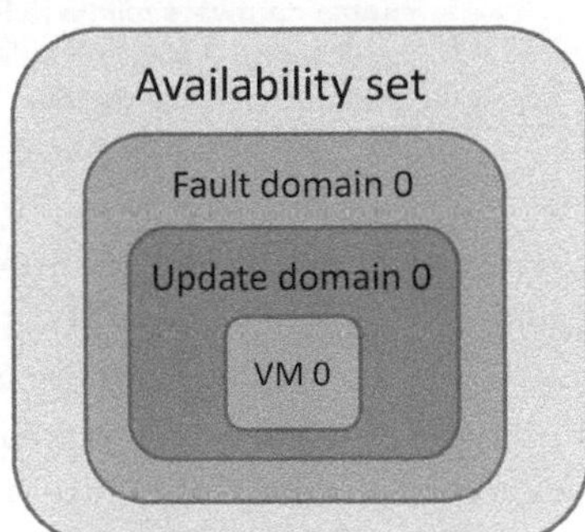

Figure 7.5 The first VM is created in fault domain 0 and update domain 0.

When the second VM is created, the Azure platform looks to see where the next available deployment position would be. This is now fault domain 1 and update domain 1, as shown in figure 7.6.

Your template creates three VMs, so what do you think happens next? The Azure platform looks again to see where the next available deployment position would be. You created only two fault domains, so the VM is created back in fault domain 0. But the VM is created in a different update domain than the first VM. The third VM is created in update domain 2, as shown in figure 7.7.

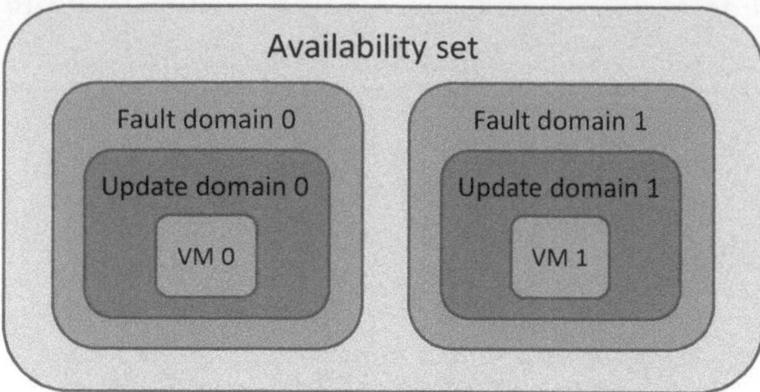

Figure 7.6 With a second VM created, the VMs are now evenly distributed across fault and update domains. This is often considered the minimal amount of redundancy to protect your applications.

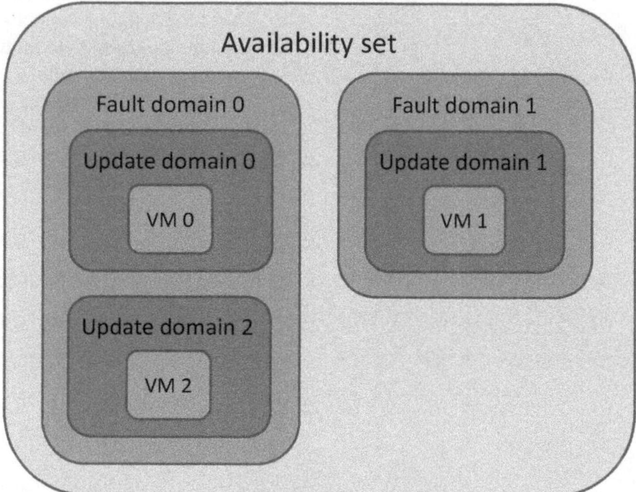

Figure 7.7 The third VM is created back in fault domain 0, but in update domain 2. Although VMs 0 and 2 potentially share the same hardware failure risk, they're in different update domains and so will not undergo regular maintenance at the same time.

VMs 0 and 2 are in the same fault domain, so potentially a hardware failure could impact both VMs. But routine maintenance impacts only one of those VMs at a time, because they're distributed across update domains. If you keep going and create more VMs, the Azure platform will continue to distribute them across different fault and update domains. When all five update domains are used, the sixth VM is created back in update domain 0, and the cycle continues.

7.2.4 View distribution of VMs across an availability set

Now that you understand the theory of how VMs are distributed across fault and update domains in an availability set, let's check what happened to your Resource Manager template deployment.

Try it now

To see how your VMs are distributed in an availability set, complete the following steps.

1. Browse to and select Resource Group from the navigation bar at left in the Azure portal. Choose the resource group you created for your template deployment, such as `azuremolchapter7`.
2. Select your availability set from the list of resources, such as `azuremolavailabilityset`.
3. In the Overview window is a list of VMs and their associated fault and update domains, as shown in figure 7.8.

NAME	STATUS	FAULT DOMAIN	UPDATE DOMAIN
vm0	Running	1	1
vm1	Running	0	2
vm2	Running	0	0

Figure 7.8 The availability set lists the VMs it contains and shows the fault domain and update domain for each VM. This table lets you visualize how the VMs are distributed across the logical domains.

If you're particularly observant, you may notice that the VMs don't line up perfectly with the expected order of fault and update domains. Is there a bug?! Probably not. If you examine the example in figure 7.8 and compare it with what the previous concepts told you, you'd expect the VMs to be distributed as shown in table 7.1.

Table 7.1 How you'd expect the VMs to be logically distributed in an availability set. The VMs are sequentially created and distributed across domains in a neat pattern.

Name	Fault domain	Update domain
vm0	0	0
vm1	1	1
vm2	0	2

So, what went wrong? Nothing. Think back to how Resource Manager creates resources from a template. The Azure platform doesn't wait for the first VM to be created before the second can be created. All three VMs are created at the same time. As such, there may be fractions of a second difference in which VM is associated with an availability set first. It doesn't matter what this order is, because you don't control what the underlying fault and update domains represent. That's all up to the Azure platform. You just need to make sure that your VMs *are* distributed, not *where*.

> **No, I must have pretty numbers**
> If the serial creation behavior of VMs bugs you and you *must* distribute the VMs in a neat order, you can instruct Resource Manager to create VMs in *serial*, rather than *parallel*. In this mode, the VMs are created one after another, so the deployment time is increased. To enable this serial behavior, use `"mode": "serial"` in your templates as part of the `copyIndex()` function. That should distribute the VMs in a nice, sequential way for you!

7.3 Infrastructure redundancy with availability zones

Availability sets only work with VMs. That limitation makes it hard to design and build applications that continue to be available if part of a datacenter has a problem. It's possible a major outage may cause issues across an entire Azure datacenter, so what happens to network resources like public IP addresses and load balancers? How can customers order their pizza if you don't have redundancy with your network resources?

Availability zones are physically separate datacenters that operate on independent core utilities such as power and network connectivity. Each Azure region that supports availability zones provides three zones. You create your resources in and across these zones. Figure 7.9 shows how Azure resources can be distributed across availability zones.

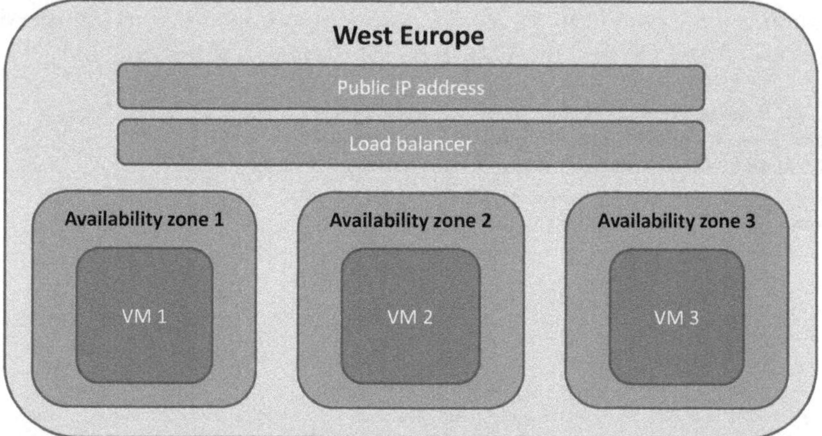

Figure 7.9 An Azure region can contain multiple availability zones: physically isolated datacenters that use independent power, network, and cooling. Azure virtual network resources such as public IP addresses and load balancers can span all zones in a region to provide redundancy for more than just the VMs.

With availability zones, your applications can tolerate an entire Azure datacenter going offline. Sure, it would take a major event for this situation to occur, but it's still possible!

In large application deployments, you may create more than one VM in each availability zone. Multiple VMs in an availability zone don't quite follow the same methodical distribution across update and fault domains as they do in availability sets. Because availability zones provide redundancy across zones, the need for update and fault domains is diminished—you don't need to worry about the individual datacenter distribution anymore. Even if a maintenance update or equipment failure inside a zone were to impact all your VMs that run in the zone, remember that zones are physically isolated from each other—the VMs in another zone would continue to run.

Now, if you feel particularly unlucky, could your VMs in different zones all experience maintenance updates at the same time? Yes, but that's unlikely. Zones within a region have staggered update cycles, just like update domains within availability sets. Updates are performed across one zone; once they're complete, updates are performed across the next zone. So again, although your VMs within a zone aren't technically distributed across the same concept of update domains, they don't need to be. Availability zones provide a higher level of abstraction and redundancy, and you should look at your application across the entire deployment, not just where VMs in one zone reside.

The inclusion of the virtual network resources in availability zones is a lot more important than it may seem at first. Figure 7.10 shows what would happen if the datacenter became unavailable for network resources such as a public IP address and load balancer that run across availability zones.

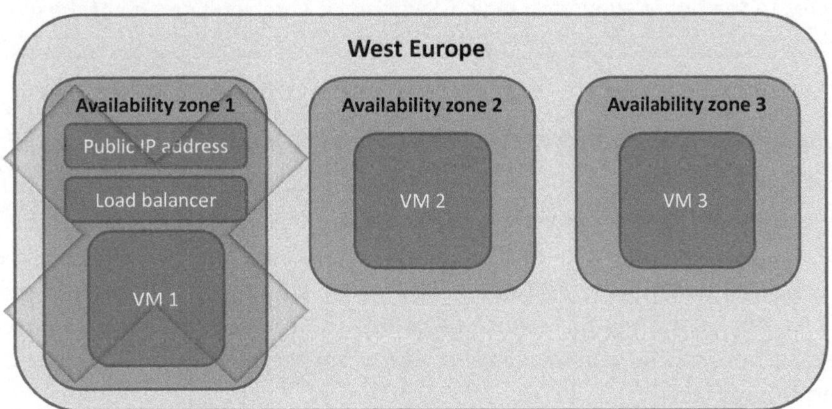

Figure 7.10 When network resources are attached to a single Azure datacenter, or zone, an outage in that facility causes the entire application to be unreachable by the customer. It doesn't matter that the other VMs continue to run in other zones. Without the network connectivity to distribute traffic from your customers, the whole application is unavailable.

I talk more about load balancers in the next chapter, but for now, all you need to understand is that the load balancer distributes traffic across all available VMs that are attached to it. The VMs report their health status at set intervals, and the load balancer no longer distributes traffic to a VM that reports as being unavailable. With a load balancer that works across availability zones, an outage in one Azure datacenter causes those VMs to become unavailable and be taken out of the load-balancer rotation.

A public IP address that spans availability zones provides a single entry point for customers to reach your load balancer and then be distributed to an available VM. In an application deployment where that public IP address resides in a single Azure datacenter, if that datacenter encounters a problem, no customer can access the public IP address. The customer can't use your application, even if there are VMs available to serve customer requests.

Supported regions for availability zones

Some availability zone regions may be in preview as you read this, so only a select number of regions, resources, and even sizes of VMs may be available for use. These limitations are likely to change over time: check out http://mng.bz/6k72 for the latest information as to what regions and resources are supported.

This chapter focuses on VMs, public IP addresses, and load balancers, but you should expect the list of supported Azure resources to grow. For example, virtual machine scale sets (covered in chapter 9) can also be created in availability zones.

For most examples throughout this book, you can select any region you wish for your resources. For these exercises on availability zones, you need to create resources in one of the supported regions. Either use the default region specified in the exercise, or refer to the list of supported regions and make sure you use one of those.

7.3.1 Creating network resources across an availability zone

Public IP addresses and load balancers can be created in one of two available tiers: *basic* and *standard*. The primary difference is that the standard tier allows the network resource to use availability zones. By default, a standard public IP address or load balancer is automatically zone redundant. There's no additional configuration for you to complete. The Azure platform centrally stores the metadata for the resource within the region you specify and makes sure the resource continues to run if one zone becomes unavailable.

Don't worry too much about what happens with the load balancer and network resources right now. Remember what I said at the start—these next two or three chapters all build on each other. In the next chapter, we dive into load balancers, and all this should start to make more sense.

> **Try it now**
> To create network resources that are redundant across availability zones, complete the following steps.

1. Select the Cloud Shell icon at the top of the Azure portal dashboard. Create a Resource group, such as azuremolchapter7az:

   ```
   az group create --name azuremolchapter7az --location westeurope
   ```

2. Create a standard public IP address in your resource group. By default, a *basic* public IP address would be created and assigned to only a single zone. The `--sku standard` parameter instructs Azure to create a redundant, cross-zone resource:

   ```
   az network public-ip create \
     --resource-group azuremolchapter7az \
     --name azpublicip \
     --sku standard
   ```

3. Create a load balancer that spans availability zones. Again, a *basic* load balancer would be created by default and assigned to a single zone, which isn't the high-availability design you want for your applications. Specify a *standard* load SKU to create a zone-redundant load balancer, as follows:

   ```
   az network lb create \
     --resource-group azuremolchapter7az \
     --name azloadbalancer \
     --public-ip-address azpublicip \
     --frontend-ip-name frontendpool \
     --backend-pool-name backendpool \
     --sku standard
   ```

7.3.2 *Creating VMs in an availability zone*

To create a VM in an availability zone, you specify which zone to run the VM in. To deploy many VMs, you ideally create and use a template. The template defines and distributes the zones for each of the VMs. As customer demand for your online pizza store grows, you can also update the template with the number of VMs you now want, and then redeploy the template. The new VMs are distributed across zones for you automatically, and there's no need to manually track which zones the VMs run in. In the end-of-chapter lab, you use a template to automatically create and distribute multiple VMs. To see the logical process to specify a zone for a VM, let's create a VM and manually specify the zone.

> **Try it now**
> The create a VM in an availability zone, complete the following steps.

1 In the Azure portal, select the Cloud Shell icon at the top of the dashboard.
2 Create a VM with the `az vm create` command you've used in previous chapters. Use the `--zone` parameter to specify zone 1, 2, or 3 for the VM to run in. The following example creates a VM named zonedvm in zone 3:

```
az vm create \
  --resource-group azuremolchapter7az \
  --name zonedvm \
  --image ubuntults \
  --size Standard_B1ms \
  --admin-username azuremol \
  --generate-ssh-keys \
  --zone 3
```

It takes a few minutes to create the VM. Once finished, the output from the command indicates the zone that the VM runs in. You can also view this information with the `az vm show` command:

```
az vm show \
  --resource-group azuremolchapter7az \
  --name zonedvm \
  --query zones
```

NOTE The examples in these "Try it now" exercises are simple, but are designed to show you that zones require little configuration to use. You didn't integrate the zone-redundant load balancer and VM, but in the next chapter, you build out a more usable application environment that's distributed across availability zones. The goal here is to show you that the Azure platform handles the redundancy and distribution of your resources, so you can focus on the application itself.

7.4 Lab: Deploying highly available VMs from a template

This lab combines and reinforce what you learned in the previous chapter on Azure Resource Manager and templates, with availability zones. Take some time to look over the example quickstart template in this exercise to see how you can use logic and functions to distribute multiple VMs across zones. Don't just deploy the template and move on—look at how the template builds on the features introduced in the previous chapter!

What's a quota?

In Azure, default quotas on your subscription prevent you from accidentally deploying a bunch of resources and forgetting about them, which would cost you a lot of money. These quotas typically vary by resource type and subscription type and are enforced at the region level. You can see a full list of quotas at http://mng.bz/ddcx.

When you start to create multiple VMs in these next few chapters, you may run into quota issues. You can also encounter quota issues if you haven't deleted resources from previous chapters and exercises. The quotas are a good system that keeps you aware of your resource usage. The error messages may not be clear, but if you see error text along the lines of

```
Operation results in exceeding quota limits of Core.
Maximum allowed: 4, Current in use: 4, Additional requested: 2.
```

then it's a good indication that you need to request an increase in your quotas. There's nothing complicated, and it's not something unique to Azure. You can view your current quota for a given region as follows:

```
az vm list-usage --location eastus
```

If you have trouble with this lab, delete the first two resource groups created in this chapter, such as azuremolchapter7 and azuremolchapter7az. If you have a low default quota set, the four VMs across those resource groups may prevent you from successfully completing this exercise.

To request an increase in your quotas for a region, follow the steps outlined at http://mng.bz/Xq2f.

3. Let's review and deploy a sample template that includes multiple VMs across availability zones. In a web browser, open the JSON file at http://mng.bz/8Oys and search for the following text:

   ```
   Microsoft.Compute/virtualMachines
   ```

   The VMs section looks similar to what you used in the previous chapter, but notice the property value for `zones`. This section combines a few different functions available in templates to pick either zone 1, 2, or 3 as the VM is created. This way, you don't need to manually track what VM runs in which zone, and how you then deploy additional VMs.
4. In your web browser, search for each of the following to see the sections on the public IP address and load balancer:

   ```
   Microsoft.Network/publicIPAddresses
   Microsoft.Network/loadBalancers
   ```

   Both resources use standard SKU, which provides zone redundancy by default. There's zero additional configuration to make this work!
5. Let's see this in action! In your web browser, open the quickstart template at http://mng.bz/O69a, and select the Deploy to Azure button.
6. Create or select a resource group, and then provide a username and password for the VMs. Enter a unique DNS name, such as azuremol.
7. Choose to create Linux or Windows VMs. Windows VMs take a little longer to create. Then, specify how many VMs to create, such as 3.
8. Check the box to agree to the terms and conditions for the template deployment, and then select Purchase, as shown in figure 7.11.

Figure 7.11 To deploy the availability zone template in the Azure portal, specify a resource group, username, and password, and then the OS type and the number of VMs you wish to create. The template uses loops, `copyIndex()`, `dependsOn`, variables, and parameters, as covered in the previous chapter on Resource Manager.

Once the VMs have been created, use the Azure portal or the `az vm show` command to see how the VMs were distributed across zones. If you're curious about what the rest of the template does with the network resources, the next chapter dives deep into load balancers for you!

Cleanup on aisle 3

Remember when, at the start of the book, I said to make sure you clean up after yourself to minimize the cost against your free Azure credits? I strongly advise you to delete the resource groups you created in this chapter. The next couple of chapters continue to create multiple VMs and web app instances, so make sure you keep costs and quotas under control.

Each time you log in to the Azure portal, you should get a pop-up notification that lets you know the status of your Azure credits. If you see your available credit reduced by a large dollar amount from day to day, examine what resource groups you may have forgotten to delete!

8 Load-balancing applications

An important component of highly available applications is how to distribute traffic across all your VMs. In the previous chapter, you learned the difference between availability sets and availability zones, and how you can create multiple VMs across Azure datacenters or regions to provide application redundancy. Even if you have all these highly available and distributed VMs, that doesn't help if only one VM receives all the customer traffic.

Load balancers are network resources that receive the incoming application traffic from your customers, examine the traffic to apply filters and load-balancing rules, and then distribute the requests across a pool of VMs that run your application. In Azure, there are a couple of different ways to load-balance traffic, such as if you need to perform SSL off-loading on large applications that use encrypted network traffic. In this chapter, you learn about the various load-balancer components, and how to configure traffic rules and filters and distribute traffic to VMs. You build on the high-availability components from the previous chapter and get ready for the next chapter on how to scale resources.

8.1 Azure load-balancer components

Load balancers in Azure can work at two different levels: layer 4, where just the network traffic is examined and distributed (the transport layer, really), and layer 7, where there's an awareness of the application data within the network traffic to help determine the distribution of data. Both levels of load balancer work the same way, as shown in figure 8.1.

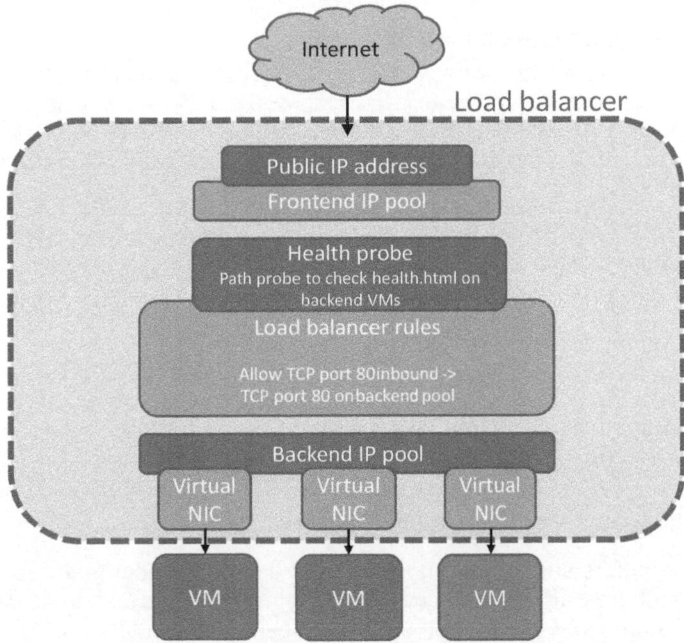

Figure 8.1 Traffic from the internet enters the load balancer through a public IP address that's attached to a frontend IP pool. The traffic is processed by load-balancer rules that determine how and where the traffic should be forwarded. Health probes attached to the rules ensure that traffic is only distributed to healthy nodes. A backend pool of virtual NICs connected to VMs then receives the traffic distributed by the load-balancer rules.

A load balancer consists of a few main components:

- *Frontend IP pool*—Entry point to the load balancer. To allow access from the internet, a public IP address can be attached to the frontend IP pool. Private IP addresses can be attached for internal load balancers.
- *Health probes*—Monitor the status of attached VMs. To make sure traffic is only distributed to healthy and responsive VMs, checks are performed on a regular basis to confirm that a VM correctly responds to traffic.
- *Load-balancer rules*—Distribute the traffic to VMs. Each incoming packet is compared against the rules, which define incoming protocols and ports, and then distributed across a set of associated VMs. If no rules match the incoming traffic, the traffic is dropped.
- *Network Address Translation (NAT) rules*—Can route traffic directly to specific VMs. For example, if you want to provide remote access via SSH or RDP, you can define NAT rules to forward traffic from an external port to a single VM.
- *Backend IP pool*—Where the VMs that run your application are attached. Load-balancer rules are associated with backend pools. You can create different backend pools for different parts of your applications.

Application Gateway: advanced load balancing

Azure load balancers can work at the network layer or the application layer. This chapter focuses on the regular Azure load balancer, which works at the network layer (layer 4, or Transport protocol). At this layer, the traffic is examined and distributed, but the load balancer has no context of what the traffic means or the applications that you run.

Azure Application Gateway is a load balancer that works at the application layer (layer 7). Application Gateway gains insight into the application that runs on the VM and can manage the traffic flows in more advanced ways. One major benefit of Application Gateway is the ability to handle encrypted, HTTPS web traffic.

When you load-balance websites with SSL certificates, you can offload the process that verifies and decrypts the traffic from the web servers. On websites with a lot of SSL traffic, the process to verify and decrypt the traffic can consume a large portion of compute time on the VMs or web apps. Application Gateway can verify and decrypt the traffic, pass the pure web request to the web servers, and then reencrypt the traffic received from the web servers and return it to the customer.

Application Gateway offers some other more advanced load-balancer features, such as the ability to distribute traffic across any IP endpoint rather than just an Azure VM. As you build applications that use more than VMs, these advanced distribution rules may be of use to you. The same core concepts apply as with a regular load balancer, which is what we focus on in this chapter so that you understand how it all works in Azure.

8.1.1 Creating a frontend IP pool

In previous chapters, you created VMs that had a public IP address assigned directly to them. You used this public IP address to then access the VM with a remote connection such as SSH or RDP, or used a web browser to access a website that ran on the VM. When you use a load balancer, you no longer connect straight to the VMs. Instead, to allow traffic to reach your load balancer and be distributed to your VMs, one or more IP addresses must be assigned to the external interface of a load balancer.

Load balancers can operate in one of two different modes:

- *Internet load balancer*—Has one or more *public* IP addresses connected to the frontend IP pool. An internet load balancer directly receives traffic from the internet and distributes it to backend VMs. A common example is for frontend web servers that customers directly access over the internet.
- *Internal load balancer*—Has one or more *private* IP addresses connected to the frontend IP pool. An internal load balancer works inside an Azure virtual network, such as for backend database VMs. You typically don't expose backend databases or application tiers to the outside world. Instead, a set of frontend web servers connects to an internal load balancer that distributes the traffic without any direct public access. Figure 8.2 shows how an internal load balancer

can distribute traffic to backend VMs that are behind a public-facing load balancer and frontend web VMs.

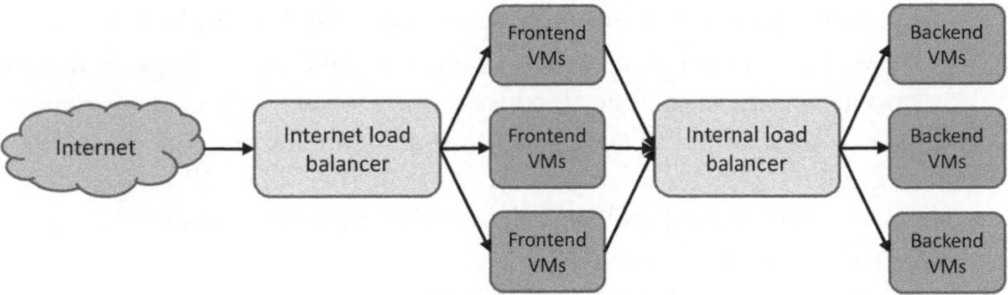

Figure 8.2 An internet load balancer may be used to distribute traffic to frontend VMs that run your website, which then connect to an internal load balancer to distribute traffic to a database tier of VMs. The internal load balancer isn't publicly accessible and can only be accessed by the frontend VMs within the Azure virtual network.

The mode for your load balancer doesn't change the behavior of the frontend IP pool. You assign one or more IP addresses that are used when access to the load balancer is requested. Both IPv4 and IPv6 addresses can be configured for the frontend IP pool. This allows you to configure end-to-end IPv6 communications between customers and your VMs as the traffic flows in and out of the load balancer.

> **Try it now**
> To understand how the load-balancer components work together, complete the following steps to create a load balancer and frontend IP pool.

1. Open the Azure portal, and select the Cloud Shell icon at the top of the dashboard.
2. Create a resource group with `az group create`. Specify a resource group name, such as `azuremolchapter8`, and a location:

   ```
   az group create --name azuremolchapter8 --location westeurope
   ```

   As you continue to build on the previous chapter and want to use availability zones, take care with the region you select, to make sure availability zone support is available.
3. Create a public IP address with `az network public-ip create`. In chapter 7, you learned that availability zones provide redundancy to network resources, so create a `standard`, zone-redundant public IP address. Specify a name, such as `publicip`:

   ```
   az network public-ip create \
     --resource-group azuremolchapter8 \
   ```

```
  --name publicip \
  --sku standard
```

To create an IPv6 public IP address, you can add `--version IPv6` to the preceding command. For these exercises, you can use IPv4 addresses.

4 Create the load balancer and assign the public IP address to the frontend IP pool. To add the public IP address, specify the `--public-ip-address` parameter. If you wanted to create an internal load balancer, you'd instead use the `--private-ip-address` parameter. As with the public IP address, create a standard, zone-redundant load balancer that works across availability zones:

```
az network lb create \
  --resource-group azuremolchapter8 \
  --name loadbalancer \
  --public-ip-address publicip \
  --frontend-ip-name frontendpool \
  --backend-pool-name backendpool \
  --sku standard
```

We dive into what the backend pool is in a few minutes.

8.1.2 Creating and configuring health probes

If one of the VMs that run your application has a problem, do you think the load balancer should continue to distribute traffic to that VM? A customer who tries to access your pizza store may get directed to that VM and be unable to order any food! A load balancer monitors the status of the VMs and can remove VMs that have issues. The load balancer continues to monitor the health, and adds the VM back into the pool for traffic distribution when the VM is shown to respond correctly again.

A health probe can work in a couple of different modes:

- *Port-based*—The load balancer checks for a VM response on a specific port and protocol, such as TCP port 80. As long as the VM responds to the health probe on TCP port 80, the VM remains in the load-balancer traffic distribution. Otherwise, the VM is removed from the load-balancer traffic distribution, as shown in figure 8.3. This mode doesn't guarantee that the VM serves the traffic as expected, only that the network connectivity and destination service returns a response.
- *HTTP path-based*—A custom page, such as health.html, is written and placed on each VM. This custom health check can be used to verify access to an image store or database connection. In this mode, the VM only remains in the load-balancer traffic distribution when the health-check page returns an HTTP code 200 response, as shown in figure 8.4. With a port-based health probe, the actual web server may run but have no database connection. With a custom health-check page, the load balancer can confirm that the VM is able to serve real traffic to the customer.

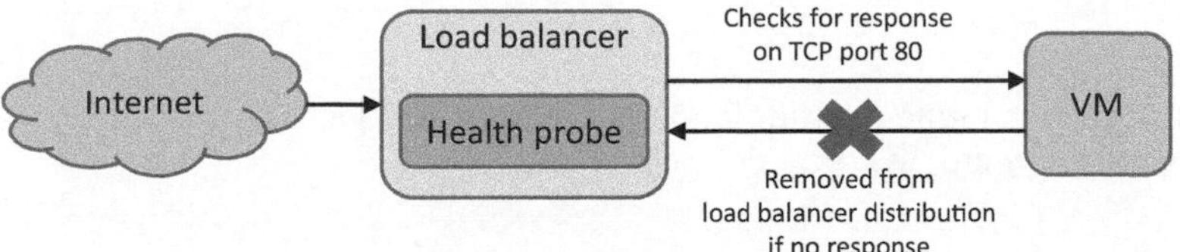

Figure 8.3 A port-based load-balancer health probe checks for a VM response on a defined port and protocol. If the VM doesn't respond within the given threshold, the VM is removed from the load-balancer traffic distribution. When the VM starts to respond correctly again, the health probe detects the change and adds the VM back into the load-balancer traffic distribution.

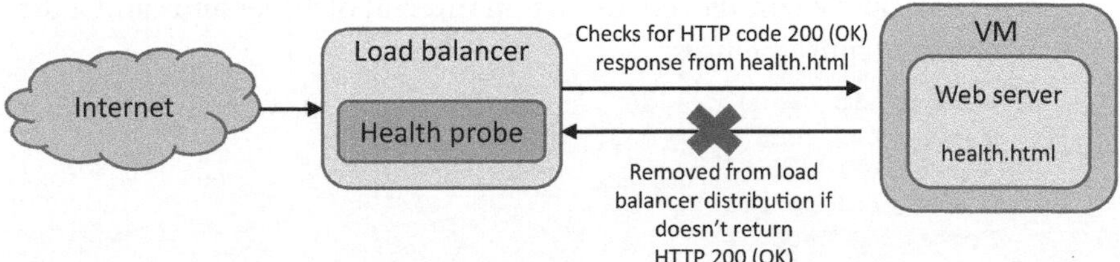

Figure 8.4 A VM that runs a web server and has a custom health.html page remains in the load-balancer traffic distribution provided that the health probe receives an HTTP code 200 (OK) response. If the web server process encounters a problem and can't return requested pages, they're removed from the load-balancer traffic distribution. This provides a more thorough check of the web server state than port-based health probes.

Additional work is required to create the custom health-check page, but the improved customer experience is worthwhile. The health-check page doesn't have to be complicated. It could be a basic HTML page that's used to confirm that the web server itself can serve pages. Without the health-check page, if the web server process has a problem, the VM would still be available on TCP port 80, so the port-based health probe would believe the VM to be healthy. An HTTP path-based health probe requires the web server to correctly return an HTTP response. If the web server process hangs or has failed, an HTTP response isn't sent, so the VM is removed from the load-balancer traffic distribution.

How often the health probe checks the VM, and what the response is, can also be configured through two parameters:

- *Interval*—Defines how frequently the health probe checks the status of the VM. By default, the health probe checks the status every 15 seconds.
- *Threshold*—Defines how many consecutive response failures the health probe receives before the VM is removed from the load-balancer traffic distribution. By default, the health probe tolerates two consecutive failures before the VM is removed the load-balancer traffic distribution.

Try it now

To create a health probe for your load balancer, as you just saw in figure 8.4, complete the following steps.

1. Open the Azure portal, and select the Cloud Shell icon at the top of the dashboard.
2. Specify a name for the health probe, such as `healthprobe`. To set up the health probe for a web server, specify HTTP port 80, and then define a custom health-check page at health.html. Later in the chapter, you create this health-check page on your VMs. To show how the interval and threshold for the health-probe response can be configured, define an interval of 10 seconds and a threshold of three consecutive failures:

```
az network lb probe create \
  --resource-group azuremolchapter8 \
  --lb-name loadbalancer \
  --name healthprobe \
  --protocol http \
  --port 80 \
  --path health.html \
  --interval 10 \
  --threshold 3
```

After the health probe is created, how do you now make it check the status of your VMs? Health probes are associated with load-balancer rules. The same health probe can be used with multiple different load-balancer rules. Remember chapter 5, where you created network security groups (NSGs) and rules? Those NSGs can be associated with multiple different VMs or virtual network subnets. A similar one-to-many relationship applies to the health probes. Let's see how to put your health probe to work and create load-balancer rules.

8.1.3 Defining traffic distribution with load-balancer rules

When traffic is directed through the load balancer to the backend VMs, you can define what conditions cause the user to be directed to the same VM. You may want the user to retain a connection to the same VM for the duration of a single session, or allow them to return and maintain their VM affinity based on the source IP address. Figure 8.5 shows an example of the default session affinity mode.

In session affinity mode, the flow of traffic is handled by a 5-tuple hash that uses the source IP address, source port, destination IP address, destination port, and protocol type. Basically, for each request a user makes to your web server on TCP port 80, they're directed to the same backend VM for the duration of that session.

What happens if the customer closes their browser session? The next time they connect, a new session is started. Because the load balancer distributes traffic across all healthy VMs in the backend IP pool, it's possible that the user connects to the same VM again; but the more VMs you have in the backend IP pool, the greater the chance that the user connects to a different VM.

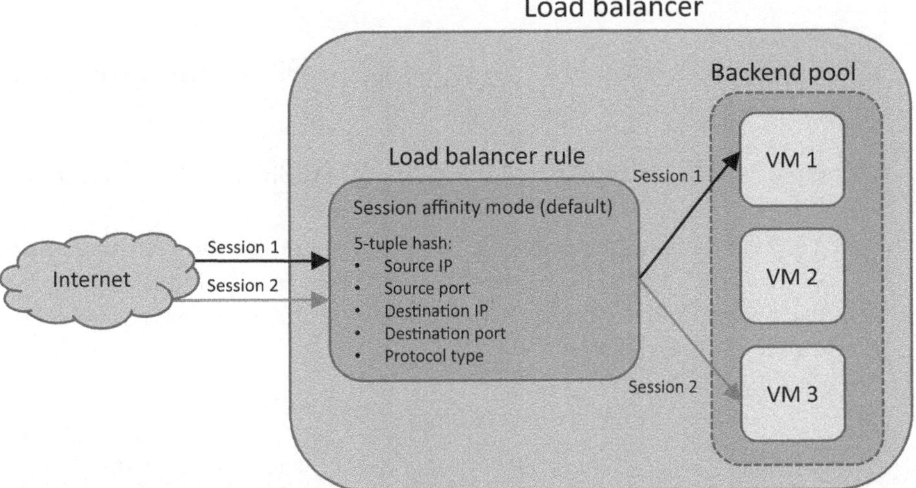

Figure 8.5 With session affinity mode, the user connects to the same backend VM only for the duration of their session.

As the application owner and developer, there may be scenarios where you may want the user to connect to the same VM as before when they start another session. For example, if your application handles file transfers, or uses UDP rather than TCP, you likely want the same VM to continue to process their requests. In these scenarios, you can configure the load-balancer rules for source IP affinity. Figure 8.6 shows an example of source IP affinity mode.

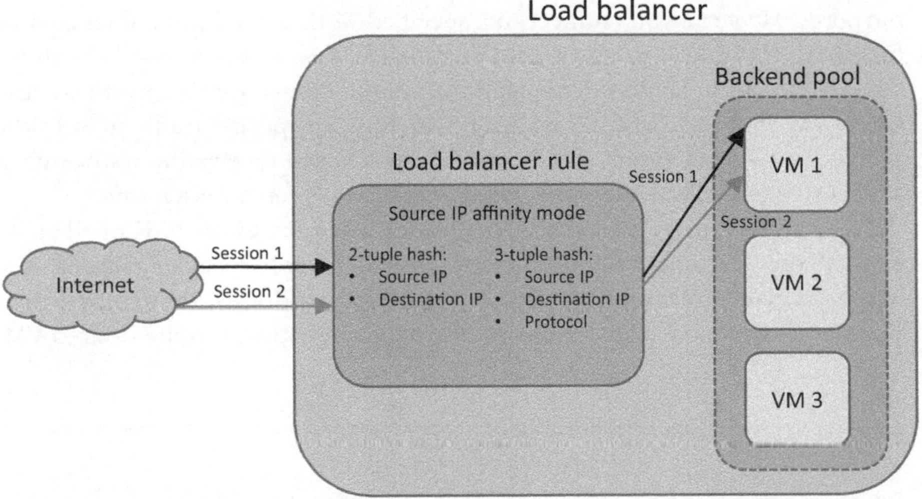

Figure 8.6 When you configure the load-balancer rules to use source IP affinity mode, the user can close and then start a new session but continue to connect to the same backend VM. Source IP affinity mode can use a 2-tuple hash that uses the source and destination IP address, or a 3-tuple hash that also uses the protocol.

Try it now

To create a load-balancer rule that uses a health probe, complete the following steps.

1 Open the Azure portal, and select the Cloud Shell icon at the top of the dashboard.
2 To create a load-balancer rule, specify a name for the rule, such as `httprule`. Provide the external port on which traffic is received and the internal port to distribute traffic to. In this basic example, traffic is received on port 80 and then distributed on port 80:

```
az network lb rule create \
  --resource-group azuremolchapter8 \
  --lb-name loadbalancer \
  --name httprule \
  --protocol tcp \
  --frontend-port 80 \
  --backend-port 80 \
  --frontend-ip-name frontendpool \
  --backend-pool-name backendpool \
  --probe-name healthprobe
```

If you run multiple websites on a VM that responds on different ports, a given rule could direct traffic to a specific website on the VM.

8.1.4 Routing direct traffic with Network Address Translation rules

The load-balancer rules distribute traffic across the backend pools of VMs, so there's no guarantee that you can connect to a given VM for maintenance or management purposes. How can you connect to a specific VM that's behind a load balancer? One final part of the load-balancer configuration to look at are Network Address Translation (NAT) rules. These rules let you control the flow of specific traffic to direct it to a single VM. Figure 8.7 shows how NAT rules forward specific traffic to individual VMs.

NAT rules work alongside NSG rules. The VM can receive the traffic only if there's a NSG rule that allows the same traffic as the load-balancer NAT rule.

Why might you create NAT rules? What if you want to use SSH or RDP to connect to a specific VM, or use management tools to connect to a backend database server? If the load balancer distributes traffic across the backend VMs, you'd have try to connect again and again and again, and you still might not connect to the desired VM.

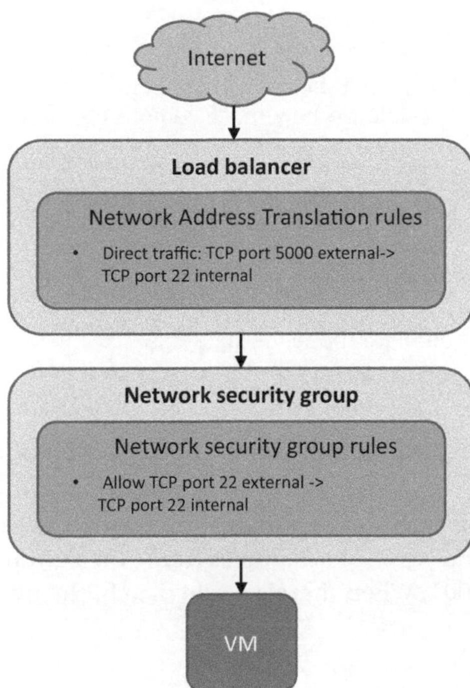

Figure 8.7 Traffic in the load balancer is processed by NAT rules. If a protocol and port match a rule, the traffic is then forwarded to the defined backend VM. No health probes are attached, so the load balancer doesn't check whether the VM is able to respond before it forwards the traffic. The traffic leaves the load balancer and is then processed by NSG rules. If the traffic is permitted, it's passed to the VM.

Keeping things secure

We dive into some security topics in part 3 of the book, but security should be an ever-present consideration as you build and run applications in Azure. Security shouldn't be something you add later. With the rise of cloud computing and disposable VMs and web apps, it's easy to overlook some basic security best practices. Especially if you work in Azure as part of a wider enterprise subscription, make sure any resources you create don't accidentally provide a way for attackers to gain access to your infrastructure.

What kind of things are bad? Well, some of things you've done already in this book! Remote management ports for SSH and RDP shouldn't be opened to the public internet as you've done, or at the very least you should restrict access to being from a specific IP address range.

The best practice would be to create one secured VM that has remote management available. As needed, you connect to this one, secured VM, and then connect over the internal Azure virtual network to additional VMs. You used this basic jump-box VM approach in chapter 5. This approach minimizes the attack footprint and reduces the need for NSG rules and load-balancer NAT rules. Chapter 16 discusses Azure Security Center and how you can dynamically request and open remote-management ports for a specific time period, which is the best of both worlds.

> ***(continued)***
> Even if you work in a private Azure subscription that has no connectivity to other Azure subscriptions at school or work, try to minimize how much remote connectivity you provide.

> **Try it now**
> To create a load balancer NAT rule, complete the following steps.

1. Open the Azure portal, and select the Cloud Shell icon at the top of the dashboard.
2. To create a load-balancer NAT rule, define a name, such as `natrulessh`, and the frontend IP pool to use. The NAT rule examines traffic on a given protocol and port, such as TCP port 50001. When there's a rule match, the traffic is forwarded to backend port 22:

```
az network lb inbound-nat-rule create \
  --resource-group azuremolchapter8 \
  --lb-name loadbalancer \
  --name natrulessh \
  --protocol tcp \
  --frontend-port 50001 \
  --backend-port 22 \
  --frontend-ip-name frontendpool
```

3. At this point, you've created a basic load balancer. Examine how the load-balancer components have come together:

```
az network lb show \
  --resource-group azuremolchapter8 \
  --name loadbalancer
```

A public IP address has been assigned to the frontend IP pool, and you created a health probe to check the status on a custom health page for a web server. A load-balancer rule was created to distribute web traffic from your customers to a backend pool, and uses the health probe. You also have a load-balancer NAT rule that permits SSH traffic. But there are no VMs to receive that traffic yet. Your pizza store customers are hungry, so let's create some VMs that can run your web application and to which the load balancer can distribute traffic!

8.1.5 Assigning groups of VMs to backend pools

The final section of the load balancer defines backend pools that include one or more VMs. These backend pools contain VMs that run the same application components, which allows the load balancer to distribute traffic to a given backend pool and trust that

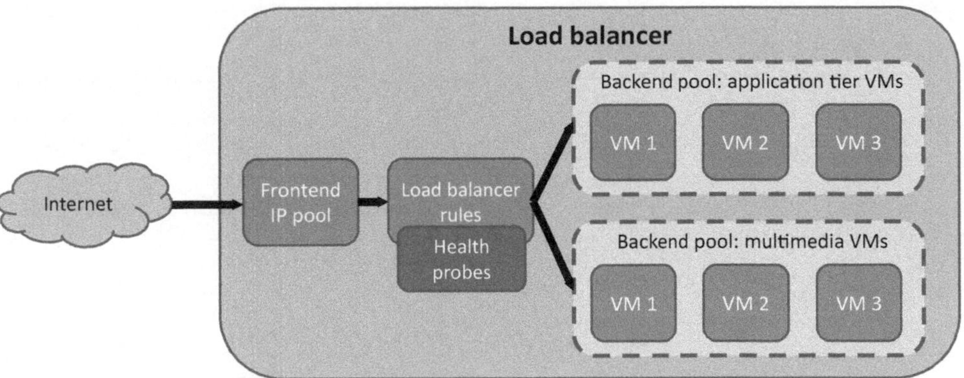

Figure 8.8 One or more backend pools can be created in a load balancer. Each backend pool contains one or more VMs that run the same application component. In this example, one backend pool contains VMs that run the web application tier, and another backend pool contains the VMs that serve multimedia, such as images and video.

any VM in that pool can correctly respond to the customer request. Figure 8.8 details how the backend pools logically group together VMs that run the same applications.

You create and use a load balancer with VMs, but everything works at the virtual network level. The frontend IP pool uses public or private IP addresses. The health probe looks at responses on a given port or protocol. Even when an HTTP probe is used, the load balancer looks for a positive network response. Load-balancer rules focus on how to distribute traffic from an external port in the frontend pool to a port on the backend pool.

When you assign VMs to the backend pool that receive traffic distributed by the load balancer, it's the virtual NIC that connects to the load balancer. The VM happens to attach to the virtual NIC. Think back to chapter 5, and this separation of VMs and virtual NIC makes sense in terms of how resources are managed. NSG rules control what traffic is permitted to flow to the VM, but they're applied to a virtual network subnet or virtual NIC, not the VM.

What does this mean for how you configure backend IP pools? You must create the rest of your virtual network resources before you can connect a VM to the load balancer. The steps to create the network resources should be a recap of what you learned a few chapters ago, so let's see how much you remember!

> **Try it now**
> To create the additional network resources, as shown in figure 8.9, complete the following steps.

1 Open the Azure portal, and select the Cloud Shell icon at the top of the dashboard.
2 Create a virtual network and subnet:

```
az network vnet create \
  --resource-group azuremolchapter8 \
  --name vnetmol \
  --address-prefixes 10.0.0.0/16 \
  --subnet-name subnetmol \
  --subnet-prefix 10.0.1.0/24
```

In practice, there's a good chance that these network resources already exist. These are also the same names and IP address ranges you used in chapter 5. You should clean up Azure resources at the end of each chapter, so such reuse of IP ranges shouldn't be a problem. Just be aware that you typically won't create a virtual network and subnet every time you create a load balancer. Rather, you can use the existing virtual network resources that are already in place.
3 Create an NSG:

```
az network nsg create \
  --resource-group azuremolchapter8 \
  --name webnsg
```

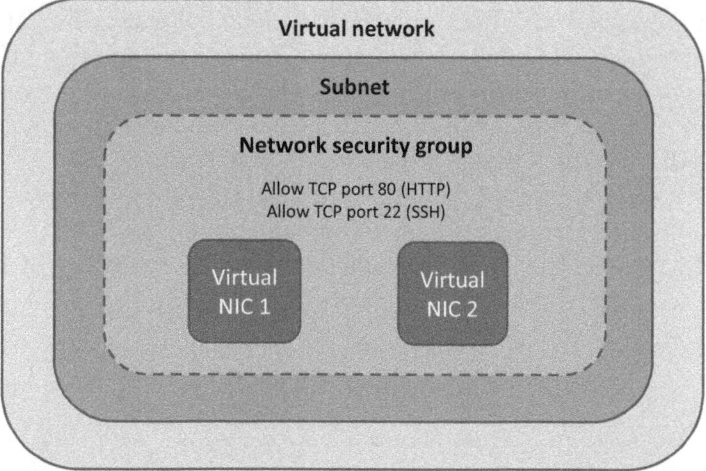

Figure 8.9 To prepare the virtual network, in this exercise you create a network, a subnet, and virtual NICs that are protected by a NSG. Rules attached to the NSG allow HTTP and SSH traffic.

4 Create an NSG rule that allows traffic from TCP port 80 to reach your VMs. This rule is needed for the web server VMs to receive and respond to customer traffic:

```
az network nsg rule create \
  --resource-group azuremolchapter8 \
  --nsg-name webnsg \
  --name allowhttp \
  --priority 100 \
  --protocol tcp \
  --destination-port-range 80 \
  --access allow
```

5 Add another rule to allow SSH traffic for remote management. This NSG rule works with the load-balancer NAT rule created in the preceding section for one of your VMs:

```
az network nsg rule create \
  --resource-group azuremolchapter8 \
  --nsg-name webnsg \
  --name allowssh \
  --priority 101 \
  --protocol tcp \
  --destination-port-range 22 \
  --access allow
```

6 Associate the NSG with the subnet created in step 2. The NSG rules are applied to all VMs that connect to this subnet:

```
az network vnet subnet update \
  --resource-group azuremolchapter8 \
  --vnet-name vnetmol \
  --name subnetmol \
  --network-security-group webnsg
```

7 The load balancer works with virtual NICs, so create two virtual NICs and connect them to the virtual network subnet. Also specify the load-balancer name and backend address pool that the virtual NICs connect to. The load-balancer NAT rule is only attached to this first virtual NIC that's created:

```
az network nic create \
  --resource-group azuremolchapter8 \
  --name webnic1 \
  --vnet-name vnetmol \
  --subnet subnetmol \
  --lb-name loadbalancer \
  --lb-address-pools backendpool \
  --lb-inbound-nat-rules natrulessh
```

8 Create the second NIC in the same way, minus the load-balancer NAT rule:

```
az network nic create \
  --resource-group azuremolchapter8 \
  --name webnic2 \
  --vnet-name vnetmol \
  --subnet subnetmol \
  --lb-name loadbalancer \
  --lb-address-pools backendpool
```

8.2 Creating and configuring VMs with the load balancer

Let's pause and explore what you've now created. Figure 8.10 shows the big picture of what your network resources and load balancer look like. Notice how integrated these resources are. The load balancer can't exist by itself. Virtual NICs must be connected to the load balancer for any traffic to be distributed. Those virtual NICs require a virtual network and subnet and should ideally be protected by an NSG. The VMs that then run your application have almost nothing to do with the steps to create and configure the load balancer!

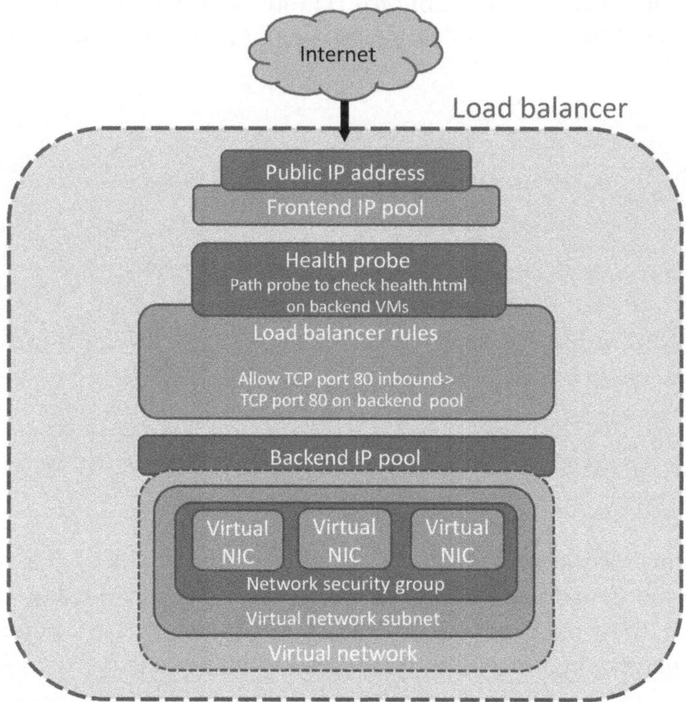

Figure 8.10 No VMs have been created here—the load-balancer configuration deals with virtual network resources. There's a tight relationship between the load balancer and virtual network resources.

You've created a lot of network resources and configured multiple parts of the load balancer. The public IP address and load balancer were created in an availability zone as zone-redundant resources, so let's create two VMs across different zones to reinforce how availability zones enhance the high availability of your applications.

If you use availability sets rather than availability zones, this is where you first create an availability set and then add your VMs to it. The Azure platform then distributes the VMs across the fault and update domains. You want to maximize the use of Azure high availability for your pizza store, so use availability zones.

> **Try it now**
> To create the VMs and attach them to the load balancer, complete the following steps.

1 Create the first VM, and assign it to an availability zone with `--zone 1`. Attach the first virtual NIC created in the preceding exercise with `--nics webnic1`. Remember, the load balancer only knows about the virtual NIC. A VM just happens to be connected to that virtual NIC:

```
az vm create \
  --resource-group azuremolchapter8 \
  --name webvm1 \
  --image ubuntults \
  --size Standard_B1ms \
  --admin-username azuremol \
  --generate-ssh-keys \
  --zone 1 \
  --nics webnic1
```

2 Create the second VM, and assign it to availability zone 2. Attach the second virtual NIC you created earlier, using `--nics webnic2`:

```
az vm create \
  --resource-group azuremolchapter8 \
  --name webvm2 \
  --image ubuntults \
  --size Standard_B1ms \
  --admin-username azuremol \
  --generate-ssh-keys \
  --zone 2 \
  --nics webnic2
```

8.2.1 Connecting to VMs and seeing the load balancer in action

To see the load balancer in action, you need to install a basic web server, as you did in chapter 2. You can also try out the load-balancer NAT rule. Can you start to see how all these components in Azure are related and build on each other?

> **Try it now**
> To install a web server on your VMs, complete the following steps.

1 Open the Azure portal, and select the Cloud Shell icon at the top of the dashboard.

2 In chapter 5, we discussed the SSH agent. The SSH agent allows you to pass an SSH key from one VM to the next. Only VM1 has a load balancer NAT rule, so you need to use the agent to connect to VM2.

Start the SSH agent, and add your SSH key so that you can connect to both VMs:

```
eval $(ssh-agent) && ssh-add
```

3 Obtain the public IP address attached to the load-balancer frontend IP pool. This is the only way for traffic to route through the VMs:

```
az network public-ip show \
  --resource-group azuremolchapter8 \
  --name publicip \
  --query ipAddress \
  --output tsv
```

4 SSH to VM 1. Specify the public IP address of the load balancer and the port that was used with the load-balancer NAT rule, such as 50001. The `-A` parameter uses the SSH agent to pass through your SSH keys:

```
ssh -A azuremol@ipAddress -p 50001
```

5 In chapter 2, you used `apt-get` to install the entire LAMP stack that included the Apache web server. Let's see something a little different from the Apache web server with the standalone but powerful NGINX web server. On a Windows VM, this is typically where you'd install IIS:

```
sudo apt-get install -y nginx
```

6 In the GitHub samples repo that you've used in previous chapters, there's a basic HTML web page and a health-check page for the load-balancer health probe. Clone these samples to the VM:

```
git clone https://github.com/fouldsy/azure-mol-samples.git
```

7 Copy the sample HTML page and health-check to the web server directory:

```
sudo cp azure-mol-samples/8/webvm1/* /var/www/html/
```

8 Repeat all this for the second VM. Remember the SSH agent? You should be able to SSH from VM 1 to VM 2 on the internal, private IP address:

```
ssh 10.0.1.5
```

Install the Nginx web server:

```
sudo apt-get install -y nginx
```

Clone the GitHub samples to the VM:

```
git clone https://github.com/fouldsy/azure-mol-samples.git
```

9 And copy the sample HTML page and health check to the web server directory:

```
sudo cp azure-mol-samples/8/webvm2/* /var/www/html/
```

Open a web browser, and connect to the public IP address of your load balancer. The basic web page loads and shows that your pizza store now has redundant VMs in availability zones that run behind a load balancer, as shown in figure 8.11! You may need to force-refresh your web browser to see that both VM 1 and VM2 respond as the load balancer distributes traffic between them.

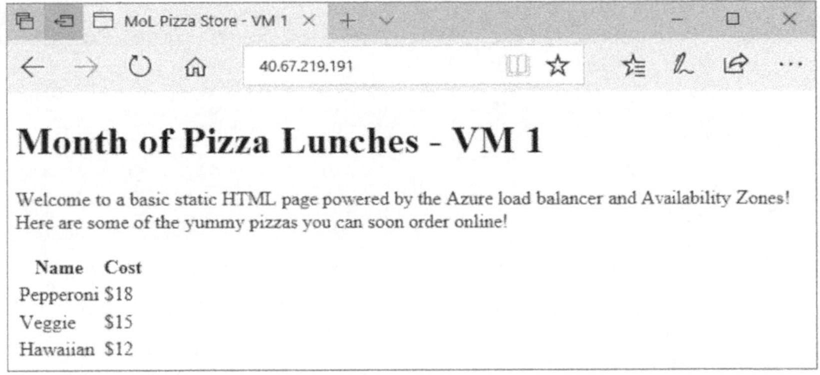

Figure 8.11 When you open the public IP address of the load balancer in a web browser, traffic is distributed to one of the VMs that run your basic website. The load-balancer health probe uses the health.html page to confirm the web server responses with an HTTP code 200 (OK). The VM is then available as part of the load-balancer traffic distribution.

8.3 Lab: Viewing templates of existing deployments

This chapter ties together what you learned in multiple previous chapters. You created network resources, as in chapter 5. You made the load balancer and VMs highly available with availability zones, as in chapter 7. And a web server was installed and sample files deployed, as in chapter 2. Your pizza store has come a long way from the basic web page on a single VM at the start of the book!

To tie in one more theme from a previous chapter, in this lab I want you to explore all the resources that make up the load balancer. To do this, you look at the Resource Manager template, as you learned about in chapter 6. The goal of this lab is to see how a single template can create and configure what's taken many pages and multiple CLI commands. And trust me, it would take even more PowerShell commands! Follow these steps:

1. Open the Azure portal. Browse to and select Resource Group from the navigation bar at left in the portal. Choose your resource group, such as azuremolchapter8.
2. Choose Automation Script from the bar at left, as shown in figure 8.12.
3. To see the relevant part of the template, select each of the resources shown in the list. Take a few minutes to explore this template and see how all the resources and components that you configured in the Azure CLI are present.

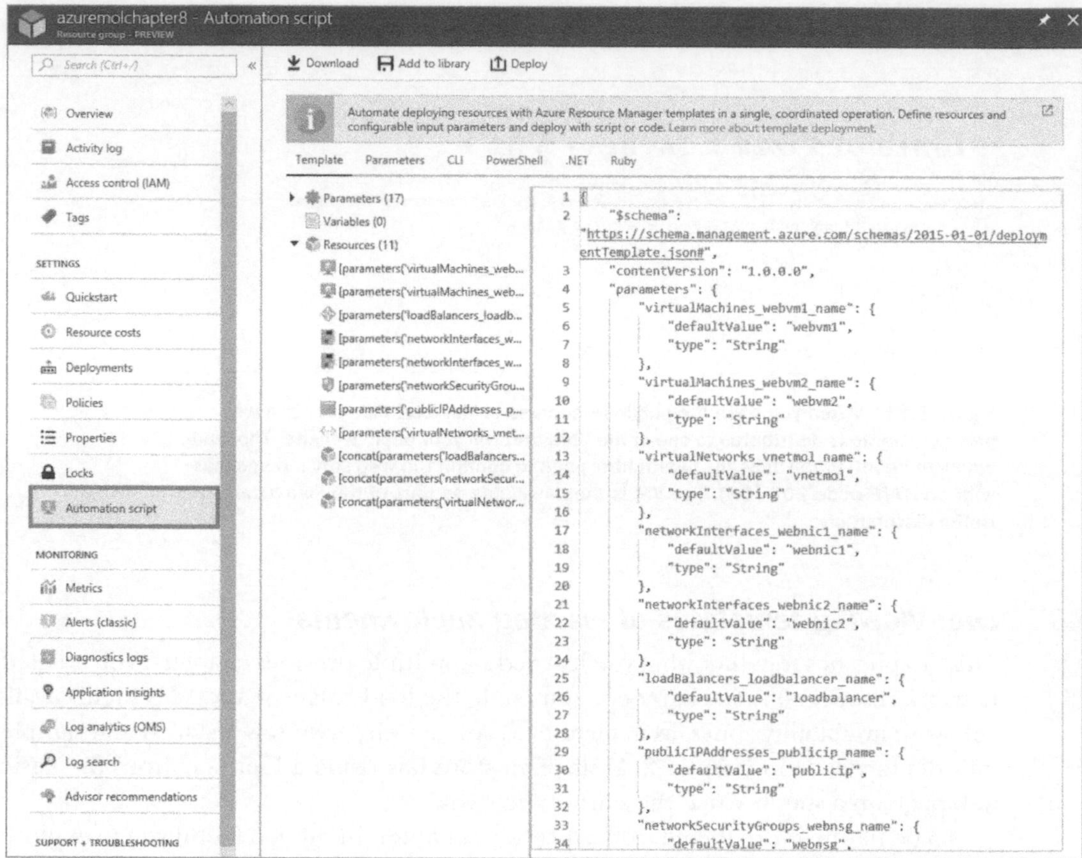

Figure 8.12 In the Azure portal, select your load-balancer resource group and view the Resource Manager template.

A template makes it a lot easier to deploy a highly available, redundant, load-balanced application environment. You can change the load balancer's name, rules, and distribution mode, and let the template deploy and configure the entire application environment for you.

Don't forget to delete this resource group to make the most of your free Azure credits!

9 Applications that scale

In the previous two chapters, we examined how to build highly available applications and use load balancers to distribute traffic to multiple VMs that run your app. But how do you efficiently run and manage multiple VMs, and run the right number of VM instances when your customers need them the most? When customer demand increases, you want to automatically increase the scale of your application to cope with that demand. And when demand decreases, such as in the middle of the night when most people without young children are asleep, you want the application to decrease in scale and save you some money.

In Azure, you can automatically scale in and out IaaS resources with virtual machine scale sets. These scale sets run identical VMs, typically distributed behind a load balancer or application gateway. You define autoscale rules that increase or decrease the number of VM instances as customer demand changes. The load balancer or app gateway automatically distributes traffic to the new VM instances, which lets you focus on how to build and run your apps better. Scale sets give you control of IaaS resources with some of the elastic benefits of PaaS. Web apps, which we haven't covered a lot in the last couple of chapters, now make a solid reappearance with their own ability to scale with application demand.

In this chapter, we examine how to design and create applications that can scale automatically. We look at why this ability to scale with demand helps you run efficient applications, and explore different ways to scale based on different metrics.

9.1 Why build scalable, reliable applications?

What does it mean to build applications that scale? It lets you grow and keep up with customer demand as the workload increases, even when you're at the movies on a weekend. It means you don't get stuck with a bill for a bunch of extra resources you don't use or, maybe worse, have your application go down due to a lack of available resources. The sweet spot for applications and the resources they need is rarely static. Usually, application demands ebb and flow throughout the day and night, or between weekdays and weekends.

There are two main ways you can scale resources, as shown in figure 9.1: vertically and horizontally. Both virtual machine scale sets and web apps can scale vertically or horizontally.

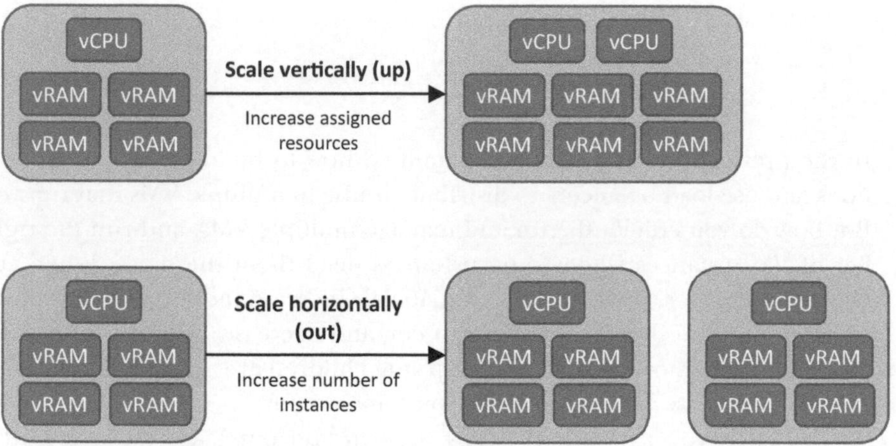

Figure 9.1 You can scale your applications up and down, or in and out. The method you use depends on how your application is built to handle scale. Vertical scale adjusts the resources assigned to a VM or web app, such as the number of CPU cores or amount of memory. This method to scale an application works well if the application runs only one instance. Horizontal scale changes the number of instances that run your application and helps increase availability and resiliency.

Scalable applications have a strong relationship with highly available applications. In chapters 7 and 8 we spent a lot of time with availability sets and availability zones, and how to configure load balancers. Both chapters centered around the need to run multiple VMs. When your applications can scale automatically, the availability of that application is also increased as those VMs are distributed across availability sets or availability zones. All of this is a Good Thing. The power of Azure is that you don't need to worry about how to add more application instances, spread those across datacenter hardware or even datacenters, and then update network resources to distribute traffic to the new application instances.

9.1.1 Scaling VMs vertically

The first way to scale resources is often the time-honored way that you may have done so in the past. If your application starts to perform slowly as more customers use it, what would you normally do? Increase the amount of CPU or memory, right? You scale *up* the resource in response to demand.

One of the most common uses of vertical scale is for database servers. Databases are notoriously hungry when it comes to compute resources—even hungrier than your pizza store customers! Database servers often consume all the resources provided to a VM, even if they don't immediately use them. This can make it hard to monitor the actual demands on the system and know when you need to scale vertically and provide more resources. Figure 9.2 shows the typical vertical scale response to a database server that needs more resources.

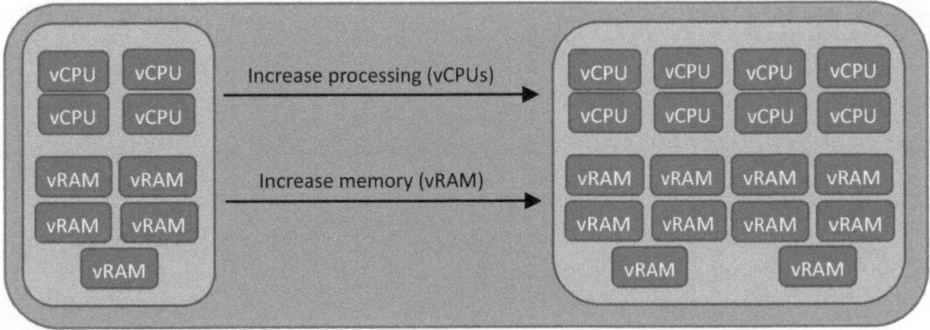

Figure 9.2 As a database grows, it needs more resources to store and process the data in memory. To scale vertically in this scenario, you add more CPU and memory.

You may need to scale beyond the demand for CPU or memory. What if you run a website that serves a lot of images or video? There may not be a lot of processing requirements, but the bandwidth demands may be high. To increase the available bandwidth, you can increase the number of NICs on your VM. And if you need to store more images and video, you add more storage. You can add or remove resources such as virtual NICs and storage as the VM continues to run.

RESIZING VIRTUAL MACHINES

In Azure, you can increase the VM size (scale up) if you need more compute resources for your application. Back in chapter 2 you created a basic VM. Its size was Standard_D2s_v3. That name doesn't tell you a lot about the compute resources assigned to a VM to determine whether you may need to increase the CPU or memory. If you want to scale vertically, you need to know what your options are.

Try it now

Follow along to see the available VM sizes and compute resources.

1 Open the Azure portal in a web browser, and then open the Cloud Shell.
2 Enter the following Azure CLI command to list available VM sizes and the compute resources they provide:

```
az vm list-sizes --location eastus --output table
```

The output from `az vm list-sizes` varies from region to region and changes over time as Azure adjusts its VM families. Here's a condensed example of the output, showing the `MemoryInMb` and `NumberOfCores` each VM size provides:

```
MaxDataDiskCount    MemoryInMb    Name                      NumberOfCores
------------------  ------------  ----------------------    ---------------
                 4          8192  Standard_D2s_v3                         2
                 8         16384  Standard_D4s_v3                         4
                16         32768  Standard_D8s_v3                         8
                32         65536  Standard_D16s_v3                       16
                 8          4096  Standard_F2s                            2
                16          8192  Standard_F4s                            4
                32         16384  Standard_F8s                            8
                 2          2048  Standard_B1ms                           1
                 2          1024  Standard_B1s                            1
                 4          8192  Standard_B2ms                           2
                 4          4096  Standard_B2s                            2
```

So, your Standard_D2s_v3 VM provides you with two CPU cores and 8 GB of memory. That's more than enough for a basic VM that runs a web server. Let's assume your online pizza store starts to get some orders, and you want to scale vertically: you can use `az vm resize` to pick another size. You specify the VM size that has the number of CPU cores and memory your application needs.

The additional CPU and memory don't magically appear on your VM. This behavior may be a little different than what you experience with Hyper-V or VMware in an on-premises world. Within reason, you can add or remove core compute resources in an on-premises environment as the VM continues to run. In Azure, a VM reboot is currently required when you resize it to register the new compute resources and trigger the appropriate billing rules. When you want to scale vertically, plan for some downtime as the VM reboots.

SCALING DOWN

What if you have a VM with more resources than it needs? This scenario is often more common than a VM that has fewer resources than needed. Application owners may choose a larger VM size than is required, to be sure their application runs smoothly. All those wasted resources cost money, and it's easy for the costs to go unnoticed until the bill arrives at the end of the month.

The ability to scale resources works in both directions. We've focused on how to scale *up* resources, but all the same concepts work to scale *down* resources. It's important to identify the VM sizes in use and how much of a demand the applications make on those resources. You can then use `az vm resize` to pick a VM size with fewer CPU cores and memory. Again, a VM restart is also currently needed for any resize operation.

9.1.2 Scaling web apps vertically

Web apps can scale up or down based on resource needs, in the same way as VMs. When you created a web app in chapter 3, the default S1 Standard size provided one CPU core and 1.75 GB RAM. Each web app tier and size provides a set amount of resources such as CPU cores, memory, and staging slots. Even if the default size or resource allocation changes, or you chose a different web app size, the concept remains the same.

If you create your web app and find the application requires more resources than the service plan provides, you can change to a different tier, as shown in figure 9.3. The same process works if you have more resources that you need. Your web app can scale up or down manually in this way as needed.

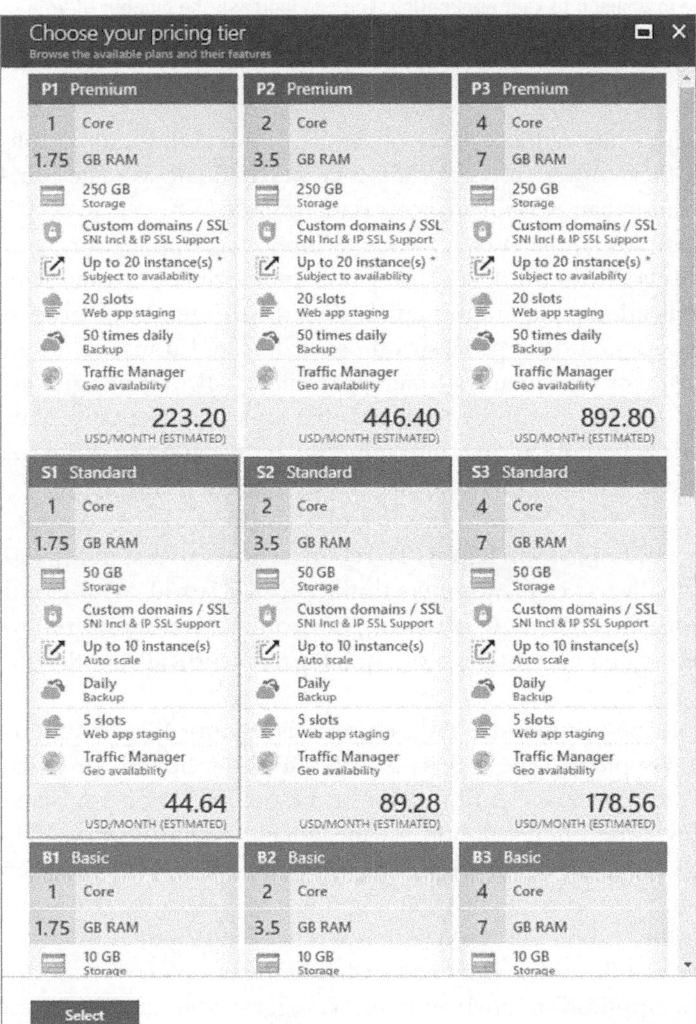

Figure 9.3 To manually scale a web app vertically, you change the pricing tier (size) of the underlying app service plan. The app service plan defines the amount of resources assigned to your web app. If your application requires a different amount of storage, number of CPUs, or deployment slots, you can change to a different tier to right-size the assigned resources to the application demand.

9.1.3 Scaling resources horizontally

A different approach to keep up with demand is to scale out, horizontally. To scale vertically, you increase the amount of CPU and memory assigned to a single resource, such as a VM. To scale horizontally, you increase the number of VMs, instead, as shown in figure 9.4.

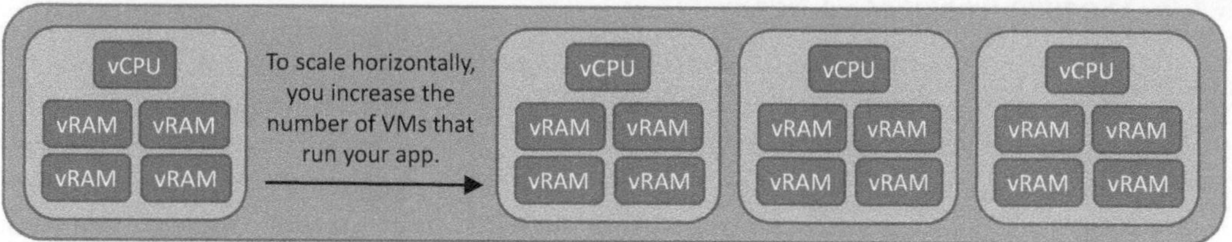

Figure 9.4 To deal with an increase in demand to your application, you can increase the number of VMs that run the application. This distributes the load across multiple VMs, rather than ever-larger single-instance VMs.

To scale horizontally, your application does need to be aware of this ability and be able to process data without conflicts. A web application is a great candidate to scale horizontally, because the application can typically process data by itself.

As you build more complex applications, you may break an application into smaller individual components. If you think back to Azure storage queues from chapter 4, you may have one application component that receives the frontend web orders, and another application component that processes those orders and transmits them to the pizza store. The use of message queues is one approach to how you design and write applications that can operate in an environment that scales horizontally. This approach also lets you scale each application component separately and use different VM sizes or web app plans to maximize efficiency and reduce your monthly bill.

Historically, you'd scale vertically because it was easier to throw more compute resources at an application and hope it was happy. To set up a cluster of resources and scale an application horizontally was often complex in the physical world. With cloud computing and virtualization, the challenges of scaling horizontally are minimized to the point that you can often scale horizontally more quickly than vertically, and without downtime.

Remember the `az vm resize` command from the previous section? What happens as the VM resize operation completes? The VM is restarted. If that's the only instance of your application, no one can access it until it comes back online. When you scale horizontally, there's no downtime when you add VM instances—when the new VMs are ready, they start to process some of the application requests. The load-balancer health probes from chapter 8 automatically detect when a new VM in the backend pool is ready to process customer requests, and traffic starts to be distributed to it.

Azure is designed to give you flexibility and choice when it comes to how you scale. If you're designing a new application environment, I suggest you implement a horizontal scale approach. VMs have a cool cousin in Azure that can help you out here: virtual machine scale sets.

9.2 Virtual machine scale sets

VMs are one of the most common workloads in Azure, for good reason. The learning curve to build and run a VM is shallow, because most of what you already know transfers straight into Azure. Web servers are one of the most common workloads for a VM, which again is convenient in that you don't have to learn new skills to transfer your knowledge of how to run Apache, IIS, or NGINX in an Azure VM.

What about a cluster of VMs that runs a web server? How would you handle that in your regular on-premises environment? There are many possible cluster solutions, to start with. What about updates to your physical servers or VMs? How would you handle those? What if you wanted to automatically increase or decrease the number of instances in the cluster? Do you need to use another tool to handle that? An outline of a virtual machine scale set is shown in figure 9.5.

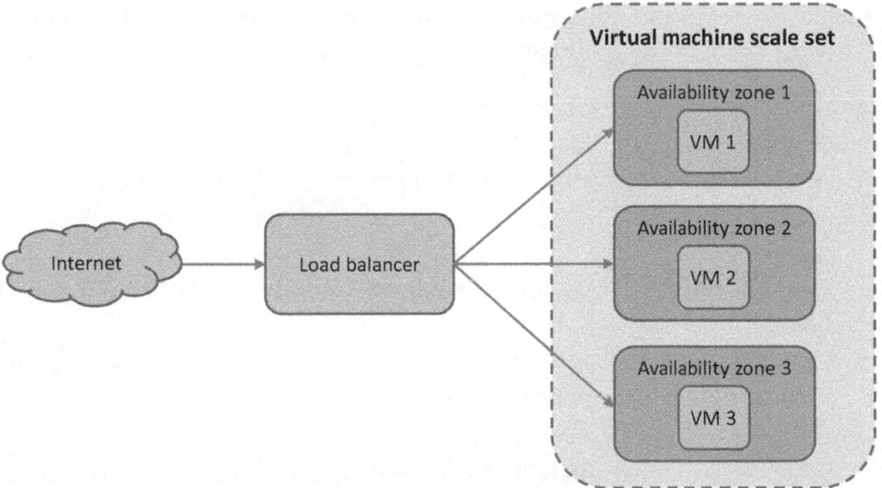

Figure 9.5 A virtual machine scale set logically groups together a set of VMs. Each VM is identical and can be centrally managed, updated, and scaled. You can define metrics that automatically increase or decrease the number of VMs in the scale set based on your application load.

A scale set simplifies how you run and manage multiple VMs to provide a highly available, load-balanced application. You tell Azure what size VM to use, a base image for the VM, and how many instances you want. You can then define CPU or memory metrics to automatically increase or decrease the number of instances in response to the application load, or on a schedule at peak customer hours. Scale sets combine the IaaS model of VMs with the power of PaaS features like scale, redundancy, automation, and centralized management of resources.

A single-VM scale set?

If you build applications on VMs, plan to start out with a scale set, even if you only need one VM. Why? A scale set can expand at any time, and it automatically creates the connections to a load balancer or application gateway. If demand for the application suddenly increases in two months, you can tell the scale set to create an additional VM instance or two.

With a regular, standalone VM, to expand, you need to add that VM to a load balancer; and if you didn't begin with the VM in an availability set or availability zone, you have to plan for how to now make those VMs highly available. By creating a scale set to begin with, even for one VM, you future-proof your application with minimal additional work required.

9.2.1 Creating a virtual machine scale set

Although a scale set makes it simpler to build and run highly available applications, you need to create and configure a few new components. That said, you can reduce the process down to two commands to deploy a scale set with the Azure CLI.

Try it now

To create a scale set with the Azure CLI, complete the following steps.

1. Open the Azure portal, and select the Cloud Shell icon at the top of the dashboard.
2. Create a resource group with `az group create`. Specify a resource group name, such as `azuremolchapter9`, and a location:.

   ```
   az group create --name azuremolchapter9 --location westeurope
   ```

   Scale sets can use availability zones, so make sure you select a region where support is available.
3. To create a scale set, specify the number of VM instances you want and how the VM instances should handle updates to their configuration. When you make a change to the VMs, such as to install an application or apply guest OS updates, the VMs can update automatically as soon as they detect the change. Or you can set the upgrade policy to `manual` and apply the updates at a suitable time of your choice. The rest of the parameters should be familiar from when you create a single VM:

   ```
   az vmss create \
     --resource-group azuremolchapter9 \
     --name scalesetmol \
     --image UbuntuLTS \
     --admin-username azuremol \
   ```

```
    --generate-ssh-keys \
    --instance-count 2 \
    --vm-sku Standard_B1ms \
    --upgrade-policy-mode automatic \
    --lb-sku standard \
    --zones 1 2 3
```

That's it! You created multiple VMs across an availability zone that can scale. Get ready for what's really cool about the scale set you just created with the Azure CLI. Remember that entire previous chapter about load balancers, and all those CLI commands you had to use, and how you looked at templates to simplify how you create a load balancer? That `az vmss create` command created and configured a load balancer for you!

Remember your quota limits

I mentioned this a couple of chapters ago, but it's worth repeating in case you run into problems. In Azure, default quotas on your subscription prevent you from accidentally deploying resources and forgetting about them, which will cost you money! You can see the list of quotas at http://mng.bz/ddcx.

When you create multiple VMs, you may run into quota issues. You may also have issues if you don't delete resources from previous chapters and exercises. If you see error text along the lines of

```
Operation results in exceeding quota limits of Core.
Maximum allowed: 4, Current in use: 4, Additional requested: 2.
```

it's a good indication that you need to request an increase in your quotas. You can view your current quota for a given region as follows:

```
az vm list-usage --location westeurope
```

To request an increase in your quotas for a region, follow the steps outlined at http://mng.bz/Xq2f.

The Azure CLI helps you create a scale set with minimal prompts. A load balancer has been created and configured, a public IP address assigned, and the scale set VM instances added to the backend IP pool.

Try it now

Check out the resources created with your scale set, as described next.

To see what resources were created with your scale set, run the following command:

```
az resource list \
  --resource-group azuremolchapter9 \
  --output table
```

The output is similar to the following example. Look at the Type column for proof that a virtual network, public IP address, and load balancer were created:

```
Name       ResourceGroup       Type
------     ----------------    ----------------------------------
mol        azuremolchapter9    Microsoft.Compute/virtualMachineScaleSets
molLB      azuremolchapter9    Microsoft.Network/loadBalancers
molLBIP    azuremolchapter9    Microsoft.Network/publicIPAddresses
molVNET    azuremolchapter9    Microsoft.Network/virtualNetworks
```

What does all this magic mean? When you create a scale set with the Azure CLI, a zone-redundant load balancer and public IP address are created for you. The VMs are created and added to a backend IP pool on the load balancer. NAT rules are created that allow you to connect to the VM instances. The only thing missing are load-balancer rules, because they vary based on the applications you want to run. As you add or remove VMs to the scale set, the load-balancer configuration automatically updates to allow traffic to be distributed to the new instances. This magic isn't limited to the Azure CLI—if you use Azure PowerShell or the Azure portal, these supporting network resources are created and wired up to work together.

Try it now

Your scale was created with two instances. You can manually scale the number of VM instances in your scale set. When you do, the load balancer automatically updates the backend IP pool configuration. Set the `--new-capacity` of the scale set to four instances as follows:

```
az vmss scale \
    --resource-group azuremolchapter9 \
    --name scalesetmol \
    --new-capacity 4
```

9.2.2 Creating autoscale rules

When you created your scale set, a fixed number of instances were deployed. One of the biggest features of scale sets is the ability to automatically scale in or out the number of VM instances that the scale set runs.

As shown in figure 9.6, the number of instances in a scale set can automatically increase as the application load increases. Think about a typical business application in your environment. Early in the workday, users start to access the application, which causes the resource load on those VM instances to increase. To ensure optimum application performance, the scale set automatically adds more VM instances. The load balancer automatically starts to distribute traffic to the new instances. Later in the workday, as users go home, application demand goes down. The VM instances use less resources, so the scale set automatically removes some VM instances to reduce unnecessary resources and lower cost.

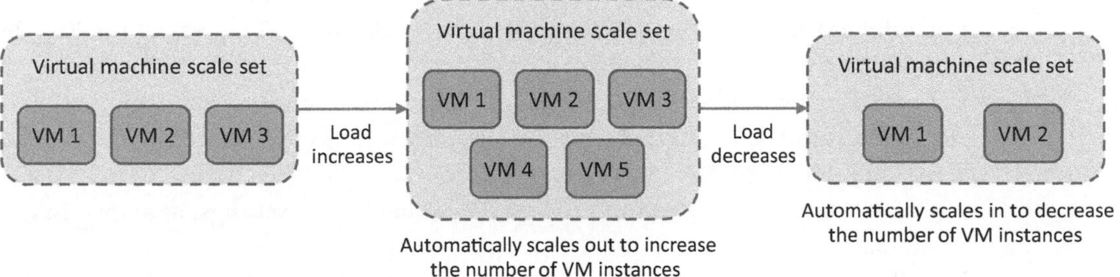

Figure 9.6 Scale sets can automatically scale in and out. You define rules to monitor certain metrics that trigger the rules to increase or decrease the number of VM instances that run. As your application demand changes, so does the number of VM instances. This maximizes the performance and availability of your application, while also minimizing unnecessary cost when the application load decreases.

You can base your scale-set rules on various metrics. You can look at host metrics for basic resource consumption, configure in-guest VM metrics collection for analysis of specific application performance counters, or use Azure Application Insights to monitor deep within the application code.

Schedules can also be used to define a certain number of VM instances in a scale set for a time window. Back to the example of a common business application where demand is higher in the work hours than evening, you may want to define a higher fixed number of instances to run during business hours. In the evening, you then define a lower fixed number of instances to run.

Autoscale rules based on metrics monitor performance over a defined time interval, such as 5 minutes, and may then take another few minutes to spin up the new VM instances and configure them for application use. If you use fixed schedules to autoscale the number of VM instances in your scale set, those additional resources are already in use, and the load balancer distributes traffic to them throughout the day.

The use of schedules requires a baseline for the typical application demand and doesn't account for higher or lower demand at certain parts of the business account or sales cycle. You may end up with more resources than you need at times, so you pay more than needed. And you may have situations where the application load is higher than the number of VM instances in the scale set can provide.

Try it now

To create autoscale rules for a scale set, complete the following steps.

1. Browse to and select Resource Group from the navigation bar at left in the Azure portal. Choose the resource group you created for your template deployment, such as `azuremolchapter9`.

2 Select your scale set from the list of resources, such as scalesetmol.
3 Under Settings at left in the Scale Set window, choose Scaling. Select the Enable Autoscale button.
4 Enter a name, such as `autoscale`, and then define a minimum, maximum, and default instance count. For this exercise, set the minimum to 2, maximum to 10, and default to 2.
5 Choose Add a Rule, and then review the available rule settings, as shown in figure 9.7.

   The default parameters look at the average CPU consumption. The rule triggers when the load is greater than 70% over a 10-minute interval. The scale set is increased by 1 VM instance, and the rules then wait for 5 minutes before they begin to monitor and can trigger the next rule.

   This cool-down period gives the new VM instances time to deploy and begin to receive traffic from the load balancer, which should decrease the overall application load in the scale set. Without this cool-down period, the rules may trigger another VM instance to be added before the load has started to be distributed across the previous VM instance created. To create the rule, select Add.
6 Choose Add a Rule again. This time, configure the rule to Decrease Count By 1 when the average CPU load is less than 30% over a 5-minute duration. To create the rule, select Add.
7 Review your rules, as shown in figure 9.8, and then select Save.

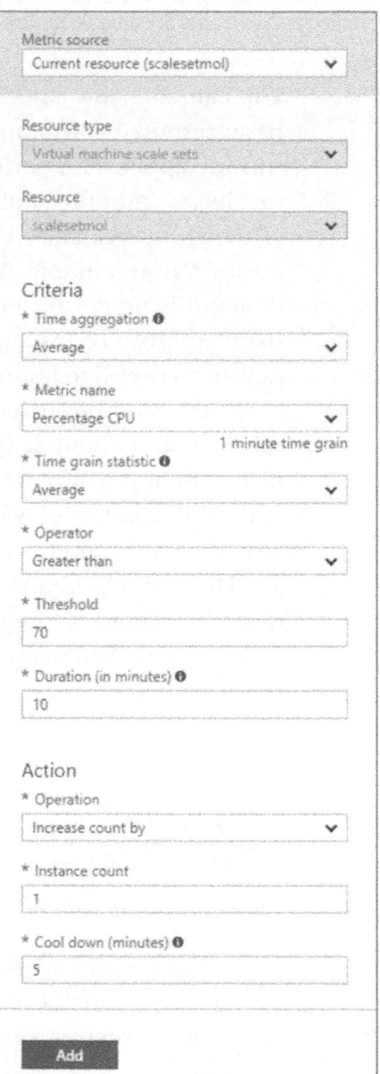

Figure 9.7 When you add an autoscale rule, you define the exact behavior required for the rule to trigger.

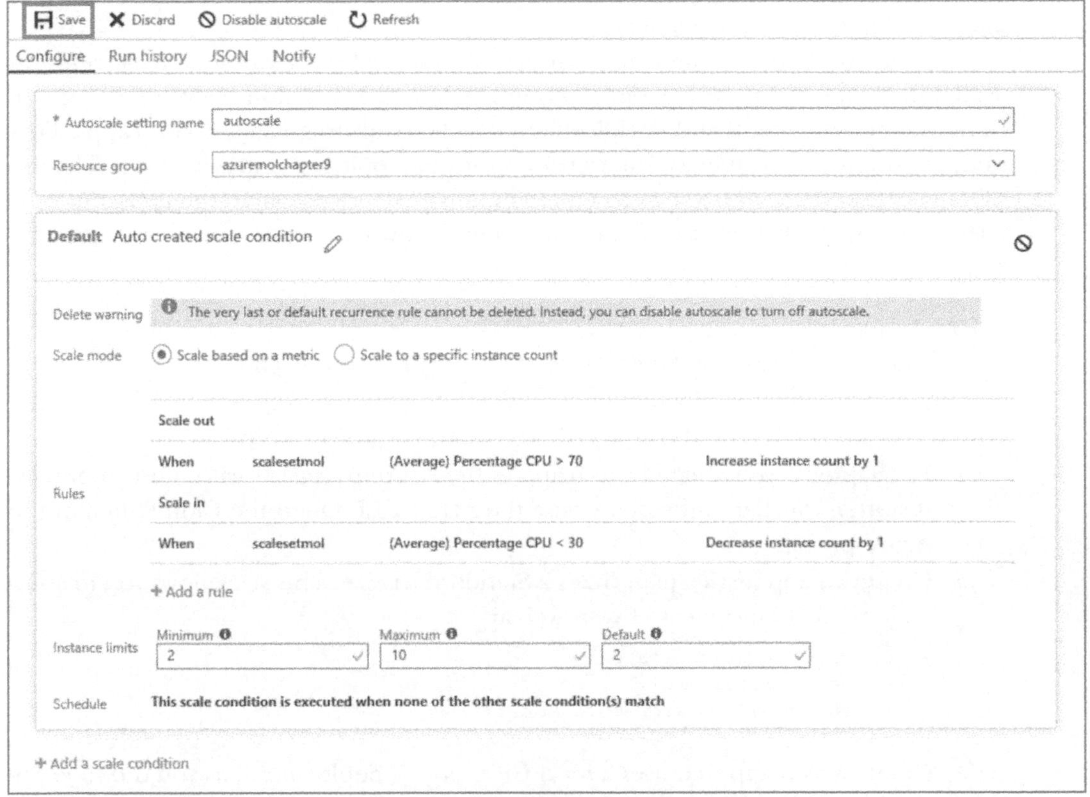

Figure 9.8 You should now have one rule that increases the instance count by one when the average CPU load is greater than 70%, and another rule that decreases the instance count by one when the average CPU load is less than 30%.

You can also configure autoscale rules with the Azure CLI, Azure PowerShell, or in templates. The portal provides a nice visual way to review the rules and see available options for each parameter. As you build more complex rules, templates provide a way to create scale sets with the same set of rules in a reproducible fashion.

9.3 Scaling a web app

If you were super interested in web apps in chapter 3, or Azure tables and queues in chapter 4, these last three chapters that have been heavy on IaaS VMs may have left you scratching your head. Wasn't the cloud meant to be easier than this? For PaaS components like web apps, absolutely!

I don't want you to feel like the next few pages rush through how to provide the same high availability and autoscale capabilities to web apps. The truth is, it's a lot easier to do! Like all things, the choice between IaaS and PaaS is a balance between flexibility and ease of management. Much of the underlying redundancy is abstracted in

PaaS services like web apps, so you don't need a whole chapter on high availability and another chapter on load balancers.

The IaaS path to build and run your own VMs or scale sets with load balancers and availability zones may come from a business need or restriction. Developers, operations engineers, or tools and workflows may not be ready to go all-in to web apps. That said, I strongly urge you to look at web apps for new application deployments. The use of PaaS components like web apps gives you more time to focus on the apps and your customers rather than infrastructure and administration.

Try it now

To create a web app with the Azure CLI, complete the following steps.

1. In chapter 3, you created a web app in the Azure portal. As with most resources, it's often quicker and easier to use the Azure CLI. Open the Cloud Shell in the Azure portal.
2. Create an app service plan that's a Standard S1 size. This size allows you to autoscale up to 10 instances of your web app:

```
az appservice plan create \
  --name appservicemol \
  --resource-group azuremolchapter9 \
  --sku s1
```

3. Create a web app that uses a local Git repo for deployment, as you did in chapter 3:

```
az webapp create \
  --name webappmol \
  --resource-group azuremolchapter9 \
  --plan appservicemol \
  --deployment-local-git
```

   All the concepts and scenarios discussed in the previous section around autoscale rules and schedules for scale sets apply to web apps. As a quick recap, these are a couple of common scenarios for autoscaling web apps:

   - Automatically increase or decrease the number of web app instances based on performance metrics, to support application demand throughout the workday.
   - Schedule a web app to automatically increase the number of instances at the start of the workday and then decrease the number of instances at the end of the workday.

In the case of the pizza store, the web app may receive more traffic later in the day and through the evening, so there isn't one set of autoscale rules that applies to every situation. Again, you need to baseline your application performance to understand how it runs under normal use and the performance metric at which the app needs to scale out or in. Even when you use autoscale schedules, you should continue to monitor and track when your peak application demands are, to create rules that support that usage pattern.

Try it now
To create autoscale rules for a web app, complete the following steps.

1. Browse to and select Resource Group from the navigation bar at left in the Azure portal. Choose the resource group you created for your web app, such as azuremolchapter9.
2. Select your web app from the list of resources, such as webappmol.
3. Under Settings at left in the web app window, choose Scale Out (App Service Plan). Select the Enable Autoscale button.
4. Enter a name, such as `autoscalewebapp`, and then define a minimum, maximum, and default instance count. For this exercise, set the minimum to 2, maximum to 5, and default to 2.
5. Choose Add a Rule, and then review the available rule settings. This window looks the same as the autoscale rules for scale sets. The default parameters look at the average CPU consumption, and trigger when the load is greater than 70% over a 10-minute interval. The web app is increased by one instance, and the rules then wait for 5 minutes before they begin to monitor and can trigger the next rule. To create the rule, select Add.
6. Choose Add a Rule again. This time, configure the rule to Decrease Count by 1 when the average CPU load is less than 30% over a 5-minute duration. To create the rule, select Add.
7. Review your rules, as shown in figure 9.9, and then select Save.

When your autoscale rules trigger the web app to scale out or scale in, the Azure platform updates the traffic distribution to the available web app instances. There's no load balancer, like you have with scale set. The concept is similar, just abstracted away from you because you're meant to enjoy the PaaS approach and not worry so much!

Both scale sets and web apps provide a way to build rules that automatically scale the number of instances that run your applications. With multiple instances to run your application, you also increase the availability of your app. Scale sets are a good middle ground between developers and business decision makers who want or need to build applications on VMs, while using the PaaS-like features to autoscale and reconfigure the flow of customer traffic.

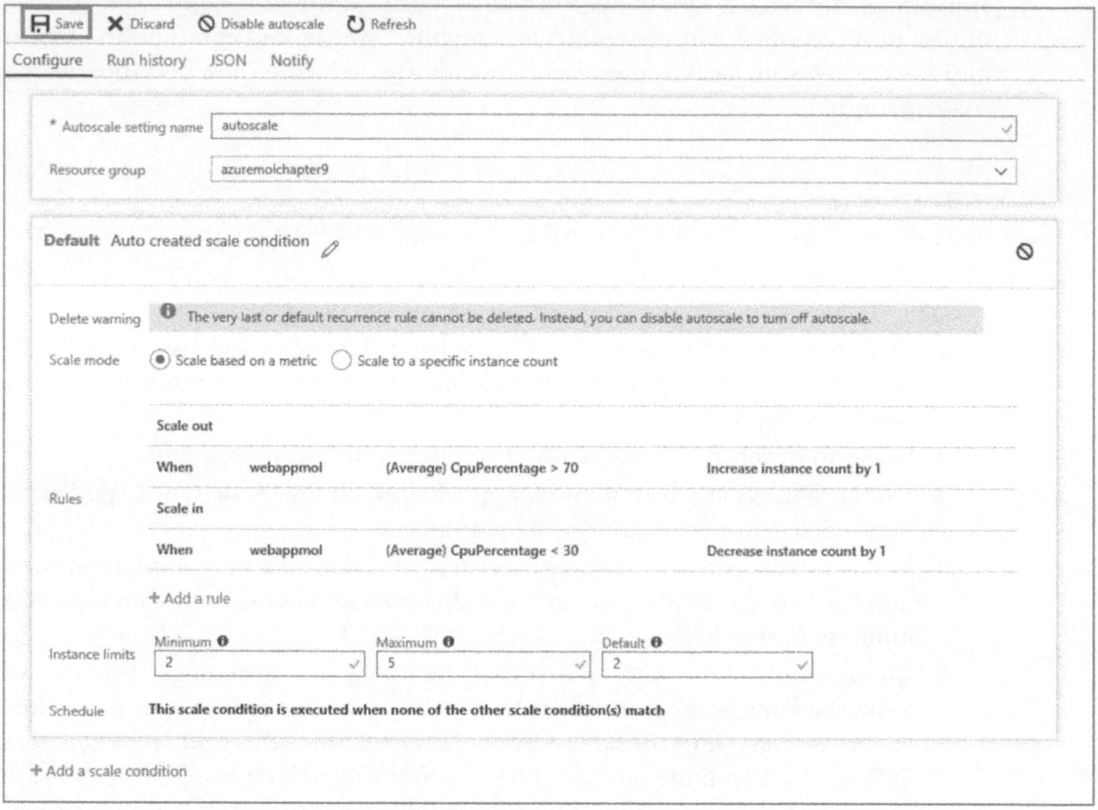

Figure 9.9 You should now have one rule that increases the instance count by one when the average CPU load is greater than 70%, and another rule that decreases the instance count by one when the average CPU load is less than 30%.

9.4 Lab: Installing applications on your scale set or web app

We covered a lot in this chapter, so now you can choose a quick final lab for either scale sets or web apps. Or, if you want to extend your lunch break, do both!

9.4.1 Virtual machine scale sets

You have multiple VM instances in your scale sets, but they don't do a lot right now. For an overview of the different ways to install applications to VM instances in a scale set, see http://mng.bz/9Ocx. In practice, you'd use one of those automated deployment methods; but for now, manually install a web server on the VM instances as you did in chapter 8:

1 Remember load-balancer NAT rules? By default, each VM instance in a scale set has a NAT rule that allows you to SSH directly to it. The ports aren't on the

standard TCP port 22. You can view the list of VM instances in a scale set and their port numbers as follows:

```
az vmss list-instance-connection-info \
  --resource-group azuremolchapter9 \
  --name scalesetmol
```

2 To connect to a specific port via SSH, use the `-p` parameter as follows (provide your own public IP address and port numbers):

```
ssh azuremol@40.114.3.147 -p 50003
```

3 Install a basic NGINX web server on each VM instance with `apt install`. Think back to how you did that in chapter 8.
4 To see the scale set in action, open the public IP address of the scale set load balancer in a web browser.

9.4.2 Web apps

To deploy your application to a web app that runs multiple instances, the process is the same as the single web app from chapter 3. You push the application to the local Git repository for the web app, and, thanks to the power of PaaS, the Azure platform deploys that single codebase to multiple web app instances:

1 Initialize a Git repo in azure-mol-samples/9, and then add and commit the sample files as you did in chapter 3:

```
cd azure-mol-samples/9
git init && git add . && git commit -m "Pizza"
```

2 Your web app has a local Git repository. Add a remote for your web app in the same way you did in chapter 3:

```
git remote add webappmolscale <your-git-clone-url>
```

3 Push this sample to your web app. This makes a single code commit, but your app is then distributed across the multiple web app instances:

```
git push webappmolscale master
```

10 Global databases with Cosmos DB

Data. You can't get by without it. Almost every application that you build and run creates, processes, or retrieves data. Traditionally, this data has been stored in a structured database such as MySQL, Microsoft SQL, or PostgreSQL. These large, structured databases are established and well-known, have ample documentation and tutorials, and can be accessed from most major programming languages.

With great power comes great responsibility, and a lot of infrastructure overhead and management typically goes with these traditional structured databases. That's not to say you shouldn't use them—far from it—but when it comes to applications that run on a global scale, it's no easy feat to also then build clusters of database servers that replicate your data and intelligently route customers to your closest instance.

That's where Azure Cosmos DB becomes your best friend. You don't need to worry about how to replicate your data, ensure consistency, and distribute customer requests. Instead, you add data in one of the many models available and then choose where you want your data to be available. In this chapter, you learn about unstructured database models in Cosmos DB, how to create and configure your database for global distribution, and how to build web applications that use your highly redundant and scalable Cosmos DB instance.

10.1 What is Cosmos DB?

Chapter 4 started to explore unstructured databases with Azure storage tables. The example was basic, but the concepts are the foundations of Cosmos DB. First, let's take a step back and examine what we mean by *structured* and *unstructured* databases.

10.1.1 Structured (SQL) databases

Structured databases are the more traditional approach to storing data. A *structure*, or *schema*, to the database defines how the data is represented. Data is stored in tables, with each row representing one item and a fixed set of values assigned to it. If we take the pizza store model, each row in a table that stores the types of pizza may indicate the name of the pizza, its size, and the cost. A basic SQL database is shown in figure 10.1.

Structured database

Table

id	pizzaName	size	cost
1	Pepperoni	16"	$18
2	Veggie	16"	$15
3	Hawaiian	16"	$12

Figure 10.1 In a structured database, data is stored in rows and columns within a table. Each row contains a fixed set of columns that represent the schema for the database.

In structured databases, each server typically must contain the entire database in order for queries and data retrieval to succeed. The data is joined in queries to pull from different tables based on criteria the developer builds as part of the structured query. This is where the term *Structured Query Language* (SQL) comes from. As databases grow in both size and complexity, the servers that run the database must be sufficiently sized to handle that data in memory. That becomes difficult, and costly, with very large datasets. Given that they need a structure, it also makes it difficult to add properties and change the structure later.

10.1.2 Unstructured (NoSQL) databases

The unstructured data in NoSQL databases isn't stored in tables of rows and columns; rather, it's stored in dynamic arrays that allow you to add new properties for an item as needed. One big advantage of this approach is that you can quickly add a new pizza type or specialty topping without changing the underlying database structure. In a structured database, you'd need to add a new column to a table and then update the application to handle the additional column. In NoSQL databases, you add another property to a given entry from your code; see figure 10.2.

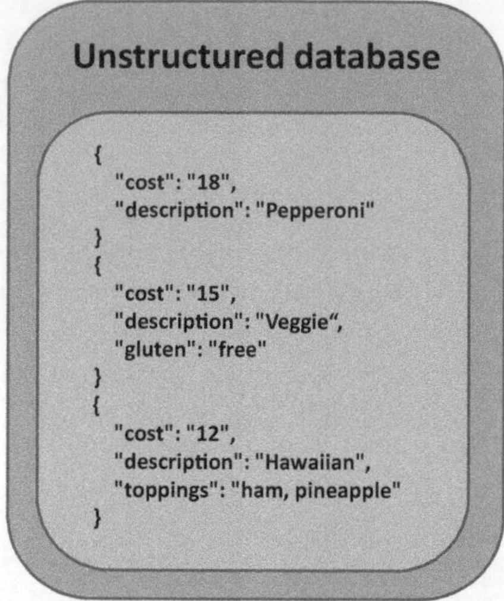

Unstructured database
{
"cost": "18",
"description": "Pepperoni"
}
{
"cost": "15",
"description": "Veggie",
"gluten": "free"
}
{
"cost": "12",
"description": "Hawaiian",
"toppings": "ham, pineapple"
}

Figure 10.2 In an unstructured database, data is stored without fixed mappings of columns to a row in a table. You can add toppings to a single pizza, for example, without updating the entire schema and other records.

NoSQL databases also offer different database models. These models give an indication of how the data is stored and retrieved in the database. Which model you use varies based on the size and format of data you work with, and how you need to represent the data in your application. These models include document, graph, and table. Don't caught get too caught up in the models for now; different models work better for different sets of unstructured data, depending on how you need to relate and query the data. The key takeaway is that unstructured, NoSQL databases have a different underlying concept to how they store and retrieve data, which you can use to your advantage as you build and run cloud applications in Azure.

10.1.3 Scaling databases

Remember how I said that for a structured database, the entire database typically needs to exist on each server? As you get into very large databases, you need ever-larger servers to run them. You may never work with databases that grow to hundreds of gigabytes or even terabytes in size, but NoSQL databases approach how databases grow and scale differently than SQL databases. The difference is that NoSQL databases typically scale horizontally rather than vertically.

There's a limit to how much you can vertically scale a VM—that is, give it more memory and CPU. You start to encounter performance issues in other parts of the compute stack as you squeeze out the maximum in storage throughput and network bandwidth. And that's without the hit to your wallet (or your boss's wallet) when you see the bill for such large VMs. As a recap from chapter 9, vertical scaling is illustrated in figure 10.3. Now imagine a cluster of such large database VMs, because you want redundancy and resiliency for your application, right?

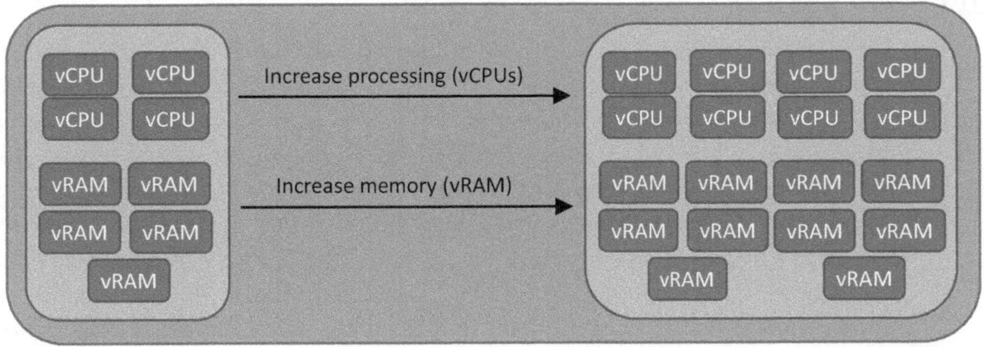

Figure 10.3 Traditional structured databases scale vertically. As the database grows, you increase the amount of storage, memory, and CPU power on the server.

In contrast, scaling horizontally allows you to run database VMs with less resources and a lower price to go along with them. To do this, NoSQL databases split data across database nodes and route requests from your application to the appropriate node. The other nodes in the cluster don't need to be aware of where all the data is stored; they just need to respond to their own requests. You can quickly add nodes to a cluster in response to customer demand as needed.

As a result, in a NoSQL database, the entire database doesn't need to fit in the memory of a host. Only part of the database, a *shard*, needs to be stored and processed. If your application works with large amounts of *structured* data, a NoSQL database may hurt performance because the different hosts are queried for their pieces of information to then return to the customer. If you have a large amount of *unstructured* data to process, NoSQL databases may offer a performance improvement, if not a management and efficiency benefit. An example of how unstructured databases scale horizontally across hosts is shown in figure 10.4.

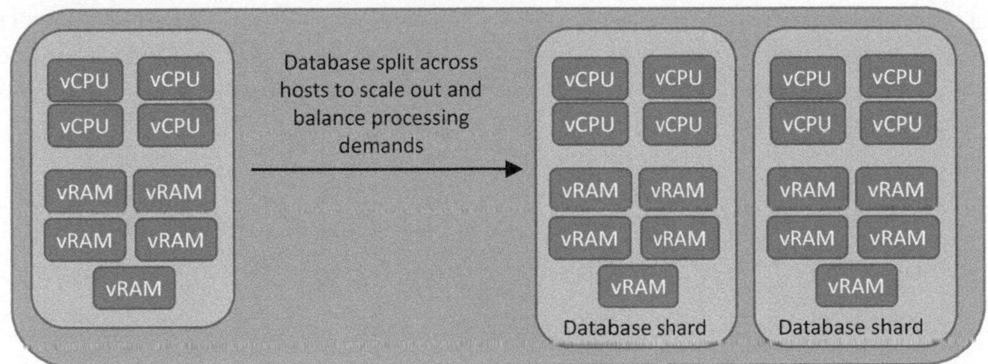

Figure 10.4 Unstructured NoSQL databases scale horizontally. As the database grows, it's sharded into segments of data that are distributed across each database server.

10.1.4 Bringing it all together with Cosmos DB

So, what is Cosmos DB? It's an autoscaling, globally distributed database platform that allows you to use various forms of NoSQL databases. As with services like Web Apps, Cosmos DB abstracts a lot of the management layer from you. When you create a web app, you don't need to configure load balancing or clustering—you choose your regions and can configure autoscaling and then upload your application code. The Azure platform handles how to replicate and distribute the web app traffic in a highly available way. With Cosmos DB, you don't worry about how large a database you need, how much memory to assign, or how to replicate data for redundancy. You choose how much throughput you may need and what regions to store your data in, and then you start adding data.

This chapter uses an SQL model for Cosmos DB, but the data is stored in a NoSQL, JSON format. These may be new concepts, but stick with me. Other models can be used, including Mongo, Cassandra, Gremlin, and Table. The functionality is the same for all of them: pick your model, choose your regions, and add your data. That's the power of Cosmos DB.

10.2 Creating a Cosmos DB account and database

Let's see Cosmos DB and unstructured databases in action. There are a couple of different ways to do this. The first is to use the Azure portal to create an account, and then select and create a database model. You then enter data into the database so that your app can query it. Or, you can use the Azure CLI, Azure PowerShell, or language-specific SDKs to create it all in code. Let's use the Azure portal so that you can also visually create and query your data.

10.2.1 Creating and populating a Cosmos DB database

In chapter 4, you created your first NoSQL database with an Azure storage table. Let's use Cosmos DB to create a similar database, this time one that offers all the geo-redundancy and replication options to make sure your online store allows customers to order pizza without any downtime. Let's create a Cosmos DB account and a document database, and then add some data entries for three types of pizza, as shown in figure 10.5.

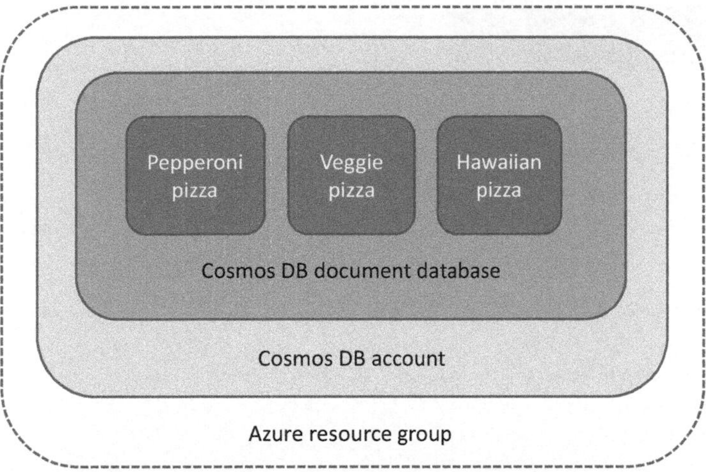

Figure 10.5 In this section, you create a resource group and a Cosmos DB account. A document database is then created in this account, and you add three entries to represent a basic menu for your pizza store.

> **Try it now**
> To see Cosmos DB in action, create an account as shown in figure 10.6.

1. Open the Azure portal, and select Create a Resource in the upper-left corner of the dashboard.
2. Search for and select Azure Cosmos DB, and then choose Create.
3. Enter a unique name for your Cosmos DB account, such as `azuremol`.
4. The type of model you can use for your database is referred to as the API. For this example, choose SQL from the drop-down menu.
5. Choose Create New under Resource Group, and then enter a name, such as `azuremolchapter10`.
6. For Location, select East US. Cosmos DB is available in all Azure regions, but for this example, the web application you deploy in the end-of-chapter lab expects you to use East US.
7. Leave the Enable Geo-Redundancy box unchecked. The next section dives more into how to replicate your database globally.
8. Select Create. It takes a couple of minutes to create your Cosmos DB account.

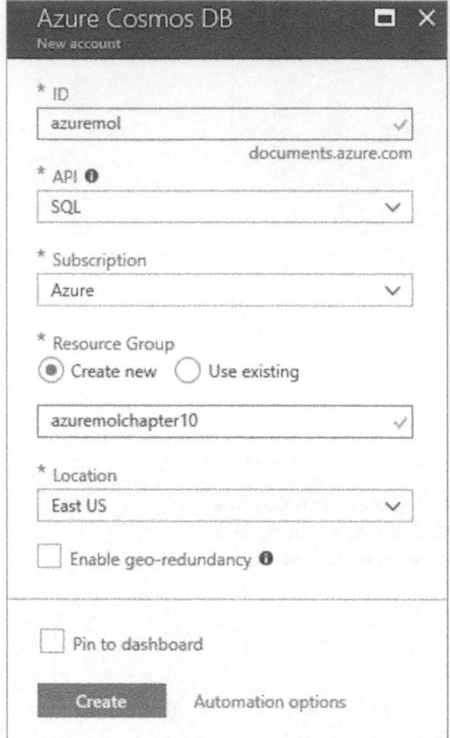

Figure 10.6 Create a Cosmos DB database with the SQL model type (API). You can also automatically enable geo-redundancy across a paired region as you create the database, but you'll do that in separate step later.

Your database is empty right now, so let's explore how you can store some basic data for your pizza store menu. In Cosmos DB databases that use the document model, data is logically grouped into containers called *collections*. These collections store related pieces of data that can be quickly indexed and queried, as shown in figure 10.7. Collections aren't totally dissimilar to how you organize a traditional SQL database into tables, but collections offer a lot more flexibility when it comes to distributing the data for performance or redundancy.

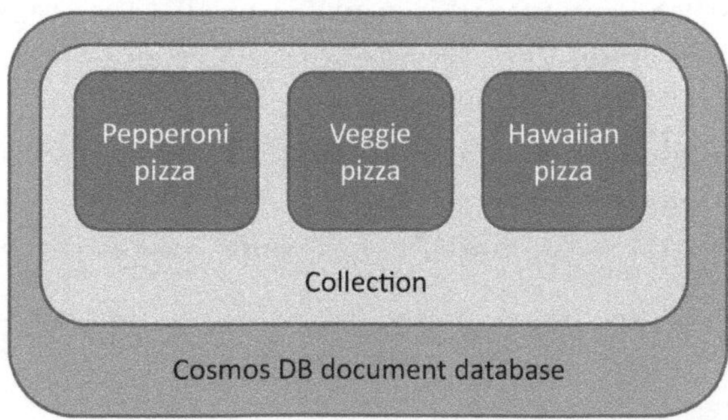

Figure 10.7 A Cosmos DB database that uses the document model stores data in collections. These collections let you group data for quicker indexing and querying.

Because Cosmos DB is designed to handle very large amounts of data and throughput, you can choose how to size and control the flow, and cost, of that data. Throughput is calculated in request units per second (RU/s), and one request unit is the equivalent of 1 KB of document data. Essentially, you define how much bandwidth you want your database to have. In case you haven't guessed, the more bandwidth (RU/s) you want, the more you pay. Cosmos DB shows you how much data you're using and how much throughput your application uses, and you typically don't need to worry too much about right-sizing things. For your pizza store, let's not start out too crazy, though!

Try it now

To create a collection and populate some entries in the database, complete the following steps as shown in figure 10.8.

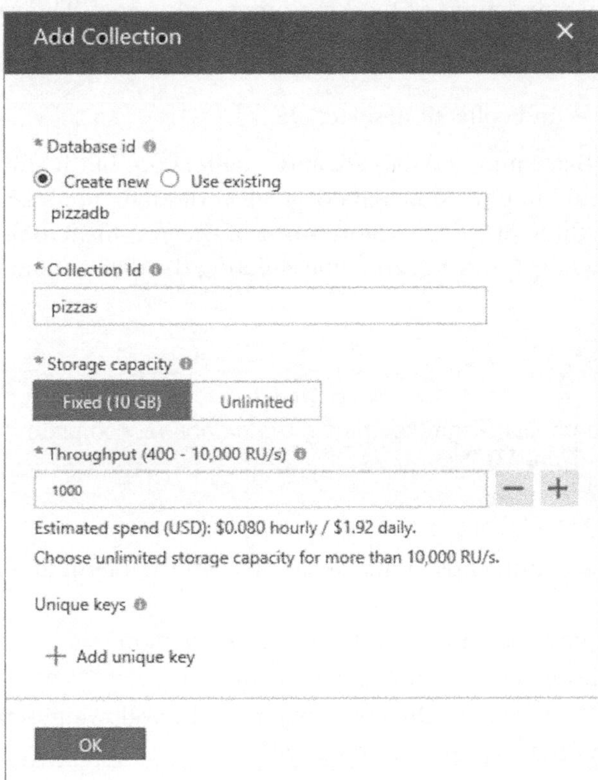

Figure 10.8 Create a collection to hold your pizza store menu items. You can choose how much storage to reserve and how much bandwidth (RU/s) you want your application to use.

1. Browse to and select Resource Group from the navigation bar at left in the Azure portal. Choose the resource group in which you created your Cosmos DB database, such as azuremolchapter10.
2. Select your Cosmos DB account from the list of resources, and then choose the Overview page.
3. At the top of the Cosmos DB account overview, choose Add Collection.
4. This is your first database, so choose Create New, and then enter a name, such as `pizzadb`.
5. For Collection ID, enter `pizzas`. This creates a logical container that you can use to store the items on your pizza store menu.
6. Under Storage Capacity, choose Fixed (10 GB). This creates a balanced database and provisions a smaller amount of bandwidth (RU/s), thus reducing operating costs.
7. Leave Throughput set to the default value.
8. Don't choose Add Unique Key. Keys are a way to further logically define the container, such as for subsections of food customers can order. The wider collection is for your menu, but you may want partition keys for pizzas, drinks, and desserts.
9. To create the database and collection, select OK.

You now have a Cosmos DB account, a database, and a collection, but it still doesn't contain your pizzas. You could import some data or write code that enters a bunch of data. Let's manually create three pizzas to explore some of the graphical tools built in to the Azure portal for browsing, querying, and manipulating the data in your Cosmos DB database.

Try it now

To create a collection and populate some entries in the database, complete the following steps as shown in figure 10.9.

1. In your Cosmos DB account, chose Data Explorer from the menu at left in the Overview window.
2. Expand the `pizzadb` database and then the `pizzas` collection.
3. To add some data, choose Documents > New Document.
4. Data is added in JSON format. In the text box, enter the following data to create a new menu item for a basic pepperoni pizza:

   ```
   {
       "description": "Pepperoni",
       "cost": "18"
   }
   ```

   To add the data to the database, select Save.

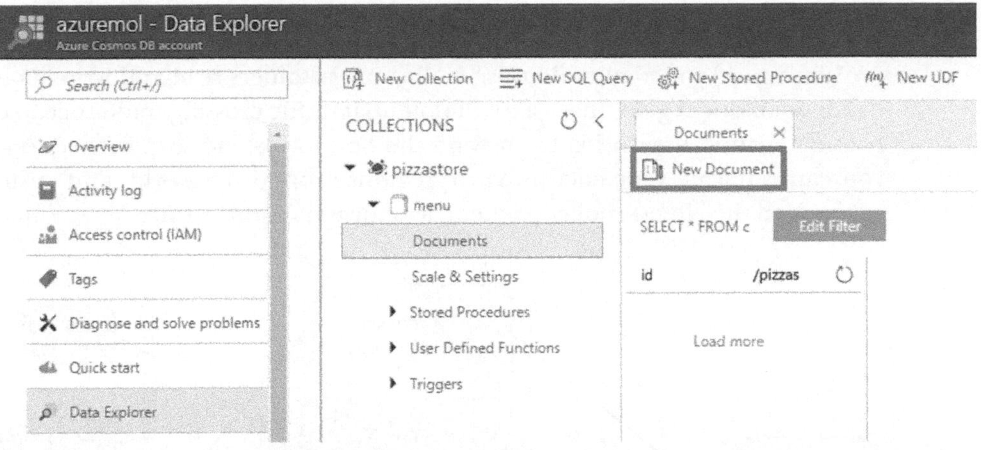

Figure 10.9 With the Data Explorer in the Azure portal, you can browse your collections to query or create new documents. This graphical tool lets you quickly manage your database from a web browser.

5 Add another pizza to your menu. This time, add a property to indicate that this pizza has a gluten-free crust. You don't need to do anything special to the underlying database—just add another property to your data. Select New Document again, and then enter the following data and select Save:

```
{
    "description": "Veggie",
    "cost": "15",
    "gluten": "free"
}
```

6 Add one final type of pizza. This time, add a property that includes what toppings are on the pizza. Select New Document again, and then enter the following data and select Save:

```
{
    "description": "Hawaiian",
    "cost": "12",
    "toppings": "ham, pineapple"
}
```

These three entries show the power of a NoSQL database. You added properties to the entries without needing to update the database schema. Two different properties showed that the veggie pizza has a gluten free crust, and what toppings are on the Hawaiian pizza. Cosmos DB accepts those additional properties, and that data is now available to your applications.

10.2.2 Adding global redundancy to a Cosmos DB database

You now have a Cosmos DB database that stores a basic pizza menu in the East US region. But your pizza store is ready to open franchises all around the world! You want to replicate the data about your pizzas to Azure regions in different locations, close to your new customers.

Why would you want to do this? If all your customers read and write data from the database in one region, that's a lot of potential traffic crossing under-ocean cables and routing around the world. To provide the best low-latency experience to customers, you can replicate your data to Azure regions around the world, and customers can connect to the closest replica to them, as shown in figure 10.10.

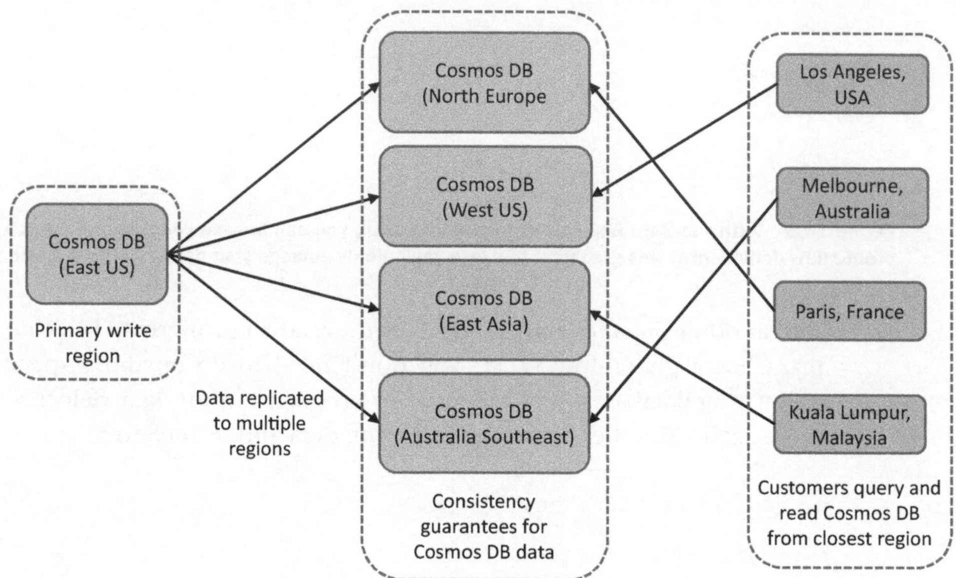

Figure 10.10 Data is replicated from one primary Cosmos DB instance to multiple Azure regions around the world. Web applications can then be directed to read from their closet region, and customers are dynamically routed to their closest location to minimize latency and improve response times.

Consistency models and guarantees are built into the Cosmos DB platform to handle this data consistency and replication for you. You designate one or more regions as the primary write location. This book's examples use a single write point, but you can use multimaster support to write data to the closest endpoint that's then propagated asynchronously to other regions. The data is also rapidly replicated to the read regions that you designate. You can control the order of failover, to designate read regions, and, with your application, either automatically or manually specify regions to read from.

You can define a consistency model—which is more of a design consideration than an operational one— that defines how quickly writes across multiple regions are replicated. The consistency models range from *strong*, which waits on replicated writes to be confirmed by replicas and so guarantees reads are consistent, to *eventual*, which is more relaxed: it guarantees that all the data is replicated, but there may be a slight delay when reads from replicas return different values until they're all in sync.

There's a balance between a more limited geographic distribution, such as with the strong consistency model, to wider geographic replication with the eventual consistency model, but with the understanding that there's a slight delay as the data is replicated. There are also bandwidth and processing costs, depending on how consistently and timely you wish the data to be replicated. The Azure platform handles the underlying replication of data from your write point; you don't need to build your applications to replicate the data or determine how best to read data from replicated endpoints.

On a global scale, this means you could have multiple VMs or web apps as you created in previous chapters, but in different regions around the world. Those apps connect to a local Cosmos DB instance to query and read all of their data. Through some cool Azure network traffic features we discuss in the next chapter, users can be automatically routed to one of these local web application instances, which also use a local Cosmos DB instance. In the event of regional outages or maintenance, the entire platform routes the customer to the next-closest instance.

In the traditional structured database world where you manage the VMs, database install, and cluster configuration, such a setup takes serious design planning and is complicated to implement. With Cosmos DB, it takes three mouse clicks. Honestly!

Try it now

To replicate your Cosmos DB data globally, complete the following steps.

1. Browse to and select Resource Group from the navigation bar at left in the Azure portal. Choose the resource group in which you created your Cosmos DB database, such as azuremolchapter10.
2. Select your Cosmos DB account from the list of resources. Those two mouse clicks were free, but start counting from here!
3. On the Overview page, the Regions map shows that your database is currently available in the East US region. Select the map to open the Replicate Data Globally window.
4. The map shows all the available Azure regions, as shown in figure 10.11. Choose West Europe, and then select Save. You can choose any Azure region you wish, but the end-of-chapter lab expects your data to be replicated to West Europe. It takes a few moments to replicate the data to the region you selected and bring the data online for your applications to use.

Okay, count those mouse clicks! Three clicks, right? Let's be generous and consider the first two mouse clicks to select the resource group and Cosmos DB account. So, in

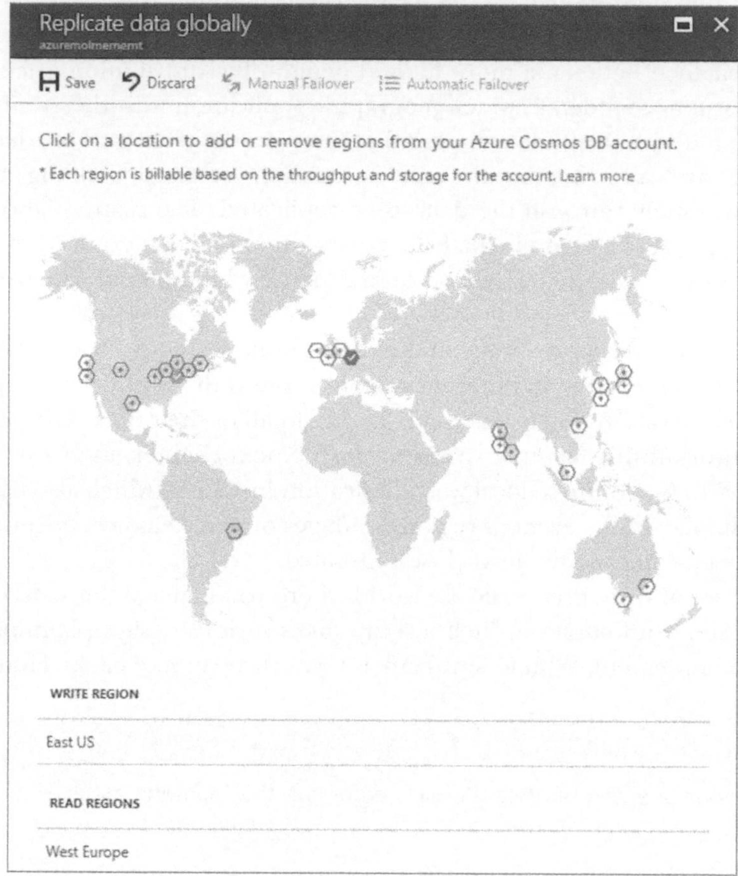

Figure 10.11 Select an Azure region around the world to replicate your Cosmos DB database to, and then choose Save. Those are all the steps required to globally distribute your data.

no more than five mouse clicks and a matter of seconds, you created a replica instance of your database that allows your applications to access data from the closest region to them. Can you do that with a traditional MySQL cluster? Please tweet me @fouldsy if you can do that this quickly outside of Cosmos DB!

With your database now distributed globally, does it take a lot of changes to your code to determine which Cosmos DB region to connect to? How can you maintain all these different versions of your applications based on what Azure region they run? Easy—let the Azure platform determine it all for you!

10.3 Accessing globally distributed data

For the most part, the Azure platform determines the best location for your application to talk to. An application typically needs to read and write data. You can define the failover policies for your Cosmos DB database, which controls the primary write location. This write location acts as the central hub to ensure that data is consistently replicated across regions. But your web app can then typically read from multiple available regions to speed up the queries and return data to the customer, as you saw in figure 10.10. All of this is handled by REST calls.

Let's see what happens from the Azure CLI when you ask for information about a Cosmos DB database. This is like an application making a connection to a database, but it stops you from getting too deep into the code.

Try it now

Use `az cosmosdb show` to find information about your read and write location, as shown next.

Open the Azure portal in a web browser, and then open the Cloud Shell. Use `az cosmosdb show` to view the read and write locations for your Cosmos DB database. Enter the resource group name and database name you created in the previous "Try it now" exercises. In the following example, the resource group is `azuremolchapter10` and the Cosmos DB database name is `azuremol`:

```
az cosmosdb show \
  --resource-group azuremolchapter10 \
  --name azuremol
```

A lot of output is returned from this command, so let's examine the two key parts: read locations and write locations. Here's some example output for the `readLocations` section:

```
"readLocations": [
    {
      "documentEndpoint":"https://azuremol-eastus.documents.azure.com:443/",
      "failoverPriority": 0,
      "id": "azuremol-eastus",
      "locationName": "East US",
      "provisioningState": "Succeeded"
    },
    {
      "documentEndpoint":
➥"https://azuremol-westeurope.documents.azure.com:443/",
      "failoverPriority": 1,
      "id": "azuremol-westeurope",
      "locationName": "West Europe",
      "provisioningState": "Succeeded"
    }
  ],
```

When your application makes a connection to a Cosmos DB database, you can specify a connection policy. If databases aren't normally your thing, think of a basic ODBC connection you may create on a Windows machine. The connection string typically defines a hostname, a database name, a port, and credentials. Cosmos DB is no different. You can connect to Cosmos DB from multiple languages, including .NET, Python, Node.js, and Java. The languages may differ, but all the SDKs share a similar setting: endpoint discovery. Two main properties of the connection policy are important:

- *Automatic endpoint discovery*—The SDK reads all the available endpoints from Cosmos DB and uses the failover order specified. This approach ensures that your application always follows the order you specify at the database-level. For example, you may want all reads to go through East US and only use West Europe when there's maintenance in the primary location.
- *Preferred endpoint locations*—You specify the locations you wish to use. An example is if you deploy your app to West Europe and want to ensure that you use the West Europe endpoint. You lose a little flexibility as endpoints are added or removed, but you make sure your default endpoint is close to your app without needing more advanced network routing to help determine this for you.

Typically, your application lets the Cosmos DB SDK handle this. Your application doesn't change how it handles the connection to the database: it just knows that there are different locations it *can* connect to. But the SDK is what *makes* the connection and uses this location awareness.

Figure 10.12 shows a simplified approach to how this location awareness is used between your application and the SDK. Again, the language doesn't matter, and the approach is the same—the figure uses the Python SDK because that's what a couple of the examples have been written in. This example also assumes you're using automatic endpoint locations.

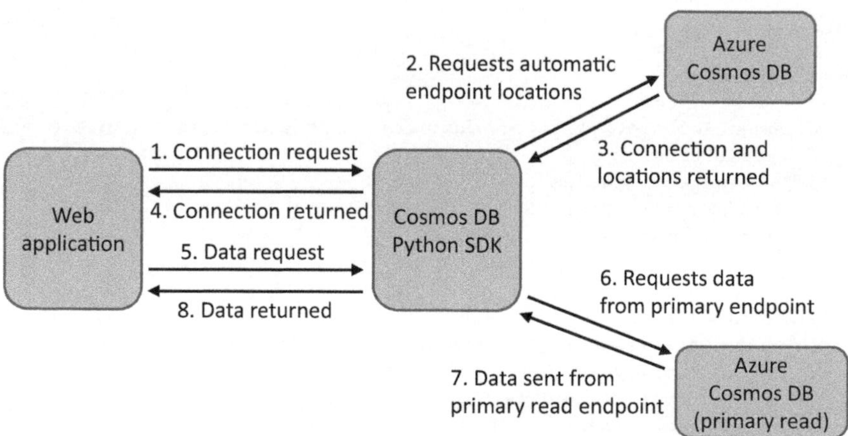

Figure 10.12 The flow of requests through a Cosmos DB SDK when an application uses location awareness to query Cosmos DB

The steps illustrated in figure 10.12 are as follows:

1. Your application needs to make a connection to a Cosmos DB database. In the connection policy, you enable automatic endpoint discovery. The application uses the Cosmos DB SDK to make a database connection.
2. The Cosmos DB SDK makes a connection request and indicates that it wishes to use automatic endpoint locations.
3. A connection is returned based on the credentials and database requested.
4. The SDK returns a connection object for the application to use. The location information is abstracted from the application.
5. The application requests some data from the Cosmos DB database. The SDK is again used to query and obtain the data.
6. The SDK uses the list of available endpoints and makes the request to the first available endpoint. The SDK then uses the connection endpoint to query the data. If the primary endpoint is unavailable, such as during a maintenance event, the next endpoint location is automatically used.
7. Cosmos DB returns the data from the endpoint location.
8. The SDK passes the data from Cosmos DB back to the application to parse and display as needed.

One last thing to look at with Cosmos DB are access keys. These keys allow you to control who can access the data and what permissions they have. Keys can be regenerated; and, as you do with passwords, you may want to implement a policy to regularly perform this key-regeneration process. To access the distributed data in Cosmos DB, you need to get your keys. The Azure portal provides a way to view all the keys and connection strings for your database.

Try it now

To view the keys for your Cosmos DB account, complete the following steps.

1. Browse to and select Resource Group from the navigation bar at left in the Azure portal. Choose the resource group in which you created your Cosmos DB database, such as azuremolchapter10.
2. Select your Cosmos DB account from the list of resources.
3. At left, choose Keys. As shown in figure 10.13, make a note of the URI and primary key. You use these values in the end-of-chapter lab.

A lot in Cosmos DB happens under the hood to distribute your data and allow your applications to read and write from the most appropriate locations. But that's the whole point. An awareness of what the Cosmos DB service does helps you to design

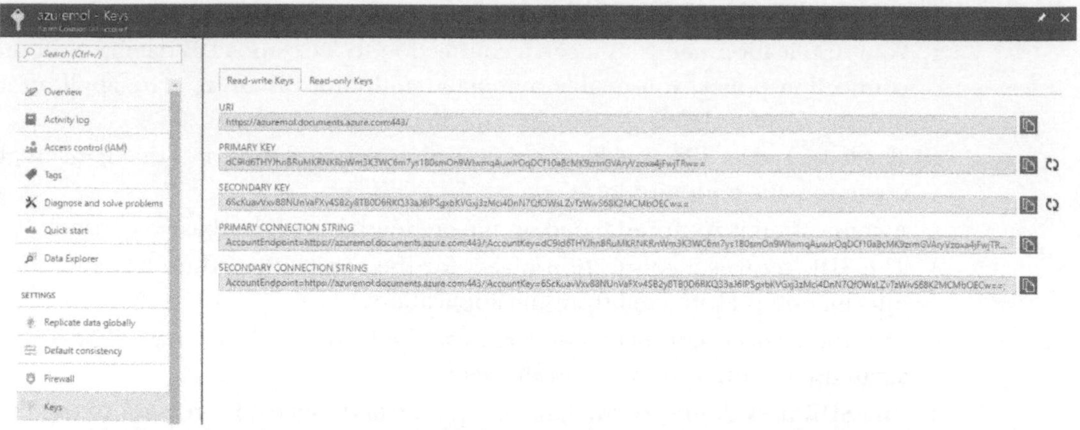

Figure 10.13 The Keys section of your Cosmos DB account lists the connection information and access keys. You need this information when you build and run applications, such as in the end-of-chapter lab.

and plan your application, or troubleshoot if you try to make a write request directly to the wrong location rather than the SDK passing information back and forth. But you don't need to worry about the how and when—focus on your applications, and use Azure services like Cosmos DB to provide the cloud functionality and benefits that allow you to operate on a global scale.

10.4 Lab: Deploying a web app that uses Cosmos DB

In section 10.2.2, you distributed your Cosmos DB database globally. We then went over a bunch of theory as to how web applications can read from locations around the world—but you probably want to see it in action. Now's your chance! In this lab, a basic web app uses a preferred-endpoint location list to force the read location to a different region than the write endpoint. It takes only one line in the connection policy to make the app read from a database on a different continent:

1. In the Azure portal, create a web app, and then create a deployment source (local Git repository). The steps are the same as when you created one in previous chapters, such as chapter 3, so check those exercises if you need a refresher.
2. Open the Cloud Shell. In earlier chapters, you obtained a copy of the Azure samples from GitHub. If you didn't, grab a copy as follows:

   ```
   git clone https://github.com/fouldsy/azure-mol-samples.git
   ```
3. Change into the directory that contains the Cosmos DB web app sample:

   ```
   cd ~/azure-mol-samples/10/cosmosdbwebapp
   ```
4. Edit the configuration file with the database URI and access key that you copied in the previous "Try it now" exercise to view your Cosmos DB keys:

   ```
   nano config.js
   ```

5 Add and commit your changes in Git with the following command:

```
git init && git add . && git commit -m "Pizza"
```

6 Create a link to the new Git repository in your staging slot with `git remote add azure` followed by your Git deployment URL.
7 Use `git push azure master` to push your changes to your web app.
8 Select the URL to your web app from the Azure portal Overview window.
9 Open this URL in a web browser to see your pizza store, which is now powered by Cosmos DB, along with the location your data was returned from, as shown in figure 10.14.

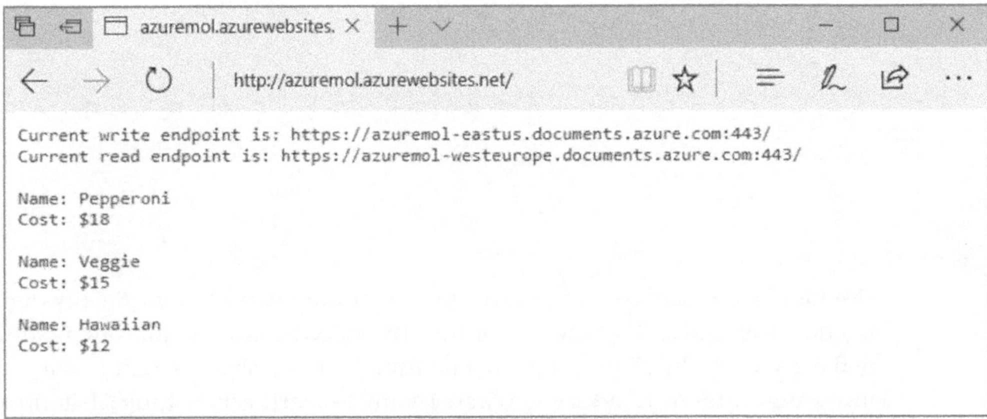

Figure 10.14 The basic Azure web app shows your short pizza menu based on data in the Cosmos DB database. The write endpoint is shown as East US, and you used a preferred location list to set West Europe as the primary read endpoint. This approach lets you pick locations as you deploy your app globally, without the need for complex traffic routing.

11 Managing network traffic and routing

Domain Name Service (DNS) resolution is at the heart of almost every digital connection you make. It's how you browse the web, receive email, watch Netflix, and make Skype calls. DNS is the mechanism that translates a name, such as manning.com, into an IP address. When I want to learn a new topic, I don't need to remember 35.166.24.88—I just enter `manning.com` in a web browser and browse some books! Network devices route traffic based on IP addresses, so you need an approach that helps those of us with bad memories to do things like buy books or pizza online.

Over the last few chapters, we've spent a lot of time learning about how to build applications that can scale, are highly available, and are globally distributed. One of the last missing pieces is how to direct customers from around the world to the most appropriate application instance, typically the instance closest to them. Azure Traffic Manager makes it easy to automatically route customers to your application instances based on performance or geographic location. In this chapter, we discuss how you can create and manage DNS zones in Azure, and then how to use Traffic Manager to route customers with DNS queries, as shown in figure 11.1.

11.1 What is Azure DNS?

You don't need a deep understanding of how DNS works to complete this chapter and use Azure DNS. Figure 11.2 shows a high-level overview of how a user queries a DNS service to obtain the IP address for a web application. A lot of substeps could happen around steps 1 and 2, so if you have a little time left in your lunch break at the end of this chapter, feel free to read up on how DNS queries and recursion work.

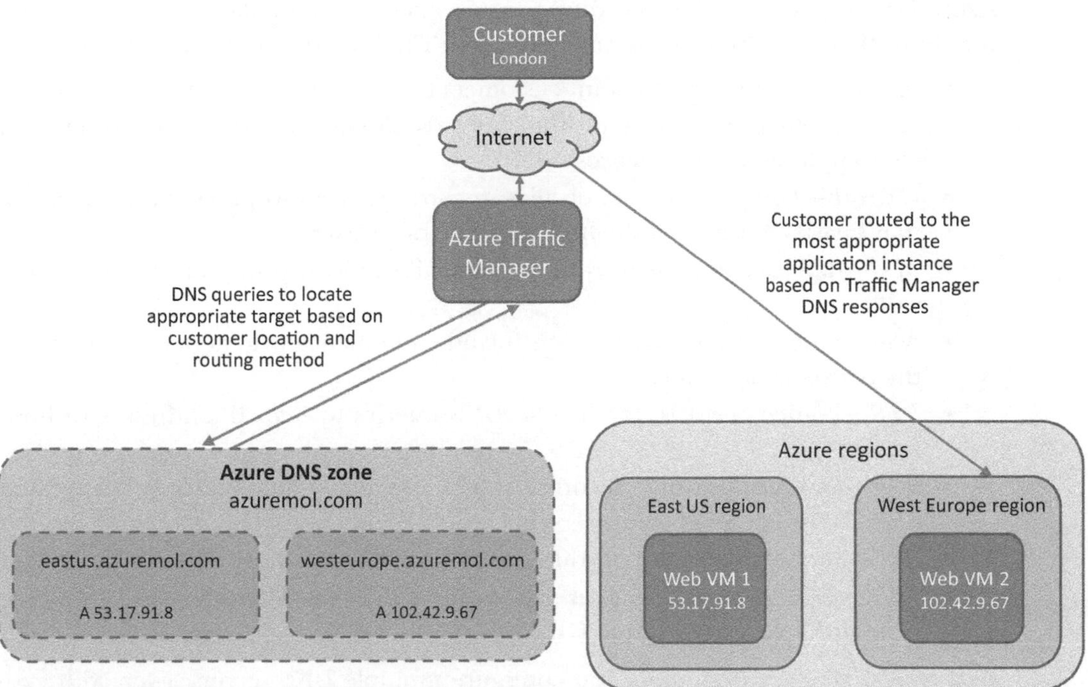

Figure 11.1 In this chapter, we examine how you can create DNS zones in Azure DNS. To minimize latency and improve response times, Traffic Manager can then be used to query DNS and direct customers to their closet application instance.

Azure DNS functions the same as any existing DNS solution you may use or be familiar with. Your zone and records are stored in Azure, and the name servers that respond to DNS queries are globally distributed across the Azure datacenters.

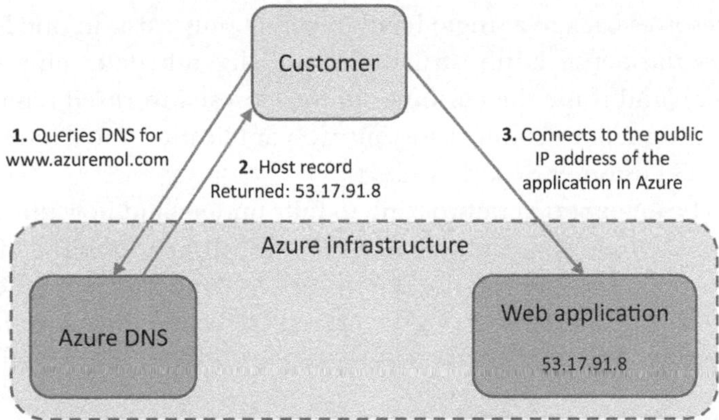

Figure 11.2 This simplified flow of DNS traffic shows how a user sends a DNS request for www.azuremol.com to a DNS server, receives a response that contains the associated IP address, and then can connect to the web application.

Azure DNS supports all the record types you'd expect in a regular DNS service offering. Both IPv4 and IPv6 records can be created. The record types are as follows:

- *A*—IPv4 host records, to point customers to your applications and services
- *AAAA*—IPv6 host records, for the cool kids who use IPv6 to point customers to your applications and services
- *CNAME*—Canonical name, or alias, records, such as to provide a short name that's easier to use than the full hostname of a server
- *MX*—Mail exchange records to route email traffic to your mail servers or provider
- *NS*—Name server records, which include automatically generated records for the Azure name servers
- *PTR*—Pointer records, for reverse DNS queries to map IP addresses to hostnames
- *SOA*—Start-of-authority records, which include automatically generated records for the Azure name servers
- *SRV*—Service records, to provide network services discovery, such as for identity
- *TXT*—Text records, such as for Sender Protection Framework (SPF) or DomainKeys Identified Mail (DKIM)

In a typical DNS configuration, you configure multiple DNS servers. Even with geographic distribution of those servers for redundancy, customers may query a name server on the other side of the world. Those milliseconds to query, resolve, and then request a response for the web application can add up when you have lots of customers wanting to order pizza.

An Azure DNS zone is replicated globally across the Azure datacenters. *Anycast* networking ensures that when a customer makes a DNS query to your domain, the closest available name server responds to their request. How does anycast routing do this? Typically, a single IP address is advertised across multiple regions. Rather than a simple DNS query that resolves back to a single IP address that only exists in one location, anycast routing allows the network infrastructure to intelligently determine where a request is coming from, and route the customer to the closest advertised region. This routing allows your customers to connect to your web application more quickly and provides a better overall customer experience.

You don't need to be an expert at networking to fully understand how this works—Azure handles it for you! When you combine Azure DNS with Azure Traffic Manager, which we look at in the next section, you not only return DNS queries from the closest name servers, but also connect customers to the closest application instance to them. Make those milliseconds count!

11.1.1 Delegating a real domain to Azure DNS

When you register a real domain, your provider gives you a management interface and tools to manage that domain. To allow customers to access your services and use the Azure DNS zone and records, you delegate authority of your domain to the Azure name servers. This delegation causes all DNS queries to immediately be directed to those Azure name servers, as shown in figure 11.3. Azure doesn't currently allow you to purchase and register domains within the platform, so you need to purchase the domain name through an external registrar and then point the NS records to the Azure name servers.

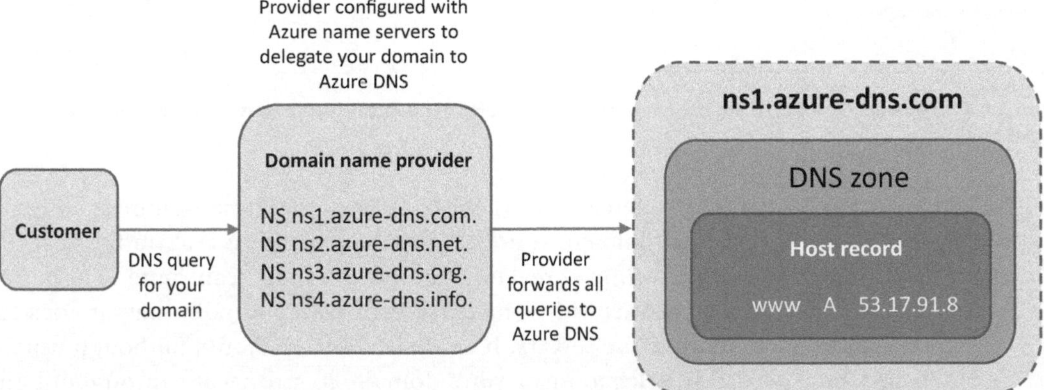

Figure 11.3 To delegate your domain to Azure, configure your current domain provider with the Azure name server addresses. When a customer makes a DNS query for your domain, the requests are sent directly to the Azure name servers for your zone.

Why delegate your DNS to Azure? To simplify management and operations. If you create additional services, adjust the load-balancer configuration, or want to improve response times with globally replicated DNS, Azure provides that single management interface to complete those tasks. When your DNS zones are hosted in Azure, you can also implement some of the Resource Manager security features discussed in chapter 6: features such as role-based access control (RBAC) to limit and audit access to the DNS zones, and resource locks to prevent accidental, or even malicious, zone deletion.

Most domain registrars provide rather basic interfaces and controls to manage DNS zones and records. To reduce management overhead and improve security, Azure DNS allows you to use the Azure CLI, Azure PowerShell, or the REST APIs to add or edit records. Operations teams can use the same tools and workflows to onboard new services; and if problems occur, it's often easier to troubleshoot when you can verify that DNS operates as you expect without introducing the variable of a third-party DNS provider.

So, if you're convinced there's logic to delegating your domain to Azure DNS, what Azure name servers do you point your domain to? If you create an Azure DNS zone, the name servers are listed in the portal, as shown in figure 11.4. You can also access these name server address with the Azure CLI or Azure PowerShell.

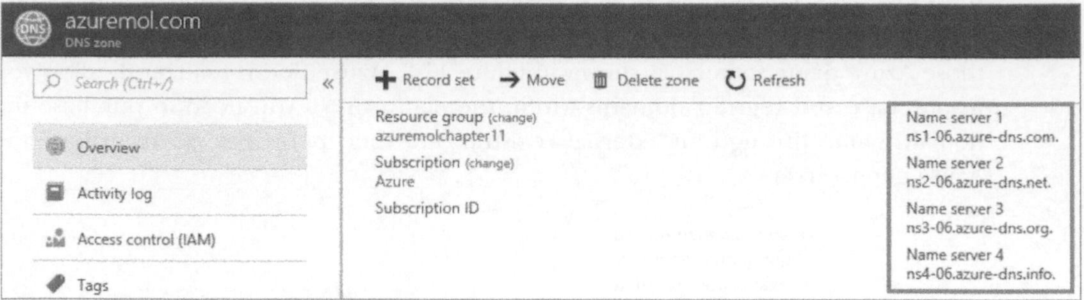

Figure 11.4 You can view the Azure name servers for your DNS zone in the Azure portal, Azure CLI, or Azure PowerShell.

There are no "Try it now" exercises for these last few pages, because unless you purchase and configure a real domain, you can't test how to route real traffic. You can create an Azure DNS zone without a real domain, but no traffic can route to it. In real life, you update the NS records with your current provider to point any queries for your domain to the Azure name servers. It can take 24 to 48 hours (although usually much less time) for the delegation of your domain to propagate throughout the global DNS hierarchy, so plan accordingly—this may cause brief interruptions for customers who access your application.

11.2 Global routing and resolution with Traffic Manager

In previous chapters, you learned about highly available applications that are globally distributed. The end goal is multiple web app or VM instances, in different regions or continents, that connect to a Cosmos DB instance close to them. But how do you get your customers to connect to the closest VM or web app that runs your application?

Azure Traffic Manager is a network service that acts as a central destination for your customers. Let's use the example of a web application at the address www.azuremol.com. Figure 11.5 provides an overview of how Traffic Manager routes users to the closest available application.

Traffic Manager doesn't perform the role of a load balancer that you learned about in chapter 8. As figure 11.5 shows, Traffic Manager routes traffic to a public IP. Let's examine the flow of traffic a little more closely:

1. The user makes a DNS query for www.azuremol.com. Their DNS server contacts the name servers for azuremol.com (which could be Azure name servers if you use Azure DNS!) and requests the record for www.
2. The www host resolves to a CNAME record that points to azuremol.trafficmanager.net.
3. DNS service forwards the DNS request the Azure name servers for trafficmanager.net.

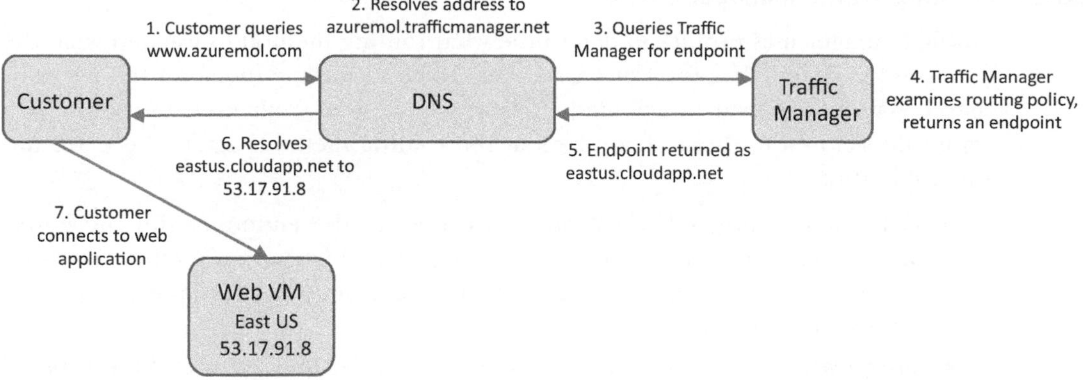

Figure 11.5 A customer sends a DNS query to a DNS service for www.azuremol.com. The DNS service forwards the query to Traffic Manager, which returns an endpoint based on the routing method in use. The endpoint is resolved to an IP address, which the customer uses to connect to the web application.

4. Traffic Manager then examines the request and determines an endpoint to direct the user toward. Endpoint health and status are examined, as with Azure load balancers. The Traffic Manager routing method is also reviewed. The routing methods that Traffic Manager can use are as follows:
   a. *Priority*—Controls the order in which endpoints are accessed
   b. *Weighted*—Distributes traffic across endpoints based on an assigned weight metric
   c. *Performance*—Latency-based routing of users to an endpoint so that the user receives the quickest possible response time
   d. *Geographic*—Associates endpoints with a geographic region, and directs users to them based on their location
5. The endpoint eastus.cloudapp.net is returned to the DNS service by Traffic Manager.
6. The DNS service looks up the DNS record for eastus.cloudapp.net and returns the result of the query to the customer.
7. With the IP address of their requested endpoint, the customer contacts the web application directly. At this point, the traffic could hit the public IP address of an Azure load balancer rather than a VM directly.

As you can see, the role of Traffic Manager is to determine a given application endpoint to direct customers to. There are some health checks that monitor the status of endpoints, similar to the load-balancer health probes you learned about in chapter 8. And you can define a priority or weighted traffic-routing mechanism to distribute users across a set of available endpoints—again, similar to a load balancer. Traffic Manager typically directs traffic to an Azure load balancer or application gateway, or to a web app deployment.

11.2.1 Creating Traffic Manager profiles

Traffic Manager uses profiles to determine what routing method to use and what the associated endpoints are for a given request. To continue the theme of the previous chapters about a globally distributed application, you want your users to use the web application closest to them. If you look at the routing methods again, there are two ways to do this:

- *Performance routing*—The customer is routed to the endpoint with the lowest latency, relative to the source of the request. This routing method provides some intelligence and always allows Traffic Manager to forward the customer to an available endpoint.
- *Geographic routing*—The customer is always routed to a given endpoint, based on the source of their request. If the customer is in the United States, they're always directed to East US, for example. This routing method requires you to define geographic regions to be associated with each endpoint.

When you use geographic routing, you get a little more control over the endpoints that customers use. There may be regulatory reasons that state customers in a given region must always use endpoints in the same region. The exercises use geographic endpoints to show a more real-world example, because there's a trick to geographic routing—you should specify a child *profile*, not an endpoint directly.

The sky won't fall if you use the geographic routing method with endpoints, but the recommended practice is to use another Traffic Manager profile to pass traffic to the final endpoint. Why? Regions can only be associated with one Traffic Manager profile. In the previous chapters on high availability, you always wanted to make sure you have redundancy. If you associate a region with a given endpoint and use geographic routing, you have no failover option should that endpoint encounter a problem, or if you perform maintenance.

Instead, nested child profiles allow you to set a priority that always directs traffic to a healthy endpoint. If the endpoint is unhealthy, traffic goes to an alternate endpoint. Figure 11.6 shows traffic failing over to a different region, although you could also create multiple web app instances in West US and use a weighted routing method on the child profile. As you start to scale out your application environment, take time to think about how best to provide high availability to endpoints behind Traffic Manager. For these examples, you create failover between regions to clearly see the differences in behavior.

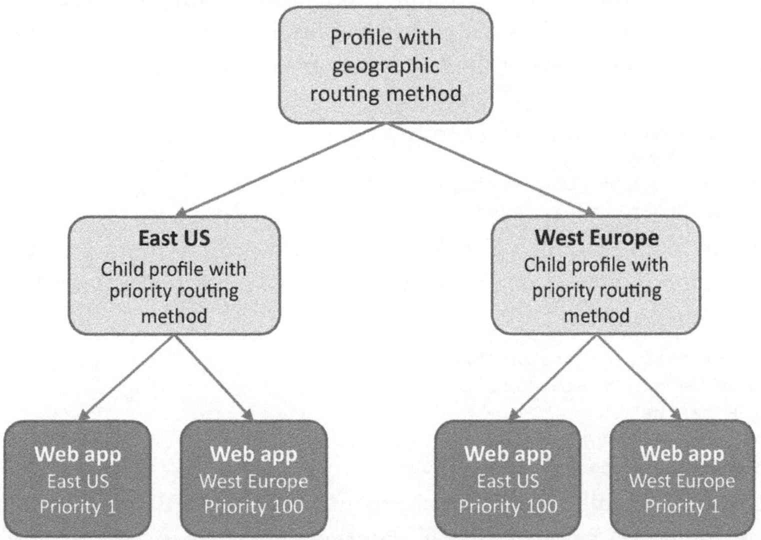

Figure 11.6 A parent Traffic Manager profile with the geographic routing method should use child profiles that contain multiple endpoints. Those child endpoints can then use priority routing to always direct traffic to the preferred endpoint. For example, the East US child profile always sends traffic to the endpoint in East US, provided the endpoint is healthy. If the endpoint is unhealthy, traffic is then directed to West Europe. Without this child profile, customers in East US couldn't fail over to an alternate endpoint and would be unable to access your web application.

Try it now

To create the Traffic Manager profiles for your distributed application, complete the following steps.

The rest of the exercises use East US and West Europe. If you don't live in one of those regions, pick a different region that's more appropriate. Just remember to be consistent throughout the exercises! The end-of-chapter lab shows how this all comes together and works, but you won't be correctly directed to your web apps if you live outside of North America or Europe and don't change the regions accordingly.

1. Open the Azure portal, and select the Cloud Shell icon across the top of the dashboard.
2. Create a resource group, specifying a resource group name, such as `azuremolchapter11`, and a location, such as `eastus`:

```
az group create --name azuremolchapter11 --location eastus
```

3. Create the parent Traffic Manager profile. You want to use the geographic routing method and then specify a name, such as `azuremol`. The parameter for the

DNS name tells you it must be unique, so provide a unique name. The following domain creates the hostname azuremol.trafficmanager.net, which you use to configure the web apps in the lab at the end of the chapter:

```
az network traffic-manager profile create \
  --resource-group azuremolchapter11 \
  --name azuremol \
  --routing-method geographic \
  --unique-dns-name azuremol
```

4 Create one of the child Traffic Manager profiles. This time, use the priority routing method and the name eastus, and specify another unique DNS name, such as `azuremoleastus`:

```
az network traffic-manager profile create \
  --resource-group azuremolchapter11 \
  --name eastus \
  --routing-method priority \
  --unique-dns-name azuremoleastus
```

5 Create one more child Traffic Manager profile with the name westeurope, and another unique DNS name, such as `azuremolwesteurope`:

```
az network traffic-manager profile create \
  --resource-group azuremolchapter11 \
  --name westeurope \
  --routing-method priority \
  --unique-dns-name azuremolwesteurope
```

6 You've created a web app a couple of times now, so let's use the CLI to quickly create two app service plans and then a web app in each plan. One of these web apps is in East US, the other in West Europe. In the end-of-chapter lab, you upload sample web pages to these web apps, so for now just create the empty website and get them ready to use a local Git repository.

Create the web app in East US as follows:

```
az appservice plan create \
  --resource-group azuremolchapter11 \
  --name appserviceeastus \
  --location eastus \
  --sku S1

az webapp create \
  --resource-group azuremolchapter11 \
  --name azuremoleastus \
  --plan appserviceeastus \
  --deployment-local-git
```

Create a second web app in West Europe:

```
az appservice plan create \
  --resource-group azuremolchapter11 \
  --name appservicewesteurope \
  --location westeurope \
  --sku S1

az webapp create \
```

```
--resource-group azuremolchapter11 \
--name azuremolwesteurope \
--plan appservicewesteurope \
--deployment-local-git
```

11.2.2 Globally distributing traffic to the closest instance

You've created the Traffic Manager profiles and endpoints, but no traffic that can flow. If customers were directed to the profiles, there would be no association with your endpoints. The diagram in figure 11.7 shows how you need to associate endpoints with profiles.

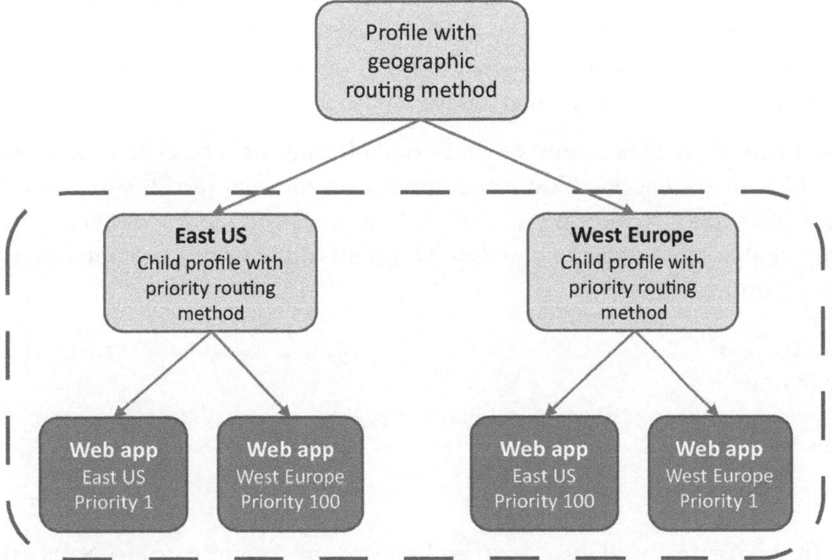

Figure 11.7 In this section, you associate your endpoints with the Traffic Manager profiles, and define the priority for the traffic to be distributed.

The first associations you make are for your web app endpoints. Remember that for high availability, you want both web apps to be available to each Traffic Manager profile. You use a priority routing method to direct all traffic to the primary web app for each profile. If that web app is unavailable, the traffic can then fail over to the secondary web app endpoint.

When you created the Traffic Manager profiles in the previous section, a few defaults were used for the health-check options and endpoint monitoring. Let's explore what those options are:

- *DNS Time to Live (TTL): 30 seconds*—Defines how long the DNS responses from Traffic Manager can be cached. A short TTL ensures that customer traffic is routed appropriately when updates are made to the Traffic Manager configuration.

- *Endpoint Monitor Protocol: HTTP*—You can also choose HTTPS or a basic TCP check. As with load balancers, HTTP or HTTPS ensures that an HTTP 200 OK response is returned from each endpoint.
- *Port: 80*—The port to check on each endpoint.
- *Path: /*—By default, checks the root of the endpoint, although you could also configure a custom page, like the health-check page used by load balancers.
- *Endpoint Probing Interval: 30 seconds*—How frequently to check endpoint health. The value can be 10 seconds or 30 seconds. To perform fast probing every 10 seconds, there's an additional charge per endpoint.
- *Tolerate Number of Failures: 3*—How many times an endpoint can fail a health check before the endpoint is marked as unavailable.
- *Probe Timeout: 10 seconds*—The length of time before a probe is marked as failed and the endpoint is probed again.

You don't need to change any of these default options. For critical workloads when you build your own application environments in the real world, you could lower the number of failures to tolerate or the probing interval. These changes would ensure that any health issues were detected quickly, and traffic would be routed to a different endpoint sooner.

Try it now

To associate endpoints with profiles and finish the geographic routing, complete the following steps.

1. In the Azure portal, browse to and select your resource group. Select the Traffic Manager profile you created for East US.
2. Choose Endpoints from the navigation bar at left in the profile, and then select Add, as shown in figure 11.8.
3. Create an endpoint, as shown in figure 11.9. For Type, select Azure Endpoint. Enter a name, such as `eastus`, and then choose App Service as the Target Resource Type.
4. Select Target Resource, and then select your web app in East US, such as azure-moleastus.
5. Leave Priority as 1, and then select OK.

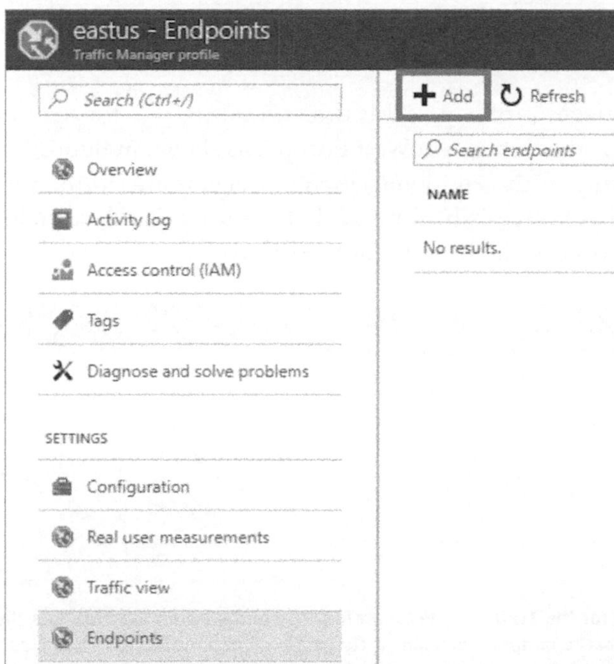

Figure 11.8 Select your resource group, and then choose the Traffic Manager profile for East US. Under Settings, select Endpoints, and then choose Add.

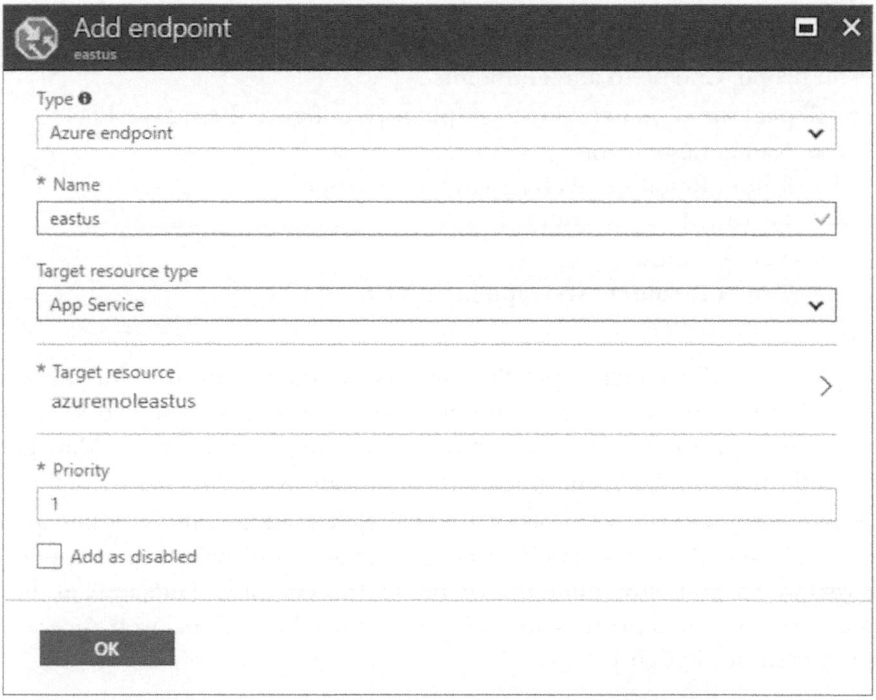

Add endpoint
eastus
Type
Azure endpoint
* Name
eastus
Target resource type
App Service
* Target resource
azuremoleastus
* Priority
1
Add as disabled
OK

Figure 11.9 Create an endpoint named `eastus`. The target resource type is App Service. Select the web app you created in East US. With a priority of 1, all traffic is directed to this endpoint, provided the endpoint remains healthy and can serve traffic.

6 Repeat the process to add another endpoint. This time, name the endpoint `westeurope`, select your web app in West Europe as the Target Resource, and set a priority of 100.

  Your Traffic Manager profile now lists two endpoints: one for the web app in East US, and one for the web app in West Europe, as shown in figure 11.10. This priority-based routing of the endpoints always directs traffic to the web app in East US when that resource is healthy. If that resource is unavailable, there's redundancy to fail over to the web app in West Europe.

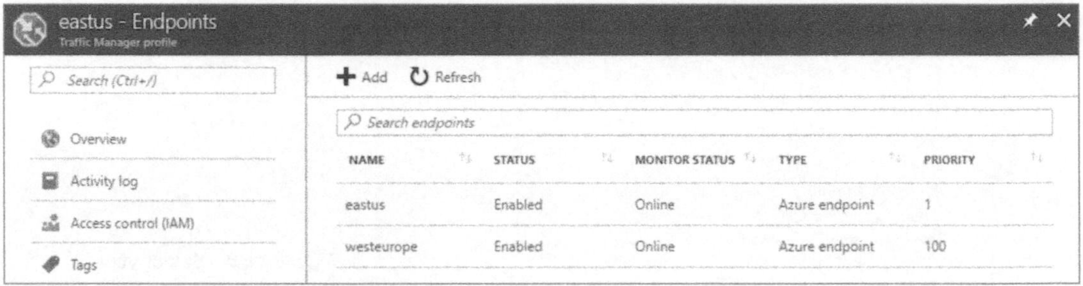

Figure 11.10 Two endpoints are listed for the Traffic Manager profile. The endpoint for East US has the lower priority, so it always receives traffic when the endpoint is healthy. Redundancy is provided with the West Europe endpoint, which is used only when the East US endpoint is unavailable

7 Go back to your resource group, and select the Traffic Manager profile for West Europe. Choose to add endpoints.

8 Repeat the steps to add two endpoints. Configure them as follows:

   a Name: westeurope
     Target Resource: Web app in West Europe
     Priority: 1

   b Name: eastus
     Target Resource: Web app in East US
     Priority: 100

  Your Traffic Manager profile now lists two endpoints: one for the web app in West Europe, and one for the web app in East US, as shown in figure 11.11. You've provided the same redundancy as the previous Traffic Manager profile, this time with all traffic going to West Europe when healthy and East US if not.

Just one more part to this process, I promise! Remember, this is a best practice for high availability if you use Traffic Manager for global distribution of applications. In the real world, your environment may not be this complex. Let's look at the diagram again to see the child profiles and association with the regional web apps you need to create, as shown in figure 11.12.

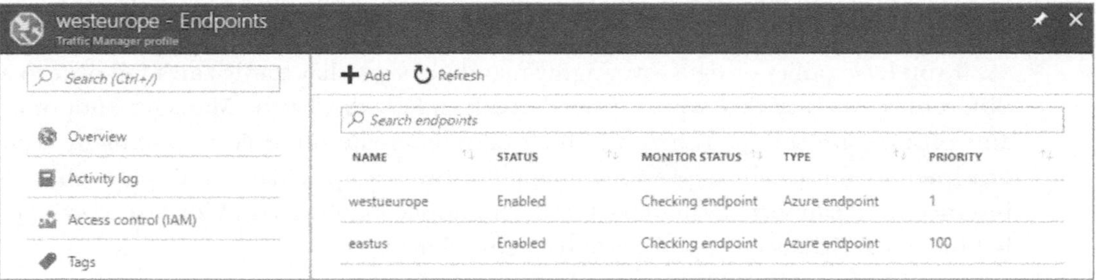

Figure 11.11 The same configuration of endpoints as the previous Traffic Manager profile, this time with the location of the web apps reversed. These child profiles can be used to always route customers to the web app in either East US or West Europe, but you now have redundancy to fail over to another endpoint if the primary endpoint in the region is unavailable.

To direct traffic based on geography, you define a region, such as North America, and a nested profile, such as eastus. All customers in the North America region are directed to this child profile. You configured the priorities on that child so that the web app in East US always serves the traffic. But you've provided a redundant option to fail over to the web app in West Europe as needed.

The inverse happens for customers in West Europe. Another endpoint for the parent Traffic Manager profile can be added, this time with Europe as the region to be associated with the endpoint, and then the `westeurope` nested profile. All European

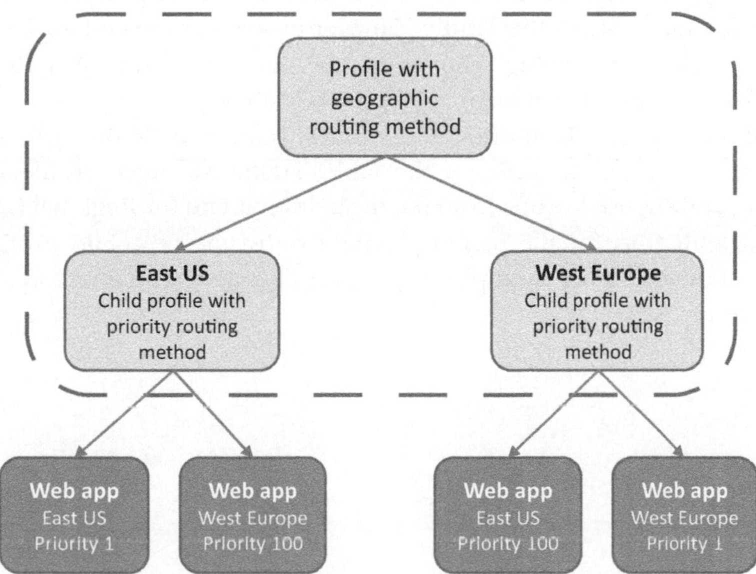

Figure 11.12 The child Traffic Manager profiles for East US and West Europe have been created, with the regional web apps and priorities configured as needed. Now you need to associate the child profiles with the parent profile.

traffic is routed to this profile, and the web app in West Europe always serves the web application. In the event of a problem, the traffic can fail over to East US.

If you have policy or data sovereignty mandates such that traffic can't fail over to a different region like this, you may need to adjust how the Traffic Manager endpoints and profiles are set up. You could, for example, create multiple web apps in West Europe, as you saw in a previous chapter. This way, you have multiple web app instances that can serve customers. Or, if your application runs on VMs, use a scale set behind a load balancer to profile similar redundancy.

Try it now

To associate the child profiles with the parent profile, complete the following steps.

This is where your own regional location matters! If you live outside one of the regional groupings shown in the Traffic Manager profiles, make sure you select your own region, or you won't be able to access the web app in the end-of-chapter lab.

1. In the Azure portal, browse to and select your resource group. Select the parent Traffic Manager profile. In the earlier examples, that was called azuremol.
2. Choose Endpoints from the navigation bar at left in the profile, and then select Add.
3. Create an endpoint that uses the first child profile, as shown in figure 11.13. For Type, choose Nested Endpoint. Provide a name, such as `eastus`, and then select Target Resource. Select the Traffic Manager profile you created for East US.
4. Under Regional Grouping, choose North America/Central America/Caribbean from the drop-down menu, and then select OK.
5. Repeat the steps to add another endpoint. This time, name the endpoint westeurope, set Target Resource to the child Traffic Manager profile for West Europe, and choose Europe from the drop-down menu for Regional Grouping.

   Your endpoints for the parent profile now list the two child profiles, with each an endpoint associated with the appropriate geographic region, as shown in figure 11.14.

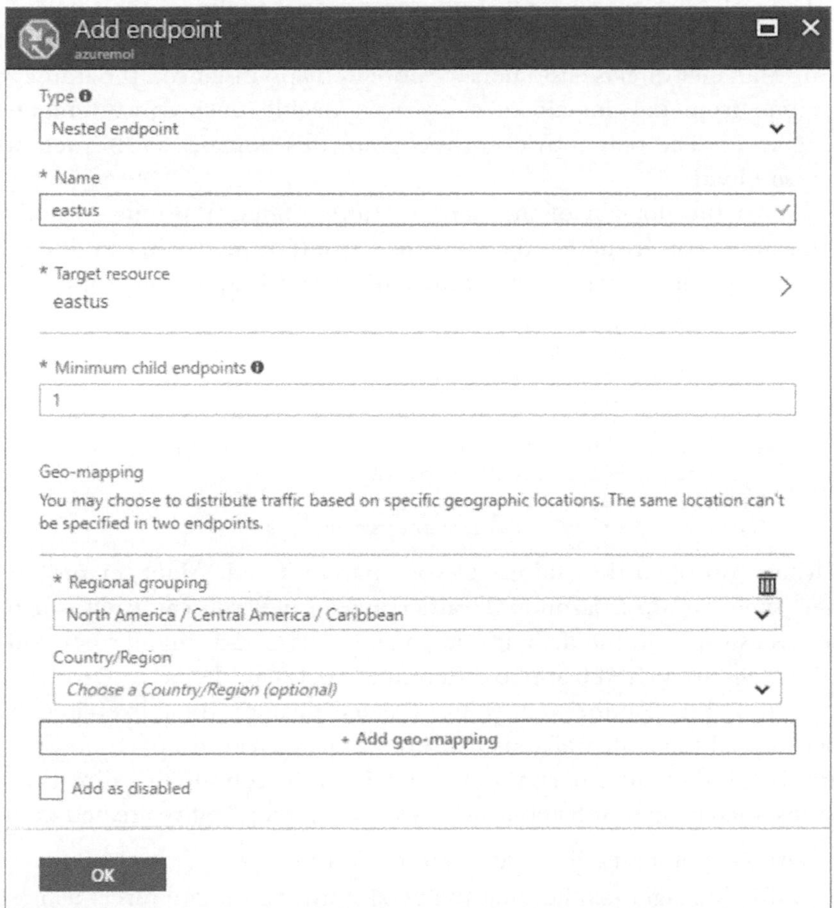

Figure 11.13 This endpoint uses the nested profile for East US. The regional grouping directs all customers from North America/Central American/Caribbean to the endpoints configured in the child profile.

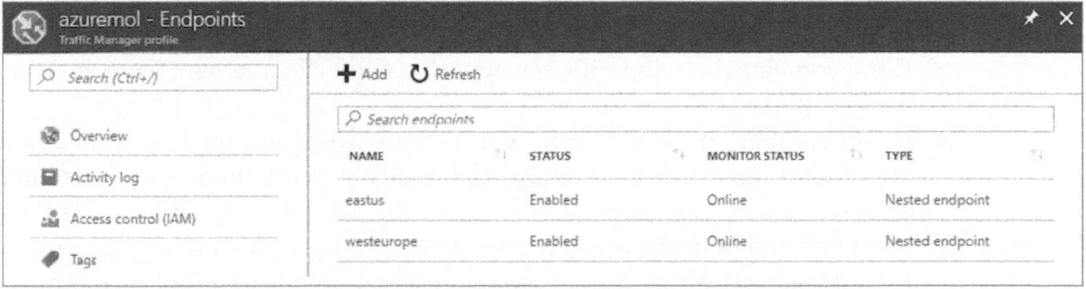

Figure 11.14 Nested child profiles with associated geographic regions. This parent Traffic Manager profile now directs all traffic from Europe to the web app in West Europe, with redundancy to use East US if there's a problem. The opposite is true for customers in North America/Central America/Caribbean.

6 The web apps are currently set to only accept traffic on their default domain. This default domain is in the form of *webappname*.azurewebsites.net. When Traffic Manager directs customers to those web app instances, the traffic appears to come from the domain of the parent profile, such as azuremol.trafficmanager.net. The web apps don't recognize this domain, so the web application won't load.

Add the domain of the parent Traffic Manager profile to both web app instances you created in the previous steps. If needed, you can find the domain name on the Overview page of the parent Traffic Manager profile:

```
az webapp config hostname add \
  --resource-group azuremolchapter11 \
  --webapp-name azuremoleastus \
  --hostname azuremol.trafficmanager.net

az webapp config hostname add \
  --resource-group azuremolchapter11 \
  --webapp-name azuremolwesteurope \
  --hostname azuremol.trafficmanager.net
```

Now, when you open the address of your parent Traffic Manager profile in a web browser, such as https://azuremol.trafficmanager.net, you can't tell which web app you access as they run the default web page. In the end-of-chapter lab, you upload a basic web page to each web app to differentiate between them!

Let's stop and examine what you've created through these exercises. It's important, because all the high-availability and redundancy features from previous chapters can now be used by customers, with automatic traffic routing that directs them to the closest instance of your web application. In this chapter, you've created the following:

- A web app in East US and another in West Europe.
- Traffic Manager profiles that use geographic routing to direct all customers in North and Central America to the East US web app, and all customers in Europe to the West Europe web app.
- Child Traffic Manager policies with priority routing to provide failover use of the alternate region if the primary web app for the region is unavailable.

In terms of high availability:

- If you combine this setup with web apps that autoscale, you have a ton of redundancy right now.
- If you combine these web apps with Cosmos DB, you now have your entire application automatically scaling and globally distributed, with customers always accessing resources close to them for the lowest latency on response times and best performance.
- Even if you stuck with VMs, you can use scale sets with load balancers to provide the same highly available, globally distributed environment.

I know these last few chapters have contained a lot of new stuff, and each chapter has taken up pretty much all of your lunch break each day! But look at where you've come in the past week. You can now create a web application with either IaaS VMs or PaaS web apps, make them highly available and load balanced, and let them automatically scale, as shown in figure 11.15. You can use a globally distributed Cosmos DB backend for your database needs, and you can automatically route customers to the closest regional instance of your application, all with DNS that's hosted in Azure.

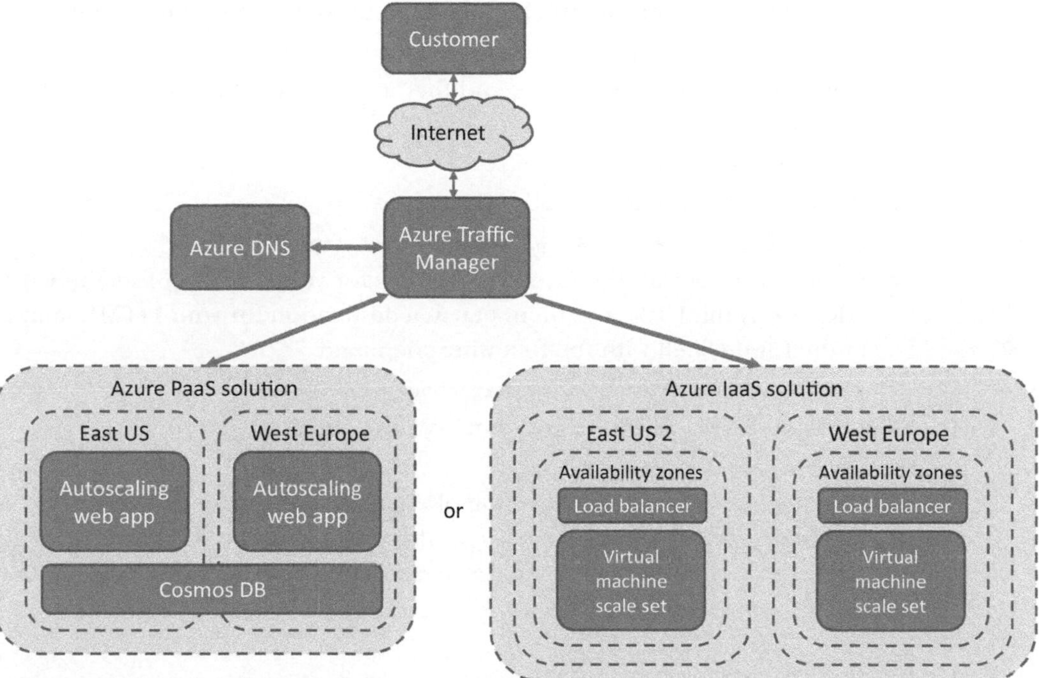

Figure 11.15 After the last few chapters, you should understand how to create highly available IaaS or PaaS applications in Azure. The IaaS solutions can use availability zones, load balancers, and scale sets. The PaaS solutions can use autoscaling web apps and Cosmos DB. Traffic Manager and Azure DNS can route customers to the most appropriate application instance automatically, based on their geographic location.

The end-of-chapter lab uploads a couple of basic websites to your web apps, just to prove that Traffic Manager works and the appropriate endpoint serves your traffic. If you have time, feel free to complete the exercise; otherwise pat yourself on the back and go take a nap. I won't tell your boss! We have one more chapter in this second section of the book, and it talks about how to make sure your applications remain healthy: how to monitor and troubleshoot your applications and infrastructure.

11.3 Lab: Deploying web apps to see Traffic Manager in action

This has been another chapter where we covered a lot, so this exercise should be one that keeps building mental muscle of your Azure skills with web apps. In the Azure samples GitHub repo are two basic web pages for the online pizza store application. Each web page's title shows the location of the web app. Upload these web pages to the relevant web app instance to see your Traffic Manager flows in practice:

1. If needed, clone the GitHub samples repo in your Cloud Shell as follows:

   ```
   git clone https://github.com/fouldsy/azure-mol-samples.git
   ```

2. Start with the eastus web page, and then repeat the following steps in the westeurope directory:

   ```
   cd ~/azure-mol-samples/11/eastus
   ```

3. Initialize the Git repo, and add the basic web page:

   ```
   git init && git add . && git commit -m "Pizza"
   ```

4. In the Azure portal, the Overview window for your web app lists the Git clone URL. Copy this URL, and then set it as a destination for your HTML sample site in the Cloud Shell with the following command:

   ```
   git remote add eastus <your-git-clone-url>
   ```

5. Push the HTML sample site to your web app:

   ```
   git push eastus master
   ```

6. Repeat these steps for the azure-mol-samples/11/westeurope directory. When finished, open your web browser to the domain name of your parent Traffic Manager profile, such as https://azuremol.trafficmanager.net, to see the traffic flow.

12 Monitoring and troubleshooting

In the previous chapters, you learned how to make your applications highly available and route customers from around the world to globally distributed instances of your application. One goal was to minimize the amount of interaction with your application infrastructure and let the Azure platform automatically manage health and performance for you. Sometimes, you still need to roll up your sleeves and review diagnostics or performance metrics. In this chapter, you learn how to review boot diagnostics for a VM, monitor performance metrics, and troubleshoot connectivity issues with Network Watcher.

12.1 VM boot diagnostics

With web apps, you deploy your code and let the Azure platform handle the rest. In chapter 3, we looked at the basics of how to troubleshoot and diagnose problems with web app deployments. You learned how to see real-time application events to monitor performance. When you work with VMs in the cloud, it's often hard to troubleshoot a problem when you can't physically see the computer screen the way you can get web app diagnostics.

One of the most common issues with VMs is lack of connectivity. If you can't SSH or RDP to a VM, how can you troubleshoot what's wrong? One of the first things you may want to check is whether the VM is running correctly. To help with this, Azure provides VM boot diagnostics that includes boot logs and a screenshot of the console.

Interactive boot-console access

For specific troubleshooting scenarios, you can also access a live serial console for VMs in Azure. This serial console allows for interactive logons and troubleshooting in the event of boot problems. You can reconfigure your VM to correct for failed boot scenarios or misconfigurations of services and applications that prevent your VM from booting correctly.

This chapter doesn't go into specific scenarios for serial console use, but it's a great resource that lets you virtually sit in front of the screen of a VM as it starts up. You also need boot diagnostics enabled, so these exercises are prerequisites for the serial console.

Try it now

To create a VM and enable boot diagnostics, complete the following steps.

1. In the Azure portal, select Create a Resource in the upper-left corner. Select Windows Server 2016 VM.
2. Enter a Name, such as `molvm`, a User Name, such as `azuremol`, and a Password. The password must be a minimum of 12 characters long and contain three of the following: a lowercase character, an uppercase character, a number, and a special character.
3. Choose Create New Resource Group. Enter a name, such as `azuremolchapter12`. Select the most appropriate Azure region closest to you.
4. Select a VM size, such as D2S_v3.
5. On the Settings page, review the default resources created for the virtual network, public IP address, and network security group (NSG). These should be familiar resources from the previous VMs you've created. Leave the defaults—there's nothing you need to change.

   One thing you may have skipped over previously was the Monitoring section. As shown in figure 12.1, the Boot Diagnostics option is enabled by default, and a storage account is created. For now, leave the Guest OS Diagnostics option disabled.
6. To create your VM, select OK in the Settings window and then Create in the Summary window.
7. It takes a few minutes to create and configure the VM, so let's continue to explore the boot diagnostics.

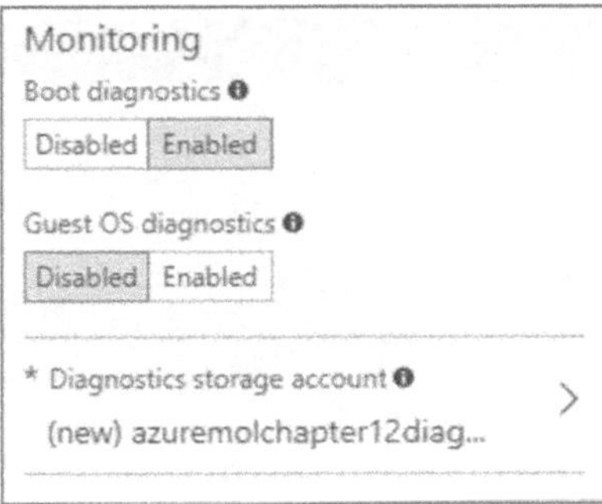

Figure 12.1 By default, boot diagnostics are enabled when you create a VM in the Azure portal. A storage account is created, which is where the boot diagnostics are stored. In a later exercise, you review and enable guest OS diagnostics, so don't enable them right now. For production use, I recommend that you enable both boot diagnostics and guest OS diagnostics for each VM you create.

If you don't have boot diagnostics enabled but run into a problem, you likely can't boot the VM to successfully enable diagnostics. It's a fun chicken-and-egg scenario, right? As a result, boot diagnostics are automatically enabled for VMs created in the Azure portal. For Azure PowerShell, Azure CLI, and the language-specific SDKs, you need to enable boot diagnostics. I recommend that you enable boot diagnostics on your VMs when you create them.

You do need to create a storage account for the boot logs and console screenshots, but the cost is likely less than $0.01 per month to store this data. The first time you run into a VM problem and need access to the boot diagnostics, that penny per month will be worth it! This storage account can also be used to hold additional VM-level performance metrics and logs, which we examine in the next section. Again, the storage costs are minimal. Even as your VM environment grows, it's worth the additional minor cost to be able to quickly troubleshoot an issue when things go wrong.

Try it now

To view the boot diagnostics for your VM, complete the following steps.

1 In the Azure portal, select Virtual Machines from the menu on the left. Choose the VM you created in the previous exercise.
2 Under the Support Troubleshooting section of the VM menu, choose Boot Diagnostics. The boot diagnostics and VM status are displayed, as shown in figure 12.2. The health report would indicate if there were boot problems with the VM and allow you to hopefully diagnose the root cause of the issue.

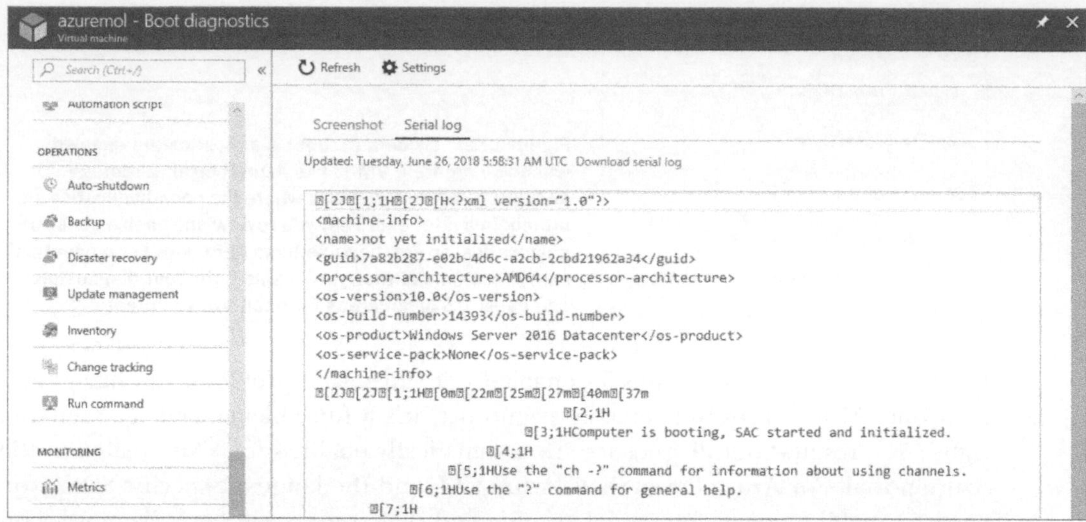

Figure 12.2 The boot diagnostics for a VM report on the health and boot status. If errors are displayed, you should be able to troubleshoot and diagnose the root cause. You can also download the logs from the portal for analysis on your local computer.

12.2 Performance metrics and alerts

One of the first steps to troubleshoot an issue starts with a review of performance. How much memory is available, how much CPU is consumed, and how much disk activity is there?

As you build and test your applications in Azure, I recommend that you record performance baselines at various points. These baselines give you an idea as to how your application should perform under different amounts of load. Why is this important? In three months, how can you determine if you encounter performance problems without some data to compare the current performance against?

When you learned how to autoscale applications in chapter 9, you used basic performance metrics, such as CPU usage, to tell the Azure platform when to increase or decrease the number of instances of your application. These basic metrics only give you a small insight as to how the VM performs. For more detailed metrics, you need to look at the performance of the VM. To do this, you need to install the Azure diagnostics extension.

12.2.1 Viewing performance metrics with the VM diagnostics extension

To add functionality to your VMs, Azure has dozens of extensions that you can seamlessly install. These extensions install a small agent or application runtime into the VM that often then reports information back to the Azure platform or third-party solutions. VM extensions can automatically configure and install components, or run scripts on your VMs.

The VM diagnostics extension is a common extension that's used to stream performance metrics from inside the VM to a storage account. These performance metrics can then be analyzed in the Azure portal, or downloaded and used in an existing monitoring solution. You can use the diagnostics extension to gain a deeper understanding of the performance of CPU and memory consumption from within the VM, which can typically provide a more detailed and accurate picture than the host.

Automation and VM extensions

In chapter 18, we discuss Azure Automation to perform tasks on your VMs in an automated, scheduled manner. One powerful feature of Azure Automation is acting as a PowerShell Desired State Configuration (DSC) pull server. PowerShell DSC is used to define a given state of how a system should be configured, what packages should be installed, files and permissions, and so on. You create definitions for the desired configuration and apply them to VMs or physical servers. You can then report on and enforce compliance with those policies. The Azure PowerShell DSC extension is used to apply DSC configurations, such as from an Azure Automation pull server.

Other extensions that can apply configurations and run scripts on VMs include the Azure Custom Script Extension. With the Custom Script Extension, you either define a simple set of commands or point to one or more external scripts, such as those hosted in Azure Storage or GitHub. These scripts can run complex configuration and installation tasks, and ensure that all deployed VMs are configured consistently.

Both the Azure PowerShell DSC extension and Custom Script Extension are commonly used with virtual machine scale sets. You apply one of these extensions to the scale set, and then as VM instances are created within the scale set, they're automatically configured to run your application. The goal of these extensions is to minimize the required manually configuration of VMs, which is an error-prone process and requires human interaction.

Other ways to automate VM configurations include Puppet and Chef, both of which have Azure VM extensions available. If you already have a configuration-management tool in use, check with the vendor for its supported approach for use in Azure. There's a good chance a VM extension is available to make your life easier.

Try it now

To enable the VM diagnostics extension, complete the following steps.

1. In the Azure portal, select Virtual Machines from the menu on the left. Choose the VM you created in a previous exercise.
2. Under the Monitoring section of the VM menu, choose Diagnostic Settings.

3 Select the button to Enable Guest-Level Monitoring.

It takes a couple of minutes to enable guest-level monitoring. Behind the scenes, here's what Azure does:

- Installs the VM diagnostics extension
- Configures the extension to stream guest-level metrics for the following areas:
  - Logical disk
  - Memory
  - Network interface
  - Process
  - Processor
  - System
- Enables application, security, and system logs to be streamed to Azure Storage

Once the diagnostics extension is installed, you can limit what data is collected by selecting only certain performance counters to report. For example, you may wish to only collect memory usage, or enable the collection of Microsoft SQL Server metrics. By default, metrics are collected every 60 seconds. You can adjust this sample rate as desired for your applications and infrastructure.

The VM diagnostics extension can also stream log files from your VM. This allows you to centralize the application, security, and system logs for analysis or alerts, as shown in figure 12.3. By default, application and system logs that generate Critical, Error, or Warning are logged, along with security events for Audit Failure. You can change the log levels to record, as well as enable log collection from IIS, application logs, and Event Tracing for Windows (ETW) events. As part of your application planning and deployment, determine what logs you want to collect.

There's nothing unique to Windows VMs here. You can use the diagnostics extension on Linux VMs in the same way, to obtain performance metrics and stream various logs.

If your VM encounters a problem, often the only way to analyze what happened is to review the *crash dumps*. Support channels often request these dumps if you want to get to the root cause for a problem. As with the boot diagnostics, there's no way to retroactively enable crash dumps to see why something failed, so determine whether you need to monitor certain processes and be proactive about configuring crash dumps. For example, you could monitor the IIS process and record a full crash dump to Azure Storage if the process fails.

Here are a couple of other areas that you can configure for guest metrics:

- *Sinks* allow you to configure the VM diagnostics extension to send certain events to Azure Application Insights. With Application Insights, you can gain visibility directly into how your code performs.
- *Agent* lets you specify a storage quota for all your metrics (the default is 5 GB). You can also enable the collection of logs for the agent itself, or uninstall the agent.

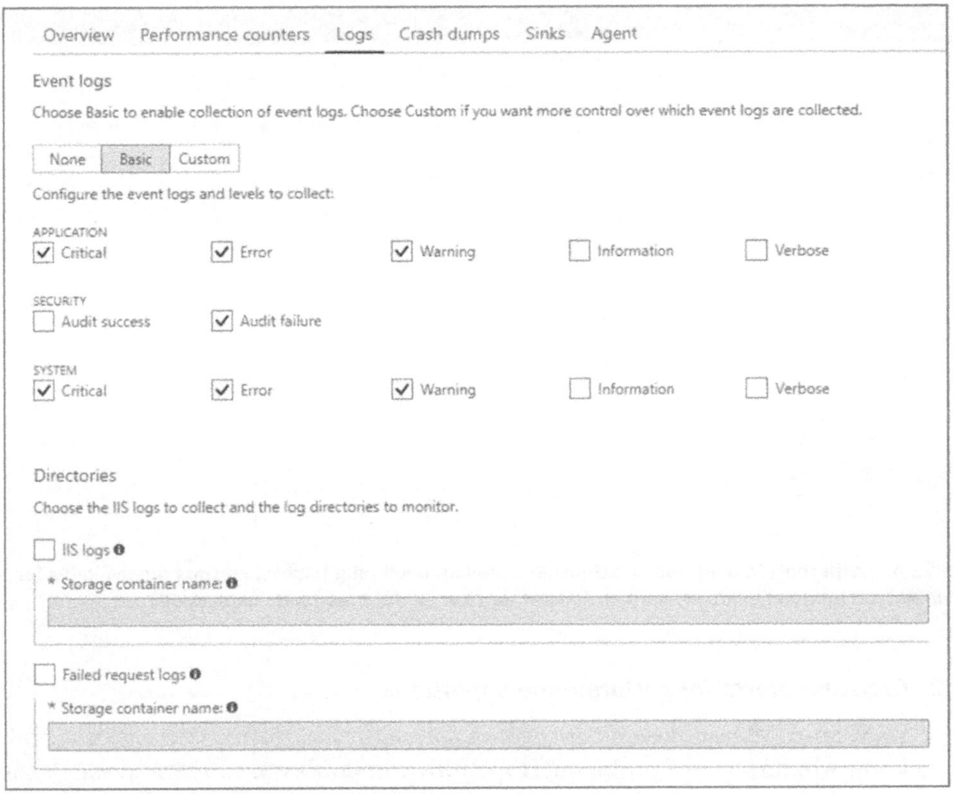

Overview Performance counters Logs Crash dumps Sinks Agent

Event logs

Choose Basic to enable collection of event logs. Choose Custom if you want more control over which event logs are collected.

None Basic Custom

Configure the event logs and levels to collect:

APPLICATION

- [x] Critical
- [x] Error
- [x] Warning
- [ ] Information
- [ ] Verbose

SECURITY

- [ ] Audit success
- [x] Audit failure

SYSTEM

- [x] Critical
- [x] Error
- [x] Warning
- [ ] Information
- [ ] Verbose

Directories

Choose the IIS logs to collect and the log directories to monitor.

- [ ] IIS logs

* Storage container name:

- [ ] Failed request logs

* Storage container name:

Figure 12.3 You can configure events and log levels for various components within the VM. This ability lets you centralize your VM logs for analysis and to generate alerts. Without the need to install complex, and often costly, monitoring systems, you can review and receive notifications when issues arise on your Azure VMs.

Try it now

To view guest-level metrics, complete the following steps.

1. In the Azure portal, select Virtual Machines from the menu on the left. Choose the VM you created in a previous exercise.
2. Under the Monitoring section of the VM menu, choose Metrics.
3. Many more metrics are now available, compared to the host-based metrics from chapter 9. In the Filter Metrics text box at the top of the list of available metrics, enter `memory`. From the filtered list, select [Guest] \Memory\% Committed Bytes in Use, as shown in figure 12.4.

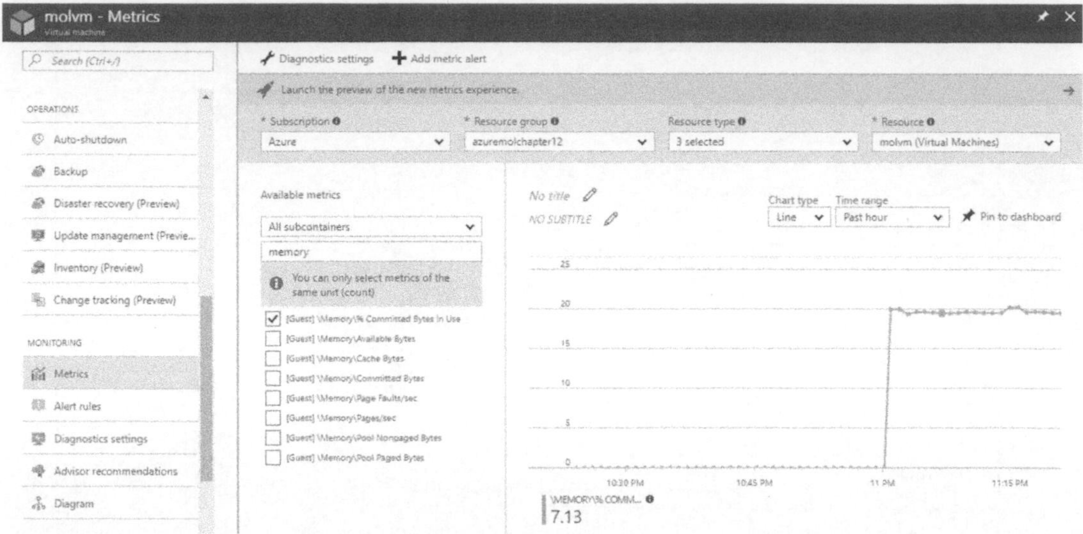

Figure 12.4 With the VM diagnostics extension installed, additional [Guest] metrics are available for review. You can search for and select the metrics to view, or change the time range as desired.

12.2.2 Creating alerts for performance conditions

With your VM configured to expose guest-level performance metrics, how do you know when there's a problem? Hopefully, you don't want to sit and watch the performance graphics in real time and wait until a problem occurs! I'm not your boss, if that's your thing. But there's a much better way: metric alerts.

Metric alerts let you select a resource, metric, and threshold, and then define who and how you want to notify when that threshold is met. Alerts work on more than just VMs. For example, you can define alerts on public IP addresses that watch for inbound distributed denial of service (DDoS) packets and warn you when a certain threshold is met that could constitute an attack.

When alerts are generated, you can choose to send an email notification to owners, contributors, and readers. These users and email addresses are obtained based on the RBAC policies applied. In larger organizations, this could send email notifications to a large group of people, so use with care! Another option is to specify email addresses, which could be the application owners or specific infrastructure engineers, or a distribution list or group targeted to the directly involved parties.

A couple of other options exist for actions to take when an alert is triggered:

- *Execute a runbook*—In chapter 18, we examine Azure Automation. The Automation service allows you to create and use runbooks that execute scripts. These scripts could perform a basic remedial action on the VM, such as to restart a process or even reboot the VM. They could also run Azure PowerShell cmdlets to enable Azure Network Watcher features like capture packets, which we explore in the rest of this chapter.

- *Run a logic app*—Azure logic apps allow you to build workflows that run serverless code. You could write information to a support ticket system or initiate an automated phone call to an on-call engineer. In chapter 21, we explore the wonderful world of serverless computing with Azure logic apps and Azure functions.

In the end-of-chapter lab, you configure some alerts for your VM. Azure can do more than help to troubleshoot and monitor your VMs, though. Let's discuss another common cause for things to go wrong: the network.

12.3 Azure Network Watcher

VM performance metrics and boot diagnostics are great ways to monitor your Azure IaaS applications. Web app application logs and App Insights provide awareness of the performance of your PaaS applications. Network traffic is often less glamorous, but it's more likely to be the cause of application connectivity issues that you or your customers encounter.

Back in chapter 5, I joked that the network team always gets the blame for problems that the operations team can't explain. Here's where we can try to make friends again, or at least get some solid proof of the network being to blame! Azure Network Watcher is one of those features that helps bring teams together for a nice group hug. With Network Watcher, you can monitor and troubleshoot using features such as these:

- Capturing network packets
- Validating IP flow for NSGs
- Generating network topology

What's great about these features is that they put different teams in the driver's seat for how to troubleshoot problems. If you create some VMs and then can't connect to them, you can verify that there's network connectivity. For developers, if your application can't connect to a backend database tier, you can examine the NSG rules to see if there's a problem. And network engineers can capture packets to examine the complete communication stream between hosts for more in-depth analysis.

Additional network troubleshooting

Network Watcher works in tandem with the diagnostic logs and metrics discussed earlier in the chapter. Network resources such as load balancers and application gateways can also generate diagnostic logs. These logs work the same as application and system logs from a VM or web app. Logs are collated in the Azure portal for you to determine if there are errors in the configuration or communications between hosts and applications.

DNS and Traffic Manager also have a Troubleshoot area in the Azure portal. The portal guides you through some common errors that you may encounter, offers configuration advice, and provides links to additional documentation. If all else fails, you can open a support request with Azure Support.

(continued)

Although it may often be easier to build large application deployments with Azure Resource Manager templates or with Azure CLI or PowerShell scripts, the Azure portal has a lot of great tools and features when things go wrong. Especially with complicated network configurations and security policies, a few seconds of your time to review the output from Network Watcher tools can identify an issue and let you resolve it quickly. All these tools help to improve the overall health and experience of your applications for your customers.

What are some scenarios where you may want to use Network Watcher and the troubleshooting features it offers? Let's look a few common issues and see how Network Watcher could help.

12.3.1 Verifying IP flows

Here's a common problem: customers can't connect to your application. The application works fine when you connect from the office, but customers can't access the application over the public internet. Why?

VPNs and ExpressRoute

Azure virtual private networks (VPNs) provide secure communications between on-premises offices and Azure datacenters. Azure ExpressRoute provides high-speed, dedicated private connections from on-premises offices to the Azure datacenters and is often used in large organizations.

Both connections are a little more complicated to set up than we can cover in a single lunch break, and they're also often things that you set up and configure only once. The network team is usually responsible for configuring these, and you may not even realize that you access Azure over a private connection.

All the testing of your application works great. You can access the application through a web browser, place orders, and receive email notifications. When your customers then go to place an order, the application doesn't load.

How can Network Watcher help? By verifying IP flows. Network Watcher simulates traffic flow to your destination and reports back as to whether the traffic can successfully reach your VM.

Try it now

To enable Network Watcher and verify IP flows, complete the following steps.

1. In the Azure portal, select All Services from the top of the Services navigation menu at left.

2 Filter and select Network Watcher from the list of available services. You enable Network Watcher in the region(s) that you wish to monitor. When you enable Network Watcher in a region, Azure uses role-based access controls (RBACs) for the various resources and network traffic.

3 Expand the list of regions for your account, and then choose Enable Network Watcher for the same region as the VM you created in a previous exercise, as shown in figure 12.5.

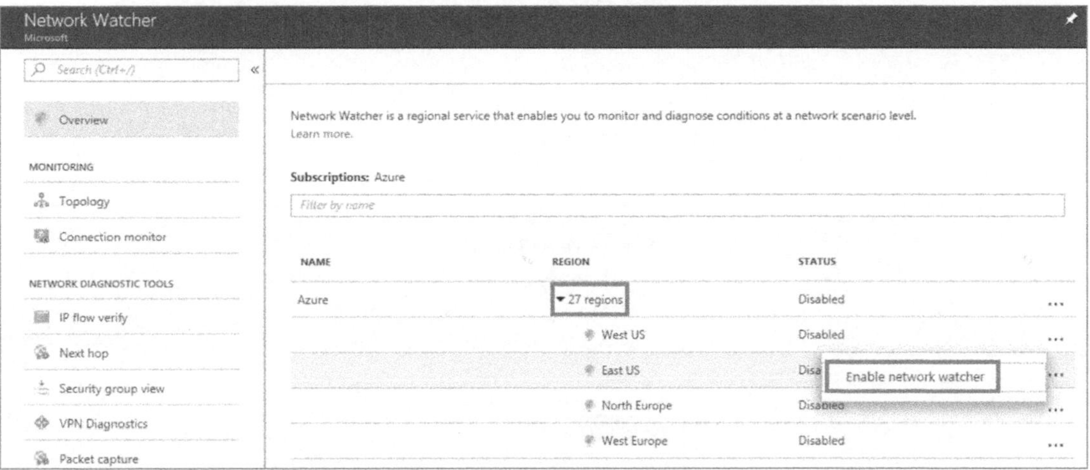

Figure 12.5 From the list of Azure subscriptions (you probably have only one), expand the list of regions. From a security perspective, you should only enable Network Watcher in Azure regions that you need to monitor for a given problem. Network Watcher can be used to capture packets for other applications and services across your subscription if you enable the feature in many regions.

4 It takes a minute or two for Network Watcher to be enabled in your region. Once it's enabled, select IP Flow Verify under Network Diagnostic Tools at left in the Network Watcher window.

5 Select your resource group, such as azuremolchapter12, and VM, such as molvm. By default, Protocol is set to TCP and Direction is Inbound. The Local IP Address of the virtual NIC is also populated.

6 For Local Port, enter port 80. If you accepted the defaults when you created the VM in the previous exercise, you didn't open port 80, so this is a good test of what happens when traffic is denied.

7 Under Remote IP Address, enter `8.8.8.8`. This address may seem familiar—it's an open DNS server provided by Google. You aren't doing anything with this server; you just need to give Network Watcher an external IP address to simulate traffic flow. You could also go to https://whatsmyip.com and enter your real public IP address. Set Remote Port to port 80, and then select Check, as shown in figure 12.6.

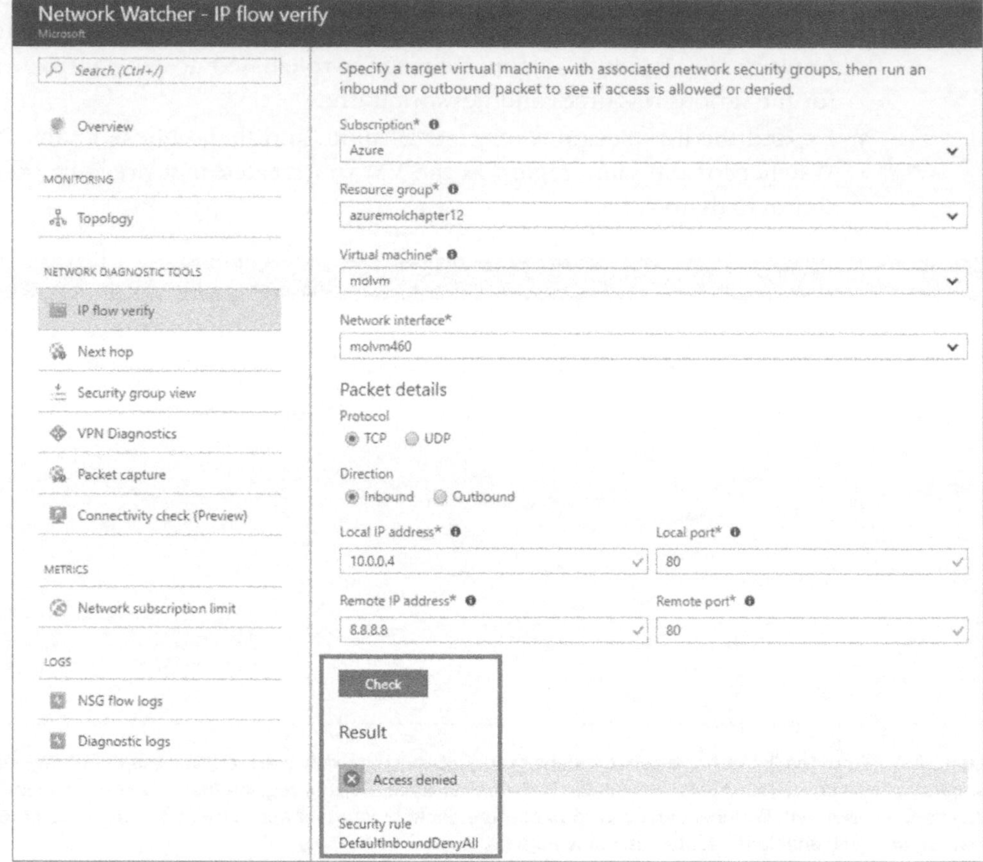

Figure 12.6 Select your VM, and provide a local port on the VM to test. In this example, you want to test connectivity to port 80 to simulate a common web application on the VM. The remote IP address can be any external address for Network Watcher to simulate traffic. What really happens is that Network Watcher examines the effective security group rules to validate if traffic could flow to the VM based on the source and destination IP addresses and ports.

The result of your IP flow check should be "Access denied." Helpfully, Network Watcher then tells you which rule caused the traffic flow to fail: the DefaultInbound-DenyAll rule. You know there's a network security rule that blocks traffic, but where is this rule applied? At the subnet, virtual NIC, or application security group? There's another Network Watcher feature that can tell you!

12.3.2 Viewing effective NSG rules

NSG rules can be applied to a single virtual NIC, at the subnet level, or against a group of VMs in an application security group. Rules are combined, which allows you to specify a common set of rules across an entire subnet and then get more granular for application security groups (such as "allow TCP port 80 on all webservers") or an individual VM.

Here are some common examples of how NSG rules may be applied:

- *Subnet level*—Allow TCP port 5986 for secure remote management from management subnet 10.1.10.20/24.
- *Application security group level*—Allow TCP port 80 for HTTP traffic to web applications, and apply the application security group to all web application VMs.
- *Virtual NIC level*—Allow TCP port 3389 for remote desktop access from management subnet 10.1.10.20/24.

These are basic rules, and they explicitly allow certain traffic. If no *allow* rules match a network packet, the default *DenyAll* rules are applied to drop the traffic.

During the testing of the application discussed in the example, you may have configured that HTTP rule to only traffic from one of your on-premises subnets. Now, customers over the public internet can't connect.

Try it now

To determine where an NSG rule is applied, complete the following steps.

1. In Network Watcher, select Security Group View at left.
2. Select your resource group, such as azuremolchapter12, and your VM, such as molvm. It takes a few seconds for the effective rules to be displayed, as shown in figure 12.7.

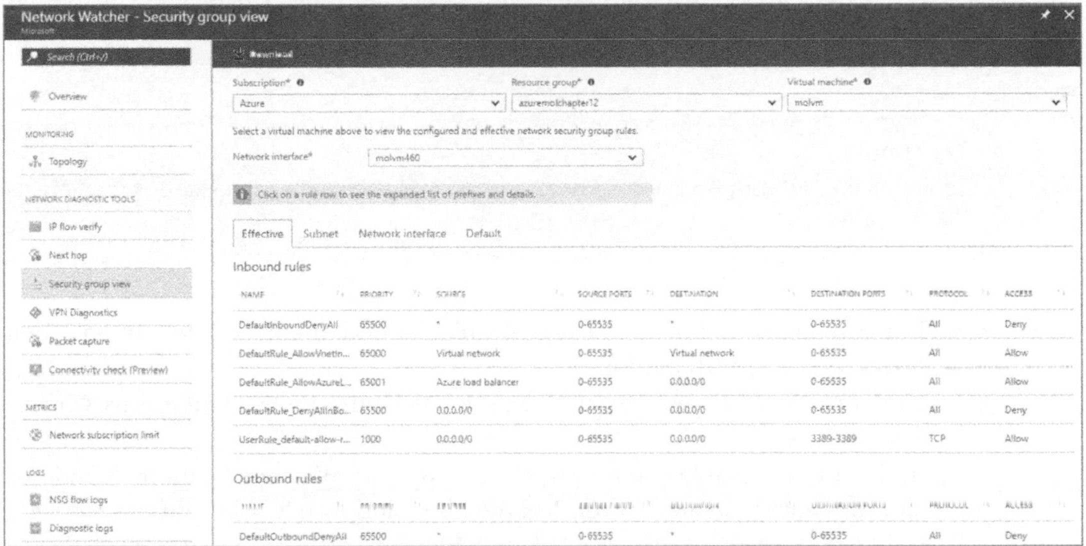

Figure 12.7 When you select a VM, Network Watcher examines how all the NSG rules are applied and the order of precedence, and shows what effective rules are currently applied. You can then quickly drill down to the subnet, virtual NIC, and default rules to find and edit where a given rule is applied.

The default rules from the VM you created earlier aren't exciting, but you can move through subnet, network interface, and default rules to get a feel for the way that effective rules are combined and how you could identify where rules are applied if you need to make changes.

12.3.3 Capturing network packets

Let's assume that you updated your network security rules to allow access to your application for public internet customers, but one customer reports they experience odd behavior. The web application sometimes doesn't load, or displays broken images. Their connection often appears to time out.

Intermittent problems are often the hardest to troubleshoot, especially if you have limited, or no, access to the computer that encounters a problem. One common troubleshooting approach is to capture the network packets and review them for signs of any problems such as network transmission errors, malformed packets, or protocol and communication issues.

With network packet captures, you get the raw stream of data between two or more hosts. There's an art to analyzing network captures, and it's not for the faint hearted! Special third-party tools such as Riverbed's Wireshark, Telerik's Fiddler, and Microsoft's Message Analyzer provide a graphical way for you to view and filter the network packets, typically grouping them by related communications or protocols. Figure 12.8 shows an example of what a network packet capture looks like.

To enable Network Watcher to capture packets to and from your VMs, first install the Network Watcher VM extension. As you saw in the previous section, VM extensions provide a way for the Azure platform to reach inside a VM to perform various management tasks. In the case of the Network Watcher extension, it examines network traffic to and from the VM.

> **Try it now**
> To install the Network Watcher VM extension and capture network packets, complete the following steps.

1. In the Azure portal, select Virtual Machines in the menu on the left, and then select your VM, such as molvm.
2. Under the Settings category at left in the VM window, select Extensions. Choose Add an Extension.
3. In the list of available extensions, choose Network Watcher Agent for Windows, and then select Create. To confirm the extension install, select OK.
4. It may take a few minutes for Network Watcher Agent to be installed on your VM. To go back to the Network Watcher menu in the Azure portal, select All

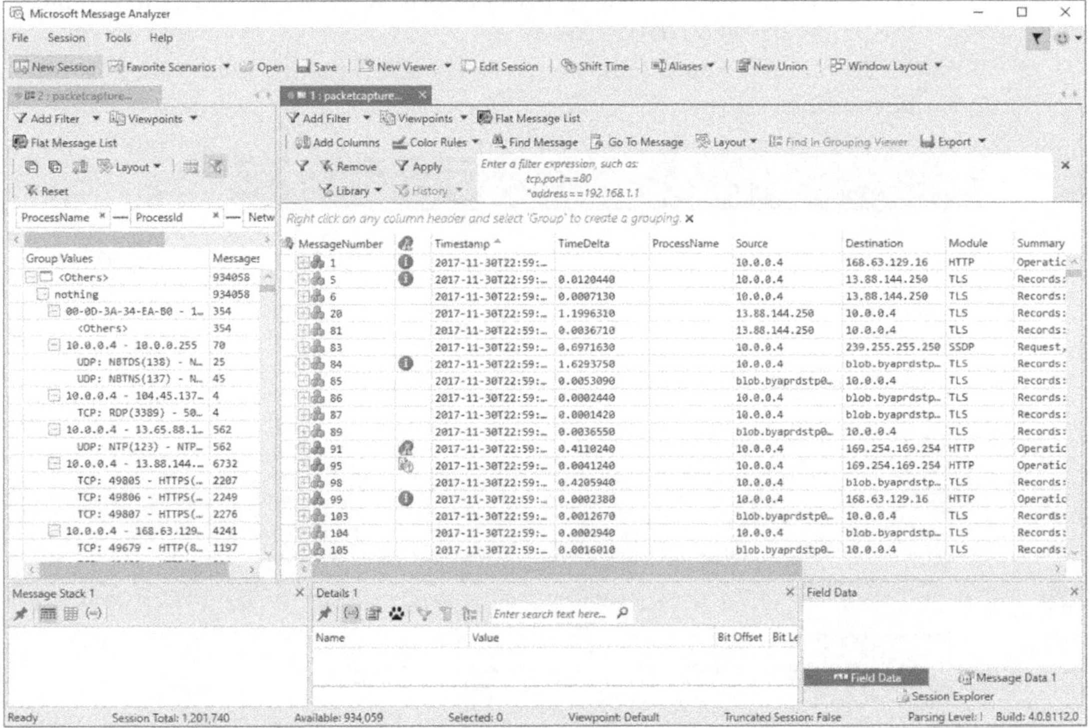

Figure 12.8 A network capture when viewed in Microsoft's Message Analyzer. Each individual packet is available for inspection. You can group and filter by communication protocol or client-host. This depth of network data allows you to examine the actual packets that flow between nodes to troubleshoot where an error occurs. A former colleague once told me, "The packets never lie." The puzzle is to figure out what the packets tell you.

Services at the top of the Services navigation menu at left in the portal, and then choose Network Watcher.

5 Under Network Diagnostic Tools at left in the Network Watcher window, select Packet Capture, and then choose Add a New Capture.
6 Select your resource group, such as azuremolchapter12, and VM, such as molvm. Enter a name for your packet capture, such as `molcapture`.

   By default, packet captures are saved to Azure Storage. You can also choose Save to File and specify a local directory on the source VM. The Network Watcher Agent extension then writes the packet capture file to disk in the VM.
7 If it isn't already selected, choose the storage account name that starts with the name of your resource group, such as azuremolchapter12diag739. This is the storage account created and used by the VM diagnostics extension that you enabled earlier.
8 You can specify a maximum file size for the packet capture (default is 1 GB) and maximum duration for the packet capture (default is 30 minutes). To only

capture traffic from specific sources or ports, you can also add a filter to narrow the scope of your packet captures.

9 Set Duration to 60 seconds. To start the packet capture, select OK, as shown in figure 12.9.

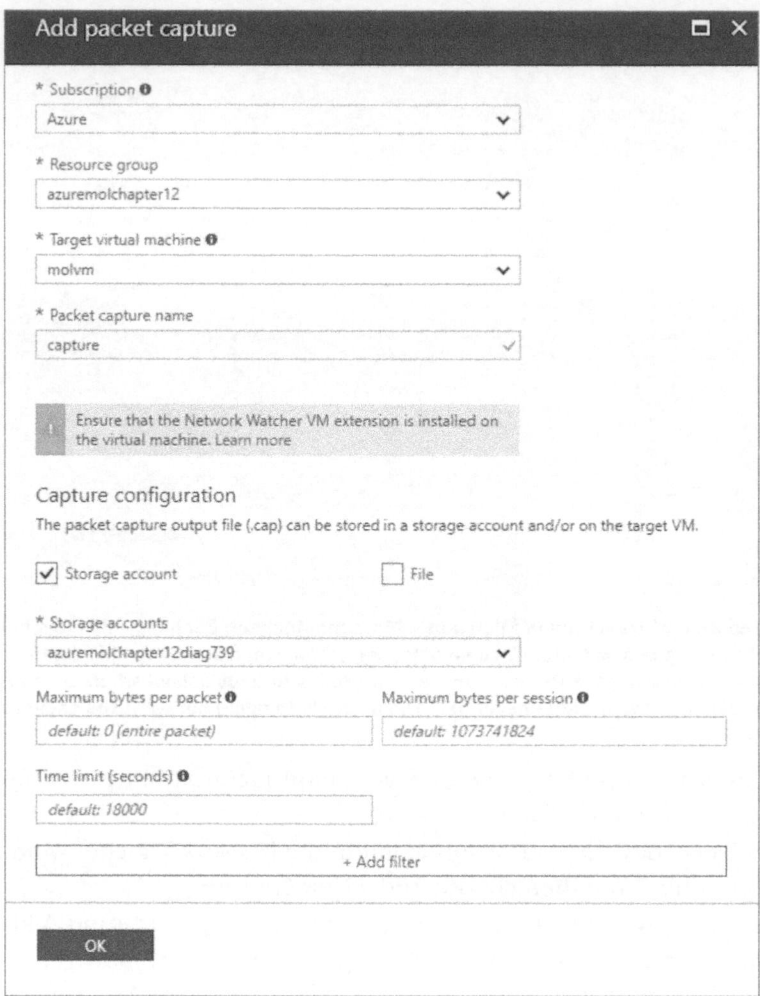

Figure 12.9 When you start a packet capture, you can save the data to Azure Storage or a local file on the VM. You can also specify a maximum size or duration of the packet captures. To limit captures to particular addresses or ports, you can add filters and define your specific needs.

It takes a minute or two to start the capture. When the capture is in progress, the data is streamed to the Azure Storage account or local file on the VM. The list of captures is shown in the Network Watcher portal page. If you stream the logs to Azure Storage, you can have the capture go straight to the Storage account and download the .cap capture file. You can then open the packet capture in an analysis program as discussed earlier. In fact, the example network capture shown earlier in figure 12.8 was from an Azure Network Watcher packet capture!

12.4 Lab: Creating performance alerts

The VM diagnostics, metrics, and Network Watcher features have hopefully given you some insight into what's available in Azure to help you troubleshoot application problems. Some things, like boot diagnostics and the VM diagnostics extension, make the most sense when you enable and configure them as you deploy VMs. In this lab, you configure some metric alerts to see what you can be notified about and what the alerts look like when you receive them:

1. In the Azure portal, browse to the VM you created in the previous exercises. Under the Monitoring section for the VM, select Alerts.
2. Choose Add Metric Alert, and then create an alert when the Metric of \Memory\% Committed Bytes in Use is Greater Than a Threshold of 10 Percent Over the Last 5 minutes. A chart should show you what the latest metrics are, so adjust the threshold if 10% wouldn't trigger an alert.
3. Check the box to Email Owners, Contributors, and Readers.
4. Wait a few minutes for the alert notification to come through. Anyone with RBAC permissions to the VM would receive this notification.
5. To scope the alert notifications, edit the alert rule to instead notify via Additional Administrator Email(s), and specify a different email account than the one associated with your Azure subscription. This approach simulates how you can send notifications to a specific support address or a distribution list of application owners, for example.
6. Depending on your role and involvement in the VM and application management, you can explore how to generate alerts based on Azure log entries. Select your VM, and then Alert rules again. This time, choose Add Activity Log Alert. Look at the available options for what Azure services and actions can be used to generate alerts. Try to create an alert when your VM is restarted, as shown in figure 12.10.

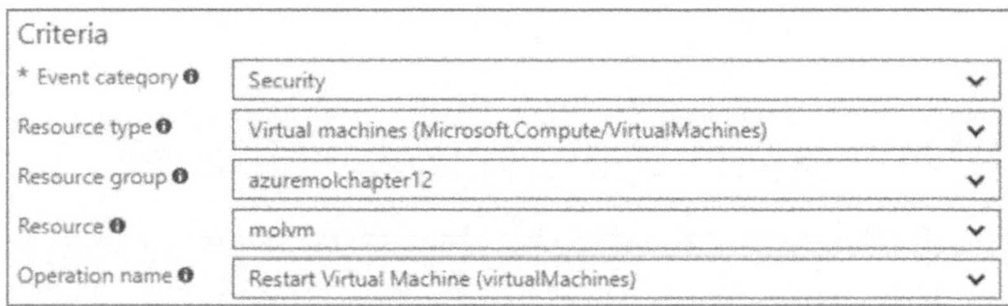

Figure 12.10 Create an alert when a security event for your VM records a Restart Virtual Machine operation.

Part 3

Secure by default

In an online world where applications are typically connected to the internet 24/7, the threat of a digital attack is all too real. These attacks cost time, money, and customer trust. A central part of building highly redundant and distributed applications includes how to secure them and protect your data. Azure has several built-in features to secure your data, including encryption, monitoring, digital key vault, and backups. In this part of the book, you learn how to secure and protect your applications right from the start.

13 Backup, recovery, and replication

The next few chapters introduce some of the core Azure features and services that allow you to build security into your applications. That's probably too subjective: security shouldn't be an add-on feature or consideration. Rather, security should be inherently built into the heart and soul of your application from the start. In this chapter, you begin your journey into Azure security with how to back up and recover your data. Backups may not seem like a common security topic, but think about security as more than data encryption or website SSL certificates. What about the safety of your data from outages, data loss, and hacking? A discussion of backups and replication also acts as a good topic to bridge from the previous section on high availability into this section on security.

Backups may seem trivial, and as a former backup administrator, I can tell you there isn't much exciting about backup jobs and rotations! But timely backups that work are crucial to protect your applications and ensure that in the worst-case scenario, you can restore your data quickly and reliably. You can also replicate your VMs from one Azure region to another. This ability builds on the high-availability concepts we looked at back in chapter 7.

In this chapter, you learn how to back up and restore VMs and then replicate VMs automatically across Azure. All these backups and restore points are encrypted to secure your data.

13.1 Azure Backup

One of the cool things about Azure Backup is that it's both a service and a big bucket of storage for the actual backups. Azure Backup can protect VMs in Azure, on-premises VMs or physical servers, and even VMs in other providers such as Amazon Web Services (AWS). The data backups can be stored on your own on-premises storage arrays or within an Azure recovery vault. Figure 13.1 shows how the Azure Backup service can protect and orchestrate all of your backup needs.

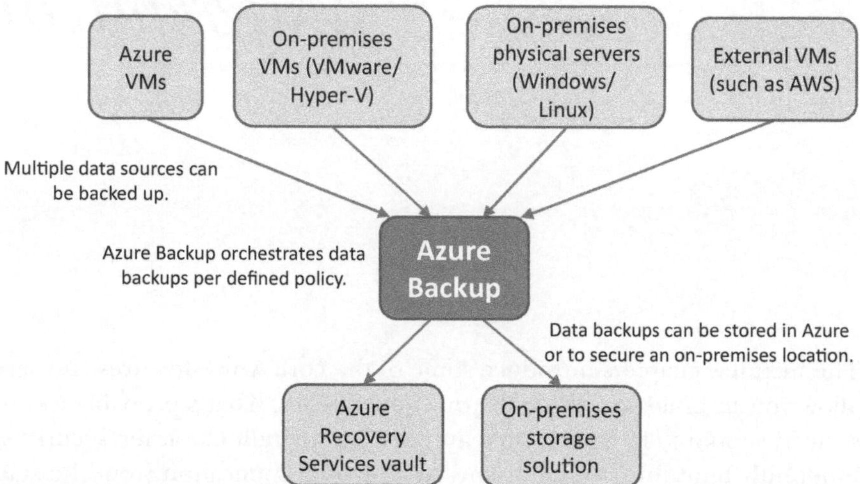

Figure 13.1 Multiple VMs or physical servers, from various providers and locations, can be backed up through the central orchestration service. Azure Backups uses defined policies to back up data at a given frequency or schedule. These backups can then be stored in Azure or to an on-premises storage solution. Throughout, data is encrypted for added security.

At its core, Azure Backup manages backup schedules and data retention, and orchestrates the backup or restore jobs. To back up Azure VMs, there's no server component to install and no agent to manually install. All the backup and restore operations are built into the Azure platform.

To back up on-premises VMs or physical servers, or VMs in other providers such as AWS, you install a small agent that enables secure communication back and forth with Azure. This secure communication ensures that your data is encrypted during transfer.

For data stored in Azure, the backups are encrypted using an encryption key that you create and retain sole access to. Only you have access to those encrypted backups. You can also back up encrypted VMs, which we look at in the next chapter, to really make sure your data backups are safe.

There's no charge for the network traffic flow to back up or restore data. You only pay for each protected instance, and then however much storage you consume in

Azure. If you use an on-premises storage location, the cost to use Azure Backup is minimal, because there are no Azure Storage or network traffic costs.

13.1.1 Policies and retention

Azure Backup uses an incremental backup model. When you protect an instance, the first backup operation performs a full backup of the data. After that, each backup operation performs an incremental backup of the data. Each of these backups is called a *recovery point*. Incremental backups are a time-efficient approach that optimizes the storage and network bandwidth usage. Only data that has changed since the previous backup is securely transferred to the destination backup location. Figure 13.2 details how incremental backups work.

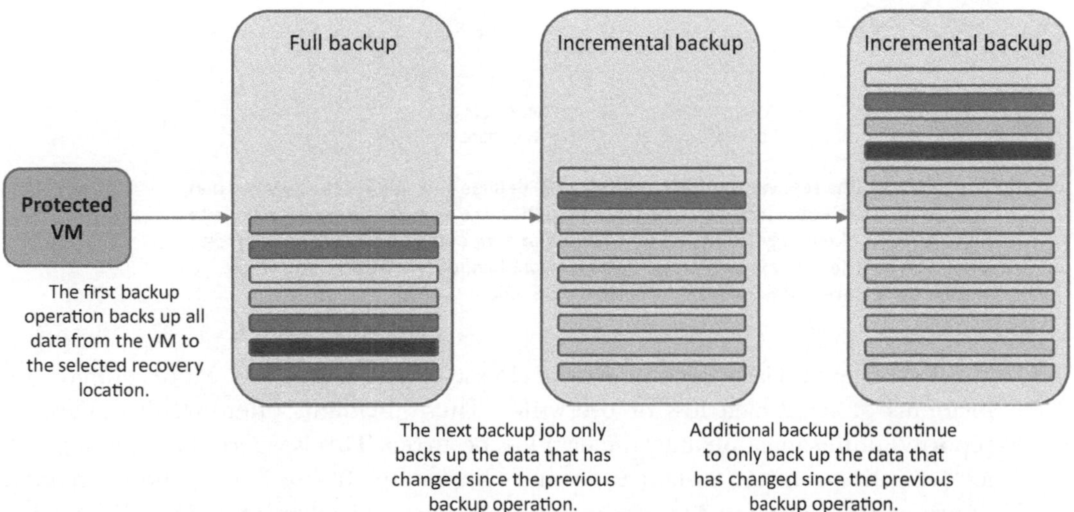

Figure 13.2 Incremental backups only back up the data that has changed since the previous operation. The first backup is always a full backup. Each subsequent backup job only backs up data that has changed since the previous job. You control the frequency of full backups with policies. This approach minimizes the amount of data that needs to securely travel across the network and be housed in the destination storage location. Azure Backup maintains the relationship of incremental backups to each other to ensure that when you restore data, it's consistent and complete.

With Azure Backup, you can store up to 9,999 recovery points for each instance that you protect. For some context, if you made a regular daily backup, you'd be set for over 27 years. And you could keep weekly backups for almost 200 years. I think that would cover most audit situations! You can choose to retain backups on a daily, weekly, monthly, or yearly basis, which is typically in line with most existing backup policies.

To implement the optimal backup strategy for your workload, you need to understand and determine your acceptable *recovery point objective* (RPO) and *recovery time objective* (RTO).

RECOVERY POINT OBJECTIVE

The RPO defines the point that your latest backup allows you to restore. By default, Azure Backup makes a daily backup. You then define retention policies as to how many days, weeks, months, or years you wish to keep these recovery points. Although the RPO is typically used to define the maximum amount of acceptable data loss, you should also consider how far back in time you may wish to go. Figure 13.3 shows how the RPO defines the amount of acceptable data loss.

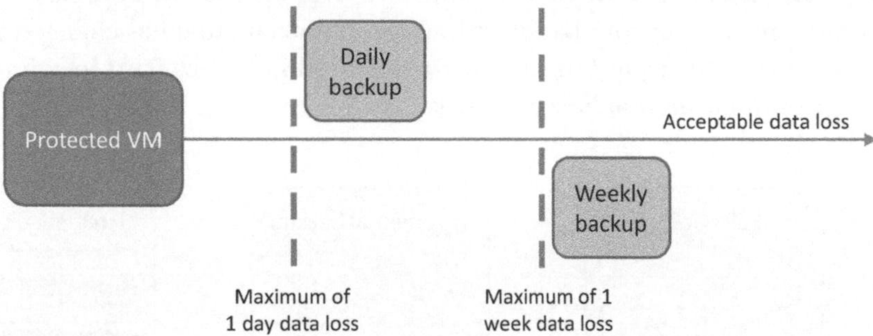

Figure 13.3 The recovery point objective (RPO) defines how much data loss you can sustain for a protected instance. The longer the RPO, the greater the acceptable data loss. An RPO of one day means up to 24 hours of data could be lost, depending on when the data loss occurred in relation to the last backup. An RPO of one week means up to seven days' worth of data could be lost.

Major outages and large amounts of data loss are rare occurrences. More common are incidents of small data loss or overwrites. These incidents often aren't noticed or reported until sometime after the data loss occurred. This is where the retention policy for your protected instances becomes important. If you have a short retention policy, you may be unable to restore data from the required point in time. You need to determine a balance between retaining multiple recovery points and the storage costs to retain all those recovery points.

Azure storage is relatively cheap: typically less than $0.02 per gigabyte of storage. This equates to approximately $2 per month for a 100 GB VM data backup. Depending on how much your data changes, the size of the incremental recovery points could add up quickly. Retaining recovery points for weeks or months could run into tens of dollars per month per protected instance. This isn't to discourage you—but it's important to plan your needs and be smart with your costs. Storage looks cheap at less than $0.02 per gigabyte until you have hundreds of gigabytes per protected instance and dozens or even hundreds of instances to protect.

I'm a former backup administrator, and storage capacity was often a central factor when I determined how many recovery points to retain. That storage capacity often created compromises with those RPOs. If you use Azure Storage rather than an on-premises storage solution, you don't need to worry about available storage capacity. I can all but guarantee there's more storage than your credit card limit!

RECOVERY TIME OBJECTIVE

The RTO dictates how quickly you can restore your data. If you choose to back up Azure VMs and store the recovery points in an on-premises storage solution, it takes much longer to restore those backups than if they were housed directly in Azure Storage. The inverse would be true if you backed up on-premises VMs or physical servers to Azure Storage. Figure 13.4 outlines the RTO.

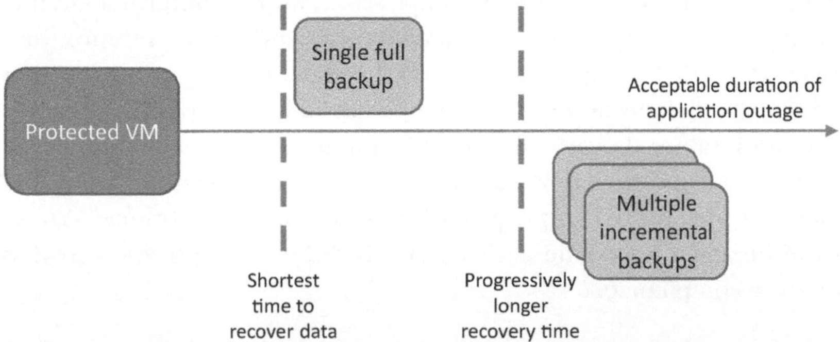

Figure 13.4 The RTO defines how long it's acceptable for the data-restore process to take and the application to be unavailable. The more recovery points are involved in the restore process, the longer the RTO. In a similar manner, the closer the backup storage is to the restore point, the shorter the RTO.

In either scenario, the recovery-point data would need to be transferred from the recovery-point storage location to the restore location. For large restore operations, where you may need to transfer hundreds of gigabytes, your network bandwidth becomes a real bottleneck for how quickly you can make applications available again.

The same is true for long retention policies with many successive incremental recovery points. Restoring the data may require that multiple recovery points be mounted and restored. Your job is to determine how far back in time you need to be able to travel, and how much time you can take to restore the data.

Both RPO and RTO vary based on your applications and business use. An application that processes real-time orders can't tolerate much outage or downtime, so the RPO and RTO are likely to be very low. You typically use a database to hold your data, so you'd typically design tolerances into the application rather than rely on recovery points. If you think back to Cosmos DB, there isn't anything to back up—the Azure platform performs the replication and data protection for you. If you built a custom solution on MySQL or Microsoft SQL Server, you'd typically use a similar type of clustering and replication to ensure that multiple copies of the database exist, so the loss of one instance wouldn't require you to restore from a backup. Backups are primarily to protect against a major outage or data corruption.

13.1.2 Backup schedules

How do you control the frequency of your backups and the retention of the recovery points? In Azure Backup, these settings are defined in policies. You build these policies to cover the various scenarios you wish to protect against, and you can reuse the policies for multiple protected instances.

For example, a backup policy may define that you want to make a backup at 6:30 p.m. each day. You wish to keep daily backups for six months and rotate them to retain weekly backups for two years. For compliance purposes, you retain monthly backups for five years. A yearly backup is retained for 10 years. Figure 13.5 shows these retention policies as the default options when you create a backup policy.

The retention values shown in figure 13.5 may appear excessive, but for an application that involves communication and messaging, you often need to retain backups for regulatory and compliance purposes for these long time frames. Azure Backup provides the flexibility to define policies to suit different application workloads and quickly enforce compliance.

> **Try it now**
>
> All your Azure backups are stored in a Recovery Services vault. To create a vault and backup policy, complete the following steps.

1. Open the Azure portal, and select Create a Resource at upper left in the menu.
2. Search for and select Backup and Site Recovery (OMS), and then choose Create.
3. Provide a name, such as `azuremol`, and then choose Create New Resource Group. Enter a resource group name, such as `azuremolchapter13`.
4. Select a location, and then choose Create.
5. Select Resource Groups from the menu at left in the portal, and then choose the resource group you created.
6. Select your Recovery Services vault from the list of available resources, choose Backup Policies from the menu at left, and then select Add a Policy.
7. Select the Azure Virtual Machine policy type, and then provide a name for your new policy, such as `molpolicy`. By default, a backup is created each day. Select the most appropriate time zone from the drop-down menu. By default, Azure uses Universal Coordinated Time (UTC).

   If you wish, review and adjust the retention policies for daily, weekly, monthly, and yearly. The previous section on backup schedules detailed these retention values;these options typically vary as you create and apply backup policies to protect your VM instances.
8. When you're ready, select Create.

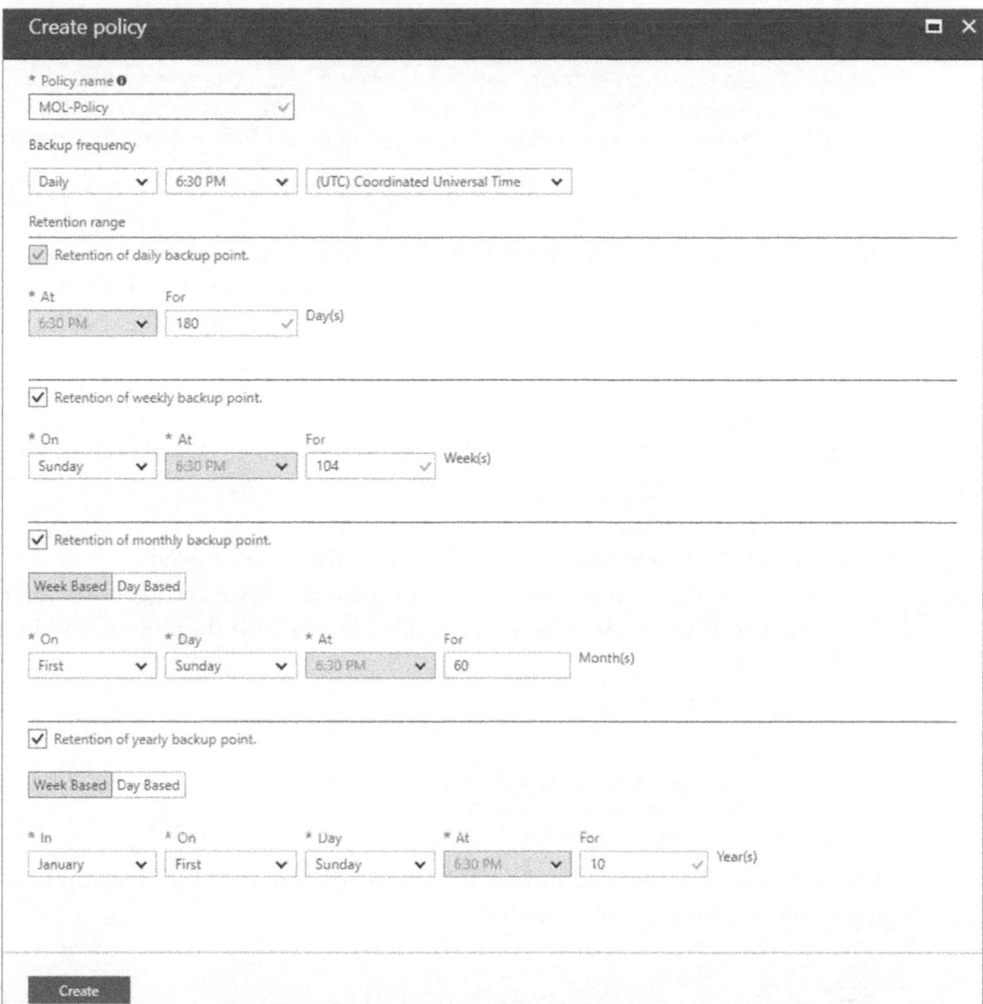

Figure 13.5 When you create an Azure Backup policy, you can define how long to retain recovery points. These retention values allow you to build policies to fit various compliance and audit requirements that you must adhere to.

> **The simple life**
>
> You can also configure VM backups when you create a VM in the Azure portal. On the Settings page where you configure virtual network settings or diagnostics and troubleshooting options, you can enable Azure Backup. You can pick an existing Recovery Services vault or create one, and create or use a backup policy. You can't currently enable backups as part of the VM deployment in the Azure CLI or Azure PowerShell, but it's usually a single command post-deployment to do so.

(continued)

I like to plan a backup strategy, retention policies, and schedules, which is why these exercises created the Recovery Services vault and policies first. But, if you want to quickly create a VM and enable backups, you can do that in the Azure portal in one step.

You now have a backup policy, which also defines retention policies for various periods, but you have nothing to back up yet. Let's create a VM with the Cloud Shell so that you can create a backup and, in a later exercise, replicate the data.

Try it now

To create a test VM for backup and replication, complete the following steps.

1. Select the Cloud Shell icon at the top of the Azure portal.
2. Create a VM with `az vm create`. Provide the resource group name created in the previous lab, such as `azuremolchapter13`, and then enter a VM name, such as `molvm`:

```
az vm create \
  --resource-group azuremolchapter13 \
  --name molvm \
  --image win2016datacenter \
  --admin-username azuremol \
  --admin-password P@ssw0rdMoL123
```

A backup policy is defined, and a test VM is ready. To see Azure Backup in action, let's apply your backup policy to the VM.

Try it now

To back up a VM with your defined policy, complete the following steps.

1. Select Resource Groups from the menu at left in the portal. Choose the resource group and then the VM you created.
2. Under Operations, select Backup.
3. Make sure your Recovery Services vault is selected, and then choose your backup policy from the drop-down menu. Review the schedule and retention options, and then choose Enable Backup, as shown in figure 13.6.
4. It takes a few seconds for the backup policy to be applied. Once it's enabled, go back to the backup settings. The VM status reports "Warning (Initial backup pending)." To create the first backup, choose the Backup Now button, as shown in figure 13.7.

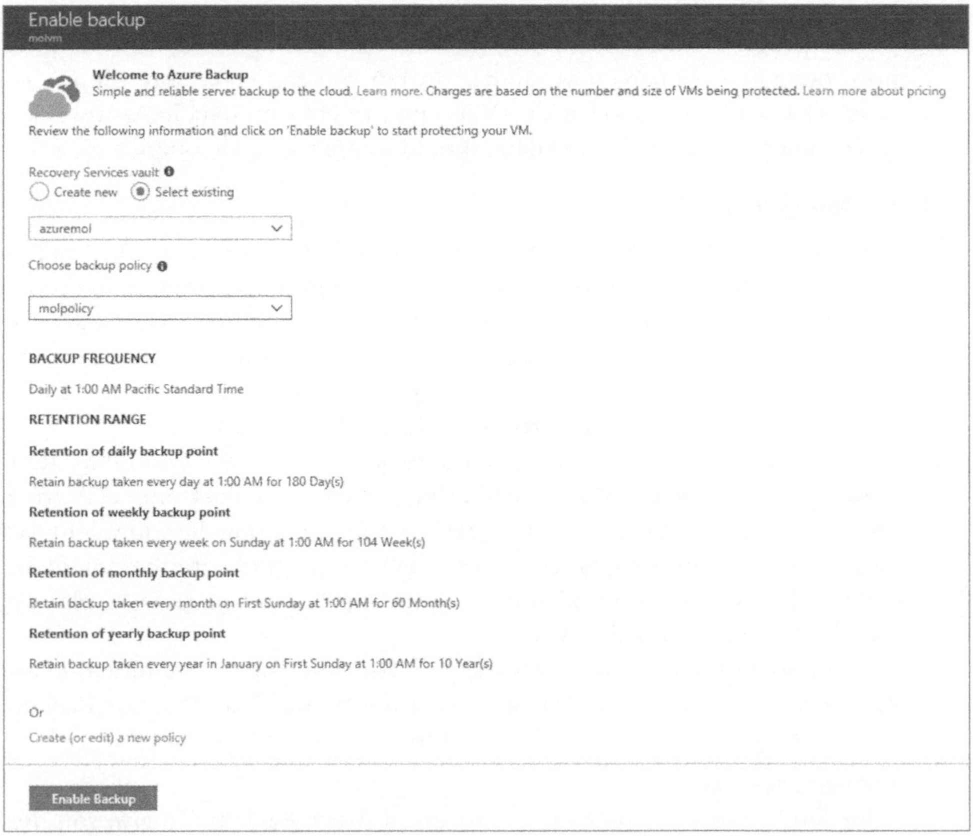

Enable backup

molvm

Welcome to Azure Backup

Simple and reliable server backup to the cloud. Learn more. Charges are based on the number and size of VMs being protected. Learn more about pricing

Review the following information and click on 'Enable backup' to start protecting your VM.

Recovery Services vault

Create new Select existing

azuremol

Choose backup policy

molpolicy

BACKUP FREQUENCY

Daily at 1:00 AM Pacific Standard Time

RETENTION RANGE

Retention of daily backup point

Retain backup taken every day at 1:00 AM for 180 Day(s)

Retention of weekly backup point

Retain backup taken every week on Sunday at 1:00 AM for 104 Week(s)

Retention of monthly backup point

Retain backup taken every month on First Sunday at 1:00 AM for 60 Month(s)

Retention of yearly backup point

Retain backup taken every year in January on First Sunday at 1:00 AM for 10 Year(s)

Or

Create (or edit) a new policy

Enable Backup

Figure 13.6 If needed, choose your Recovery Services vault, and then select your backup policy from the list of available policies. The backup schedule and retention options are shown for review.

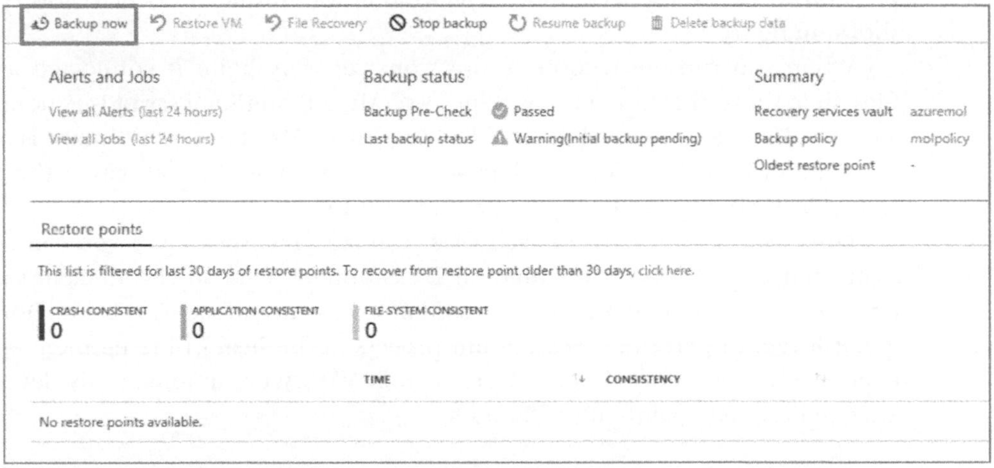

Backup now Restore VM File Recovery Stop backup Resume backup Delete backup data

Alerts and Jobs

View all Alerts (last 24 hours)

View all Jobs (last 24 hours)

Backup status

Backup Pre-Check Passed

Last backup status Warning(Initial backup pending)

Summary

Recovery services vault azuremol

Backup policy molpolicy

Oldest restore point -

Restore points

This list is filtered for last 30 days of restore points. To recover from restore point older than 30 days, click here.

CRASH CONSISTENT 0 APPLICATION CONSISTENT 0 FILE-SYSTEM CONSISTENT 0

TIME CONSISTENCY

No restore points available.

Figure 13.7 To create the first backup, select the Backup Now button. The status updates when complete and shows the latest backup time, latest restore point, and oldest restore point.

It can take 15 to 20 minutes for the first complete backup operation to complete. To see the progress of the backup job, you can select the option to View All Jobs. There's no progress bar or percentage indicator, but you can make sure the job is still running. That's all it takes to back up VMs and protect your data in Azure! Keep reading to see how you can restore the data, should something go wrong.

13.1.3 Restoring a VM

Azure Backup allows you to restore a complete VM or perform a file-level restore. In all my years, file-level restore operations were the more common of the two. This type of restore job is usually performed when files are deleted or accidentally overwritten. File-level restores usually determine the retention policies for your backups. The more important the data, the more likely you want to retain backups for longer, in case you get a late-night call to restore a file from six months ago.

A complete VM restore, as you might expect, restores the entire VM. Rarely have I performed a complete VM restore to bring a deleted VM back online. A great use case for a complete VM restore is to provide a test VM, functionally equivalent to the original. You can restore a VM and then test a software upgrade or other maintenance procedure. This can help you identify potential problems and create a plan for how to handle the real, production VM.

It's also important to regularly test your backups. Don't wait until a situation arises when you need to restore data in a real-world scenario. Trust in Azure Backup, but verify that you know how and where to restore the data when needed!

FILE-LEVEL RESTORE

A file-level restore is a pretty cool process in Azure Backup. To give you flexibility in how and where you restore files, Azure creates a recovery script that you download and run. This recovery script is protected with a password so that only you can execute the recovery process. When you run the recovery script, you're prompted to enter the password before you can continue. The window for downloading the recovery script is shown in figure 13.8.

When you run the recovery script, your recovery point is connected as a local filesystem on your computer. For Windows VMs, a PowerShell script is generated, and a local volume is connected, such as F:. For Linux VMs, the recovery point is mounted as a data disk, such as /dev/sdc1 in your home volume. In both cases, the recovery script clearly indicates where you can find your files.

Once you've finished restoring files from the recovery vault, you return to the Azure portal and select the Unmount Disks option. This process detaches the disks from your local computer and returns them for use in the recovery vault. Don't worry if you forget to perform this unmount process in the heat of the moment when you need to quickly restore files for a production VM! Azure automatically detaches any attached recovery points after 12 hours.

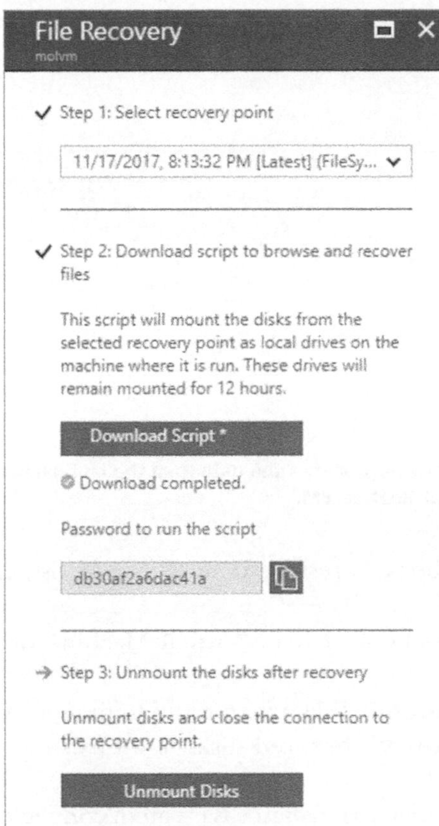

Figure 13.8 When you perform a file-level restore, you choose a recovery point to restore. A recovery script is then downloaded to your computer, which can only be executed by entering the generated password. The recovery script mounts the recovery point as a local volume on your computer. Once you've restored the files you need, you unmount the disks from your computer, which returns them for use in the recovery vault.

Complete VM restore

A complete VM restore creates a VM, connects the VM to the virtual network, and attaches all the virtual hard disks. Let's try the process for a complete VM restore. Because it's always best to test maintenance updates before you perform them for real, this restore exercise is good practice.

> **Try it now**
> To restore a complete VM, complete the following steps.

1. From your resource group, select the VM that you backed up in the previous exercise.
2. Select the Backup option from the menu at left in the VM. The backup overview should report that a recovery point has been created, as shown in figure 13.9. If not, wait a few minutes and then come back to this exercise. Or, just read through what the process entails.

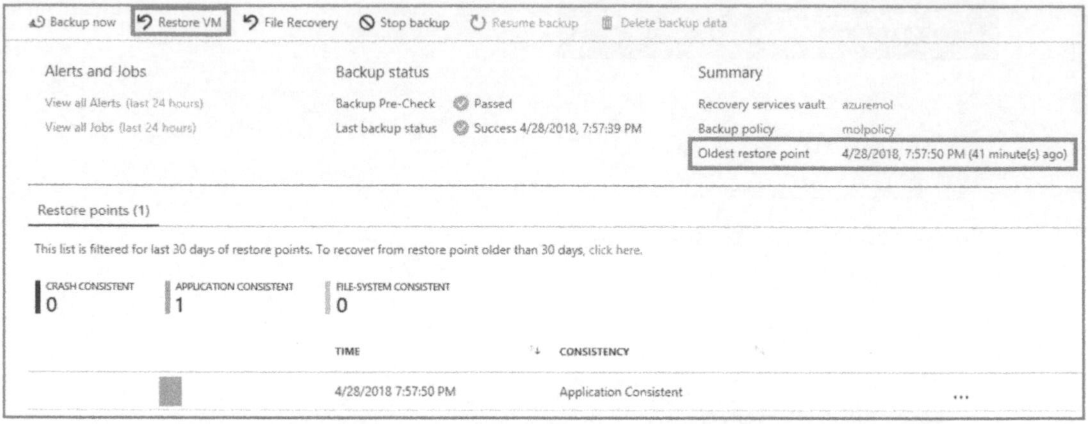

Figure 13.9 When the VM backup is complete, the overview page shows the data from the last backup and available restore points. To start the restore process, select Restore VM.

3. Select the Restore VM button. Choose a restore point from the list, and then select OK.
4. Choose a Restore Type. You can choose Create Virtual Machine or Restore Disks.

   When you choose to restore disks, the disks are restored to the specified storage account. You can then attach these restored disks to an existing VM and obtain the data you need.

   If you restore a complete VM, a new VM instance is created, connected to the virtual network, and the disks are reattached. For this exercise, choose Create Virtual Machine, as shown in figure 13.10. Provide a name for the restored VM, such as `restoredvm`, and then review the settings for virtual network and storage. In production, you typically connect the restored VM to a segregated virtual network so you don't impact production traffic.
5. Select OK and then Restore.

It takes a few minutes to connect the recovery point and create a restored VM with the previous disks attached. At this point, you could connect to the restored VM to test software upgrades or restore large amounts of data as needed.

You can also back up a web app, so this isn't just a VM approach. The process is a little different, but the concepts are the same. Moving your application model to a PaaS solution like a web app doesn't mean you can forget the basics of data backups and retention!

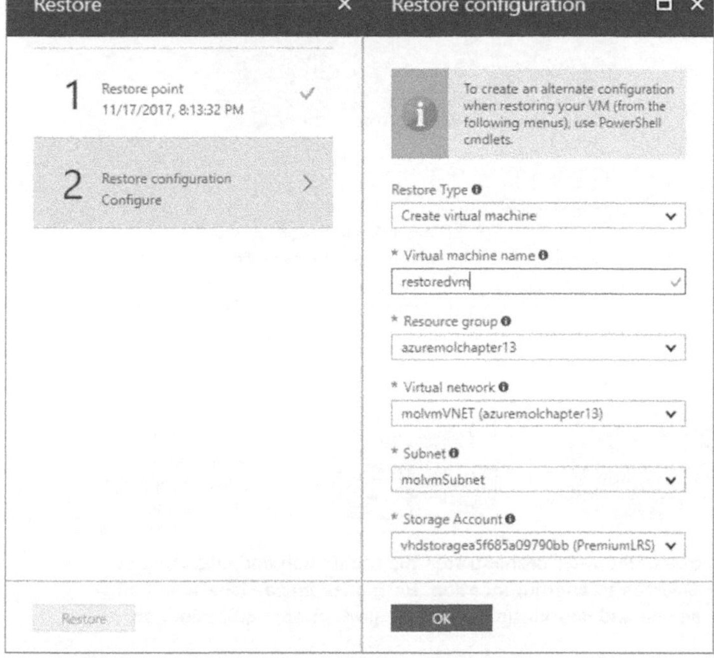

Figure 13.10 You can restore a complete VM or just the data disks. This example restores a complete VM and connects it to the same virtual network and subnet as the original VM. In practice, you should connect to a different subnet to keep the network traffic separate from production workloads.

13.2 Azure Site Recovery

Remember when we discussed Cosmos DB, and you learned that with the click of a button your data is replicated to a completely different Azure region for redundancy and fault tolerance? You can do that with entire VMs, too! Azure Site Recovery is a powerful service that can do way more than replicate VMs to a different region. Figure 13.11 outlines how Azure Site Recovery acts to orchestrate workloads between locations.

An important aspect is that Azure Site Recovery is for more than just Azure VMs—Site Recovery can be used to replicate on-premises VMware or Hyper-V VMs to Azure for disaster recovery (DR) or as part of a migration to Azure. You can also use Azure Site Recovery purely as the orchestrator to replicate on-premises VMs from one location to a secondary on-premises location.

In the same way that Azure Backup doesn't mean "only works with Azure," Azure Site Recovery doesn't mean "only replicates Azure VMs." Both Azure Backup and Azure Site Recovery can be used as hybrid solutions for backup and disaster recovery. These Azure services can be used to protect all your workloads, both on-premises and in Azure. A single reporting structure for compliance and validation can then be

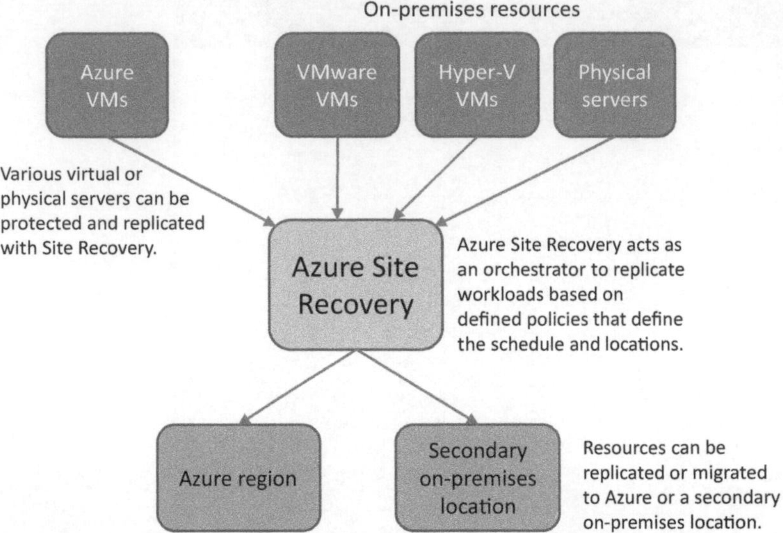

Figure 13.11 Azure Site Recovery orchestrates the replication and migration of physical or virtual resources to another location. Both on-premises locations and Azure can serve as source and destination points for protection, replication, or migration.

generated to make sure all the workloads that you think are protected are indeed safe from data loss.

Why would you use Azure Site Recovery? Two primary reasons are most common: replication and migration. Replication protects you from a complete Azure region outage. It would take a catastrophic event for an entire region to go offline, but when you work in IT, you know that anything is possible. Even availability sets and availability zones, which we talked about in chapter 7, typically only protect you from a smaller outage within an Azure region. If the entire region goes down, your app will go down. With Site Recovery, your entire application environment, including virtual network resources, is replicated to a secondary Azure region. At the click of a button, that secondary location can be brought online and made active. Traffic can then route to this secondary location and begin to serve your customers. Figure 13.12 shows a high-level overview of how Azure Site Recovery protects your environment.

The VM is just metadata that defines what the VM size is, what disks are attached, and what network resources the VM connects to. This metadata is replicated, which allows the VMs to be quickly created when a failover is initiated. The virtual disks are replicated to the recovery environment and are attached when a recovery VM is created during a failover event.

For Azure-to-Azure replication, there's no defined replication schedule. The disks replicate in almost real time. When data on the source virtual disks changes, it's replicated to the recovery environment. For hybrid workloads, where you protect

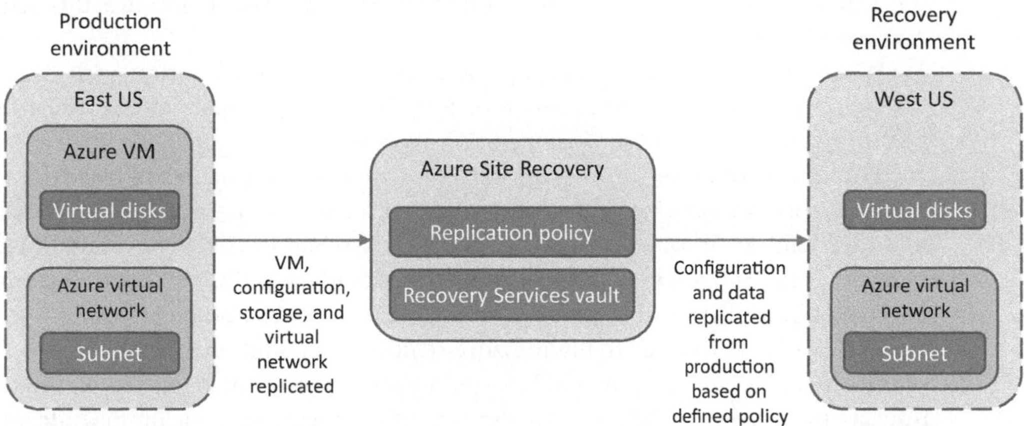

Figure 13.12 Azure Site Recovery replicates configuration, data, and virtual networks from the production environment to a recovery environment. The VMs aren't created in the recovery environment until a failover is initiated. Only the data replicates.

on-premises VMware or Hyper-V VMs, you define policies that control the replication schedule.

If we focus on Azure-to-Azure replication, how does the data replicate in near real time? A storage account cache is created in the production environment location, as shown in figure 13.13. Changes written to the production virtual disks are immediately replicated to this storage account cache. The storage account cache is then replicated to the recovery environment. This storage account cache acts as a buffer so that any replication delays to the distant recovery location don't impact performance on the production workload.

The process to configure Site Recovery for Azure-to-Azure replication is straightforward but takes some time to create all the necessary replicated resources and complete

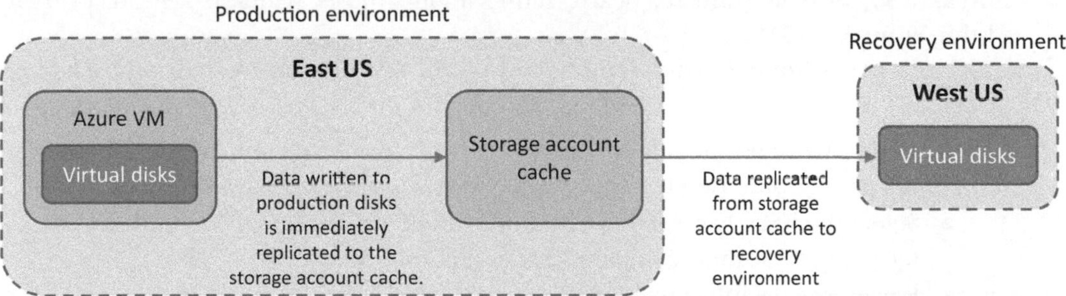

Figure 13.13 Changes on the production disks are immediately replicated to a storage account cache. This storage account cache prevents performance impacts on the production workloads as they wait to replicate changes to the remote recovery location. The changes from the storage account cache are then replicated to the remote recovery point to maintain data consistency.

the initial data replication. In the end-of-chapter lab, you configure this Azure-to-Azure replication.

What can you do with VMs replicated to a secondary location with Azure Site Recovery? For the most part, cross your fingers and hope that you don't need them! But there are a couple of scenarios when you would need them.

The first should be obvious: in the event of a major outage. If an Azure region becomes totally unavailable, such as because of a natural disaster in the area, you can initiate a failover of your resources. This tells Azure Site Recovery to create VMs in the recovery location based on the replicated VM metadata and then attach the appropriate virtual hard disks and network connections. You could also be proactive here—if a natural disaster is forecast to hit an Azure region, you could initiate a failover *before* the event takes place. This approach lets you decide when to incur some potential downtime as the resources fail over to the secondary location, typically outside primary business hours. Once the forecast event has passed in the primary Azure region, you can then fail-back your resources and continue to run as normal.

The second scenario where you may fail over is to test that the process works. In the same way backups should be regularly tested, you should test a replication and failover plan. It would be pretty embarrassing and stressful to find that when you need to bring a secondary location online, there's some misconfiguration on the virtual networks, or one of the applications doesn't fail over gracefully. Helpfully, Azure provides an option specifically for testing failover. An isolated Azure virtual network is typically used in the secondary location, and the production workloads continue to run as normal in the primary location. If you use Azure Site Recovery, be sure to regularly test the failover process!

13.3 Lab: Configuring a VM for Site Recovery

There are a number of prerequisites to configure on-premises VMware or Hyper-V replication with Azure Site Recovery. It's a great feature, both for disaster-recovery purposes and to migrate VMs to Azure. But it takes up way more than your lunch break! So, if you want to learn more about those scenarios, head over to http://mng.bz/x71V.

Let's set up Azure-to-Azure replication with the test VM you created and backed up earlier:

1. In the Azure portal, select Resource Groups from the menu at left. Choose the resource group used in the previous exercises, such as azuremolchapter13.
2. Select the VM you created in the earlier exercises, such as molvm. Choose Disaster Recovery from the menu at left in the VM window.
3. Review the defaults provided by Azure Site Recovery, as shown in figure 13.14. A resource group and a virtual network are created in the destination location. A storage account cache is created to replicate from the source virtual disks, and a Recovery Services vault and policy are created to control the replication process.

There's nothing you need to change here, although if you use this in production and have multiple VMs to protect, you'll need to review how the VMs map to existing replicated virtual networks and subnets. For this lab, click Enable Replication.

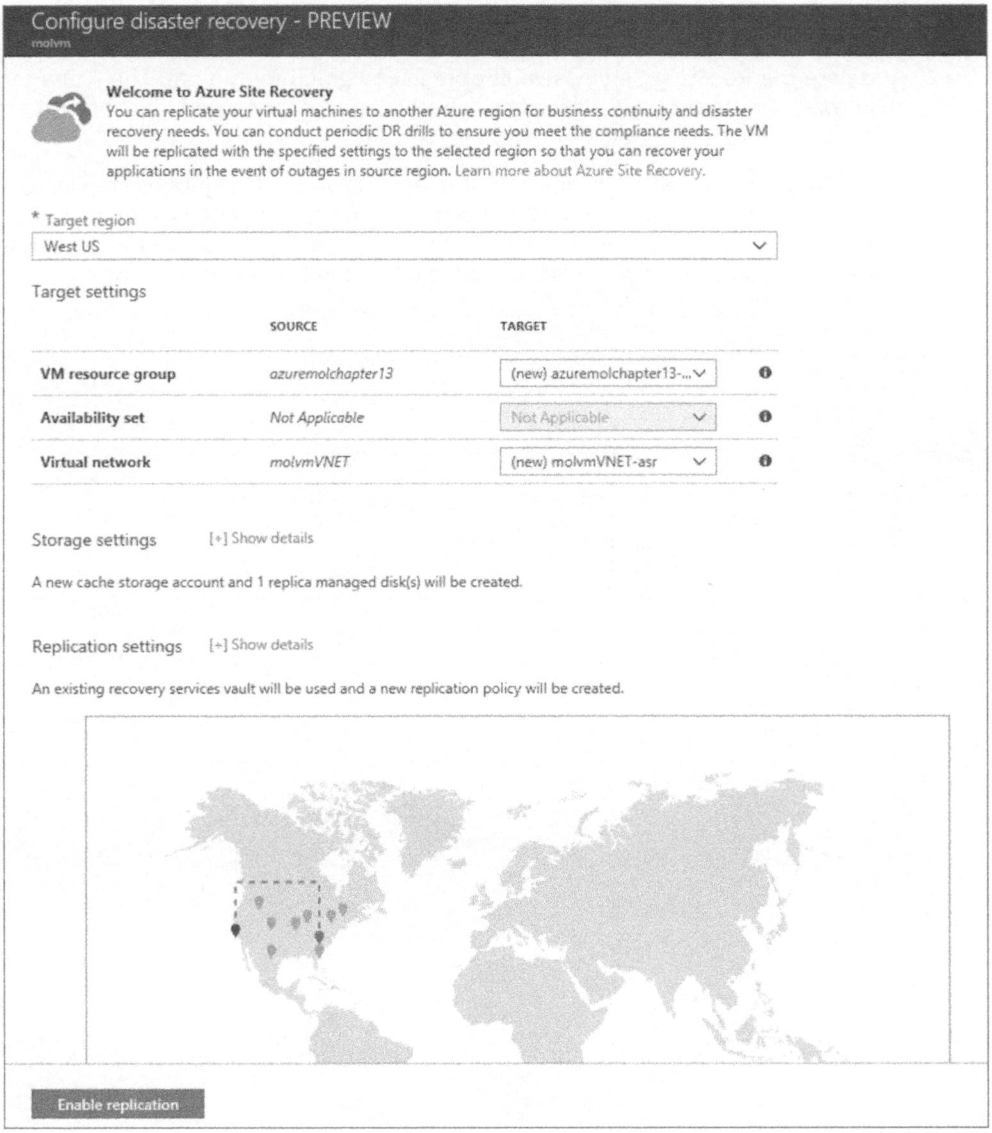

Configure disaster recovery - PREVIEW
molvm

Welcome to Azure Site Recovery
You can replicate your virtual machines to another Azure region for business continuity and disaster recovery needs. You can conduct periodic DR drills to ensure you meet the compliance needs. The VM will be replicated with the specified settings to the selected region so that you can recover your applications in the event of outages in source region. Learn more about Azure Site Recovery.

* Target region
West US

Target settings

	SOURCE	TARGET
VM resource group	*azuremolchapter13*	(new) azuremolchapter13-...
Availability set	*Not Applicable*	Not Applicable
Virtual network	*molvmVNET*	(new) molvmVNET-asr

Storage settings [+] Show details

A new cache storage account and 1 replica managed disk(s) will be created.

Replication settings [+] Show details

An existing recovery services vault will be used and a new replication policy will be created.

Enable replication

Figure 13.14 Site Recovery populates these default values automatically for all the replicated resources, vaults, and storage cache it needs. To replicate a VM, select Enable Replication.

Now, go back to work. Seriously! It takes a while to configure all the replicated resources and complete the initial data sync. Don't wait around unless your boss is fine with you taking a really long lunch break today!

Keeping your backups safe from deletion

If you have VMs that are protected with Azure Backup or Site Recovery, you can't delete the Recovery Services vault or resource group for the VM. The Azure platform knows you have active data that's backed up or replicated and prevents those resources from being deleted.

To delete protected VMs, first disable any active backup jobs or replicated VMs. When you do so, you can choose to retain the protected data or remove it. Once the VMs are no longer protected, the Recovery Services vault can be deleted as normal to keep your free Azure credits available for use in the rest of the book.

14 Data encryption

The security of your data is important. More specifically, the security of your customers' data is critical. We hardly go a week without a major company in the news after they encountered a data breach. Often, these incidents are caused by a lack of security, misconfiguration, or plain carelessness. In this digital age, it's all too easy for attackers to automate their attempts to gain access to your data. The time to recover from a security incident at an application level may be nothing compared to how long it takes the business to regain the trust of its customers if *their* data was exposed.

Azure includes encryption features that make it hard to claim you don't have the time or expertise to secure your data. In this chapter, we examine how to encrypt data stored in Azure Storage, on managed disks, or the complete VM. Entire books have been written about data encryption, and this chapter doesn't dive deep into encryption methods and considerations. Instead, you see how to enable some of the core Azure features and services to secure your data throughout the application lifecycle.

14.1 What is data encryption?

When you purchase something online, do you check that there's a little padlock icon in the address bar to indicate the website uses HTTPS? Why is it bad to send your credit details over a regular, unsecured HTTP connection? Every bit of data in a network packet that flows between devices could potentially be monitored and examined. Figure 14.1 shows how shopping online without an HTTPS connection could be bad for your credit card statement.

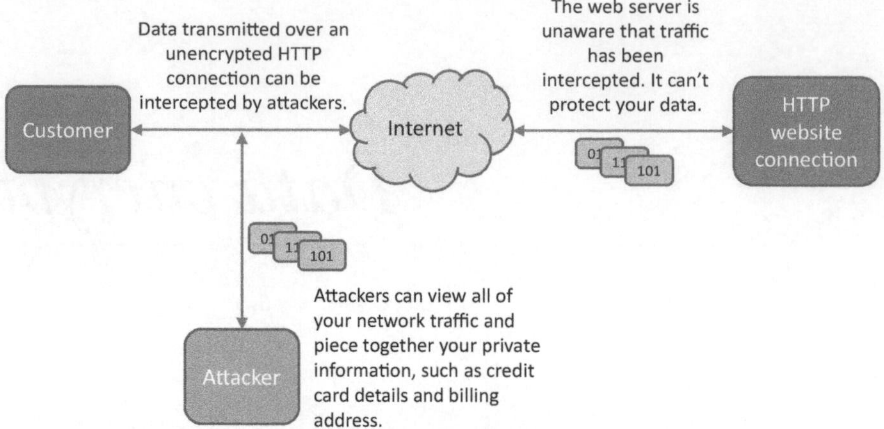

Figure 14.1 In this basic example, an attacker could intercept network traffic that's sent over an unencrypted HTTP connection. Because your data isn't encrypted, the attacker could piece together the network packets and obtain your personal and financial information. If you instead connect to the web server over an encrypted HTTPS connection, an attacker can't read the contents of the network packets and view the data.

There's no excuse for web servers to use unsecure connections. Every web app that you create in Azure automatically has a wildcard SSL certificate applied to it. An *SSL certificate* is digital component that's used to secure the web server and allow a web browser to validate the connection. A wildcard SSL certificate can be used across an entire domain, such as *.azurewebsites.net, the default domain for web apps. When you created a web app in chapter 3, you could have added https:// to the web address and started to use encrypted communications with your web apps. That's all there is to it!

Custom SSL certificates are relatively cheap and easy to implement. Through projects such as Let's Encrypt (https://letsencrypt.org), you can obtain a certificate for free and automatically configure your web server in minutes. Azure doesn't currently provide custom SSL certificates, in the same way you can't purchase a custom domain name through Azure. You need to purchase a domain name and SSL certificate from a third party and then apply them to your web apps. You can then upload and apply the SSL certificate to your web app, as shown in figure 14.2.

As you design and build applications in Azure, you should implement secure communications wherever possible. This approach helps secure the data while it's in transit, but what about when that data is written to disk? A similar process exists for disks and VMs that secures and protects your data at rest. Figure 14.3 shows how disk and VM encryption works.

azuremol - SSL certificates
App Service

Search (Ctrl+/)

Overview
Activity log
Access control (IAM)
Tags
Diagnose and solve problems

DEPLOYMENT
Quickstart
Deployment credentials
Deployment slots
Deployment options
Continuous Delivery (Preview)

SETTINGS
Application settings
Authentication / Authorization
Managed service identity
Backups
Custom domains
SSL certificates

SSL

Certificates must be associated with your application before you can use them to create a binding. You can upload a certificate you purchased externally, or import an App Service Certificate.

Import App Service Certificate
Upload Certificate

Public Certificates
You have no certificates. Upload a certificate now to get started.

Private Certificates
You have no certificates. Upload a certificate now to get started.

SSL bindings
Add binding

HOST NAME	CERTIFICATE	SSL TYPE
No results		

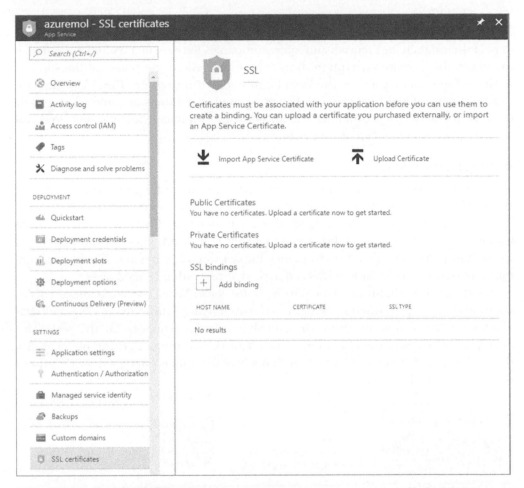

Figure 14.2 You can easily upload and apply a custom SSL certificate to your web apps. A default wildcard certificate is already available at https://yourwebapp.azurewebsites.net; but if you use a custom domain name, you need to purchase and apply a custom SSL certificate.

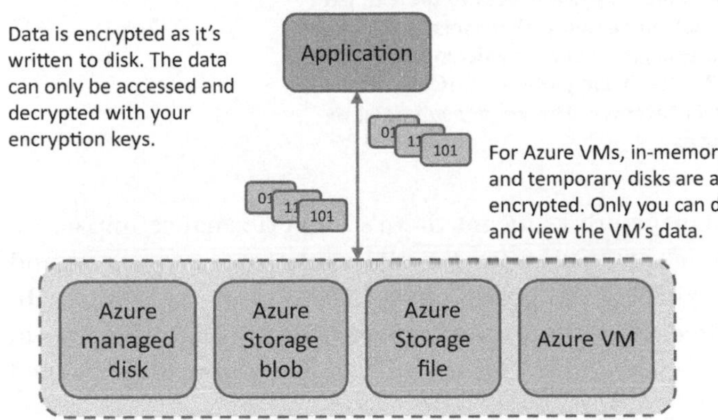

Figure 14.3 When you encrypt your data, only you can decrypt and view the contents. If an attacker were to gain access to a virtual disk or individual files, they wouldn't be able to decrypt the contents. Encryption methods can be combined: customers can connect to your web over HTTPS, you can force traffic to storage accounts to be over HTTPS, and you can then encrypt the data that's written to disk.

These simplified examples of data encryption in Azure hopefully motivate you to implement encryption as you design and build applications in Azure. Most customers expect their data to be secured, and many companies have regulatory and compliance mandates that require encryption. Don't think only about the potential fines to the business for a data breach, or the loss of customer trust. Consider the risk of the customers' personal and financial data being exposed, and how that could impact their daily lives. You probably don't like the idea of your own data being exposed, so do all you can to protect the data of your customers.

14.2 Encryption at rest

If data encryption is so important, how do you use it in Azure? Just keep doing what you've already learned in this book! Right at the start, I mentioned that all of your VMs should use managed disks, right? There are many good reasons for that, one of which is security. A managed disk is automatically encrypted. There's nothing for you to configure, and there's no performance impact when it's enabled. There's no opt-out here—your data is automatically encrypted at rest with managed disks.

What does it mean for the data to be *encrypted at rest*? When you use managed disks, your data is encrypted when it's written to the underlying Azure storage. The data that resides on the temporary disks, or data that exists in memory on the VM, isn't encrypted. Only once the OS or data disk's data *rests* on the underlying physical disk does it become encrypted. Figure 14.4 shows how the data is encrypted as it's written to a managed disk.

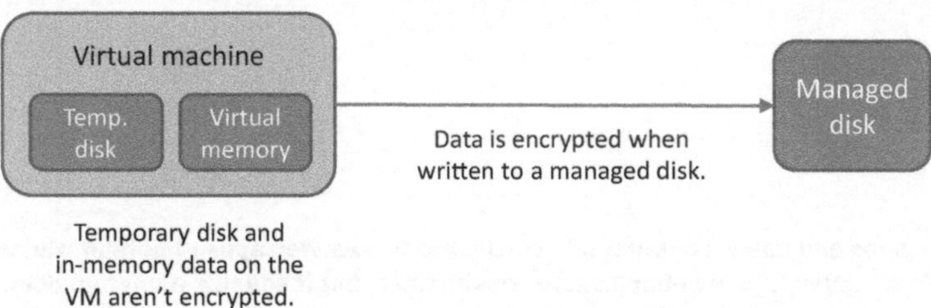

Figure 14.4 As data is written to a managed disk, it's encrypted. In-memory data on the VM, or data on temporary disks local to the VM, isn't encrypted unless the entire VM is enabled for encryption, which we look at later in this chapter. The automatic encryption of data written to managed disks causes no overhead to the VM. The Azure platform performs the encryption operation on the underlying storage. The VM doesn't need to handle any encrypt/decrypt processes.

This encryption at rest for managed disks means there's no performance impact on the VMs. There's no additional processing for the VM to perform to encrypt and decrypt the data, so all the available CPU power can be used to run applications. In typical VM encryption scenarios, the VM uses a certain amount of compute power to process and manage the data encryption. The trade-off to the automatic managed disk encryption is that only the OS and data disks are secured. Potentially, other in-memory or temporary disk data on the VM could be exposed.

Microsoft manages the digital encryption keys within the Azure platform with the automatic encryption of managed disks. This does create another trade-off in that you can automatically encrypt your data without the need to create, manage, rotate, or revoke keys, but you have to trust in Microsoft to protect those keys.

14.3 Storage Service Encryption

Automatic managed disk encryption is great, but what if you use Azure Storage for blob or file storage? Azure Storage Service Encryption (SSE) lets you encrypt data at the storage account level. Data is encrypted as it's written to the account. Microsoft again handles the encryption keys, so no management overhead or configuration is required. The Azure platform abstracts the key generation and management for you. If you prefer, you can create and use your own encryption keys, with a little additional management overhead.

The goal with both automatic managed disk encryption and SSE is to make it as easy as possible for you to encrypt your data and spend more time on how to design, build, and run your applications. Figure 14.5 shows how SSE protects your data and can also force secure communications when data is in transit.

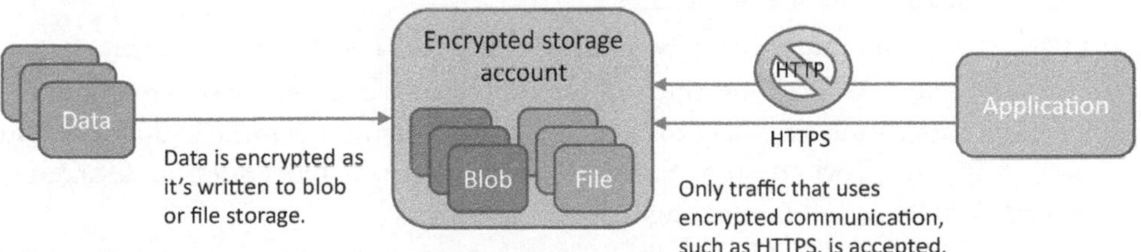

Figure 14.5 When you enable SSE, Azure blobs and files are encrypted as the data is written to disk. Azure tables and queues aren't encrypted. For additional data security, you can force all communications with a Storage account to use secure communication protocols, such as HTTPS. This protects the data in transit until the moment it's encrypted on disk.

> **Forcing storage traffic to use secure transfers**
>
> Along with enabling SSE, you can force all storage requests and transfers to use a secure communication method. This setting forces all REST API calls to use HTTPS, and all Azure file connections that don't enable encryption, such as older versions of the SMB protocol, to be dropped.
>
> Azure SDKs, such as the Python examples we examined in chapter 4, can use encrypted connections. The reference docs for each language-specific SDK provides guidance on how to implement secure communications.

(continued)
The use of secure communications should be built into applications from the start. It may cause problems to enable secure communications on an existing application if some components weren't originally configured appropriately. At the very least, test secure communications for an existing application in a development environment first.

One minor catch with SSE is that if you enable encryption on an existing storage account that already contains data, only new data written to the storage account is encrypted. If you plan your application needs carefully, enable SSE when you create the storage account to ensure that all data then written to the account is encrypted.

Try it now

To create a storage account and enable both encryption and secure communications, complete the following steps.

1. Open the Azure portal, and select the Cloud Shell icon from the top menu.
2. Create a resource group. Provide a name, such as `azuremolchapter14`, and a location, such as `eastus`:

   ```
   az group create --name azuremolchapter14 --location eastus
   ```

3. Create a storage account with `az storage account create`. Provide a unique name, such as `azuremolstorage`, and enter the resource group that you created in the previous step. Enter a storage account type, such as `Standard_LRS` for locally redundant storage.

   To enable SSE, use the `--encryption-services blob` parameter. To force secure communications, set `--https-only` to `true`:

   ```
   az storage account create \
     --name azuremolstorage \
     --resource-group azuremolchapter14 \
     --sku standard_lrs \
     --encryption-services blob \
     --https-only true
   ```

4. Verify that the storage account is encrypted and enabled for secure communications. Query for `enableHttpsTrafficOnly` and the encryption parameters:

   ```
   az storage account show \
       --name azuremolstorage \
       --resource-group azuremolchapter14 \
       --query [enableHttpsTrafficOnly,encryption]
   ```

   The output is similar to the following:

   ```
   [
     true,
     {
   ```

```
      "keySource": "Microsoft.Storage",
      "keyVaultProperties": null,
      "services": {
        "blob": {
          "enabled": true,
          "lastEnabledTime": "2017-11-21T04:41:05.127074+00:00"
        },
        "file": {
          "enabled": true,
          "lastEnabledTime": "2017-11-21T04:41:05.127074+00:00"
        },
        "queue": null,
        "table": null
      }
    }
  ]
```

14.4 VM encryption

The automatic encryption of Azure managed disks helps provide a level of VM security. For a comprehensive approach to VM data security, you can encrypt the VM itself. This process involves more than encrypting the underlying virtual hard disks. The OS disk and all attached data disks, along with the temporary disk, are encrypted. The VM memory is also encrypted to further reduce the attack surface. You use two new Azure components to encrypt a VM:

- *Azure Key Vault* stores encryption keys used to encrypt VMs.
- *Azure Active Directory service principals* control access to the encryption keys.

Figure 14.6 shows the VM encryption overview process.

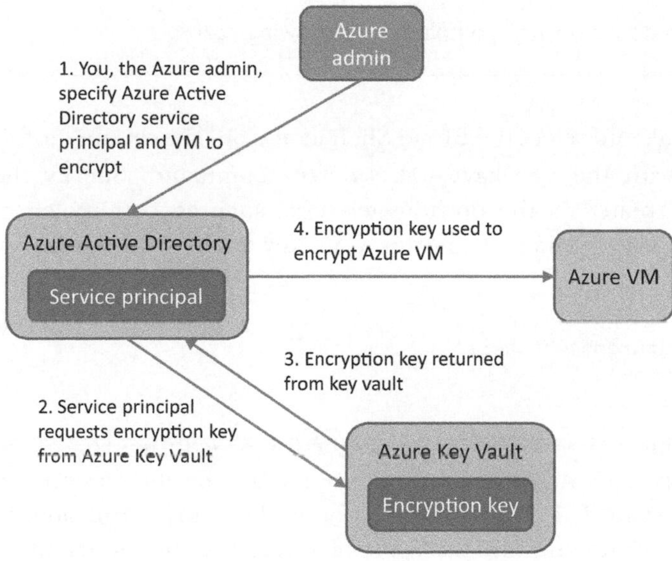

Figure 14.6 When you encrypt a VM, you specify a service principal and encryption key to use. The credentials you provide for the service principal are used to authenticate against Azure Key Vault and request the specified key. If your credentials are valid, the encryption key is returned and used to encrypt the VM.

One advantage of encrypting the entire VM is that you manage the encryption keys. These encryption keys are securely stored in Azure Key Vault, and you can choose between using software- or hardware-generated keys. You control these keys, so you can define access to them and use role-based access controls (RBACs) and auditing to track usage. You can also rotate the encryption keys on a defined schedule, much like changing your password every 60 or 90 days. These additional controls and management tasks for encryption keys add some management overhead but provide maximum flexibility for securing your data, and they may be required for certain regulatory purposes. Let's look a little more at Azure Key Vault and Azure Active Directory service principals.

14.4.1 Storing encryption keys in Azure Key Vault

We spend the next chapter on Azure Key Vault, but I wanted to show you the power of data encryption and VM encryption first. As a quick overview, Azure Key Vault is a digital vault that allows you to securely store encryption keys, SSL certificates, and secrets such as passwords. For redundancy, key vaults are replicated across Azure regions. This replication protects your keys and secrets, and ensures that they're always available for use.

Only you have access to your key vaults. You generate and store objects in key vaults and then define who has access to those vaults. Microsoft manages the underlying Key Vault service but has no access to the contents of the vaults. This security boundary means when you encrypt your data in Azure, you are the only one who can decrypt and view it.

> **Try it now**
> To create a key vault and encryption key, complete the following steps.

1. Open the Azure portal, and select the Cloud Shell icon from the top menu.
2. Create a key vault with the `az keyvault create` command. Specify the resource group you created in the previous exercise, such as azuremolchapter14, and then provide a unique name for your key vault, such as `azuremolkeyvault`:

```
az keyvault create \
  --resource-group azuremolchapter14 \
  --name azuremolkeyvault \
  --enabled-for-disk-encryption
```

Let's pause and think about why you add a parameter for `--enabled-for-disk-encryption`. When you encrypt a VM, the Azure platform needs to be able to start and decrypt the VM so that it can run. The Azure platform doesn't have any permissions to access that data, and Microsoft doesn't have access to view and use those encryption keys for anything other than starting a VM. When you enable a key vault for disk encryption, you grant permissions for Azure to access the key vault and use the encryption key associated with a VM.

Again, Microsoft doesn't have access to these keys or your data, only the ability to start your encrypted VM. It's pretty hard to do much with an encrypted VM when it can't boot. Figure 14.7 shows how the Azure platform uses the encryption key to start an encrypted VM.

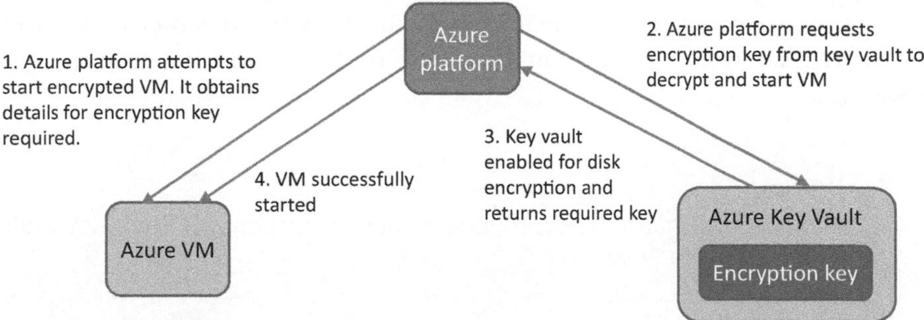

Figure 14.7 When a key vault is enabled for disk encryption, it grants permission for the Azure platform to request and use the encryption key to successfully start an encrypted VM.

Keys can be created and stored in software, or they can be stored in hardware security modules (HSMs) for additional security. For many purposes, software keys work great, although you may have security mandates that require the use of HSMs. We discuss this more in the next chapter.

3. To create a key, specify the vault you created in the previous step, such as azuremolkeyvault, and then provide a key name, such as `azuremolencryptionkey`:

```
az keyvault key create \
  --vault-name azuremolkeyvault \
  --name azuremolencryptionkey \
  --protection software
```

14.4.2 Controlling access to vaults and keys with Azure Active Directory

Chapter 6 looked at how you secure and control access to resources with role-based access controls (RBACs). These controls let you specify users and groups, and define granular permissions as to what they can do with each resource. At the heart of those controls is Azure Active Directory (AAD).

AAD could fill an entire book. It could probably fill an entire series of books! It builds on the enterprise-proven identity and management solution, Active Directory. With AAD, you can create and manage user or group permissions to resources in Azure, Office 365, or a hybrid scenario for on-premises file shares or network resources such as printers.

It's hard to cover AAD in a single chapter of a *Month of Lunches* series book. There's so much to cover that I'd almost certainly leave you wanting more. Hybrid scenarios with an on-premises Active Directory environment, multifactor authentication for cloud applications, and user and group management in AAD are specific administration tasks that only a small number of Azure admins may use. There's a wealth of excellent documentation at https://docs.microsoft.com/azure/active-directory if you want to dive into AAD.

For now, you want to use AAD to authenticate with Azure Key Vault and access encryption keys. To do this, you use a special type of user account called a *service principal*. A service principal can't be used to log in to a VM with a username and password like a regular user account, but it can be used to authenticate with services and resources.

Try it now

To create an Azure Active Directory service principal for use with Azure Key Vault, complete the following steps.

1. Open the Azure portal, and select the Cloud Shell icon from the top menu.
2. Create a default service principal, and view the ID and secret (a password). You use these credentials to authenticate against Azure resources, such as your key vault. This service principal can be used for resources across your entire subscription. As with network resources, in the real world you should plan the long-lived key vaults you'll need, create service principals that are assigned to them, and then use these credentials with your applications:

```
az ad sp create-for-rbac \
  --query "{spn_id:appId,secret:password}"
```

   The sample output from this command is as follows. Make a note of your own values, because you need them in the remaining steps:

```
{
  "secret": "2575580b-3610-46b2-b3db-182d8741fd43",
  "spn_id": "4d1ab719-bd14-48fd-95d0-3aba9500b12f"
}
```

3. Grant your service principal access to the key vault with permissions to wrap, or use, the encryption key. Specify your key vault name, such as `azuremolkeyvault`, and then the SPN provided in the output from the preceding step:

```
az keyvault set-policy \
  --name azuremolkeyvault \
  --spn 4d1ab719-bd14-48fd-95d0-3aba9500b12f    \
  --key-permissions wrapKey   \
  --secret-permissions set
```

14.4.3 Encrypting an Azure VM

Figure 14.8 repeats figure 14.6, to see how you've created an AAD service principal with permissions to use an encryption key that was created in an Azure key vault. This service principal and encryption key can be used to encrypt many VMs. One approach is to use the same encryption key for all the VMs within a given application deployment. This minimizes the overhead of key management and, if you use virtual machine scale sets, allows you to autoscale the number of VM instances without the need to generate encryption keys each time. In the end-of-chapter lab, you encrypt a single VM, although the same process can work with a scale set. Especially when you work with larger, autoscaling applications, be sure to design and build in security features.

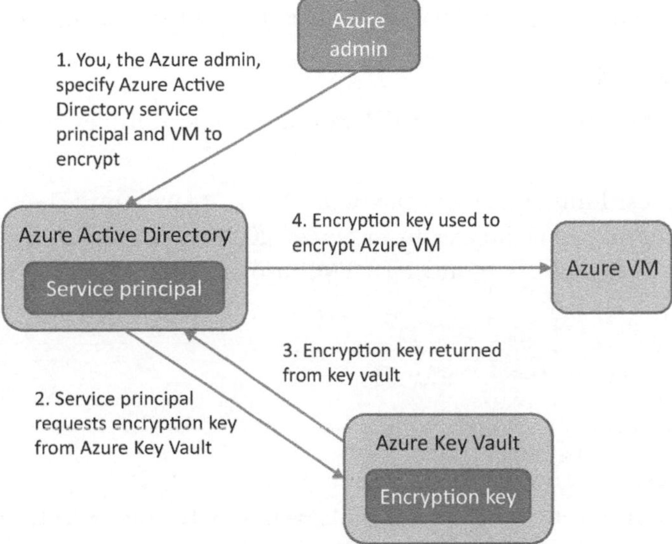

Figure 14.8 (Repeats figure 14.6) You can now use your AAD service principal to request the use of an encryption key stored in a key vault. This encryption key can be used to encrypt a VM. You create and encrypt this VM in the end-of-chapter lab.

When you encrypt a VM, an Azure VM extension is installed. The extension controls the encryption of the OS disk, temporary disk, any attached data disks, and in-memory data, as shown in figure 14.9. For Windows VMs, the BitLocker encryption mechanism is used. For Linux VMs, dm-crypt is used to process the encryption. The VM extension can then report back on the status of encryption and decrypt the VM as desired.

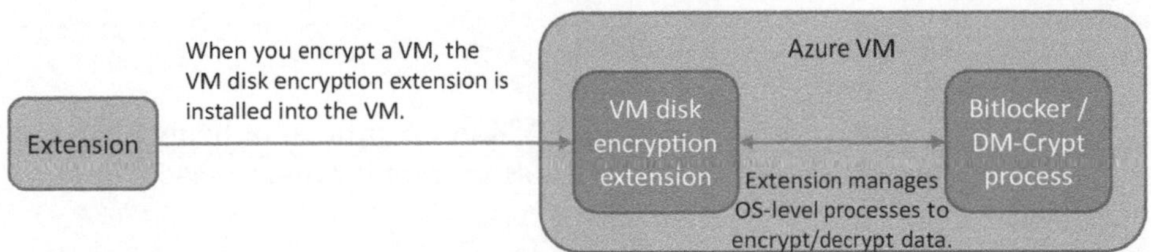

Figure 14.9 When you encrypt a VM, the Azure disk encryption extension is installed. This extension manages the use of BitLocker on Windows VMs or dm-crypt on Linux VMs, to perform the data encryption on your VM. The extension is also used when you query the encryption status for a VM.

Because the VM disk encryption extension relies on BitLocker or dm-crypt, there are some limitations around the use of VM encryption. Most Azure Marketplace images support disk encryption, although some restrictions exist on VM sizes that support encryption or encryption of connected network file shares such as Azure files. For the most comprehensive information on supported limitations and considerations for VM encryption, read the latest Azure docs at http://mng.bz/NjPB.

This chapter has provided a quick intro to the data security and encryption features in Azure. Automatic encryption for managed disks and SSE doesn't require much configuration, so there's no real barrier to prevent you from using them.

14.5 Lab: Encrypting a VM

Let's see all this in action by encrypting a VM with the encryption key you stored in your key vault:

1 Create a VM. Most Linux images in the Azure Marketplace support encryption, as do the Windows Server images from Server 2008 R2 and later. To make it quick and easy, create an Ubuntu LTS VM, just as you have for most of this book:

```
az vm create \
  --resource-group azuremolchapter14 \
  --name molvm \
  --image ubuntults \
  --admin-username azuremol \
  --generate-ssh-keys
```

2 Enable encryption on the VM. Provide your own SPN ID and secret, which was output earlier, to create your service principal:

```
az vm encryption enable \
  --resource-group azuremolchapter14 \
  --name molvm \
  --disk-encryption-keyvault azuremolkeyvault \
  --key-encryption-key azuremolencryptionkey \
  --aad-client-id 4d1ab719-bd14-48fd-95d0-3aba9500b12f \
  --aad-client-secret 2575580b-3610-46b2-b3db-182d8741fd43
```

It takes a few minutes to install the Azure VM disk encryption extension and begin the process of encrypting the VM.

3 Once encryption has started, monitor the progress and be ready to restart the VM to complete the encryption process. View the status as follows:

```
az vm encryption show \
  --resource-group azuremolchapter14 \
  --name molvm
```

Here's some example output of a VM in the process of being encrypted. At the start, the status for `osDisk` reports as `EncryptionInProgress`:

```
{
      "dataDisk": "NotMounted",
      "osDisk": "EncryptionInProgress",
      "osDiskEncryptionSettings": {
```

```
            "diskEncryptionKey": {
                 "secretUrl":
➥"https://azuremolkeyvault.vault.azure.net/secrets/[CA]
➥e77098c9-8c8b-4c1b-9181-[CA]
➥3c6e3c1d865b/c6a38e90212a453f94027ebca75e5d87",
           "sourceVault": {
                "id":
➥"/subscriptions/guid/resourceGroups/
➥azuremolchapter14/providers/Microsoft.KeyVault/
➥vaults/azuremolkeyvault"
           }
            },
            "enabled": true,
            "keyEncryptionKey": {
            "keyUrl":
➥"https://azuremolkeyvault.vault.azure.net/keys/
➥azuremolencryptionkey/5be845a38dd443949bdc963dba7c84b4",
               "sourceVault": {
               "id":
➥"/subscriptions/guid/resourceGroups/
➥azuremolchapter14/providers/Microsoft.KeyVault/
➥vaults/azuremolkeyvault"
               }
            }
  },
  "osType": "Linux",
  "progressMessage": "OS disk encryption started"
}
```

It can take a while to complete the disk encryption, so this may be another good lab exercise to come back to in an hour or so—unless you want a long lunch break! Hey, I'm not your boss, but it gets boring looking at the same encryption status message.

4 When the encryption status reports as `VMRestartPending`, restart the VM:

```
az vm restart --resource-group azuremolchapter14 --name molvm
```

You can then check the status of VM encryption again with `az vm encryption show` to confirm that the VM reports as Encrypted.

Remember your housecleaning chores

These last two end-of-chapter labs didn't take long to complete, but they may have taken a while to finish. Don't forget to go back and delete resources when you're done with them.

In chapter 13, remember that you need to disable Azure Backup or Site Recovery protection before you can delete the Recovery Services vault and resource group. Make sure you go back and clean up those lab resources before they start to use up too many of your free Azure credits.

15 Securing information with Azure Key Vault

Almost every week, there's news of a cybersecurity incident with a major company. In the same way you've used various forms of automation to grow or replicate your applications and data, attackers automate their own actions. It's unlikely that a single person will manually try to compromise the security of your systems. This concept makes it difficult to defend your systems 24 hours a day, 7 days a week, 365 days a year (okay, or 366 days!).

Chapter 14 discussed how to encrypt your data and VMs. This is a great first step, and we briefly looked at how to create and use encryption keys stored with the Azure Key Vault service. Secure data, such as keys, secrets, and certificates, is best stored in a digital vault like a key vault, which can centrally manage, issue, and audit the use of your critical credentials and data. As your applications and services need access to different resources, they can automatically request, retrieve, and use these keys, secrets, and credentials. In this chapter, you learn why and how to create a secure key vault, control access, and then store and retrieve secrets and certificates.

15.1 Securing information in the cloud

As applications become more complex and the risk of cyberattacks grows, security becomes a critical part of how you design and run your services. Especially in the cloud and with internet-facing applications, making sure you minimize the risk of unauthorized data access should be one of the main design areas you focus on.

There's no point having the greatest pizza store in the world if customers don't trust you with their payment details or personal information.

A common way to provide security for applications and services is through digital keys, secrets, and certificates, as shown in figure 15.1. Rather than using a username and password that must be manually entered time and again—or, maybe worse, written in an unencrypted configuration file—you use a digital vault to store these secure credentials and data. When an application or service requires access, they request the specific key or secret they need, and an audit trail is also created to trace any possible security misuse or breach.

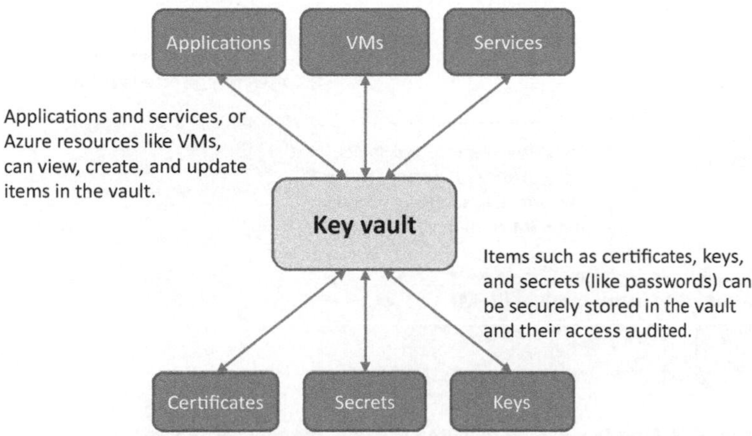

Figure 15.1 Azure Key Vault provides a secure way to store digital information such as certificates, keys, and secrets. These secure items can then be accessed directly by your applications and services, or Azure resources such as VMs. With minimal human interaction, you can centrally distribute secure credentials and certificates across your application environments.

When designed and implemented correctly, these digital vaults are almost fully automated and secure. Services can request a new digital certificate, be issued one that's then securely stored in the vault, and use it to authorize themselves against other application components. Servers can configure software by retrieving secrets such as passwords from the digital vault and then installing application components, without the credentials being stored in a text-based configuration file. An application administrator can centrally manage all the secrets, keys, and certificates for a service, and update them regularly as needed.

Azure Key Vault provides all these digital security features and allows you to tightly control which users and resources can access the secure data. Key vaults can be securely replicated for redundancy and improved application performance, and integrate with common Azure resources such as VMs, web apps, and Azure Storage accounts.

15.1.1 Software vaults and hardware security modules

Before we jump into a hands-on example of how to create and use a key vault, it's important to understand the way your secure information is stored in a vault. As shown in figure 15.2, all the keys, secrets, and certificates in a key vault are stored in a hardware security module (HSM). These devices aren't unique in Azure—they're industry-wide hardware devices that provide a high level of security for any data stored on them.

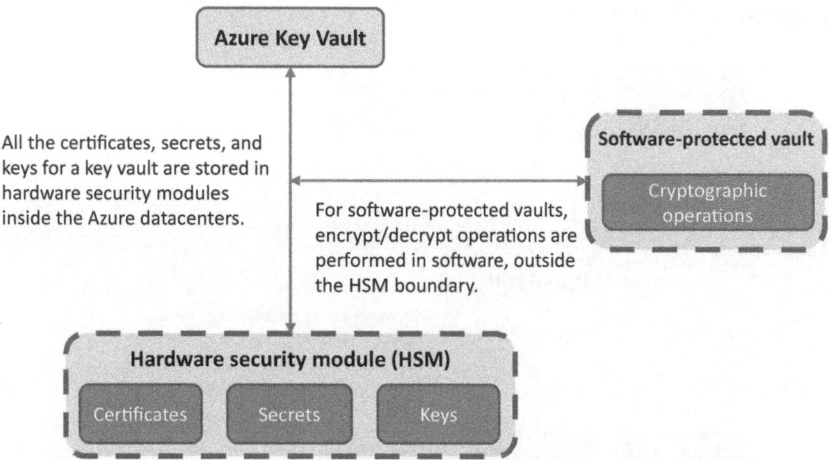

Figure 15.2 Azure Key Vault is a logical resource in Azure, but any certificates, secrets, and keys are stored in a hardware security module. For development or test scenarios, a software-protected vault can be used, which then performs any cryptograph operations—such as encrypting or decrypting data—in software, and not in hardware on the HSM. For production, you should use an HSM-protected vault, where all the processing is done on hardware.

There are currently two different types of key vault you can use: software-protected and HSM-protected. It may be confusing, which is why I want to clear up the difference before we get started:

- A *software-protected vault* stores keys, secrets, and certificates in an HSM, but any cryptographic operations that are required to encrypt or decrypt its contents are performed by the Azure platform in software. Software-protected vaults are great for development and test scenarios, although you may decide that production workloads require a slightly more secure way to perform the cryptographic operations.
- An *HSM-protected vault* again stores keys, secrets, and certificates in an HSM, but cryptographic operations that are required to encrypt or decrypt its contents are performed directly on the HSM. You can also generate your own secure keys in an on-premises HSM and then import them to Azure. There are some

additional tools and processes to follow, but this way you ensure that you completely control the keys and that they never leave the HSM boundary.

To maximize the security and integrity of your data, hardware-protected vaults are the preferred approach for production workloads.

Regardless of which type of vault you use, it's important to remember that all of your data is stored securely on a Federal Information Processing Standard (FIPS) 140–2 Level 2 validated (at a minimum) HSM, and that Microsoft can't access or retrieve your keys. There's an additional cost for HSM-protected vaults, so as with anything in Azure and cloud computing, balance the cost versus the risk of your data being compromised.

15.1.2 Creating a key vault and secret

A digital vault sounds great, but you may be a little unsure how to make use of the power that Azure Key Vault provides. Let's build an example of a basic server that runs a database such as MySQL Server, as shown in figure 15.3.

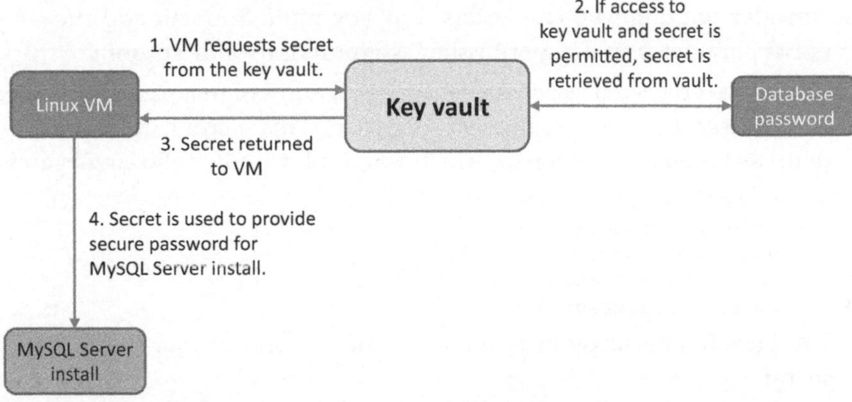

Figure 15.3 In the next few exercises, you'll build an example of a secret stored in a key vault that can be used as the database password for a MySQL Server install. A VM is created that has permissions to request the secret from the key vault. The retrieved secret is then used to automatically enter a secure credential during the application install process.

At the start of this book, one of the first exercises was to create a VM and then install the LAMP web server stack. You were likely prompted for a MySQL Server password, or a blank password was automatically used. Now that you know all about key vaults, you can automatically retrieve a password from the vault and dynamically use it to install and configure the server.

Try it now

To create a key vault and add a secret, complete the following steps.

1 Open the Azure portal, and then launch the Cloud Shell. Create a resource group, such as `azuremolchapter15`:

```
az group create --name azuremolchapter15 --location eastus
```

2 Create a key vault, such as `azuremol`, and enable it for deployment so that you can use the vault to inject keys and certificates into a VM:

```
az keyvault create \
  --resource-group azuremolchapter15 \
  --name azuremol \
  --enable-soft-delete \
  --enabled-for-deployment
```

By default, your Azure user account is assigned full permissions to the key vault. For these exercises, this is fine, although as a security best practice you should consider limiting who can access your key vault. You can add the `--no-self-perms` parameter to skip permission assignment to your account.

3 Create a secret, such as `databasepassword`, and assign a password value, such as `SecureP@ssw0rd` (yep, really secure, right?) This secret can be used as the credentials for a database server, which you deploy in the following exercises:

```
az keyvault secret set \
  --name databasepassword \
  --vault-name azuremol \
  --description "Database password" \
  --value "SecureP@ssw0rd"
```

4 You have full permissions to the key vault, so you can view the contents of your secret:

```
az keyvault secret show \
  --name databasepassword \
  --vault-name azuremol
```

From a management perspective, you can also perform common actions such as backing up and restoring, downloading, updating, and deleting items stored in a key vault. One additional property that you set when the key vault was created is the option to `--enable-soft-delete`. If your applications and services can't retrieve the secrets they need from the key vault, you could have a pretty large application outage to deal with! A key vault can store metadata for secrets for up to 90 days after they're truly deleted, which allows you to recover data that's incorrectly or maliciously deleted.

5 Delete the key you just created to simulate a mistake, or possibly someone with malicious intent:

```
az keyvault secret delete \
  --name databasepassword \
  --vault-name azuremol
```

6 Recover the secret so that you can continue to use the database password with your application and services:

```
az keyvault secret recover \
  --name databasepassword \
  --vault-name azuremol
```

If you truly want to remove a secret, there's also the option to purge a deleted secret. This option permanently removes the secret without waiting for the default 90-day recovery period to elapse.

Feel free to use `az keyvault secret show` again to view the information on your secret and confirm that the password you stored is there. Now let's move on to see how a VM can access a key vault and use the secret to install the MySQL Server.

15.2 Managed service identities

The ability to use Azure Key Vault to store secrets or keys is great, but how do you access these secrets? The Azure CLI or Azure PowerShell can access the information stored in a key vault, but it's often more convenient to allow your VMs or applications to directly retrieve secrets or keys when they need them. One way to do this is with a managed service identity (MSI), as shown in figure 15.4.

An MSI (not to be confused with the .msi Windows Installer package to install applications) lets you create a special kind of account, or identity, that identifies a VM resource. If you've used a directory service such as Active Directory, a computer

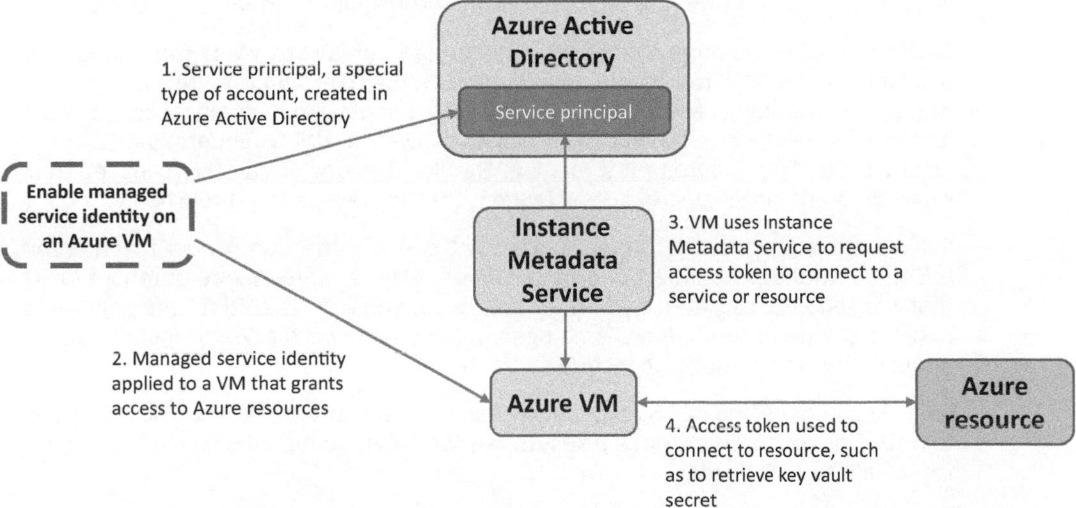

Figure 15.4 When you create a managed service identity for a VM, a service principal is created in Azure Active Directory. This service principal is a special type of account that can be used for resources to authenticate themselves. This VM then uses the Instance Metadata Service endpoint to makes requests for access to resources. The endpoint connects to AAD to request access tokens when the VM needs to request data from other services. When an access token is returned, it can be used to request access to Azure resources, such as a key vault.

account is often used to identify and grant access to various network resources that a computer needs. You don't create and use regular user accounts for this type of authentication, which improves security: you can grant a restrictive set of permissions just to a computer rather than also needing to worry about user permissions and shared folder access, for example.

An MSI is like a computer account, but it's stored in Azure Active Directory (AAD). The identity, called a *service principal*, is unique to each VM and can be used to assign permissions to other Azure resources, such as an Azure Storage account or key vault. The VM has permissions to access those resources, so you can script tasks (such as with Azure Automation, which we explore in chapter 18) that require no user intervention or prompts for usernames and passwords. The VMs authenticate themselves, and the Azure platform authorizes access to their assigned resources.

Let's see how you can use an MSI to request the `databasepassword` secret from a key vault. Once the VM can retrieve the secret, the password can be used to automatically install a MySQL database server. With a key vault and MSIs, you can run a couple of commands to retrieve the secret from the key vault, run the MySQL Server installer, and automatically provide the secure password.

Azure Instance Metadata Service

A VM that's enabled with an MSI uses a REST endpoint through the Instance Metadata Service (IMDS) to request an access token from AAD that it can then use to request data from Azure Key Vault. But what is the Instance Metadata Service?

IMDS is a REST endpoint that's only accessible internally to VMs. The endpoint is available at the non-routable address of 169.254.169.254. A VM can make a request to the IMDS endpoint to retrieve information about itself, such as Azure region or resource group name. This ability allows the VM to understand how and where in the Azure platform it's running. The IMDS endpoint can be accessed from many different languages, including Python, C#, Go, Java, and PowerShell.

For maintenance events, the IMDS endpoint can also be queried so that the VM becomes aware of a pending update or reboot event. Any pre-update or reboot tasks that are required can then be carried out. Because IMDS is a REST endpoint on a non-routable IP address, there's no agent or extension for the VM to install, and no network security or routing concerns.

For MSI purposes, the IMDS endpoint is used to relay the request for an access token to AAD. This approach provides a secure way for VMs to request access without needing to talk to AAD directly.

> **Try it now**
> To create a VM with an MSI, complete the following steps.

1 Create an Ubuntu VM. Provide your resource group, such as `azuremolchapter15`, and a name for the VM, such as `molvm`. A user account named azuremol is created, and the SSH keys that you've used in previous chapters are added to the VM:

```
az vm create \
  --resource-group azuremolchapter15 \
  --name molvm \
  --image ubuntults \
  --admin-username azuremol \
  --generate-ssh-keys
```

2 As a security best practice, you shouldn't allow accounts to access all the resources across your entire Azure subscription. Especially for MSIs, only grant the minimum amount of permissions needed. For this exercise, scope access to only your resource group, such as azuremolchapter15. You set the scope by querying for the ID of the resource group with `--query id`. This ID is then assigned to a variable named `scope`:

```
scope=$(az group show --resource-group azuremolchapter15
➥--query id --output tsv)
```

3 Create an MSI for the VM with the reader role so that it can only read resources, not make changes to them. Scope the identity to the resource group. The variable you created in the previous step that contains the resource group ID is provided:

```
az vm identity assign \
  --resource-group azuremolchapter15 \
  --name molvm \
  --role reader \
  --scope $scope
```

The output is similar to the following. Make a note of your own `systemAssignedIdentity`, because it's used to identify your VM and set permissions in the next step:

```
{
  "role": "reader",
  "scope":"/subscriptions/8fa5cd83-7fbb-431a-af16-
➥4a20dede8802/resourceGroups/azuremolchapter15",
  "systemAssignedIdentity": "f5994eeb-4be3-4cf5-83d2-552c6ccb0bed",
}
```

4 Get information on the AAD service principal for your managed identity. Query on the `objectId`, and enter you own `systemAssignedIdentity` that was shown in the output from the previous step:

```
az ad sp list \
```

```
--query "[?contains(objectId, 'f5994eeb-4be3-4cf5-83d2-
➥552c6ccb0bed')].servicePrincipalNames"
```

The output is similar to the following condensed example. Make a note of the first `servicePrincipalName`. This value is used to assign permissions on Azure resources such as your key vault and is needed in the next step:

```
[
  "887e9665-3c7d-4142-b9a3-c3b3346cd2e2",
]
```

5 Set the policy on the key vault such that the service principal for your VM can read secrets. Enter your `servicePrincipalName` from the previous step:

```
az keyvault set-policy \
  --name azuremol \
  --secret-permissions get \
  --spn 887e9665-3c7d-4142-b9a3-c3b3346cd2e2
```

One point to make here is that when the MSI was created and scoped to the resource group, that didn't mean the VM could then do anything it wanted. First, the only role created for the identity was read permissions to resources. But you still had to assign permissions to the key vault itself. These layers of security and permissions give you fine-grained control over the exact resources each identity can access.

Now that you have access to a key vault, you probably want to know how to retrieve the secret, right?

15.2.1 Obtaining a secret from within a VM with managed service identity

You've stored a secret in a key vault for a database password, and you have a VM with an MSI that provides access to read that secret from the key vault. Now what? How do you retrieve the secret and use it? Figure 15.5 shows how a VM uses the IMDS to request access to a resource, such as a key vault. Let's go through the steps to see how the VM retrieves the secret.

> **Try it now**
> To retrieve and use a secret on a VM with an MSI, complete the following steps.

1 Get the public IP address of the VM you created in the previous exercise, such as molvm:

```
az vm show \
  --resource-group azuremolchapter15 \
  --name molvm \
  --show-details \
  --query [publicIps] \
  --output tsv
```

2 SSH to your VM, such as `ssh azuremol@publicIps`.

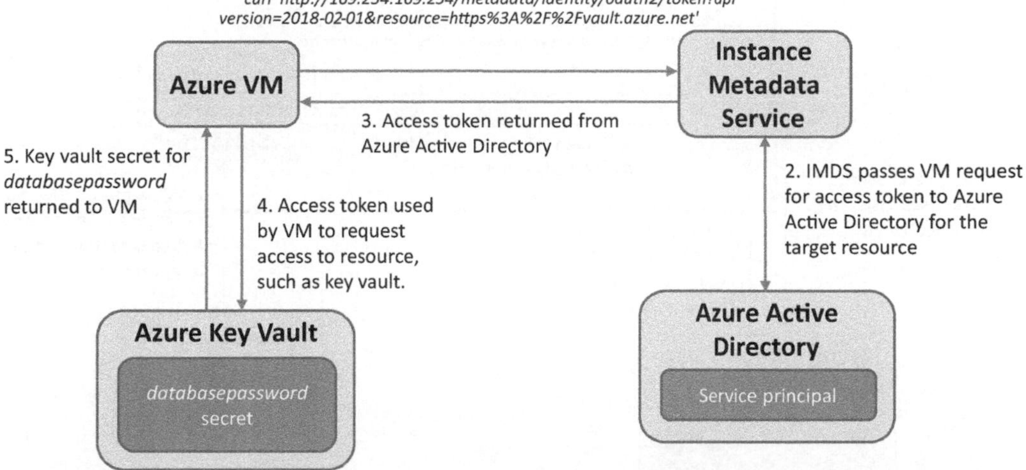
1. VM makes HTTP request to Instance Metadata Service (IMDS) endpoint
curl 'http://169.254.169.254/metadata/identity/oauth2/token?api version=2018-02-01&resource=https%3A%2F%2Fvault.azure.net'
Azure VM
Instance Metadata Service
3. Access token returned from Azure Active Directory
5. Key vault secret for databasepassword returned to VM
4. Access token used by VM to request access to resource, such as key vault.
2. IMDS passes VM request for access token to Azure Active Directory for the target resource
Azure Key Vault
databasepassword secret
Azure Active Directory
Service principal

Figure 15.5 The VM uses the IMDS to request access to a key vault. The endpoint communicates with AAD to request an access token. The access token is returned to the VM, which is then used to request access from the key vault. If access is granted by the key vault, the secret for `databasepassword` is returned to the VM.

3 To access a key vault, you need an access token. This access token is requested from the IMDS. It's a simple HTTP request, and on a Linux VM you can use the `curl` program to make the request. The IMDS passes your request on to AAD:

```
curl 'http://169.254.169.254/metadata/identity/oauth2/token?
➥api-version=2018-02-01&resource=https%3A%2F%2Fvault.azure.net'
➥-H Metadata:true
```

4 The output is a little hard to read, because it looks like a jumble of text. It's in the JSON Web Token (JWT) format. To process the JSON output and make things more human-readable, install a JSON parser called `jq`:

```
sudo apt-get -y install jq
```

5 Make your `curl` request again, but this time view the output with `jq`:

```
curl 'http://169.254.169.254/metadata/identity/oauth2/token?
➥api-version=2018-02-01&resource=https%3A%2F%2Fvault.azure.net'
➥-H Metadata:true --silent | jq
```

These first few steps are for you to be able to see how the requests are made and what the output looks like, as shown in figure 15.6. If you still log in to the VM and manually request an access token, what's the point of using an MSI? You could just provide your own credentials. In production use, you'd likely use a script that runs on the VM to automatically make the request for an access token and then retrieve the secret from the key vault. Let's keep going and see how you automate this process and retrieve the secret.

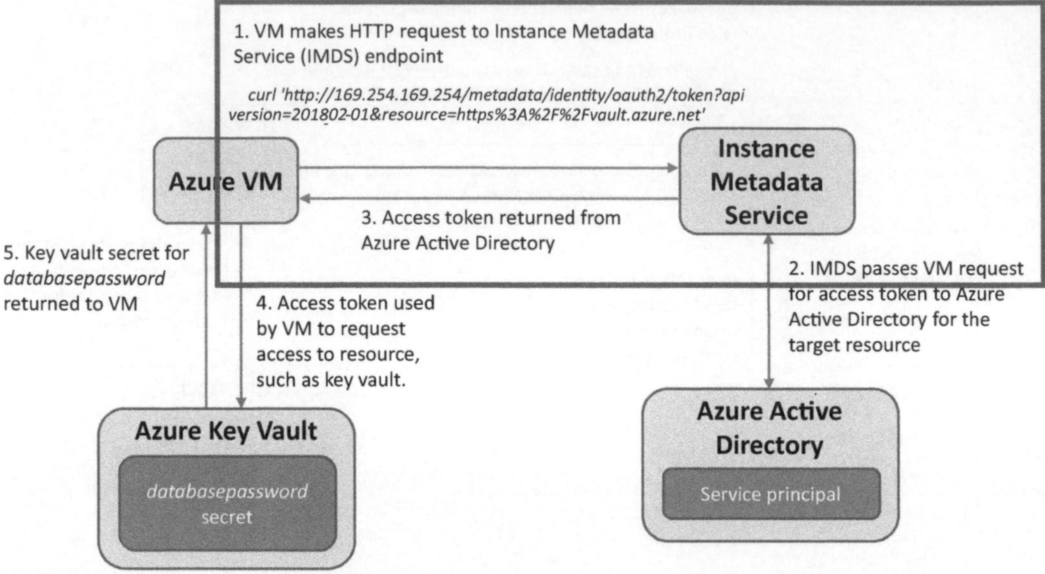

1. VM makes HTTP request to Instance Metadata Service (IMDS) endpoint
curl 'http://169.254.169.254/metadata/identity/oauth2/token?api version=201802-01&resource=https%3A%2F%2Fvault.azure.net'
Azure VM
Instance Metadata Service
3. Access token returned from Azure Active Directory
5. Key vault secret for databasepassword returned to VM
4. Access token used by VM to request access to resource, such as key vault.
2. IMDS passes VM request for access token to Azure Active Directory for the target resource
Azure Key Vault
databasepassword secret
Azure Active Directory
Service principal

Figure 15.6 The `curl` request covers the first three steps on this diagram. The `curl` request is made, the endpoint communicates with AAD, and an access token is issued.

6 To make things easier—and if you were going to do all this in a script—you can use `jq` to process the `curl` response, extract only the access token, and set it as a variable named `access_token`:

```
access_token=$(curl
➥'http://169.254.169.254/metadata/identity/oauth2/token?
➥api-version=2018-02-01&resource=https%3A%2F%2Fvault.azure.net'
➥-H Metadata:true --silent | jq -r '.access_token')
```

7 As a manual step to help you understand what this looks like, view the `access_token` variable:

```
echo $access_token
```

8 Now the fun part! Use the access token to request your secret from the key vault. Let's first do this manually so you understand what happens. Retrieve the secret with another `curl` request, and format the output with `jq`:

```
curl https://azuremol.vault.azure.net/secrets/databasepassword?
➥api-version=2016-10-01 -H "Authorization: Bearer $access_token"
➥--silent | jq
```

The output is similar to the following, which shows the value of the password stored in the secret, along with some additional metadata about the secret that you don't need to worry about:

```
{
  "value": "SecureP@ssw0rd!",
  "contentType": "Database password",
  "id":
```

```
➥"https://azuremol.vault.azure.net/secrets/databasepassword/
➥87e79e35f57b41fdb882c367b5c1ffb3",
}
```

This curl request is the second part of the workflow, as shown in figure 15.7.

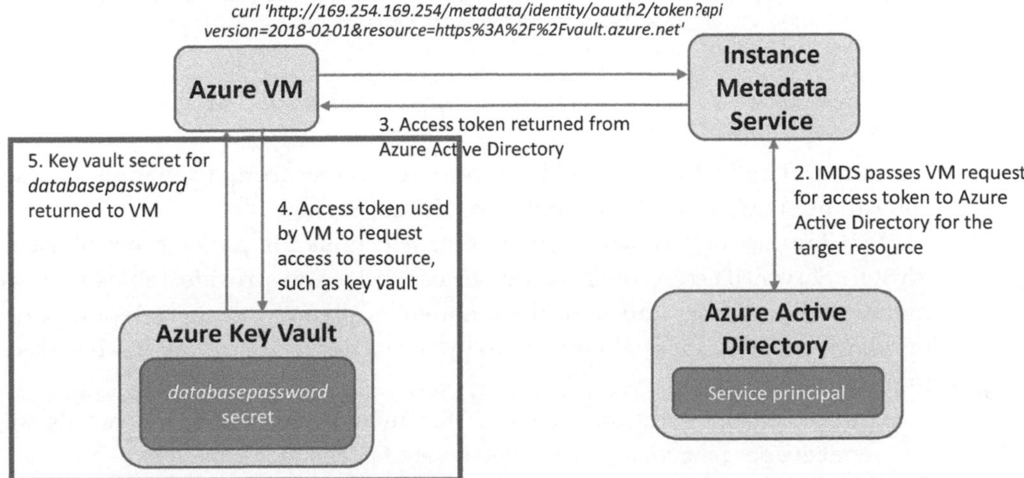
1. VM makes HTTP request to Instance Metadata Service (IMDS) endpoint
curl 'http://169.254.169.254/metadata/identity/oauth2/token?api version=2018-02-01&resource=https%3A%2F%2Fvault.azure.net'
Azure VM
Instance Metadata Service
3. Access token returned from Azure Active Directory
5. Key vault secret for databasepassword returned to VM
4. Access token used by VM to request access to resource, such as key vault
2. IMDS passes VM request for access token to Azure Active Directory for the target resource
Azure Key Vault
databasepassword secret
Azure Active Directory
Service principal

Figure 15.7 This second `curl` request covers the last two steps in the diagram. The access token is used to request the secret from the key vault. The JSON response is returned, which includes the value of the secret.

9 In the same way that you used a variable to store the access token, in a script you can assign the value of the secret to a variable as well. This time, use `jq` to process the response, extract only the value secret, and set it as a variable named `database_password`:

```
database_password=$(curl
➥https://azuremol.vault.azure.net/secrets/databasepassword?
➥api-version=2016-10-01 -H "Authorization: Bearer $access_token"
➥--silent | jq -r '.value')
```

10 Again, as a manual step to help you understand the process, view the contents of the `database_password` variable:

```
echo $database_password
```

Hopefully, you're following along! If you write an application in Python, ASP.NET, or Node.js, for example, the process will be similar as you make a request for the access token and then use the token to request a secret from a key vault. There are likely other libraries you could use you in your code rather than the `jq` utility from the command line.

As a quick recap, all these steps can be condensed down into two lines, as shown in the following listing.

Listing 15.1 Requesting an access token and then a secret from a key vault

```
access_token=$(curl
➥'http://169.254.169.254/metadata/identity/oauth2/token?
➥api-version=2018-02-01&resource=https%3A%2F%2Fvault.azure.net'
➥-H Metadata:true --silent | jq -r '.access_token')
database_password=$(curl
➥https://azuremol.vault.azure.net/secrets/databasepassword?
➥api-version=2016-10-01 -H "Authorization: Bearer $access_token"
➥--silent | jq -r '.value')
```

Now what? The MSI for your VM can retrieve a secret from a key vault; let's see how you can use that to install and configure MySQL Server.

In Ubuntu, you can set configuration selections for package installers, such as MySQL Server. These configuration selections let you provide values such as usernames and passwords and have them automatically used at the relevant part of the install process. The manual prompts to provide a password, as you may have seen back in chapter 2, are gone:

11 Set the configuration selections for the MySQL Server passwords with the `database_password` variable you created in the previous steps:

   ```
   sudo debconf-set-selections <<< "mysql-server mysql-server/root_password
   ➥password $database_password"
   sudo debconf-set-selections <<< "mysql-server mysql-
   ➥server/root_password_again password $database_password"
   ```

12 Install MySQL Server. There are no prompts, because the password is provided by configuration selections:

   ```
   sudo apt-get -y install mysql-server
   ```

13 Let's prove that all this worked! View the `database_password` variable so you can clearly see what your password should be:

   ```
   echo $database_password
   ```

14 Log in to MySQL Server. When prompted for a password, enter the value of `database_password`, which is the value of the secret from the key vault:

   ```
   mysql -u root -p
   ```

   You're logged in to the MySQL Server, which confirms that the secret from the key vault was used to successfully create the SQL server credentials! Type `exit` twice to close out of the MySQL Server command prompt, and then close your SSH session to the VM.

This was a basic example, and you'd still need to secure the MySQL Server and provide additional credentials for applications to access databases or tables, for example. The advantage of using a secret from a key vault is that you guarantee all the passwords are the same. If you use virtual machine scale sets, for example, each VM instance can automatically request the secret and install MySQL Server so it's ready to serve your application data. Those passwords are never defined in scripts, and no one needs to see what the passwords are. You could even generate passwords at random and rotate them as secrets in a key vault.

You may be wondering: storing passwords in a key vault is great, but aren't all the cool kids using digital certificates for authentication and security? Can you use a key vault to store certificates and retrieve them automatically from your applications or VMs? Of course you can!

15.3 Creating and injecting certificates

Digital certificates are a common form of security and authentication in web services and applications. Certificates are issued by a certificate authority (CA), which is (hopefully!) trusted by end users. The certificate allows users to verify that a website or application is indeed who it says it is. Every time you see a website with a web browser address that begins with https:// and has a padlock symbol, that means the traffic is encrypted and secured by a digital certificate.

Managing digital certificates can often become a major management task. A common problem is how to store and grant access to certificates as services and applications need them. In the previous exercises, we examined how a key vault can be used to share secure secrets and keys with services and applications, but a key vault can also do the same with certificates. As shown in figure 15.8, a key vault can be used to request, issue, and store certificates.

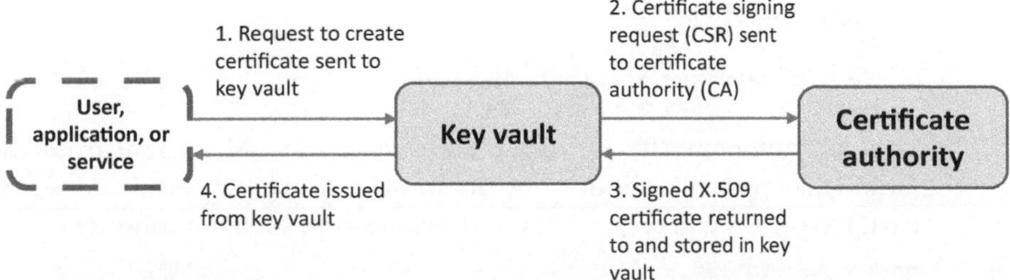

Figure 15.8 A user, application, or service can request a new certificate from a key vault. A certificate signing request (CSR) is sent by the key vault to a certificate authority (CA). This could be an external third-party CA or a trusted internal CA. Azure Key Vault can also act as its own CA to generate self-signed certificates. The CA then issues a signed X.509 certificate, which is stored in the key vault. Finally, the key vault returns the certificate to the original requestor.

In production use, you should always use a trusted CA to issue your certificates. For internal use, you can issue self-signed certificates that you create yourself. These self-signed certificates aren't trusted by other services and applications, so they typically generate a warning, but self-signed certificates let you quickly get up and running and make sure your code works as expected with encrypted traffic.

Azure Key Vault can generate self-signed certificates for you. Under the hood, Key Vault acts as its own CA to request, issue, and then store certificates. Let's use this ability to generate a self-signed certificate and see how to easily inject it into a VM. The certificate is then used for a basic web server to show you how to quickly enable SSL to secure your web traffic.

> **Try it now**
> To create and inject a certificate into a VM, complete the following steps.

1 Create a self-signed certificate in Azure Key Vault, and enter a name, such as `molcert`. Policies are used to define properties such as expiration time periods, encryption strength, and certificate format. You can create different policies to suit the needs of your applications and services. For this exercise, use the default policy that creates a 2,048-bit certificate and is valid for one year:

```
az keyvault certificate create \
  --vault-name azuremol \
  --name molcert \
  --policy "$(az keyvault certificate get-default-policy)"
```

2 To see the certificate in action, create another VM, such as `molwinvm`. This time, create a Windows VM that uses Windows Server 2016, so you spread around the OS love! Provide your own admin username and password:

```
az vm create \
  --resource-group azuremolchapter15 \
  --name molwinvm \
  --image win2016datacenter \
  --admin-username azuremol \
  --admin-password P@ssw0rd1234
```

3 You can automatically add the certificate to the VM straight from the Azure CLI. This approach doesn't rely on an MSI. Add your certificate, such as molcert, to the VM you created in the previous step, such as molwinvm:

```
az vm secret add \
  --resource-group azuremolchapter15 \
  --name molwinvm \
  --keyvault azuremol \
  --certificate molcert
```

4 Connect to the VM and verify that the certificate was injected correctly. To connect to your VM, first get its public IP address:

```
az vm show \
  --resource-group azuremolchapter15 \
  --name molwinvm \
  --show-details \
  --query [publicIps] \
  --output tsv
```

Use a local Microsoft Remote Desktop connection client on your computer to connect to your VM. Use the credentials to connect to localhost\azuremol, not the default credentials of your local computer that your Remote Desktop client may try to use, as shown in figure 15.9.

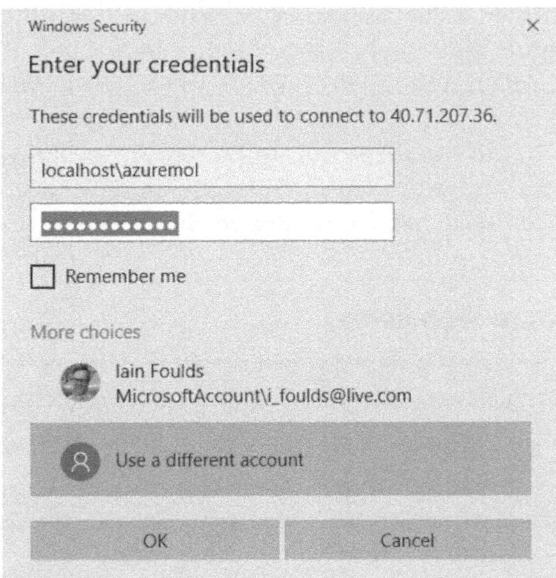

Figure 15.9 Your Remote Desktop client may try to use your default local computer credentials. Instead, select Use a Different Account, and then provide the localhost\azuremol credentials that you specified when you created the VM.

5 Once you're logged in, select the Windows Start button, and then type `mmc` and open the Microsoft Management Console. Choose File > Add / Remove Snap-in, and then select to add the Certificates snap-in.
6 Choose to add certificates for the Computer account, select Next, and then select Finish. Choose OK to close the Add / Remove Snap-in window.
7 Expand the Certificates (Local Computer) > Personal > Certificates folder. The certificate from Azure Key Vault that you injected into the VM is listed, such as CLIGetDefaultPolicy, as shown in figure 15.10.

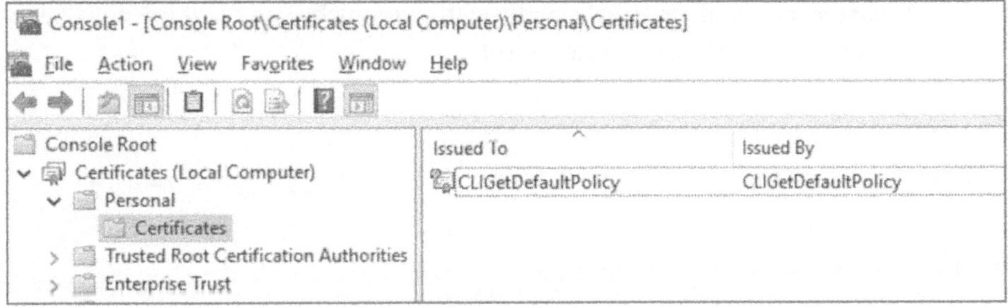

Figure 15.10 In the Microsoft Management Console, add the Certificates snap-in on the local computer. Expand the Personal > Certificates store to view installed certificates. The certificate injected from Key Vault is listed.

That's all there is to it! Create the certificate in Key Vault, and then add the certificate to the VM. The certificate is placed into the local certificate store of the computer, which allows any service or application to access it. On a Windows VM, the certificates are stored in the local certificate cache, as seen in this exercise. On Linux VMs, .prv and .crt files for the private and public parts of the certificate are stored in /var/lib/waagent/. You can then move the certificates to wherever you need to for your application or service.

Certificates can be used both for the server, to present it for authentication to other applications or services, and with their own application or service. A common example is for a web server to use an SSL certificate, which is what you do in the end-of-chapter lab.

15.4 Lab: Configuring a secure web server

In the last exercise, you injected a self-signed certificate from Azure Key Vault into a Windows VM. For this lab, install and configure the IIS web server to use the certificate:

1. Open PowerShell on your Windows VM, and then install the IIS web server:
   ```
   Add-WindowsFeature Web-Server -IncludeManagementTools
   ```
2. Open Internet Information Server (IIS) Manager. You can do this from the Tools menu in Server Manager.
3. For Default Web Site, choose to Edit Bindings.
4. Add an HTTPS binding on All Unassigned IP addresses on port 443. Select the self-signed certificate you created and injected from Key Vault, typically named something like CLIGetDefaultPolicy.
5. Open a web browser on the VM, and enter `https://localhost`. You generated a self-signed certificate in Key Vault, so the web browser doesn't trust it. Accept the warning to continue, and verify that the HTTPS binding works.
6. Back in the Azure Cloud Shell or portal, create an NSG rule for the VM on TCP port 443. Enter `https://`*`yourpublicipaddress`* in a web browser on your local computer. This is the experience your users would receive, with a warning about an untrusted self-signed certificate. For most use cases, remember to use a trusted internal or third-party certificate authority to generate trusted certificates and store them in a key vault.

16 Azure Security Center and updates

Wouldn't it be great if Azure was smart enough to monitor all of your core application resources and alert you about any security concerns? Or what if your business has security policies already defined (if you don't have any security policies, please stop right now and make a note to create some!)—how do you ensure that your Azure deployments remain compliant? If you've ever gone through an IT security audit, you know how fun it can be to look over a list of misconfigurations applied to your environment, especially the basic security lapses that you know to avoid!

Azure Security Center provides a central location for security alerts and recommendations to be grouped for your review. You can define your own security policies and then let Azure monitor the state of your resources for compliance. In this chapter, we discuss how Security Center can alert you to problems and provide steps to correct them, how you can use just-in-time VM access to control and audit remote connections, and how Update Management keeps your VMs automatically up to date with the latest security patches.

16.1 Azure Security Center

Throughout this book, we've discussed security-related topics like how to create and configure network security groups (NSGs) to restrict access to VMs, and how to only permit encrypted traffic to Azure Storage accounts. For your own deployments beyond the exercises in this book, how do you know where to start, and how can you check that you applied all the security best practices? That's where Azure Security Center can help, by checking your environment for areas you may have missed.

Azure Security Center scans your resources, recommends fixes, and helps remediate security concerns, as shown in figure 16.1. When you only have a couple of test VMs and a single virtual network in your Azure subscription, it may not seem that hard to keep track of what security restrictions you need to put in place. But as you scale up to tens, hundreds, or even thousands of VMs, manually keeping track of what security configurations need to be applied to each VM becomes unmanageable.

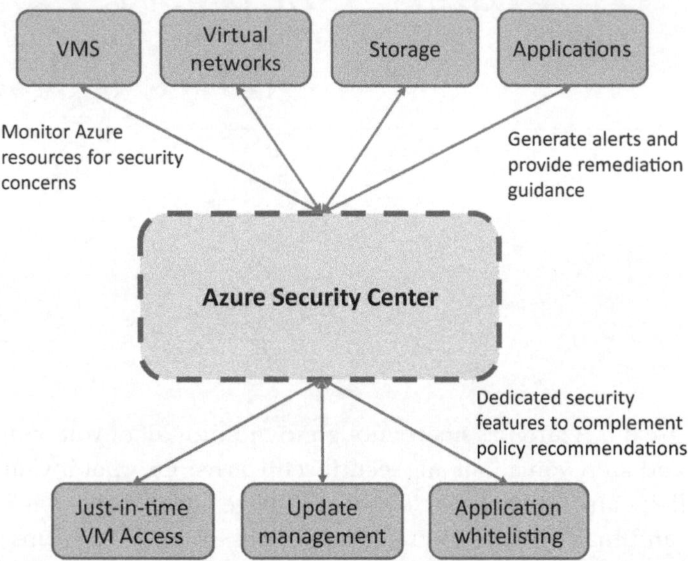

Figure 16.1 Azure Security Center monitors your Azure resources and uses defined security policies to alert you to potential threats and vulnerabilities. Recommendations and steps to remediate issues are provided. You can also use just-in-time VM Access, monitor and apply security updates, and control whitelisted applications that can run on VMs.

Security Center can also alert you to general best practices, such as if a VM doesn't have diagnostics enabled. Remember in chapter 12 when we looked at how to monitor and troubleshoot VMs? You need to install and configure the diagnostics agent *before* you have a problem. If you suspect a security breach, you may not be able to access the VM and review logs. But if you had configured the diagnostics extension to stream logs to Azure Storage, you could review what had occurred and hopefully track down the source and extent of the problem.

Try it now

To get started with Azure Security Center, complete the following steps.

1 Open the Azure portal, and select the Cloud Shell icon from the top menu.

2 Create a resource group. Provide a name, such as `azuremolchapter16`, and a location, such as `eastus`:

```
az group create --name azuremolchapter16 --location eastus
```

3 Create a basic Linux VM so that Security Center has something to monitor and provide recommendations for:

```
az vm create \
  --resource-group azuremolchapter16 \
  --name azuremol \
  --image ubuntults \
  --admin-username azuremol \
  --generate-ssh-keys
```

4 Once the VM is deployed, close the Cloud Shell. In the Azure portal, select Security Center from the list of services at left. The first time the dashboard opens, it takes a few seconds to prepare all the available components; see figure 16.2.

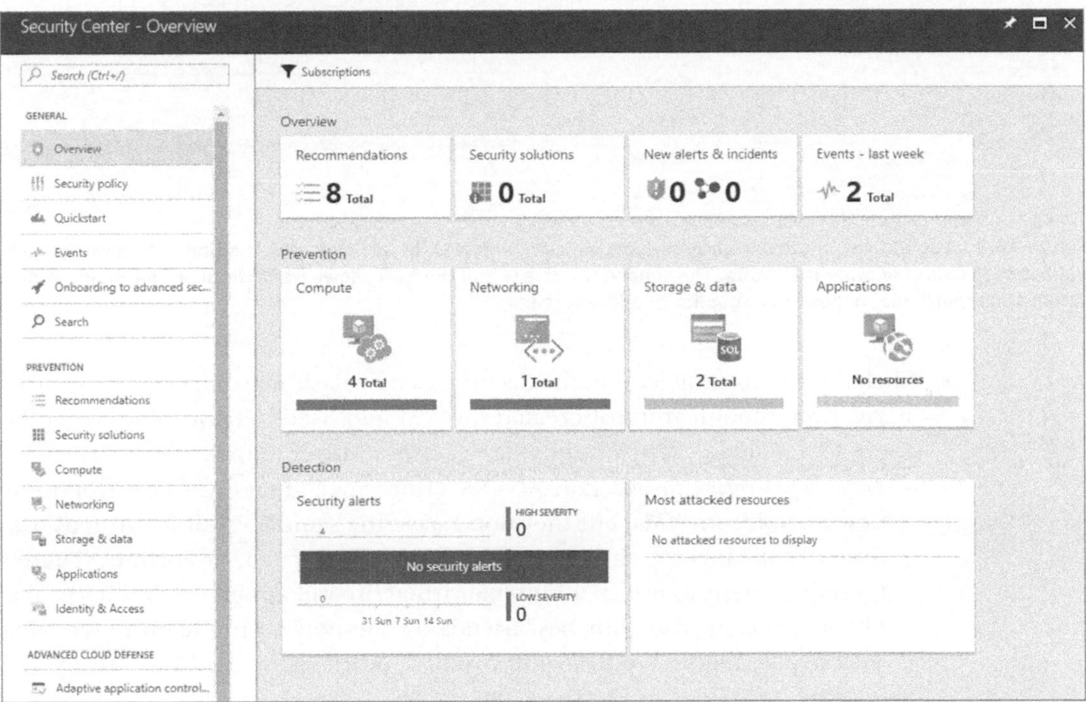

Figure 16.2 The Azure Security Center Overview window provides a list of recommendations, alerts, and events. You can select a core resource type such as Compute or Networking to view a list of security items specific to those resources.

Security Center looks at how resources such as VMs, NSG rules, and storage are deployed. Built-in security baselines are used to identify problems and provide recommendations. For example, the VM you just deployed generates a couple of warnings, as shown in figure 16.3. You can, and should, implement your own security policies that tell Azure how you want to restrict access or what needs to be done to comply with business mandates. As you then create or update resources, Azure continually monitors for deviations from these policies, and alerts you about what steps need to be taken to remediate the security issues. You use the default Azure security policies in this chapter, but think of any particular security configurations that you may want to apply to your VMs and how they could be defined in your own custom policies.

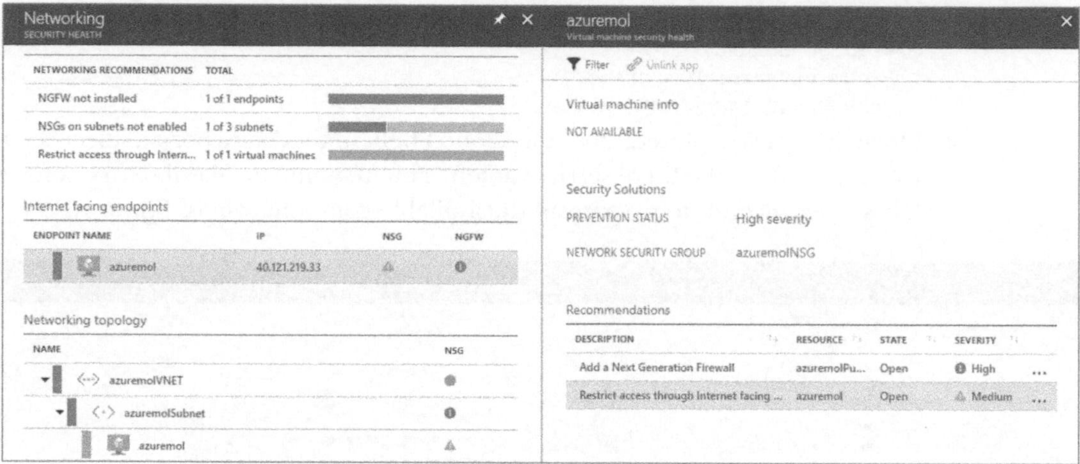

Figure 16.3 The VM you created already triggers security warnings. In this example, the first is that no firewall appliance is detected other than NSGs. The second warning is that the NSG allows traffic from any internet device, rather than restricting access to a specific IP address range.

5. Click the Networking icon in the Security Center dashboard to view the security alerts. Even though you just created this VM and used default values from the Azure CLI, some security warnings are shown in this example:
   - *No next-generation firewall detected*—NSG rules are a great way to control traffic flow to and from VMs, but they don't have the same level of features as true firewall appliances such as those from Cisco, Barracuda, or Fortinet. There's no requirement to use an additional virtual firewall appliance, but it's probably best to chat with your best friends on the networking team to see what they're planning to use to secure virtual network traffic. I told you that you'd become best friends with that team, right?
   - *Inbound access allowed from any internet location*—When you created the VM, a default NSG rule was created that allows inbound remote connections from any internet location. The recommended practice is to limit access to coming from a specific IP range or subnet. The Azure CLI (or PowerShell, portal, or templates) can't secure this rule by default unless you specify an allowed inbound range. You can edit the existing rules to limit the inbound traffic, as suggested by Security Center.

16.2 Just-in-time access

In the previous section, you learned how Security Center suggests that you limit the scope of inbound remote connectivity. You could provide an IP range to limit traffic, but ideally, you only open inbound connectivity when it's needed. That way, the VM is completely closed for remote connections and is accessible only for a short time when needed. And yes, you should still limit that brief window of connectivity to a specific IP range! That's where just-in-time (JIT) VM access comes in useful, as shown in 16.4.

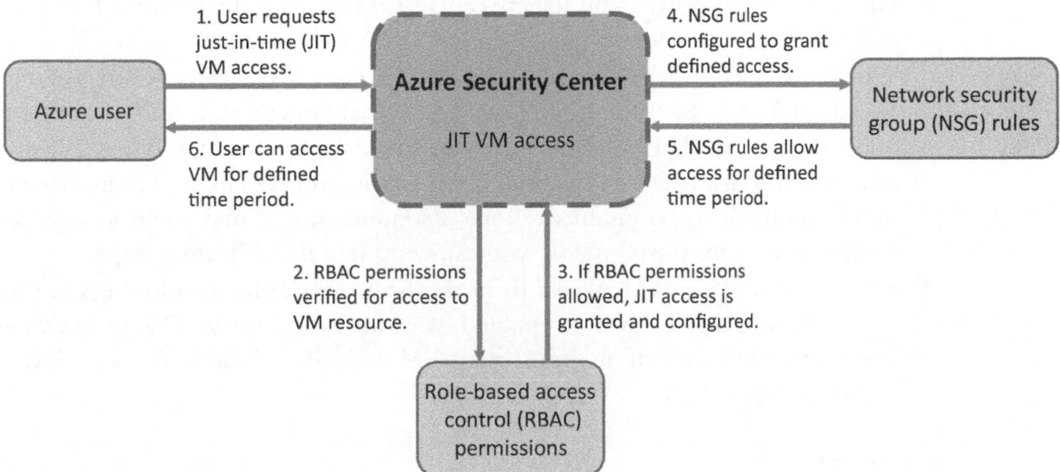

Figure 16.4 With JIT VM access, NSG rules are configured to deny remote connections to a VM. RBAC permissions are used to verify permissions when a user requests access to a VM. These requests are audited, and if the request is granted, the NSG rules are updated to allow traffic from a given IP range, for a defined period of time. The user can access the VM only during this time. Once the time has expired, the NSG rules automatically revert to a *deny* state.

With JIT access, Security Center dynamically adjusts access restrictions on a VM. When enabled, NSG rules are created that deny all remote connection traffic. A user can then request access to a VM only when needed. In combination with RBACs (discussed in chapter 6), Security Center determines whether a user has rights to access a VM when they request a connection. If the user does have permissions, Security Center updates the relevant NSG rules to allow incoming traffic. These rules are applied only for a specific time window. Once that time is up, the rules are reverted, and the VM becomes closed to remote connections again.

When would you use JIT in your fictional pizza store? Think about any VMs that would run your web application, order system, or business logic applications. Would you want those to be connected to the internet and available for people to access all the time? Hopefully not! There are valid reasons for remote access with SSH or RDP, but always try to minimize how long that access is available. Even if you have NSG rules that restrict access to certain IP ranges, JIT adds another layer of protection in terms of what Azure users can access, and then creates an easier audit trail about which Security Center can provide reports.

> **Try it now**
> To enable just-in-time VM access, complete the following steps.

1. Open the Azure portal, and select Security Center from the menu at left. Under Advanced Cloud Defense, select Just in Time VM Access.
2. If prompted, choose the option to Try Just in Time VM Access or to Upgrade to Standard Tier of Security Center. This free trial lasts 60 days and doesn't automatically extend. This overlaps with your free Azure account and won't cost you any money to use. Select the option to Apply Standard Plan, and then wait a few moments for it to be enabled. Once it's enabled, you may need to close and reopen the Azure portal before you can complete the following steps.
3. Select Just in Time VM Access from the Security Center window again. Once your standard tier account is enabled, you can view a list of VMs to use. Select Recommended, and then choose your VM and select Enable JIT on 1 VMs, as shown in figure 16.5.

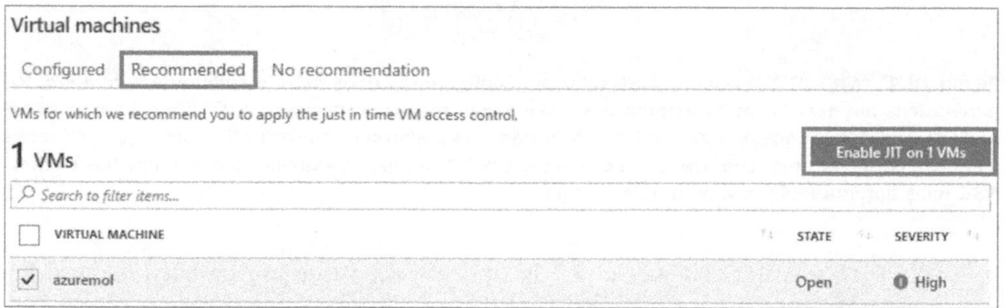

Figure 16.5 Select a VM from the Recommended options, and then choose to Enable JIT on 1 VMs. State currently shows that this VM is Open for all remote access, which flags the severity of the security concern as High.

4. By default, JIT defines rules that can open ports for SSH (port 22), RDP (port 3389), and PowerShell remoting (ports 5985 and 5986) for a period of 3 hours. If desired, select a rule and change Allowed Source IPs or Max Request Time, and then choose OK. Otherwise, leave all the defaults and choose Save, as shown in figure 16.6.
5. With JIT enabled, browse to your resource group, and then select your VM. Choose Networking to view the assigned virtual network configuration for the VM. The list of assigned NSG rules is shown, as in figure 16.7.

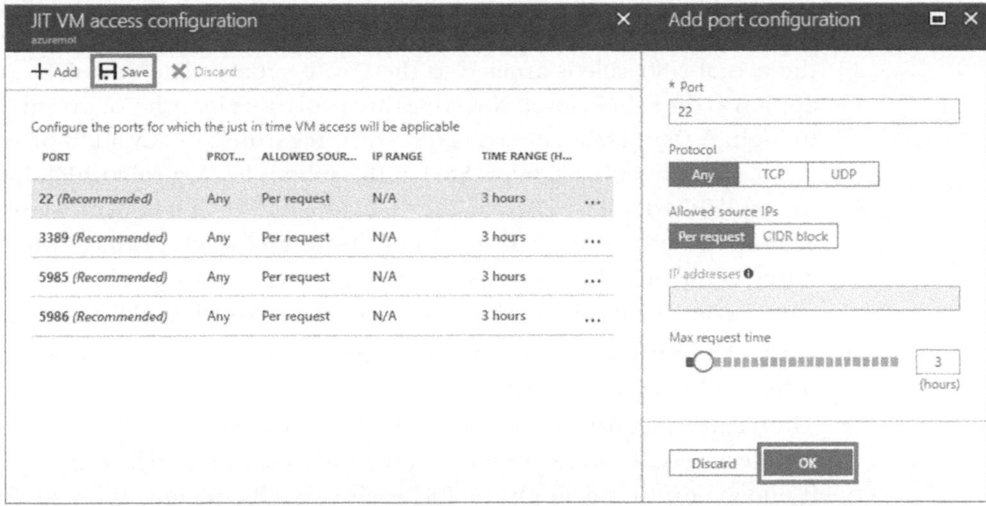

Figure 16.6 When you enable JIT, you can change the default rules to be allowed, the allowed source IPs, and a maximum request time in hours. These JIT rules allow granular control over what's permitted to allow only the bare minimum of connectivity.

The JIT rules are shown at the top of the list, because they have the lowest priority. Traffic is denied to the IP address of the VM. What may seem odd here is that a default-allow-ssh rule still exists and permits all traffic. Think back to chapter 5, when we discussed NSGs—can you tell what's happening here?

Network Interface: azuremolVMNic Effective security rules Topology

Virtual network/subnet: azuremolVNET/azuremolSubnet Public IP: **40.121.219.33** Private IP: **10.0.0.4**

INBOUND PORT RULES

Network security group azuremolNSG (attached to network interface: azuremolVMNic)
Impacts 0 subnets, 1 network interfaces

Add inbound port rule

PRIORITY	NAME	PORT	PROTOCOL	SOURCE	DESTINATION	ACTION	
1000	SecurityCenter-JITRule_-1115349600_60D7...	22	Any	Any	10.0.0.4	Deny	...
1001	SecurityCenter-JITRule_-1115349600_EED0...	3389	Any	Any	10.0.0.4	Deny	...
1002	SecurityCenter-JITRule_-1115349600_F32C...	5985	Any	Any	10.0.0.4	Deny	...
1003	SecurityCenter-JITRule_-1115349600_4D02...	5986	Any	Any	10.0.0.4	Deny	...
1004	default-allow-ssh	22	TCP	Any	Any	Allow	...
65000	AllowVnetInBound	Any	Any	VirtualNetwork	VirtualNetwork	Allow	...
65001	AllowAzureLoadBalancerInBound	Any	Any	AzureLoadBalancer	Any	Allow	...
65500	DenyAllInBound	Any	Any	Any	Any	Deny	...

Figure 16.7 The JIT rules are created with the lowest priority. These priorities make sure the JIT rules take precedence over any later rules applied at the subnet level.

JIT applies only to the VM. In the JIT rule, Destination shows the IP address of the VM. In the example shown in figure 16.7, that's 10.0.0.4. Traffic is denied. But the actual NSG rule is applied to the entire subnet. The default-allow-ssh rule applies at the subnet level. NSG rules are processed in order of priority, from low to high. A Deny action always takes effect, regardless of any additional rules.

So, even though you allow SSH at the subnet level, a rule with a lower priority explicitly denies traffic to the individual VM. This makes sense, because again, JIT works at the VM level, not the subnet level. RBAC permissions may differ between VMs connected to the same subnet, so this level of granularity lets you be specific about who can access what VMs when JIT is enabled.

6 Go back to Security Center, and select Just in Time VM Access. Choose your VM from the list, and then select Request Access.
7 The Azure platform checks your RBAC permissions to make sure you can enable access. If you're permitted, the window shown in figure 16.8 is displayed; it allows you to toggle On or Off each port. By default, JIT also only allows access from My IP. To do this, the Azure platform looks up the IP of your current connection and limits JIT access to connections from that IP.
8 Toggle On the rule for port 22, and then select Open Ports.

Go back to your VM, and look at the NSG rules again. The JIT rule is now enabled for the ports you specified, as shown in figure 16.9.

The NSG rule automatically changes back to a Deny action after the time period specified has elapsed. By default, JIT rules are applied for 3 hours. After that time, the VM returns to a more secure state, and you'd need to request access to the VM again.

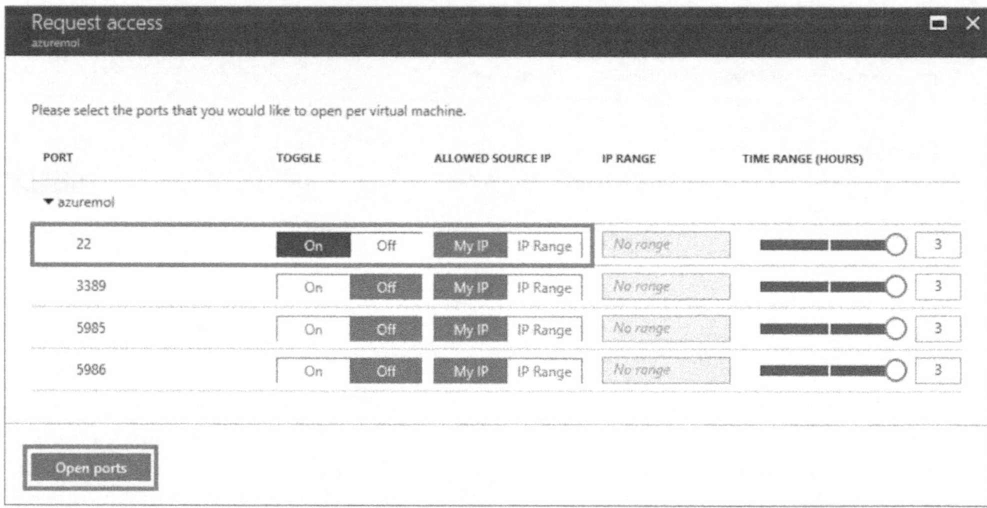

Figure 16.8 When you request access, only the specific ports and source IPs are permitted. The defaults are populated from the settings you provided when you enabled the VM for JIT, but the values can now be changed as needed for each access request.

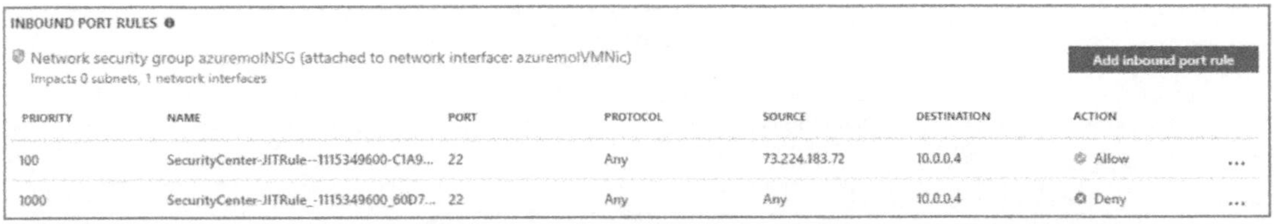

INBOUND PORT RULES

Network security group azuremolNSG (attached to network interface: azuremolVMNic)
Impacts 0 subnets, 1 network interfaces

Add inbound port rule

PRIORITY	NAME	PORT	PROTOCOL	SOURCE	DESTINATION	ACTION	
100	SecurityCenter-JITRule--1115349600-C1A9...	22	Any	73.224.183.72	10.0.0.4	Allow	...
1000	SecurityCenter-JITRule_-1115349600_60D7...	22	Any	Any	10.0.0.4	Deny	...

Figure 16.9 The JIT rule now allows traffic on port 22 to your VM, but only from your public IP address. After the time period specified (by default, 3 hours), this NSG rule reverts back to the traffic being denied.

This JIT process is to control who can request, and be granted, access to the VM. But just because a person can successfully request access to a VM doesn't mean they have permissions to log on to that VM. All that happens in Azure is that the defined NSG rules are updated. Security Center and JIT can't add, remove, or update access credentials on the VM.

All JIT requests are also logged. In Security Center, select the Just in Time VM Access option, and then choose your rule. On the right, select the ... menu option, and then choose Activity Log. This activity log helps you audit who requested access to a VM in the event of a problem.

JIT VM access is one way Security Center and Azure help keep your VMs secure. Controlling access to the VMs is a big part of security, but what about the applications, libraries, and services running on the VM? That's where you need to ensure that all the latest security updates are applied to your VMs in a timely manner.

16.3 Azure Update Management

One area that Azure Security Center can report on is the status of any required OS updates required by the VM. In your pizza store, you should try to install the latest security and application patches. You don't want to run any systems that have a known vulnerability or attack area, so a way to automate the updates of those systems and track compliance improves your security. When you work with applications that involve customer data and payment information, don't run systems without the latest patches installed. And remember to plan for a test environment that lets you safely apply security patches and validate that they don't cause problems before you apply them to production systems!

An Update Management feature is built into Azure VMs and can scan, report, and remediate OS updates. What's great about this solution is that it works across both Windows and Linux, and even within Linux, across different distributions such as Ubuntu, Red Hat, and SUSE. Figure 16.10 shows how Update Management monitors and can install required updates.

It takes a few minutes for the VM to prepare itself and report back on its update status, so let's set up your VM and then see what goes on behind the scenes.

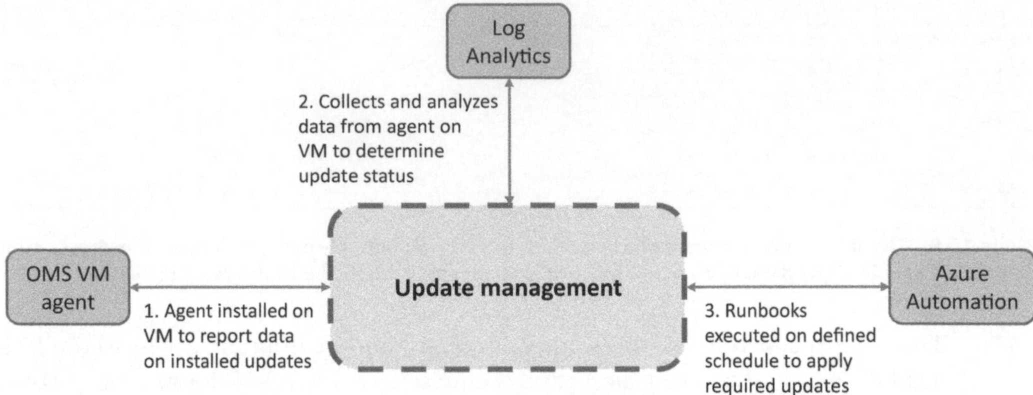

Figure 16.10 Update Management installs a VM agent that collects information on the installed updates on each VM. This data is analyzed by Log Analytics and reported back to the Azure platform. The list of required updates can then be scheduled for automatic install through Azure Automation runbooks.

> **Try it now**
> To configure your VM for Update Management, complete the following steps.

1. Open the Azure portal, and select Resource Groups from the menu at left. Select your resource group, such as `azuremolchapter16`, and then select your VM, such as azuremol.
2. Under Operations, select Update Management.
3. Leave the default options for Location and to create a Log Analytics workspace and Automation Account. We examine these components more in the remainder of this section. To turn on update management for the VM, select Enable.
4. You return to the Update Management Overview window, but it takes a few minutes to configure the VM and report back on its status. Continue reading, and let the process continue.

Let's look a little more at what happens to make this Update Management solution work. A new component was automatically installed when the VM was configured for Update Management: Operations Management Suite, which includes Azure Automation.

16.3.1 Operations Management Suite

If you've worked with any on-premises Microsoft technologies, you may have come across the System Center suite. System Center consists of multiple components such as Configuration Manager, Operations Manager, Orchestrator, and Data Protection

Manager. There are a couple of other parts, but those core components provide a way to do the following:

- Define configurations and desired state
- Install applications and updates
- Report on health and security
- Automate deployments of large services and applications
- Back up and replicate data

As businesses have moved to cloud computing providers over the last few years, those more traditional on-premises System Center components have received some updates to try to make them work in a hybrid environment. Operations Management Suite (OMS) provides a solution that was natively designed to work in the cloud but retains some of the capabilities to work with on-premises systems. We've already looked at two components of OMS in earlier chapters, even if you didn't realize it:

- *Azure Backup* provides a way to back up VMs or individual files, define retention policies, and restore data.
- *Azure Site Recovery* allows you to replicate VMs to different geographic regions in the event of a natural disaster or prolonged outage.

Both Azure Backup and Site Recovery helped you protect your data in chapter 13. Now you'll use two additional components of OMS with Update Managements:

- *Log Analytics* collects information from various sources or agents, and allows you to define policies and queries to alert you to conditions that may occur. These queries and alerts can help you track the update status of a VM, or notify you of configuration or security issues.
- *Azure Automation* allows you to build runbooks that execute commands or entire scripts. Runbooks can be large, complex deployments, and can call multiple other runbooks. We look at Azure Automation in depth in chapter 18.
- The integration of these components under the OMS umbrella is shown in figure 16.11.

Both Log Analytics and Azure Automation are powerful components and could easily fill entire chapters of a book by themselves. With only a handful of VMs to manage, it's easy to overlook the need for a centralized log repository for querying and alerting, or a way to automate configurations and deployments across VMs. If you haven't already been making a list of Azure components to follow up on when you're finished with this book, start one, and add both of these components to that list!

One thing to understand is that in Azure, there are often multiple services and components that can interact and complement each other. In the same way that Azure VMs and Azure virtual networks are individual services, both services also complement, or even rely, on each other. Azure Backup and the Azure diagnostics extension are great individual components, but they really shine if Log Analytics is used to monitor their status and collate any generated events or warnings. Hopefully, you've

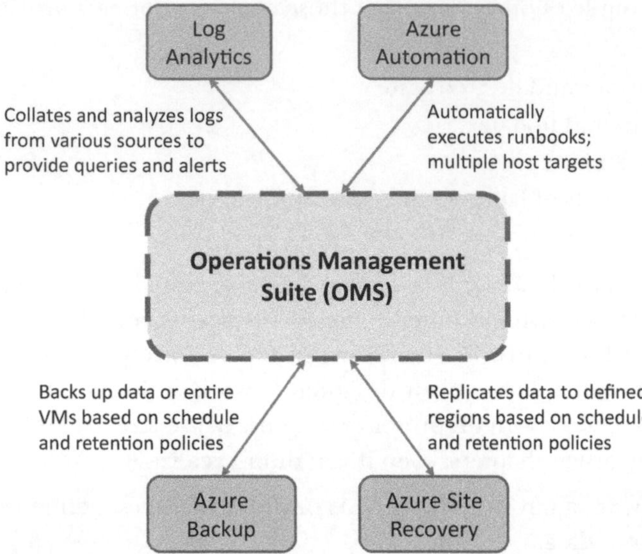

Figure 16.11 Operations Management Suite (OMS) covers multiple Azure services that work together to provide management and configuration features across your entire application environment. The services that use OMS aren't limited to Azure VMs or resources and can work across other cloud-providers or on-premises systems when appropriately configured.

begun to identify some of these related components and see how Azure services often build on each other. Now that we're into these final few chapters and looking at security and monitoring options, the goal is to ensure that the applications you run in Azure are healthy and stable.

This little thing called "Identity"

Thinking about services that complement each other, one large (and I mean *large*!) part of Azure that we've only lightly touched on is Azure Active Directory (AAD). Identity is central to everything in Azure, and AAD provides some of the security features we examined in chapter 6 with the Azure Resource Manager deployment model. The ability to use RBACs to limit what actions can be performed a resource by certain users or groups is tied into a central identity solution. Even being able to log in to the Azure portal or Azure CLI is driven by AAD.

This book doesn't cover AAD, because the scope of what it provides is broad and quite different from Azure IaaS and PaaS services like VMs, scale sets, and web apps. There may be some overlap in the topics' audience, but most developers would have a different goal for what they wanted to learn about regarding AAD compared to an application manager or an IT pro who deploys the infrastructure.

Depending on your Azure account, you may also be limited in what you can do with AAD. When you sign up for a free Azure trial account, a default AAD instance is created for you. You're the primary account in that directory, and you have full administrator rights. If you log in to Azure with an account from your business or educational institution, there's a good chance that you have little to no administrative rights. So even if we could agree on a couple of topics to focus on, you might not be able to carry out any of the exercises directly. And I really don't recommend that you go digging around in an actual AAD environment to learn how things work!

But AAD is another of those central services in Azure that binds together many other services and components. Cloud computing doesn't magically make things easier or break down operational silos—you still need the skills to work with different teams and stakeholders. Throughout these chapters, hopefully you've picked up the core skills for these different Azure services, which will help you understand how to build large, redundant applications and converse at a better level and with more awareness of what other teams may face.

For the purposes of Update Management on your VM, you don't need to interact directly with the OMS or Log Analytics. For your own awareness, there's currently a separate OMS dashboard that you can access from the Azure portal for more insights. The OMS dashboard doesn't contain a lot of information, because you have only one VM onboard and reporting information, as shown in figure 16.12; it becomes a lot more useful, the more VMs you register for monitoring. For now, you can use the regular Azure portal to update the VMs.

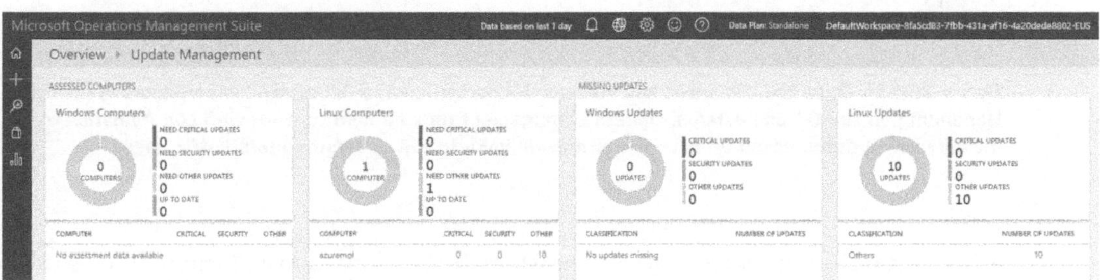

Figure 16.12 The OMS dashboard for Update Management reports the status of configured VMs. As more VMs are added to the service, you can quickly determine how many VMs require patches and how critical the missing patches are in terms of security and compliance. The pie charts show the number of Windows and Linux computers in need of updates, and then how many updates are required for each VM.

Now that you understand a little about OMS and what happens behind the scenes to make Update Management work, let's go back and discuss what your VM reports and how to perform some updates.

16.3.2 Reviewing and applying updates

It can take some time for the VM agent to perform the first scan and report back on the status of applied updates. The list of installed components must also be cross-referenced with the list of available updates for a given OS and version. If your VM hasn't finished and reported back on its status, keep reading, and check back in a few minutes. When it's ready, the overview looks like figure 16.13.

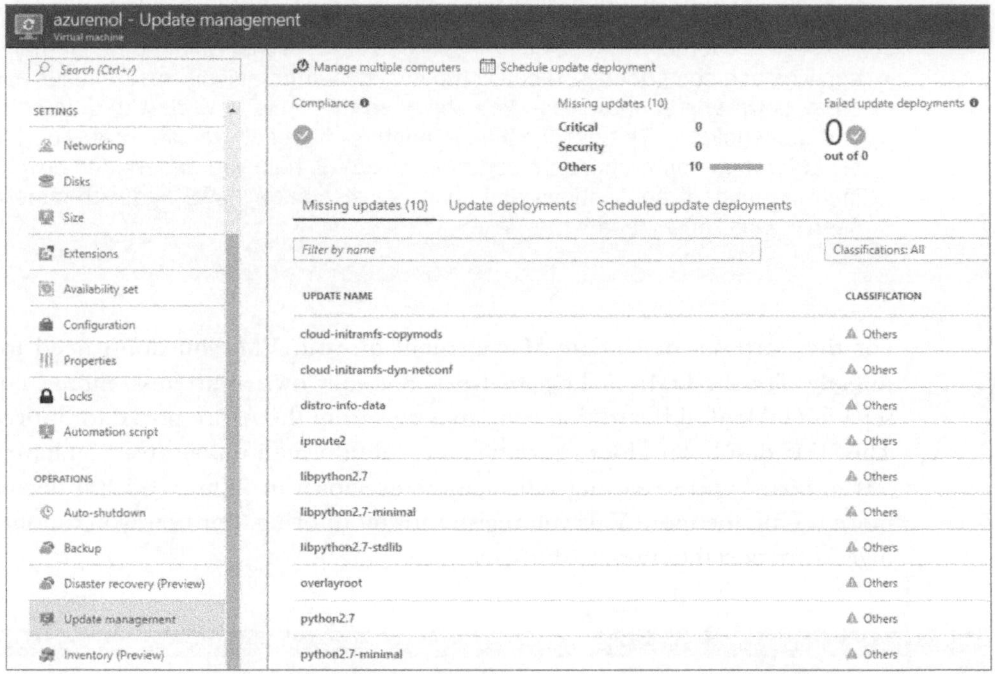

Figure 16.13 Once the VM agent has scanned for compliance, a list of available updates is provided. Depending on the OS and version, Update Management may be able to work with Log Analytics to classify the updates based on severity, or provide links to the relevant update hotfix pages.

A list of required updates is great, but what about a way to install them? That's where Azure Automation steps in! When you enabled Update Management, a number of Azure Automation runbooks were created that automatically handle the process to apply the required updates.

> **Try it now**
>
> To apply the required updates for your VM, complete the following steps.
>
> If you're lucky (or unlucky), your VM may report that no updates are required. VM images are frequently updated in Azure, and if you deploy a VM soon after the latest image was built, all the required updates are already installed. If so, read through these steps so you understand what's required when your VMs do need updating!

1. From the Update Management section of your VM, select Schedule Update Deployment.
2. Enter a name for the update deployment, such as `azuremolupdates`, and then review the Update Classifications. You can control which sets of updates are applied. For now, leave all the default options set.
3. Updates to Exclude lets you specify specific updates that you don't want to install. If you know your application requires a specific version of a package or library, you can make sure an updated package isn't installed that breaks things.
4. Select Schedule Settings, and then choose a time for the updates to be applied from the calendar and time options. The start time must be at least 5 minutes ahead of the current time, to give the Azure platform a few moments to process and schedule your runbook in Azure Automation. When you're ready, select OK.
5. Maintenance Window (Minutes) defines how long the update process can run before the VM needs to be back in operation. This maintenance window prevents long-running update processes that may cause a VM to be unavailable for hours at a time. You may want to make the maintenance window shorter or longer, depending on any service-level agreements (SLAs) for the applications that run on those VMs, or the number and size of the updates required. Leave the default value for Maintenance Window, and then select Create.
6. Back in the Update Management window, select Scheduled Update Deployments. The updates are listed as scheduled to install at the date and time you select, as shown in figure 16.14.

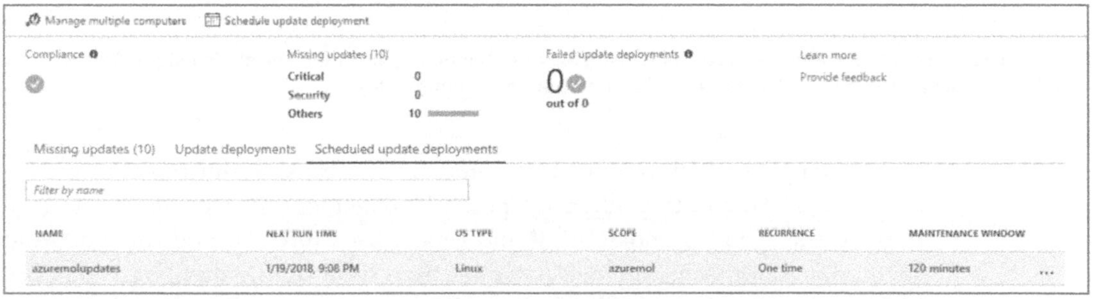

Figure 16.14 The list of scheduled deployment tasks is shown. If desired, you can delete a given task; otherwise, the updates are automatically applied at the defined time.

7 At the top of the Update Management window, select Manage Multiple Computers. The window switches to the Azure Automation account that was automatically created when Update Management was enabled for the VM. Don't worry too much for now about what the runbooks do. There's nothing for you to customize, and we examine Azure Automation in chapter 18.

Note that you can choose Add Azure VM or Add Non-Azure Machine, as shown in figure 16.15. This ability highlights how OMS is designed to provide a single approach to managing updates across your entire application environment, not just for Azure VMs.

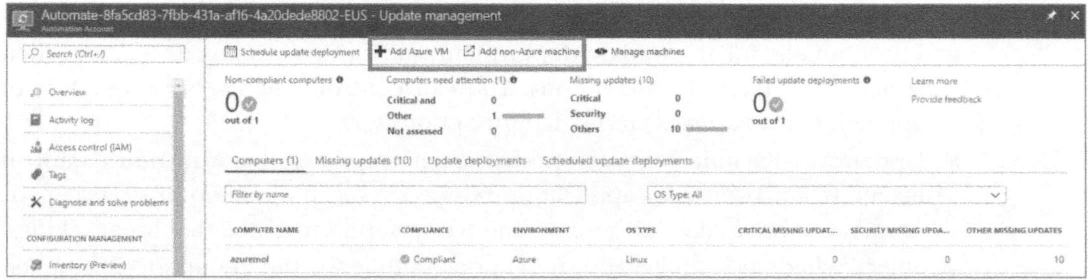

Figure 16.15 In the Azure Automation account, you can manage multiple computers and view the status or apply updates. Both Azure VMs and non-Azure computers can be monitored and controlled by the same Azure Automation account. Behind the scenes, OMS can integrate with other providers to install agents on computers in a hybrid environment. This integration allows a single dashboard and management platform to handle your update needs.

8 Under Process Automation, select Jobs. When your update deployment starts, its status is shown, as in figure 16.16. You can monitor the status of the jobs and review the output as they're executed.

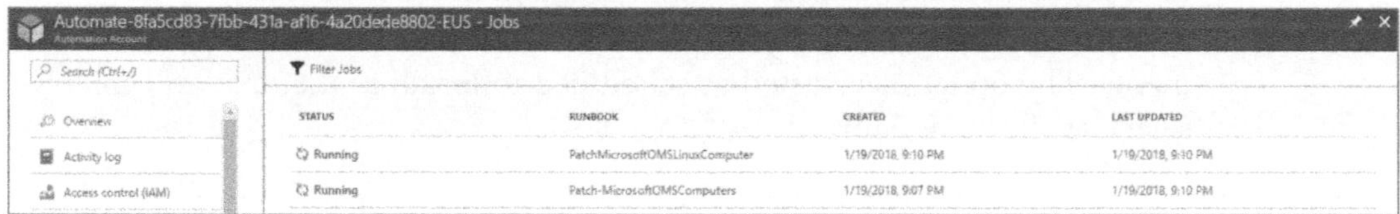

Figure 16.16 You can monitor the status of running Azure Automation jobs in the portal. To help review or troubleshoot tasks, you can click a job to view any output and generated logs.

9 Once the update deployment has finished, browse back to your resource group, select your VM, and then choose Update Management. It may take a few minutes for the agent to update itself and report back through Log Analytics that the updates have been applied; it should then show on the dashboard that the VM is up to date and no additional updates are required.

This has been a whirlwind tour of Security Center and associated components such as JIT VM access and Update Management. The goal is for you to start to think beyond just how to deploy and run a VM or web app, and instead plan for the wider application management that goes with it. Cloud computing doesn't change the need for security policies—there's arguably a greater need for resources to be secured. Let Azure features such as Security Center guide you through what needs to be done, and use the built-in tools like Update Management and Azure Automation to keep things secure at all times.

16.4 Lab: Enabling JIT for a Windows VM

This chapter covered a few different components that may have taken some time to enable themselves and report back on their expected status. This lab is optional and is more to show that there's nothing OS-specific about any of these features. If you don't have time, or you feel that you understand how you can also apply these features to a Windows VM, feel free to skip this lab. Otherwise, try the following tasks to gain some additional practice with Security Center and Update Management. Practice makes perfect, right?

1. Create a Windows Server VM of your choice in the same resource group you used for the previous exercises, such as `azuremolchapter16`.
2. Enable Just in Time VM Access on the VM. View the NSG rules, and then use your local Remote Desktop Connection client to verify that RDP connections are blocked.
3. Request JIT access, review the NSG rules again, and confirm that you can now RDP to your VM.
4. Enable Update Management on your Windows VM. This time, you should be able to use the existing OMS workspace and Azure Automation accounts. Let the OMS agent report back on required updates, and then schedule the updates to be applied through Azure Automation.

Part 4

The cool stuff

Now, the really cool stuff! In these final few chapters, let's learn about some of the upcoming technologies you can use in Azure, such as artificial intelligence and machine learning, containers and Kubernetes, and the Internet of Things. These services may not be areas you or your company are using right now, but with the current trends in computing, they probably will be soon. For me, these are some of the most exciting technologies to work with; although we move pretty quickly to cover these topics in your lunch break, it's a great way to wrap things up and show you the possibilities of what you can build in Azure.

17 Machine learning and artificial intelligence

Hopefully, we won't end up in a world where films like *The Terminator* and *The Matrix* come true. In those movies, the rise of artificial intelligence (AI) almost causes the downfall of humanity as machines fight to take control of their surroundings. One cause for concern in computing right now is how the development of AI is mostly done by large, private companies, with little or no regulation and central oversight. That's not at all to say that AI is a bad thing! Digital assistants on smartphones can help with many day-to-day tasks, and machine learning (ML) in navigation apps and home-heating controls allows the user's daily drive or room temperature to automatically adjust based on the outside temperature, time of day, and whether it's summer or winter.

As you begin this final section of the book, you'll learn about the Azure services for machine learning and artificial intelligence. In one chapter. On your lunch break. Let's set some realistic expectations: you're not going to become an expert in ML or AI in the next 45 minutes! You may, if you eat your sandwich quickly, learn enough about the many services that Azure offers to understand how to integrate some of these ML and AI services into your applications. Many of the Azure ML and AI services expect at least some prior experience in data algorithms, programming languages, batch processing, or language understanding, so don't expect to become an expert in the next hour!

In this chapter, let's go on a whirlwind tour of some of the Azure cognitive services that provide ML and AI features. You learn how to use these services to perform basic machine learning on data models, and then you use a little of the Azure

Web Apps service and the Microsoft Bot Framework to apply some of the AI services that can run a pizza store bot for customers to order pizza.

17.1 Overview and relationship of AI and ML

Hold on tight, because we're about to go from 0 to 600 mph in just a few pages! AI and ML often overlap as you build applications in Azure. Let's explore what each is, and then worry about how they work together.

17.1.1 Artificial intelligence

AI allows computers to complete tasks with some amount of flexibility and awareness, and adjust their decisions based on external factors or without the need for human interaction. The goal isn't usually to build a completely autonomous system that can evolve and develop thoughts for itself, but rather to use a set of data models and algorithms to help guide the decision-making process.

Common AI on personal computers and smartphones includes Siri, Cortana, and Google Assistant. As shown in figure 17.1, these AI resources allow you to communicate, often via voice commands, to ask for directions, set reminders, search the web, and more.

Digital assistants like this typically don't involve a large amount of what you may consider *intelligence*. They listen and respond to input you provide. But those inputs

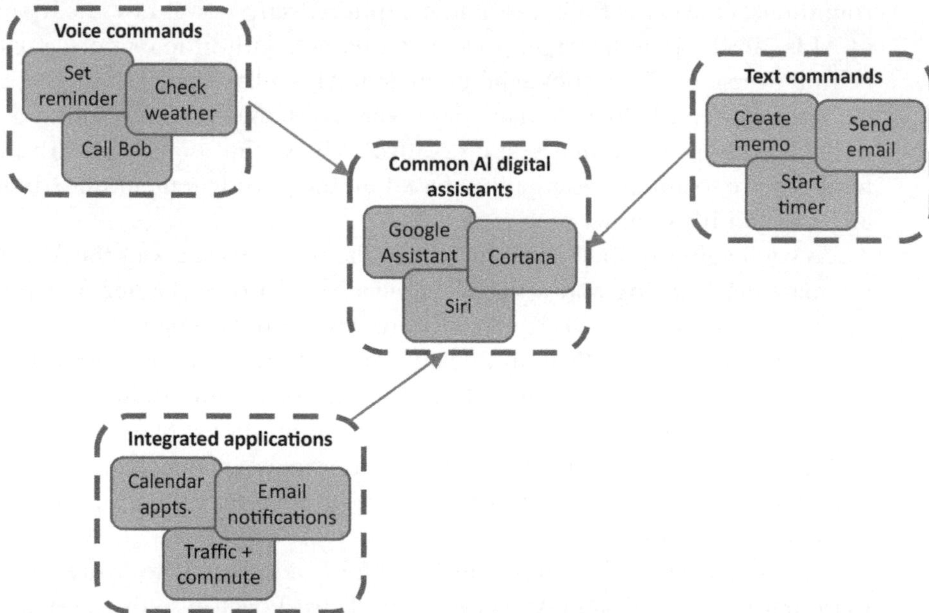

Figure 17.1 A common use of AI in everyday life is digital assistants such as Cortana, Siri, and Google Assistant. You can use voice or text commands to interact with them, and they can monitor your daily calendar and commute conditions to warn you about traffic problems.

can vary and may not always be specific commands. Think about how a digital assistant lets you set a reminder. You could use one of the following phrases:

- "Remind me at 5 to pick up milk."
- "Tell me to pick up milk on the way home."
- "I need to get milk when I'm at the store."

If you developed a traditional application, you'd need to write code that could handle all the possible variations of how a user might provide instructions. You could build regular expressions to help catch some of the variations, but what happens when the user comes up with a phrase that you didn't program? Or what if they interact via text and have a typo in their request that you didn't anticipate? These types of interactions are a great fit for AI. As shown in figure 17.2, the application is programmed for several common phrases and is then able to make an educated guess based on what it "thinks" the user is asking for.

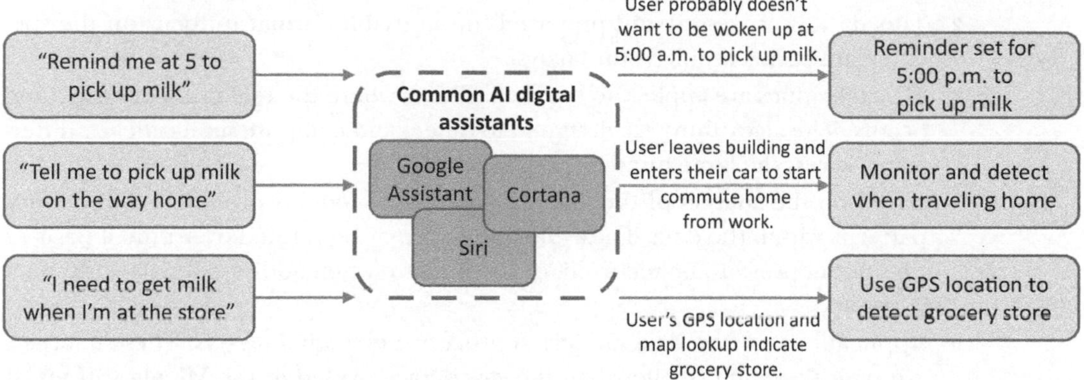

Figure 17.2 AI can take input from the user and make decisions that best suit the anticipated action. The AI isn't preprogrammed with all of these possible responses and decision trees. Instead, it uses data models and algorithms to apply context to the user input and interpret the meaning and appropriate outcome.

It's not true intelligence (yet), even in complex forms of AI; instead, it's an educated guess based on a data model that the AI has been trained with. This data model may include many different variations and phrases and may be able to learn new meanings over time. How does it learn, and where do these data models come from? That's where ML becomes important.

17.1.2 Machine learning

A great buzzword in computing over the last few years has been *big data*. The concept is that computer systems, especially in the cloud, are a great resource to process large amounts of data. *Really* large amounts of data. These processing jobs may run for a few minutes or hours, depending on the size of the data and the calculations required, and allow you to prepare and analyze large volumes of data to determine specific

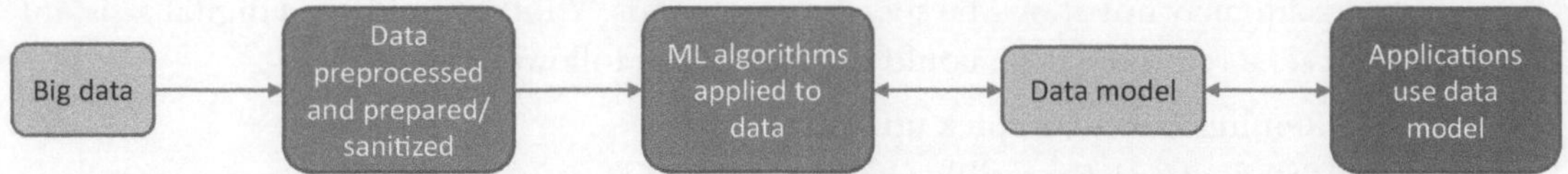

Figure 17.3 Large amounts of raw data are processed and made ready for use. Different preparation techniques and data sanitization may be applied, depending on the raw inputs. ML algorithms are then applied to the prepared data to build an appropriate data model that reflects the best correlation among all the data points. Different data models may be produced and refined over time. Applications can then use the data models on their own data inputs to help guide their decision-making and understand patterns.

patterns and correlations. These learnings form data models that other applications or AI can use to help make decisions. As shown in figure 17.3, ML involves a few different steps and includes both inputs and outputs.

Here's how the most basic form of ML works:

1. To begin the process, large amounts of raw data are provided as input.
2. This data is processed and prepared into a usable format to focus on the specific data points required for analysis.
3. ML algorithms are applied to the data. This is where the real number-crunching occurs. The algorithms are designed to detect and compute similarities or differences across the large number of data points.
4. Based on the analysis of the algorithms, a data model is produced that defines patterns within the data. These data models may be refined over time if parts of the model prove to be incorrect or incomplete when additional real-world data is applied.
5. Applications use the data models to process their own data sets. These data sets are typically much smaller than the raw data provided to the ML algorithms. If the data model is valid, then even with a small data input from the application, the correct outcome or correlation can be determined.

ML often involves complex algorithms that are designed to process all the data points provided. Hadoop and Apache Spark are two common application stacks that are used to process big data. Azure HDInsight is a managed service that allows you to analyze the large data sets processed by these application stacks. To get a little deeper into the analysis and algorithms, the R programming language is common with data scientists to help develop the models required. Don't worry too much about what Hadoop or R is. The key point is that Azure can run the common ML tools that are widely accepted within the industry.

17.1.3 Bringing AI and ML together

A common application on a smartphone is the navigation app, as shown in figure 17.4. Your provider, such as Google, can track the route you take to work each day, what time you usually leave home, and how long it takes you to get there.

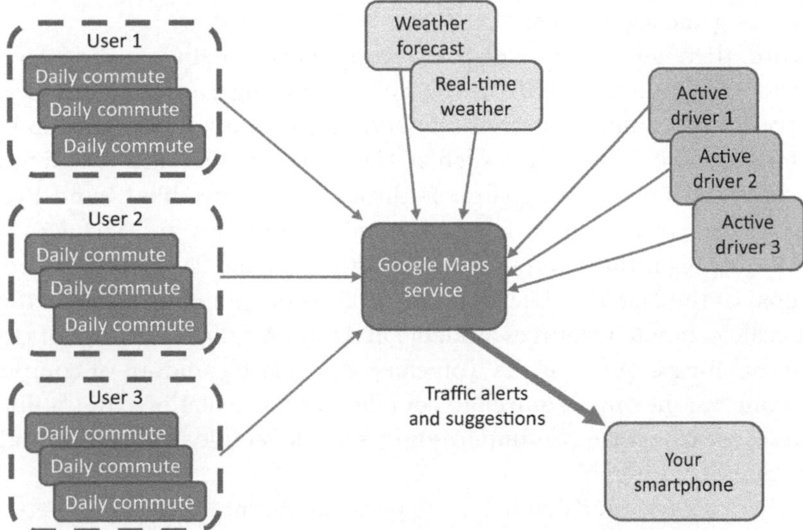

Figure 17.4 The Google Maps service receives multiple data points from users each day that record details of their commute. This data can be prepared and processed, along with the weather forecast and real-time weather during those commutes. ML algorithms can be applied to these large data sets and a data model produced. As a smaller sample of active drivers then feed their current travel conditions or weather data into the Google Maps service, the data model can be applied to predict your commute and generate a traffic alert to your smartphone that suggests an alternate route home.

This Google Maps example shows AI and ML working together. AI is applied to know when to generate a notification based on the data received after processing the ML data model. Another example of AI and ML working together is the previous idea of setting a reminder to buy milk. If the AI was trained with ML data models, the assistant would know that you probably buy milk at the grocery store, so it wouldn't remind you if you went to the hardware store. The ML data model would also be able to help the AI understand that there's a much great probability that you want to be reminded of something at 5:00 p.m., not 5:00 a.m., so it shouldn't wake you at 5:00 a.m. to buy milk. If your smartphone tracks you getting in your car at 5:00 p.m. and starting to drive away from work, ML will generate a data model that predicts you're driving home, so now's a good time for the AI to remind you about buying milk.

These are basic but powerful examples that show how ML is used to improve AI. You train AI by providing a set of data points that are processed by ML to improve accuracy or decision making.

17.1.4 Azure ML tools for data scientists

I want to quickly cover a couple of ways that some real-world number crunching and ML work can be done. To make this chapter accessible for all, the exercises use the Microsoft Bot Framework for AI, and ML with Language Understanding Intelligent Service (LUIS). To get your hands dirty with ML, we need to focus a little more on data processing and algorithms.

In Azure, there are a couple of cool components to help you dig into data on a massive scale. First, there's the Azure Machine Learning Studio, a web-based service that lets you visually build experiments by adding data sets and analysis models. These experiments can use data sources such as Hadoop and SQL, and Machine Learning Studio additional programming support through languages like R and Python. You can drag and drop data sources, data-preparation techniques, and ML algorithms. You can adjust those algorithms and then review and tweak the data models produced.

The goal of the Machine Learning Studio is to provide a low barrier for entry to the large-scale compute resources available in Azure. A primary benefit of performing ML data-crunching in Azure is that you can access a large amount of compute power and use it only for the time required to complete your calculations. In traditional environments, those expensive compute resources would sit idle for large periods of time between data-processing jobs.

One other cool resource that helps you perform serious ML and number-crunching in Azure is data science virtual machines (DSVMs). These VMs are available for both Linux and Windows. They come with many common applications preinstalled, including Azure Machine Learning Studio, Jupyter Notebooks, Anaconda Python, and R Server or SQL Server; see figure 17.5. There's no need to install all the tools and dependencies on your local computer—you can create a DSVM with as much CPU and memory resources as you need to quickly process your data, and then delete the VM when your processing job is complete and you have the data models you need.

17.2 Azure Cognitive Services

Okay, so what about AI services to make your apps smarter? In Azure, a set of related services make up the Cognitive Services suite. The services cover a few common areas of AI that let you quickly integrate these intelligent resources into your applications. The core parts of Cognitive Services are as follows:

- *Vision*, which includes
  - *Computer Vision API* for image analysis, captioning, and tagging
  - *Face API* to analyze and detect faces in images
  - *Content Moderator* to review and moderate photos, video, and text
- *Speech*, which includes
  - *Bing Speech API* to analyze and convert speech to text and vice versa
  - *Translator Speech API* for real-time language translation

- *Language*, which includes
  - *Language Understanding Intelligent Service (LUIS)* to help understand and process interaction with users. We explore LUIS later in this chapter in the lab.
  - *Bing Spell Check API* and *Translator Text API* to analyze and correct spelling mistakes or perform translations
- *Knowledge*, which includes
  - *Recommendations API* to analyze patterns and provide recommendations to customers
  - *QnA Maker API* to consume a set of information or resources and be able to provide answers to customer questions
- *Search*, which includes
  - *Bing Custom Search API* to implement search on your custom data and within applications
  - *Bing Autosuggest API* to provide automatic suggestions as users enter search phrases and queries

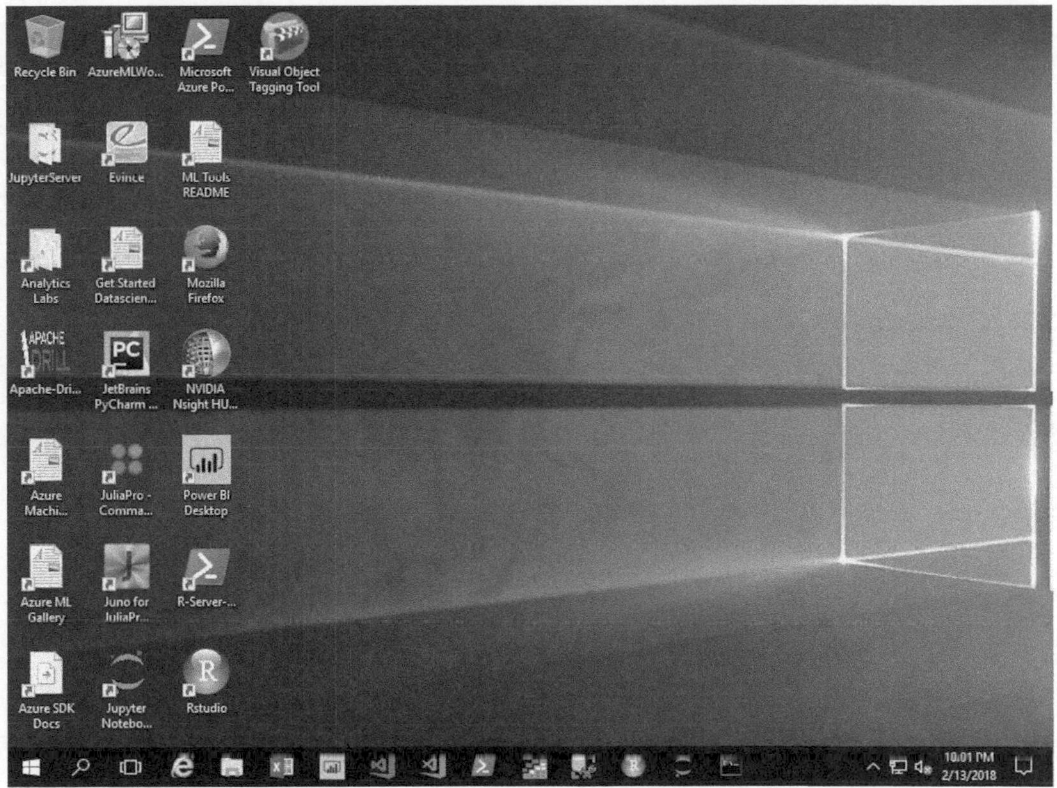

Figure 17.5 Data science virtual machines (DSVMs) are available for Windows and Linux. This Window Server 2016 DSVM comes with several data science applications preinstalled, such as R Server, Jupyter Notebooks, and Azure Machine Learning Studio. DSVMs let you quickly get up and running with processing big data and building ML algorithms.

As you can see, many Azure services combine AI and ML features. This chapter focuses on language, specifically LUIS. This service is commonly used to build an intelligent bot that can help customers on your website. You can then build an AI that can interpret phrases and questions, and provide the appropriate response to guide a user through an order process or support request.

17.3 Building an intelligent bot to help with pizza orders

A *bot* is an application that's programmed to respond to tasks and input from a user. If this sounds much like any normal application, well, it pretty much is! The difference is how the bot application determines the response.

A basic, common bot is often nothing more than an application that provides some form of automation. When a user sends a message, sets a tag on an email message, or submits a search term, the bot carries out preprogrammed tasks that perform a specific action. There's no real AI or ML here. The bot application is just responding to user input.

With the right framework, a bot can be extended and given a little more freedom and intelligence. At the start of our overview of AI, I discussed how a typical application must be preprogrammed with all the anticipated user inputs and what the corresponding output would be. But there's no flexibility if the user provides a different input phrase or a spelling mistake, for example.

Microsoft produces the Bot Framework, which allows an Azure bot to easily integrate the Bot Builder SDKs and connect to Azure Cognitive Services. With minimal code experience, you can build intelligent bots that use the power of Azure to deliver a great customer experience. Just don't try to build Skynet unless you know how *The Terminator* ends!

17.3.1 Creating an Azure web app bot

Let's deploy a bot and integrate some AI and ML services. The bot runs in an Azure web app and uses Microsoft Bot Framework to connect to LUIS and let a customer order pizza. Figure 17.6 outlines what these exercises build and what services are used.

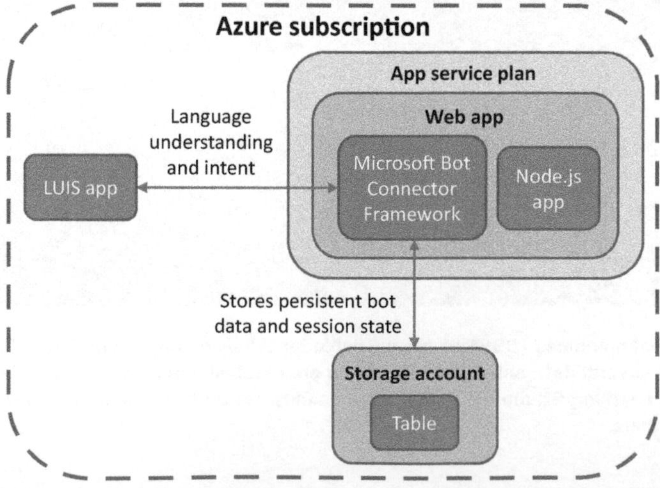

Figure 17.6 In the upcoming exercises, you create a web app bot that integrates multiple Azure AI and ML services to interact with a customer and help them order pizza.

> **Try it now**
> To create an Azure web app bot, complete the following steps.

1. Open the Azure portal, and select Create a Resource in the upper-left corner. Search for and select Web App Bot, and then select Create.
2. Enter a name for your bot, such as `azuremol`. Choose Create New Resource Group, and provide a name, such as `azuremolchapter17`.
3. Select the most appropriate region for you, and then choose the F0 pricing tier. Your bot won't process a lot of messages, so the free (F0) tier is fine.
4. Select Bot Template, and then choose the Node.js template for Language Understanding. This step creates a LUIS app you can use to perform language training and ML. Choose the most appropriate region for your LUIS app.
5. Choose App Service Plan, and then select Create New. Provide a name, such as `azuremol`, and again, select the most appropriate region for you.
6. Leave the default option to Create a Storage Account, which is used to store the state of the bot. This state includes session and message state. Your basic bot won't use it, but more complex bots do.
7. Turn off App Insights, because your bot won't use it. As with earlier chapters on web apps, for production use you may want to harness the power of App Insights to gain visibility into the performance of your application by streaming data and analytics straight from the code.
8. Leave the option checked to Auto Create App ID and Password, and then accept the agreement and choose Create.

It takes a few minutes to create the web app bot and associated components. A lot happens behind the scenes:

- An Azure App Service plan is created.
- A web app is deployed, along with a sample Node.js web application.
- A LUIS app is created, and the connection keys are configured with your web app.
- A bot is created with the Microsoft Bot Connector, and the connection keys are configured from your web app.
- An Azure Storage account and table are created for your bot to persist data as it runs and interacts with customers.

17.3.2 Language and understanding intent with LUIS

One of the Azure Cognitive Service areas that we looked at earlier was language. This makes sense, because some form of language is often used to interact with an AI. You can use LUIS to process a message or phrase from the user and determine their intent. That intent then helps your app provide an appropriate response. Let's extend your bot with LUIS.

> **Try it now**
> To build a LUIS app and use ML to train it, complete the following steps.

1. Open a web browser to www.luis.ai. Sign in with the same Microsoft credentials as your Azure subscription.
2. Select Go to My Apps, and choose your app, such as azuremol. Your LUIS app name likely has some additional numerical characters appended to it from the bot name you specified in the Azure portal.
3. Some prebuilt intents were created, but you want to overwrite the LUIS app with a more pizza-store-focused sample. First, download the azuremol.json file from GitHub at http://mng.bz/Wx0Y to your local computer. To make life easier, select the Raw button in GitHub to see only the contents of the file. Back in your LUIS app, choose Settings at upper right, and then choose Import New Version. Browse to and select the azuremol.json file you downloaded, enter a version name of `1.0`, and then select Done.
4. Go back to Build in the top menu to see the imported intents from the sample app. Choose one or two of the intents, such as `greetings` or `orderFood`, and look at some of the example phrases a customer could use to communicate with the bot.
5. Before you can see the app in action, you must train it. Select Train, and then wait a few seconds for the process to complete. Figure 17.7 shows the ML processes at work to train your LUIS app.

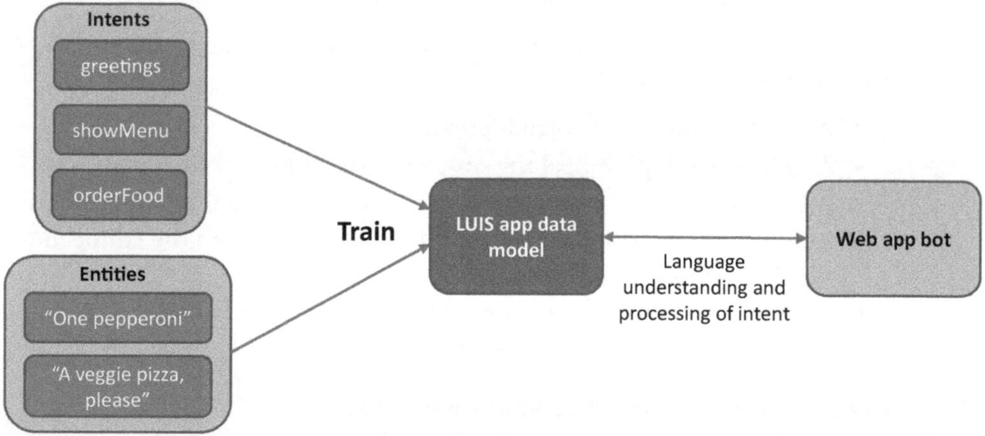

Figure 17.7 When you train the LUIS app, the intents and entities are input and processed to create a data model. This data model is then used by your web app bot to process language understanding and intent. The number of intents and entities input for processing are small, so the data model isn't perfect. In the real world, many more intents and entities would be provided, and you'd repeatedly train, test, and refine the data model to build progressively larger data sets to build an accurate model for processing language and intent.

In a more complex, real-world application, it may take longer to complete this training process as all your intents and entities are processed by the ML algorithms to build the required data model for your app to appropriately respond to customer communication.

6 With the LUIS app trained, select Test. Enter a couple of greetings, such as *hi* and *hello*. Below each of your messages is the top-scoring intent, along with the probability that the message, or utterance, you entered matches the intent. These basic greetings should correctly match the `greetings` intent.

7 Try to enter a different greeting, such as *(good) afternoon* or *(good) evening*. The single-word greeting based on the time of day may return an incorrect top-scoring intent, such as `orderStatus`. Try some other phrases until something doesn't line up with the expected intent, which indicates that the LUIS app doesn't fully understand what you mean. Select one of your incorrect messages, such as *morning*, and choose Inspect.

8 On the Inspect menu, choose to Edit the incorrect top-scoring intent. From the Assign to Intent drop-down menu, choose `greetings`, or whatever the most appropriate intent is for your incorrect phrase. You've made a change to your app, so choose to Train the LUIS app again. Figure 17.8 shows how to provide additional inputs for the ML algorithms to then process the data model and refine the language understanding and intent.

9 In the test messages window, enter the incorrect message again, such as *morning*. This time, the top-scoring internet should correctly be identified as `greetings`.

10 To make the updated LUIS app available to your web app bot, select the Publish option from the top menu. Leave all the defaults, and then select Publish to Production Slot. It takes a few seconds to complete the publish process.

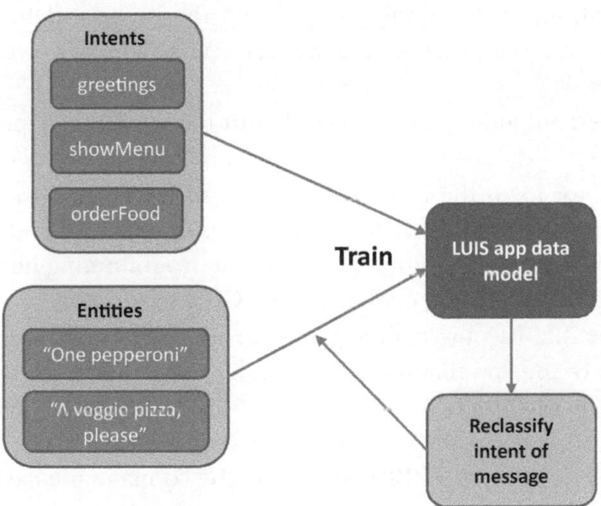

Figure 17.8 As you reclassify the intent of messages and retrain the LUIS app, the data model is refined as additional data inputs are provided to the ML algorithms. When you enter similar greetings in the future, the data model will hopefully be improved and will respond more appropriately.

Remember, your bot runs on a web app, so it has production and staging slots as you learned about way back in chapter 3. In the real world, you should publish to a staging slot, verify that everything works as expected, and then publish to the production slot. Those same PaaS features that allowed you to test and move web code between development and production lifecycles also benefits the lifecycle of your web app bot powered by LUIS.

The basic example shows that ML was able to take your data input of *(good) morning* being a greeting and understand that similar greetings, such as *(good) evening*, are also greetings. ML works best when a large set of data can be input to the data model, so it's important to thoroughly test and help train your app. The AI, in this case the LUIS app, is only as good as the size and quality of the data provided to the ML algorithms.

17.3.3 Building and running a web app bot with LUIS

You now have a basic web app bot in Azure and a LUIS app that handles the language processing and returns the customer intent. To integrate the two, the code for your bot needs to be modified to use LUIS. SDKs are available for the C# and Node.js programming languages. I find that Node.js makes it a little quicker and easier to understand what happens in the code, if this is all new to you. If you're familiar with C#, you're welcome to explore the C# SDK when you're finished with this chapter. For now, let's use a basic Node.js app from the GitHub sample repo to see your bot in action with LUIS.

> **Try it now**
> To update your web app bot with your trained LUIS bot, complete the following steps.

1. In the Azure portal, select Resource Groups from the menu at left, and then choose your resource group, such as `azuremolchapter17`. Select your web app bot, such as `azuremol`.
2. Under Bot Management at left, choose Build, and then select to Open Online Code Editor.
3. An online code editor loads the Node.js bot application that was created from the Language Understanding template in a previous exercise. If Node.js is new to you, don't worry! You're not going to do any real programming here; rather, you'll use the sample LUIS dialog code from the GitHub repo.
4. In the file explorer that lists the contents of your web app bot, select app.js to open the core part of the app that handles the integration of the LUIS app that you trained earlier.
5. Select all of the existing content of the app.js file, and delete it. Copy and paste the contents from http://mng.bz/ERJD on GitHub. To make life easier, select

the Raw button in GitHub to see only the contents of the file. The code automatically saves after you paste it back in the web app bot online editor. You can verify the save state in the upper-right corner of the online editor, which should indicate Saved.

There's nothing to build or deploy: your web app automatically runs the saved version of your bot! Your web app includes application settings that define your LUIS app ID and API key, so no code modifications are required.

NOTE The online code editor is a great way to make quick code changes, but for any real work, I suggest you use Visual Studio Code, which was introduced in chapter 1. VS Code is a lightweight editor that's great for Node.js development. If you want to use C#, there's a free Visual Studio Community edition that allows you to use the Microsoft Bot Framework and right-click-publish to Azure Web Apps (with care, for test purposes only).

Let's look at figure 17.9 to see what you've deployed. The LUIS app is now trained with ML algorithms, and your data model is ready for the Node.js app to let customers interact and order pizza.

Back in the Azure portal for your web app bot, select Test in Web Chat. It takes a few seconds the first time you connect to the bot, but you should then able to interact, view the list of pizzas on the menu, and create an order, as shown in figure 17.10. Try it yourself!

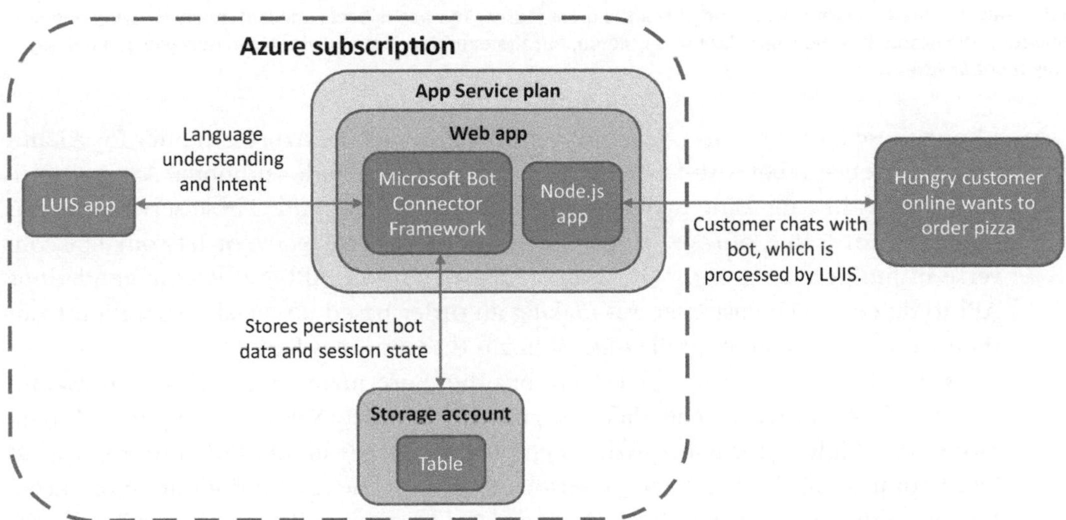

Figure 17.9 A customer can now access your bot online and ask to view the menu or order pizza. LUIS provides the language understanding, which allows the bot to process orders and send them to Azure Storage for additional processing.

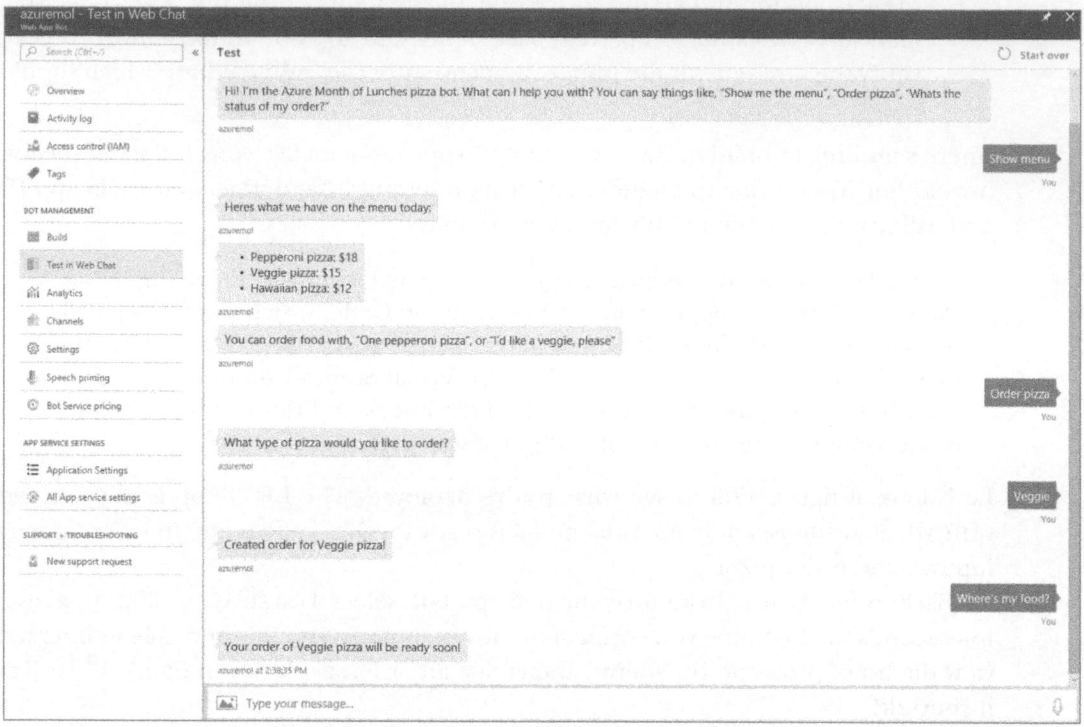

Figure 17.10 With your web app bot running, start a conversation and try to order a pizza. In this example dialog, you can view the menu, order a pizza, and check the order status. The app is basic and isn't really creating orders or updating the status beyond what pizza was ordered, but the exercise (hopefully!) shows how you can quickly deploy a bot in Azure.

I hope these basic exercises have given you an idea of what Azure can offer for AI and ML. The web app bot with LUIS can be expanded to include additional Azure Cognitive Services like the Bing Spellcheck API and Translator API. These services let you interpret words and phrases if the user spells them incorrectly, or let your bot converse in multiple languages. Or, you could use the Face API and Recommendations API to detect which customer was making an order based on facial recognition from their camera and automatically suggest pizzas that they may like.

The ML was part of the LUIS app, but there are many more ML resources and tools available in Azure. The ability to process large data sets and compute ML data models on high-performance Azure compute resources lowers the entry for you to build applications backed by some serious data sets. The applications are more accurate and efficient, and there's no hardware to buy or special tools to install, because the DSVMs include all the components required. Not all applications are a good fit for AI and ML, but as customers start to expect more what your business can offer, these Azure services can often help differentiate you.

Batch workload processing

Another area of Azure that may be of interest in terms of big-data and compute for ML are the Azure Batch and HPC services. Azure Batch lets you perform large, repetitive compute tasks without the need to manage clusters of schedulers for the work. Batch runs tasks on VMs with its own management and scheduler to help you, just as scale sets include autoscale and load balancing for VMs. Although it isn't directly related to ML, if you need other large compute-processing tasks, Batch is a great fit.

There are also high-performance computing (HPC) components in Azure for large VM sizes or access to graphical processing unit (GPU) VMs. Specific tools and suites such as DataSynapse and Microsoft HPC Pack can also be used to run applications that demand a large amount of compute power.

Areas such as ML, Azure Batch, and HPC are great examples of how to use cloud computing providers like Azure to run large compute tasks. You only pay for the compute resources you use, so you don't need to purchase and maintain expensive equipment that sees minimal use.

17.4 Lab: Adding channels for bot communication

In the earlier examples, you communicated with your bot through a test window in the Azure portal. Channels allow you to expand how you can interact with your bot. You can allow your bot to communicate with Skype or Facebook Messenger, or apps like Microsoft Teams and Slack. The Azure Bot Service simplifies the steps needed to integrate a bot with those external services:

1. In the Azure portal, select your web app bot, and then choose Channels. Pick a channel you like, such as Skype.

   Other channels often require you to create a developer connection, such as to Facebook or Slack. Skype lets you copy and paste some HTML code to make it work.
2. Provide any required information, such as Bot Application ID. You can find this ID under Settings for Bot Management.
3. If needed, use the online code editor to create a basic HTML page, such as default.htm, in the wwwroot directory, and paste any embedded code for your channel. You can open your web app from the Azure portal and then select its URL to open the default.htm page that includes your channel code, such as http://azuremol.azurewebsites.net/default.htm.

18 Azure Automation

Where possible, you shouldn't manually log in to a server and make changes. Software doesn't need to be installed by clicking buttons in a GUI, and updates don't need to be made to configuration files in a text editor. These manual actions introduce an opportunity for errors to occur, which can result in misconfigurations and application failures. If you want to replicate the configuration of a server, can you remember all the steps that were required to get the existing server up and running? What if you need to do it again in 6 months?

In chapter 16, we touched on a way to automatically check for and apply updates to servers. This magic happened with the use of Azure Automation. In this chapter, we examine how you can create, run, and edit runbooks, and use PowerShell Desired State Configuration to automatically install applications and configure servers.

18.1 What is Azure Automation?

An Azure Automation account brings together many different elements, as shown in figure 18.1. A core feature is creating and running scripts on demand or on a defined schedule. You can create scripts in PowerShell or Python, and let the Azure platform handle the scheduling and execution of those runbooks. You can share credentials and connection objects, and automatically apply and report on desired configurations of servers. Update Management, which we examined in chapter 16, keeps your servers secure and up to date with the latest host patches and updates throughout the lifecycle of your application environment.

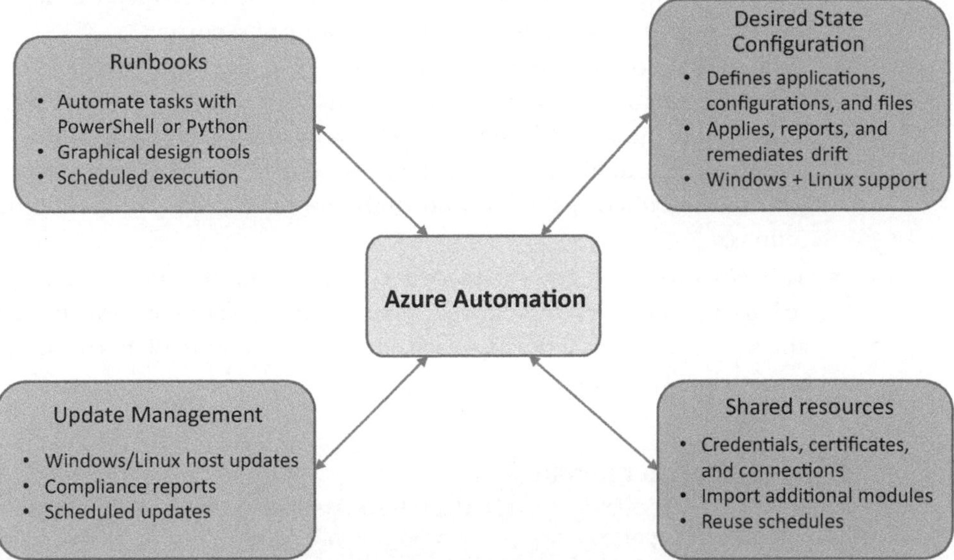

Figure 18.1 Azure Automation provides many related features. A shared set of resources, such as credentials, certificates, schedules, and connection objects can be used to automatically run PowerShell or Python scripts on target servers. You can define the desired state of a server, and Azure Automation installs and configures the server appropriately. Host updates and security patches can be automatically applied. All these features work across both Windows and Linux servers, in Azure and on-premises or other cloud providers.

To help simplify management across multiple runbooks or desired state configurations in an Automation account, you can share the following resources:

- *Schedules* let you define a set of times and recurrences that can be applied to each runbook or Update Management task. If you want to later change a regular occurrence, you can change one of the shared schedules rather than each individual runbook or Update Management task that uses it.
- *Modules* extend the core functionality by storing additional PowerShell modules. The base Windows PowerShell and Azure modules are already available, but additional modules, such as for Linux management, can be added and used in runbooks.
- *Credentials* for the different accounts that have permissions to execute various runbooks are stored as assets, not defined in each runbook. This approach lets you update and reset credentials as needed, and each runbook that uses them is automatically updated. Thus credentials aren't stored in plain text in runbooks, which increases the security of the runbooks.
- *Connections* define authentication properties to AAD service principals. This is a special type of user account that allows runbooks to access your Azure

resources. These connections typically use digital certificates, not usernames and passwords, to provide an additional layer of security.

- *Certificates* are often integrated with connection assets to provide a secure way to verify the identity of a service principal. As with basic credentials, you can regularly update these certificates in a central location, and each runbook that uses them can automatically access the new certificates. You can create and store your own certificates for use with runbooks or desired state configuration definitions.
- *Variables* provide a central place for runtime values such as names, location strings, and integers to be stored. When your runbooks are executed, these variables are injected. This approach limits the amount of hardcoded resources inside each runbook.

Work smarter, not harder

In chapter 16, we touched on how Operations Management Suite (OMS) can be used to monitor and report on servers in Azure, on-premises, or in other cloud providers. You install and configure the required agents on remote servers and then provide a way for them to connect back to the OMS infrastructure.

Azure Automation can also work across platforms and infrastructure. For example, the hybrid runbook worker can execute Automation runbooks on servers outside of Azure. You continue to use the shared Automation assets that define credentials, connections, and certificates, only this time those assets can be used to define the authentication components for the different platforms. You can also use desired state configurations on non-Azure VMs, for both Windows and Linux.

In all cases, a gateway component is installed in the remote environment to act as a proxy for the Automation commands as they're sent to the designated targets. This gateway proxy approach provides a single connection point for Automation into the remote environments and minimizes any security concerns, because there's no direct access to otherwise remote servers.

Runbooks and desired state configuration definitions may need to be edited slightly to run against on-premises physical servers compared to Azure VMs. As with OMS and Update Management, the advantage of Azure Automation is that it provides a single management plane and set of tools to deliver automation across all of your different infrastructures and servers.

18.1.1 Creating an Azure Automation account

Let's jump in and create an Azure Automation account and look at the default runbooks that are included. The demo runbooks provide a great framework to build your own runbooks, and there's also a graphical editor that you can use to drag and drop building blocks to generate automation scripts.

> **Try it now**
> To create an Azure Automation account and sample runbooks, complete the following steps.

1. In the Azure portal, select Create a Resource in the upper-left corner. Search for and select Automation, and then select Create.

   The Automation and Control option also creates an OMS workspace, as discussed in chapter 16, and configures the Automation Hybrid Worker to manage resources outside of Azure. For now, choose to create only the automation resource.
2. Enter a name, such as `azuremol`, and then create a new resource group, such as a `azuremolchapter18`. Select the most appropriate Azure region closest to you, and leave the option checked to Create Azure Run As Account.

The Create Run As Account option creates additional accounts in AAD. Security certificates are also created to allow the accounts to authenticate in an automated fashion, without the need for user prompts or saving a password. You could create and specify additional regular account credentials, defined as an Automation asset, to provide more granular control of which accounts are used to run certain runbooks.

When combined with RBACs, which we looked at in chapter 6, you can create specific Run As accounts for runbooks that provide a limited set of permissions needed to accomplish the tasks each runbook, or set of runbooks, requires. From a security perspective, this approach allows you to audit and control how and when these accounts are used. Avoid the temptation to create a single Run As account that provides admin-like permissions, because this approach provides little protection against abuse.

18.1.2 Azure Automation assets and runbooks

The Azure Automation account you created in the previous section includes some sample runbooks. Both PowerShell and Python samples are available. Connection assets and certificates are also added to the Automation account for the Run As accounts that were created. Let's explore those shared connection assets.

> **Try it now**
> To see the configured assets and sample runbooks, complete the following steps.

1. In the Azure portal, select Resource Groups at left, and then choose your group, such as `azuremolchapter18`. Select your Azure Automation account, such as `azuremol`.
2. Under Shared Resources in the menu on the left, select Connections.

3 Two Run As accounts are shown. Ignore AzureClassicRunAsAccount. As with unmanaged disks, which I mentioned as something to avoid in chapter 4, there are some traces of an older classic format of VMs in Azure. To maintain backward compatibility, some services provide management options for these classic VMs. You can no longer create classic VMs in the Azure portal, and the Azure CLI also doesn't support classic resources. So, ignore any classic references you may still see.

4 To view information about the regular account, select AzureRunAsConnection, as shown in figure 18.2.

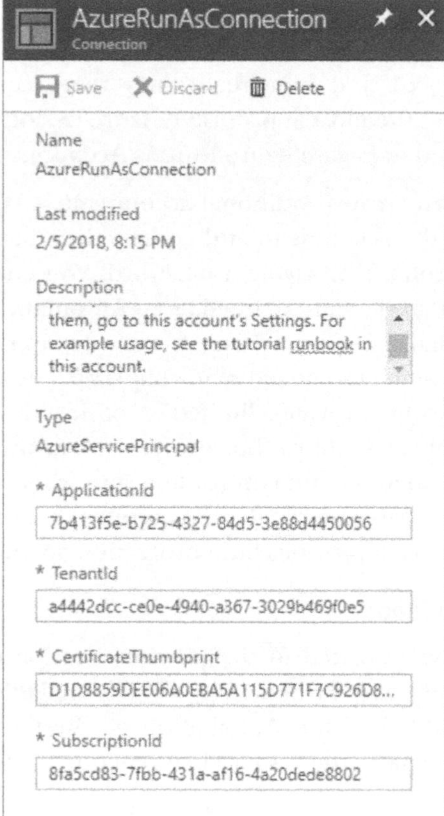

Figure 18.2 Information on the Run As account is shown, which includes an ApplicationId and TenantId. These are specific properties for AAD that help identify the credentials for this account. A CertificateThumbprint is shown, which matches up with a digital certificate we look at in the next step.

5 Select Certificates from the main menu on the Automation account under Shared Resources. Again, a classic certificate is also available, but ignore it, and choose the regular AzureRunAsCertificate. As shown in figure 18.3, the digital thumbprint matches RunAsConnection from the previous step.

6 Now that you understand the assets for connections and certificates, let's look at one of the sample runbooks. Select Runbooks from menu at left in the Automation account. A few sample runbooks are available. Choose the PowerShell runbook called AzureAutomationTutorialScript.

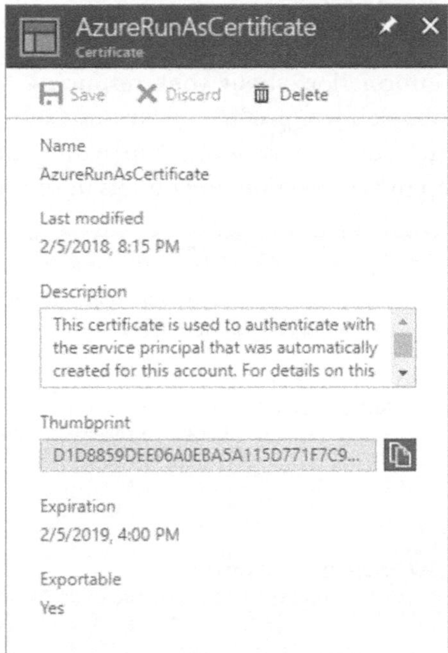

Figure 18.3 The thumbprint of the RunAsCertificate matches that shown in RunAsConnection. In your runbooks, you define which connection asset to use. The appropriate certificate is used to log in to the Azure account.

7 Across the top of the sample runbook are options to Start, View, and Edit the runbook. These should be self-explanatory!

A couple of other options include Schedule, which lets you create or select a shared resource that defines a schedule to execute the runbook at a given time, and Webhook, that lets you create a webhook URL to execute the runbook from some other script or action.

Choose View.

Azure Automation and source control with GitHub

Runbooks can be integrated with a source control system, such as GitHub. One of the great benefits of a source control system for your runbooks is that it provides a way for change management to be documented and to revert to earlier versions of the runbooks in the event of a problem.

Each time you save an Azure Automation runbook, a new version is committed to source control. You don't need to leave the runbook editor for this to happen, because the Azure platform and the configured source control system are configured to work back and forth. If you run into a problem with the new runbook, you can pull a previous version from source control that allows jobs to continue to run without delay, and then troubleshoot why the updated version has an issue.

Using source control also provides a record of what changes occurred and when. If you need to audit your runbooks or understand how they have developed over time, source control systems provide a great way to see the differences with each revision.

18.2 Azure Automation sample runbook

Let's examine how the sample PowerShell runbook, AzureAutomationTutorialScript, connects to Azure and gathers information about your resources. You can follow along with the Python sample runbook if you prefer; the layout is similar. PowerShell and Python are the only languages currently supported in Azure Automation runbooks. The following listing sets up the connection credentials in the runbook.

Listing 18.1 Setting up connection credentials

```
$connectionName = "AzureRunAsConnection"    <-- Creates an object for $connectionName
try                                         <-- Makes the connection request
{
  # Get the connection "AzureRunAsConnection "
  $servicePrincipalConnection=Get-AutomationConnection -Name
➥ $connectionName                           <-- Creates a service principal object

  "Logging in to Azure..."
  Add-AzureRmAccount `
     -ServicePrincipal `
     -TenantId $servicePrincipalConnection.TenantId `
     -ApplicationId $servicePrincipalConnection.ApplicationId `
     -CertificateThumbprint
➥ $servicePrincipalConnection.CertificateThumbprint
}
                                            Logs in to Azure
```

The code begins by creating an object for `$connectionName`. In the "Try it now" exercise, you saw that a default connection asset for AzureRunAsConnection was created. As you create your own runbooks, you may want to create additional Run As accounts and connection assets to separate the runbooks and the credentials that they use. The connection parts and exception handling that we look at next should be common across all runbooks. As needed, you can change the Run As connection asset to use.

Next, a `try` statement is used to make the connection request. A service principal object named `$servicePrincipalConnection` is created, based on `$connectionName`. The runbook then logs in to Azure with `Add-AzureRmAccount` and uses the `$servicePrincipalConnection` object to obtain the `TenantId`, `ApplicationId`, and `CertificateThumbprint`. We discussed these parameters as part of the connection asset earlier. The certificate asset that matches the thumbprint of `$servicePrincipalConnection` is then used to complete the login to Azure.

The next listing shows that if the connection fails, the runbook catches the error and stops execution.

Listing 18.2 Catching an error and stopping the runbook execution

```
catch {
    if (!$servicePrincipalConnection)
    {
        $ErrorMessage = "Connection $connectionName not found."
        throw $ErrorMessage
    } else{
```

```
        Write-Error -Message $_.Exception
        throw $_.Exception
    }
}
```

The `catch` statement handles any errors as part of the login attempt. If a service principal connection couldn't be found, an error is output. This error usually means the connection asset you specified can't be found. Double-check the name and spelling of your connection.

Otherwise, the connection object was found, and the service principal was used to log in, but that authentication process was unsuccessful. This failure could come from the certificate no longer being valid or the Run As account no longer being enabled. This functionality shows how you can revoke an account in AAD and ensure that any runbooks that use the credentials can no longer successfully run.

Now the runbook gets a list of all Azure resources.

Listing 18.3 Getting a list of Azure resources

```
$ResourceGroups = Get-AzureRmResourceGroup

foreach ($ResourceGroup in $ResourceGroups)
{
    Write-Output ("Showing resources in resource group "
➥+ $ResourceGroup.ResourceGroupName)
    $Resources = Find-AzureRmResource -ResourceGroupNameContains
➥$ResourceGroup.ResourceGroupName |
➥Select ResourceName, ResourceType
    ForEach ($Resource in $Resources)
    {
        Write-Output ($Resource.ResourceName + " of type "
➥+  $Resource.ResourceType)
    }
    Write-Output ("")
}
```

The final part of the runbook is where your runbook code would go. An object is created for `$ResourceGroups` that gets a list of all available Azure resource groups. A `foreach` loop then goes through each resource group, finds a list of resources, and writes out a list of the resource names and types.

This basic example shows how you can interact with Azure once the runbook has authenticated against the subscription. If you implement RBACs on the Run As account, only the resource groups that the account has permissions to see are returned. This approach to RBAC highlights why it's a good security principal to create and use scoped Run As accounts to limit the access the runbooks have to resources in your Azure environment. Always try to provide the least amount of privileges necessary.

If all this PowerShell or Python is new to you, don't worry. Both provide a great, basic scripting language but also can be used to develop complex, powerful applications. As a developer, either language should be relatively easy for you to pick up and use. If you're an IT pro, automating tasks helps free time for you to perform all the other jobs that are stacked up, and both PowerShell or Python are good places to start. Manning Publications has some other great books to help you, too!

18.2.1 Running and viewing output from a sample runbook

Now that you've seen what the sample runbook script contains and how the connection and certificate assets are used, let's execute the runbook and look at the output.

> **Try it now**
> To see the runbook in action, complete the following steps.

1. Close the window that shows the content of the runbook, and return to the overview of AzureAutomationScriptTutorial. Select Start at the top of the runbook window.
2. Confirm that you wish to start the runbook, and then wait a few seconds for the runbook to begin to run. Select Output, as shown in figure 18.4, and then watch the console window as the runbook logs in to Azure, gets a list of resource groups, and loops through and outputs the list of resources in each.

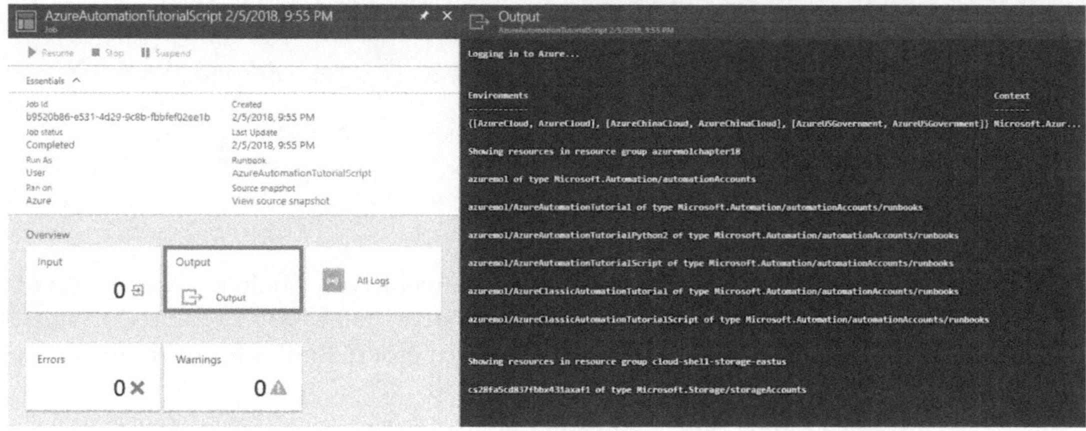

Figure 18.4 The output of the runbook can be viewed, along with any logs that are generated or errors and warnings. This basic example completes in a few seconds, but more complex runbooks may take longer. You can monitor the status of those longer runbooks and stop or pause their execution if needed.

Automation runbooks don't need to exist in isolation. One runbook can execute another runbook. This ability lets you build complex, multistep automation and minimize the duplication of code. As you design and build runbooks, try to break them down into small, discrete blocks of code. Common functions that you may reuse, such as logging in to Azure and generating a list of resources or a list of VMs, should be created as small runbooks that can be included in larger runbooks. As new PowerShell cmdlets are released or parameters are changed, you can quickly update a single shared runbook that includes those cmdlets rather than needing to update multiple different runbooks.

18.3 PowerShell Desired State Configuration (DSC)

Chapter 12 introduced the concept of VM extensions. An *extension* is a small software component that's installed in a VM to perform a given task. The VM diagnostics extension was installed on a VM to allow performance metrics and diagnostic logs to be reported back to the Azure platform from inside the VM. That's great, but we also talked a little about how you can automatically install software.

One way to install software and configure a server is to use PowerShell Desired State Configuration (DSC). With DSC, you define how you wish a server to be configured—the desired state. You can define packages to be installed, features to be configured, or files to be created, for example. What's great about DSC is that it goes beyond the first install and configure action. Over time, servers often undergo maintenance or troubleshooting events where configurations and packages are manually changed. The server would then deviate from the desired state that you initially defined. Figure 18.5 shows how Azure Automation can act as a central server that stores the DSC definitions, allowing target servers to receive their configurations and report back on their compliance.

The Local Configuration Manager (LCM) on each target server controls the process for connecting to the Azure Automation pull server, receiving and parsing the DSC definition, and applying and reporting on compliance. The LCM engine can operate without a pull server, where you locally call the process to read and apply a DSC definition. In this mode, where you manually push the configuration to the LCM

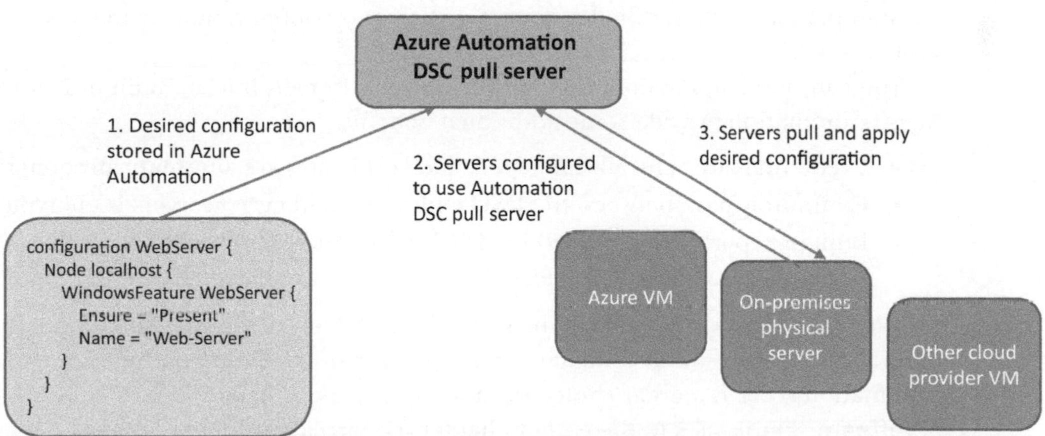

Figure 18.5 The desired state configuration for a server is created and stored in Azure Automation. The Automation account acts as a pull server, which allows connected servers to pull the required configuration from a central location. Different configuration modes can be set for the remediation behavior of the server if their configuration deviates from the desired state.

engine, you miss out on a lot of the central controls and reports that are often needed when you manage many servers.

There's also flexibility in how the target servers process the DSC definitions received from the Azure Automation pull server. You can configure DSC to operate in one of three configuration modes:

- *Apply only*—Your desired state is pushed and applied to the target server, and that's it. This is like the behavior of the Azure Custom Script Extension in that any configurations or installations are applied when first deployed, but there are no processes in place to stop those configurations manually changing over the lifecycle of the server.
- *Apply and monitor*—After the server has the desired state applied, DSC continues to monitor for any changes that cause the server to deviate from that initial configuration. A central report can be used to view servers that are no longer compliant with their desired state. This configuration is a good compromise between the need to keep a server compliant with the desired state and providing an element of human interaction to decide on remediation options.
- *Apply and autocorrect*—The most automated and self-contained configuration applies the desired state and then monitors for any deviations and automatically remediates the server should any changes occur to ensure that it remains compliant. There's a danger that legitimate manual changes will be overwritten and instead returned to the configured desired state, but this configuration mode makes sure the settings you assign always take priority.

PowerShell DSC can be used on VMs that run in other cloud providers, as well as on-premises VMs and physical servers. Thanks to .NET Core, PowerShell DSC can also be used on Linux servers, so it's not a Windows-only solution. This cross-provider, multi-OS support makes PowerShell a powerful choice to configure and manage servers at scale.

You can build and maintain your own DSC pull server, but the built-in features of Azure Automation provide some additional benefits:

- Credentials are centrally managed, and certificates are automatically generated.
- Communication between the DSC pull server and target servers is encrypted.
- Built-in reports are provided for DSC compliance, and there's integration with Log Analytics to generate more detailed reports and alerts.

This is very much a crash course in PowerShell DSC—it's a powerful component by itself and has been widely available for a few years now. When combined with Azure Automation, DSC is a great choice for automating the installation and configuration of software. Think back to the earlier chapters on virtual machine scale sets, for example. You can apply a DSC configuration to the scale set with Azure Automation, and then as each VM is created in the scale set, it will be automatically configured with the required components and application files.

18.3.1 Defining and using PowerShell DSC and an Azure Automation pull server

I hope that whirlwind tour of PowerShell DSC has given you an idea of what's possible! Let's use PowerShell DSC to automate the previous example of installing a basic web server on a VM.

> **Try it now**
> To see PowerShell Desired State Configuration in action, complete the following steps.

1 Create a Windows Server 2016 Datacenter VM, and open TCP port 80 for HTTP traffic. No more hand holding now that we're in chapter 18! You can create the VM in the Cloud Shell or Azure portal—your choice. Use the resource group you created in the previous exercises, such as `azuremolchapter18`. You can continue with the next few steps as the VM deploys.

2 On your local computer, create a file named webserver.ps1 and enter the following code:

```
configuration WebServer {
    Node localhost {
        WindowsFeature WebServer {
            Ensure = "Present"
            Name = "Web-Server"
        }
    }
}
```

Save and close the webserver.ps1 file.

3 In the Azure portal, select your resource group, and then choose your Automation account. At left, choose DSC Configurations. At the top of the DSC configuration window, choose to Add a configuration.

4 Browse to and select your webserver.ps1 file. The configuration name must match the filename, so leave the default name of webserver, and then choose OK.

5 It takes a few moments to upload and create the configuration. When it's ready, select the configuration from the list, and then choose Compile.

> **Behind the scenes of DSC**
> Let's pause to talk about what happens when you compile the configuration, as shown in the following figure. To distribute the DSC definitions, your PowerShell files are converted into a Managed Object Format (MOF) file. This file type is used for more than just PowerShell DSC and allows configuration changes on Windows components in a central, well-understood way. Any DSC definition, not just in Azure Automation, must be compiled before it can be applied to a target server. The LCM engine only accepts and processes MOF files.

(continued)

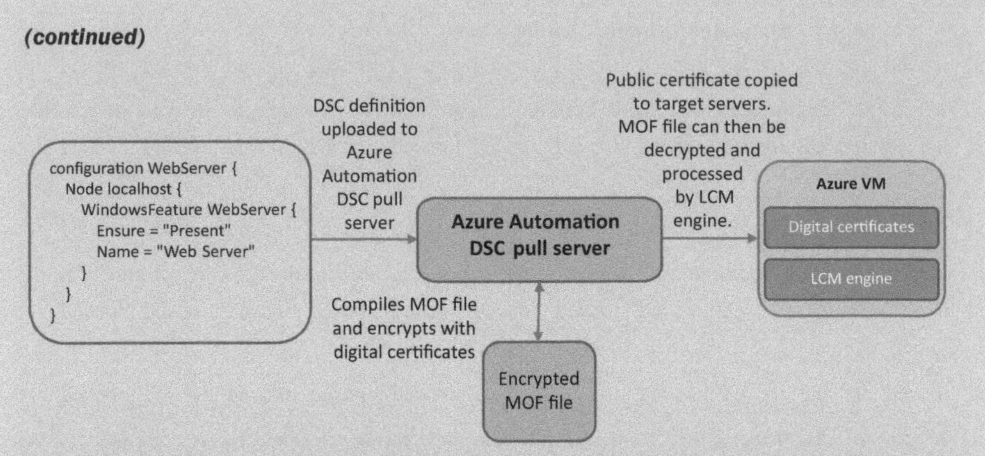

The Azure Automation DSC pull server automatically compiles the DSC definition you provide into a Managed Object Format (MOF) file. Digital certificates managed by Automation are used to encrypt the MOF file. DSC target servers receive the required public digital certificates and allows the LCM engine to decrypt and process the MOF file. The desired state can then be applied to the server.

Because the MOF file defines the complete state of your servers, you should protect its content. If an attacker knew all the application components installed and the location of various configuration files and custom code, it would increase the chance of your servers being compromised. Recent versions of PowerShell encrypt the entire MOF file. Azure Automation automatically generates the required digital certificates and keys when a target server is configured for DSC, which allows you to seamlessly use encrypted MOF files. Automation also then encrypts the traffic between the DSC pull server and target nodes, not just the MOF file.

The compile process in Azure Automation both converts the DSC definition you provide into an MOF file and encrypts the MOF file with the digital certificates and keys. The process to compile your DSC definition takes a few seconds but greatly secures your environment. Just another example of Azure securing your resources by default!

6. To apply the configuration to your VM, select DSC Nodes at left in your Automation account. Choose Add Azure VM, and then select the VM you created in previous steps.
7. Choose Connect. From the Node Configuration Name drop-down menu, select webserver.localhost. Set Default Configuration Mode to ApplyAndMonitor, and then select OK.
8. It takes a few moments to enable the VM to use the Azure PowerShell DSC pull server and apply the initial desired state. Once the Azure portal reports that the configuration is applied, can you remember how to add an inbound port rule for HTTP traffic (TCP port 80)? Check chapter 5 if you need a refresher; then, open the public IP of the VM in a web browser. The DSC process installed the IIS web server, and the default web page loads, as shown in figure 18.6.

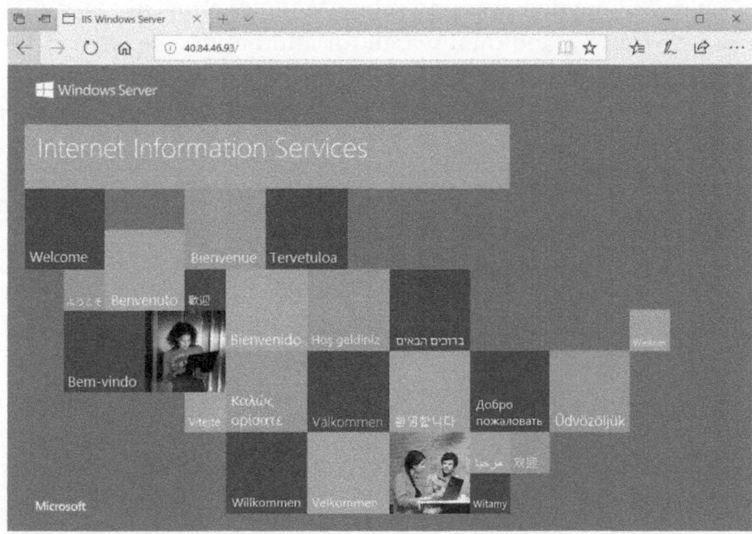

Figure 18.6 After the VM has been connected to Azure Automation DSC, the desired state is applied and the IIS web server is installed.

This basic example of PowerShell DSC only installs the web server feature. You can use PowerShell DSC to configure the IIS web server or copy your application code to the VM and run the site. Complex DSC definitions can be used to get the VM ready to serve traffic to your pizza store customers with no manual interaction. Again, think back to how you should design your applications to scale automatically—the VM can't wait for someone to log in and manually install and configure everything!

18.4 Lab: Using DSC with Linux

Just to prove that PowerShell DSC works on Linux servers, let's create an Ubuntu VM, install the necessary prerequisites, and then install a basic NGINX web server with DSC. In production, you could use a custom VM image that already had the management components installed, and then apply PowerShell DSC definitions as normal:

1. Create an Ubuntu 16.04 LTS VM, and open port 80. When you're ready, SSH to the VM.
2. Add the Microsoft Linux Software repo to the Ubuntu VM:

```
wget https://packages.microsoft.com/config/ubuntu/16.04/
➥packages-microsoft-prod.deb
sudo dpkg -i packages-microsoft-prod.deb
sudo apt-get update
```

3. Install the Open Management Infrastructure component from the Microsoft software repo:

```
sudo apt-get -y install omi
```

4 In the Azure Automation account, select Modules from the menu on the left. Select Browse Gallery, and then search for and import the nx module for managing Linux DSC resources.
5 On your local computer, create a file name nginx.ps1, and type the following code:

```
configuration nginx {
    Import-DSCResource -Module nx
    Node localhost {
        nxPackage nginx {
            Name = "nginx"
            Ensure = "Present"
            PackageManager = "apt"
        }
    }
}
```

6 Add a DSC configuration, and upload the nginx.ps1 file. When it's created, compile the configuration.
7 Add a DSC node, select your Ubuntu VM, and then choose your nginx.localhost Node Configuration name.
8 It takes a few moments for the VM to apply the desired configuration. You can view the list of connected VMs and their compliance status in the DSC nodes window. The VM reports Compliant when the LCM has accepted and applied the MOF file, but the apt-get install may take another minute or two.
9 Open TCP port 80 for HTTP traffic to your VM, and then enter the public IP address of your VM in a web browser to see the NGINX web server installed by DSC. If the website doesn't load, wait a minute or two for the install process to finish, and then refresh the page.

If you want to truly experience the brave new world of Microsoft and Linux, you can install PowerShell on your Linux VM. Complete the quick setup steps at http://mng.bz/A6Mc to understand how cross-platform PowerShell scripts can now be!

19 Azure containers

Containers, Docker, and Kubernetes have gained a huge following in a few short years. In the same way that server virtualization started to change how IT departments ran their datacenters in the mid-2000s, modern container tools and orchestrators are now shaking up how we build and run applications. There's nothing that inherently connects the growth of containers with cloud computing, but when combined, they provide a great way to develop applications with a cloud-native approach.

Entire books have been written on Docker and Kubernetes, but let's go on a whirlwind introduction and see how you can quickly run containers in Azure. There's a powerful suite of Azure services dedicated to containers that aligns more with the PaaS approach. You can focus on how to build and run your applications, rather than how to manage the container infrastructure, orchestration, and cluster components. In this chapter, we examine what containers are, how Docker got involved, and what Kubernetes can do for you. To see how to quickly run either a single container instance or multiple container instances in a cluster, we explore Azure Container Instances (ACI) and Azure Kubernetes Service (AKS).

19.1 What are containers?

There's been a huge wave of interest and adoption around containers over the last few years, and I'd be impressed if you haven't at least heard of one company that has led this charge: Docker. But what, exactly, is a container, and what does Docker have to do with it?

First, let's discuss a traditional virtualization host that runs VMs. Figure 19.1 is like the diagram we looked at back in chapter 1, where each VM has its own virtual hardware and guest OS.

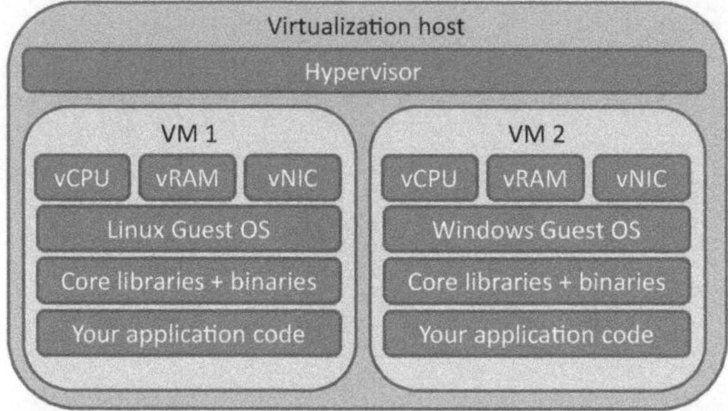

Figure 19.1 With a traditional VM infrastructure, the hypervisor on each virtualization host provides a layer of isolation by providing each VM with its own set of virtual hardware devices, such as a virtual CPU, virtual RAM, and virtual NICs. The VM installs a guest operating system, such as Ubuntu Linux or Windows Server, which can use this virtual hardware. Finally, you install your application and any required libraries. This level of isolation makes VMs very secure but adds a layer of overhead in terms of compute resources, storage, and startup times.

A container removes the virtual hardware and guest OS. All that's included in a container are the core applications and libraries required to run your app, as shown in figure 19.2.

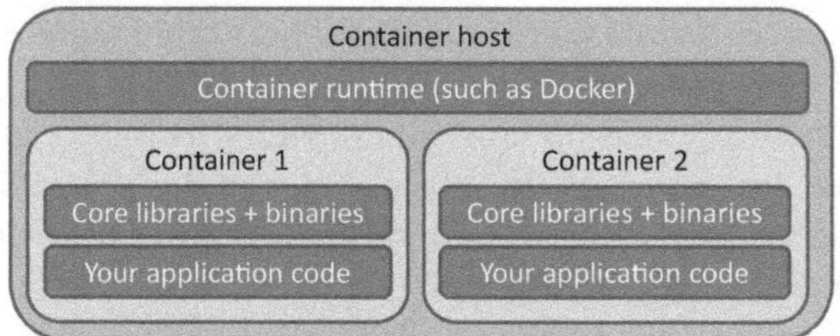

Figure 19.2 A container contains only the core libraries, binaries, and application code required to run an app. The container is lightweight and portable, because it removes the guest OS and virtual hardware layer, which also reduces the on-disk size of the container and startup times.

Many VMs can run on a single hypervisor, each VM with its own virtual guest OS, virtual hardware, and application stack. The hypervisor manages requests from the virtual hardware of each VM, schedules the allocation and sharing of those physical hardware resources, and enforces the security and isolation of each VM. The work of the hypervisor is shown in figure 19.3.

Multiple containers can also run on a single host. The container host receives the various system calls from each container and schedules the allocation and sharing of

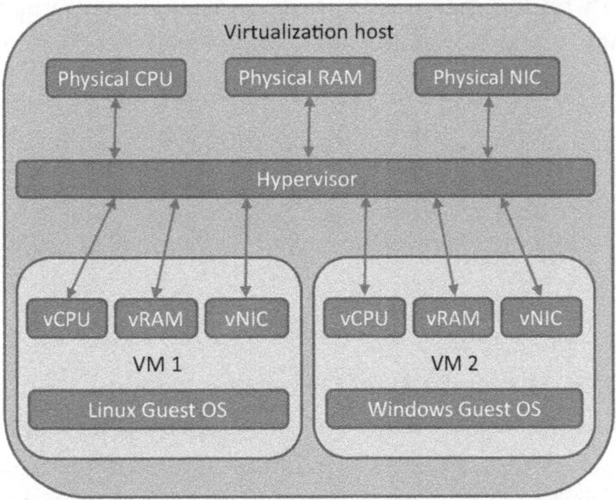

Figure 19.3 In a traditional VM host, the hypervisor provides the scheduling of requests from the virtual hardware in each VM onto the underlying physical hardware and infrastructure. The hypervisor typically has no awareness of what specific instructions the guest OS is scheduling on the physical CPU time, only that CPU time is required.

those requests across a shared base kernel, OS, and hardware resources. Containers provide a logical isolation of application processes. The work of the container runtime is shown in figure 19.4.

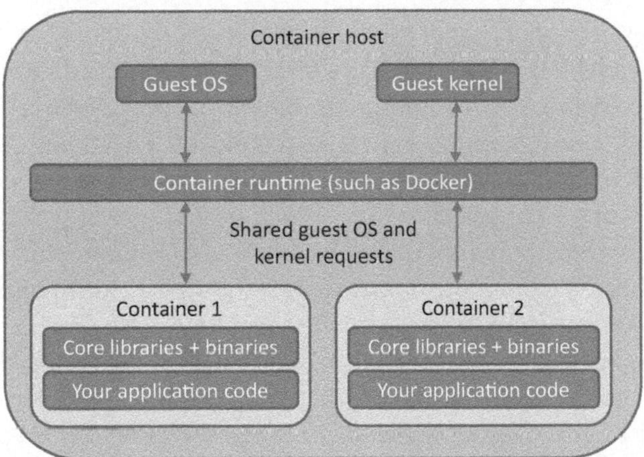

Figure 19.4 Containers share a common guest OS and kernel. The container runtime handles the requests from the containers to the shared kernel. Each container runs in an isolated user space, and some additional security features protect containers from each other.

Containers are typically much more lightweight than VMs. Containers can start up quicker than VMs, often in a matter of seconds rather than minutes. The size of a container image is typically only tens or hundreds of MBs, compared to many tens of GBs for VMs. There are still security boundaries and controls in place, but it's important to remember that each container technically shares the same kernel as other containers on the same host.

> **Try it now**
>
> It takes a few minutes to create an Azure Kubernetes Services cluster for use in the upcoming exercises, so complete the following steps and then continue reading the chapter.

1. Open the Azure portal, and select the Cloud Shell icon from the top menu.
2. Create a resource group. Provide a name, such as `azuremolchapter19`, and a location, such as `eastus`. Region availability of Azure Kubernetes Service may vary, so pick a major region such as `eastus` or `westeurope`. For an up-to-date list of region availability, see https://azure.microsoft.com/regions/services:

   ```
   az group create --name azuremolchapter19 --location westeurope
   ```

3. To create a Kubernetes cluster, all you need to specify is `--node-count`. In this example, create a two-node cluster:

   ```
   az aks create \
     --resource-group azuremolchapter19 \
     --name azuremol \
     --node-count 2 \
     --generate-ssh-keys \
     --no-wait
   ```

Why do you also generate SSH keys? Each node is a VM that has some additional components installed. These components include a container runtime, such as Docker, and some core Kubernetes components, such as the kubelet. The final `--no-wait` parameter returns control to the Cloud Shell while the rest of your cluster is created. Keep reading while the cluster is deployed.

Docker joined the container party with a set of tools and standard formats that defined how to build and run a container. Docker builds on top of existing Linux and Windows kernel-level features to provide a portable, consistent container experience across platforms. A developer can build a Docker container on their laptop that runs macOS, validate and test their app, and then run the exact Docker container, without modification, in a more traditional Linux or Windows-based server cluster on-premises or in Azure. All the required application binaries, libraries, and configuration files are bundled as part of the container, so the underlying host OS doesn't become a design factor or constraint.

The importance of Docker shouldn't be missed here. The terms *container* and *Docker* are often used interchangeably, although that's not technically accurate. Docker is a set of tools that helps build and run containers in a consistent, reliable, and portable manner. The ease of using these tools led to rapid adoption and brought the underlying container technology that had been around in one shape or another for over a decade into the mainstream. Developers embraced containers and the Docker platform, and IT departments have had to play catch-up ever since.

Docker participates in the Open Container Initiative. The format and specifications that Docker defined for how a container should be packaged and run were some of the founding principles for this project. The company's work has continued and has been built upon by others. Large contributors in the container space include IBM and Red Hat, contributing some of the core designs and code that powers the current container platforms. The Open Container Initiative and design format for container packaging and runtimes is important because it lets each vendor layer its own tools on top of the common formats, allowing you to move the underlying container between platforms and have the same core experience.

19.1.1 The microservices approach to applications

If containers offer a concept of isolation similar to VMs, can you run the same kind of workloads you do in a VM? Well, yes and no. Just because you can do something doesn't necessarily mean that you should! Containers can be used to run whatever workloads you're comfortable with, and there are benefits in terms of portability and orchestration features that we examine later in the chapter. To maximize the benefits of containers and set yourself up for success, take the opportunity to adopt a slightly different mental model when you start work with containers. Figure 19.5 compares the traditional application model with a microservices approach.

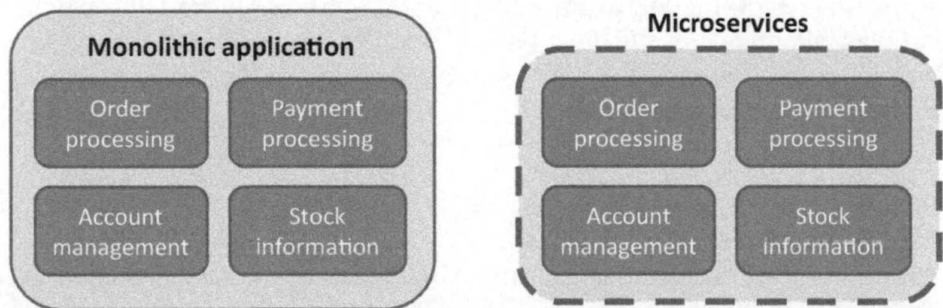

Figure 19.5 In a traditional monolithic application, the entire application runs as a single application. There may be various components within the application, but it runs from a single install and is patched and updated as a single instance. With microservices, each component is broken down into its own application service and unit of execution. Each component can be updated, patched, and scaled independently of the others.

A standard VM includes a full guest OS install, such as Ubuntu or Windows Server. This base OS install includes hundreds of components, libraries, and tools. You then install more libraries and applications, such as for the NGINX web server or Microsoft SQL Server. Finally, you deploy your application code. This VM typically runs a large part, if not all, of the application. It's one big application install and running instance. To improve performance, you may add more memory or CPU to the VM (vertical scaling, discussed in previous chapters) or increase the number of instances that run your application (horizontal scaling, as with scale sets). Creating multiple application instances only works if your application is cluster-aware, and it often involves some form of shared storage to enable a consistent state across the application instances. This traditional form of deployment is called a *monolithic* application.

A different approach to how you design, develop, and run applications is to break things down into smaller, bite-sized components. This is a *microservices* approach to application development and deployment. Each microservice is responsible for a small part of the wider application environment. Microservices can grow, scale, and be updated independently of the rest of the application environment.

Although this model may offer challenges at first while development and IT teams learn to adopt a different way to build and deploy applications, containers are a great fit for the microservice approach. Developers are empowered to deploy smaller, more incremental updates at a quicker pace than the monolithic approach to application development. Microservices and containers are also a great fit for continuous integration and continuous delivery (CI/CD) workflows where you can more easily build, test, stage, and deploy updates. Your customers receive new features or bug fixes faster than they would otherwise, and hopefully your business grows as a result.

Microservices with Azure Service Fabric

This chapter mainly focuses on Docker containers and orchestration with Kubernetes, but there's another Azure service that's similar in how it moves application development toward a microservices model. Azure Service Fabric has been around for a number of years and was historically a Windows-centric approach to building applications where each component was broken down into its own microservice. Service Fabric keeps track of where each microservice component runs in a cluster, allows the services to discover and communicate with each other, and handles redundancy and scaling.

Many large Azure services use Service Fabric under the hood, including Cosmos DB. That should give you a sense of how capable and powerful Service Fabric can be! Service Fabric itself runs on top of virtual machine scale sets. You know a thing or two about scale sets, right?

The Service Fabric platform has matured, and it can now handle both Windows and Linux as the guest OS, so you can build your app with any programming language you're comfortable with. Here's another example of choice in Azure: you have the flexibility to choose how you want to manage and orchestrate your container applications. Both Service Fabric and Azure Kubernetes Service have excellent benefits and use cases.

As a good starting point, if you currently develop, or would like to develop, microservices outside of containers, Service Fabric is a great choice. It provides a unified approach to handle both more traditional microservices applications and container-based applications. If you then choose to adopt containers for other workloads, you can use the same Service Fabric management tools and interface to manage all of your application environments. For a more container-focused application approach from the get-go, Azure Kubernetes Service may be a better choice, with the growth and adoption of Kubernetes providing a first-class container experience.

19.2 Azure Container Instances

Now that you understand a little more about what containers are and how you can use them, let's dive in and create a basic instance of the pizza store. This is the same example from earlier chapters, where you created a basic VM that ran your website, or deployed the app to web apps. In both of those cases, you had to create the VM or web app, connect to it, and then deploy a basic web page to it. Can the power of containers make your life that much easier? Absolutely!

A neat service called Azure Container Instances (ACI) lets you create and run containers in a matter of seconds. There are no upfront network resources to create and configure, and you pay for each container instance by the second. If you've never used containers and don't want to install anything locally on your computer, ACI is a great way to try the technology.

19.2.1 Creating a single container instance

To see how you can quickly run your pizza store, let's create a container instance. It takes only one command to run a container instance, but figure 19.6 shows how you bring together many components to make this happen behind the scenes. We look at the components of a Dockerfile and Docker Hub after you have the container instance up and running.

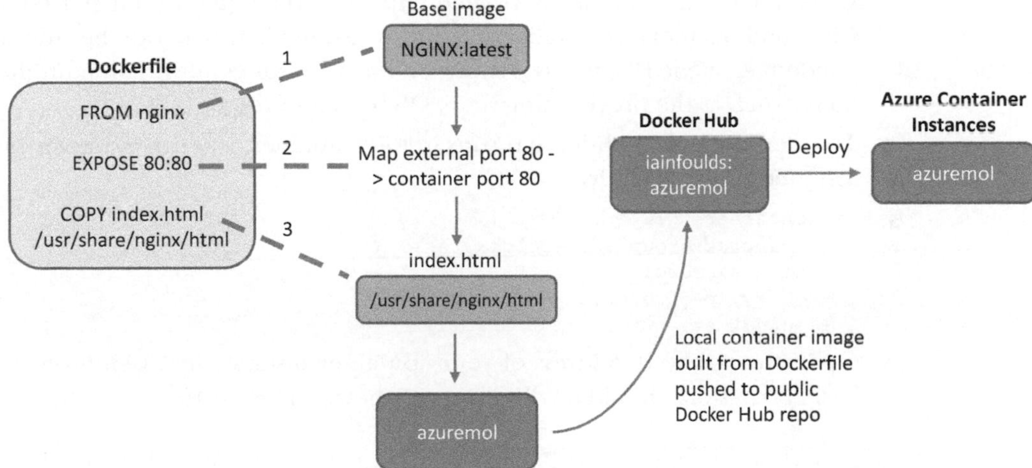

Figure 19.6 A Dockerfile was used to build a complete container image, azuremol. This image was pushed to an online public registry called Docker Hub. You can now create a container instance using this prebuilt public image from Docker Hub, which provides a ready-to-run application image.

Try it now

To create an Azure container instance that runs a basic website, complete the following steps.

1. Open the Azure portal, and select the Cloud Shell icon from the top menu.
2. Create a container instance. Specify that you'd like a public IP address and to open port 80. This exercise uses a sample image that I've created for you, which we'll examine a little more once the container is up and running:

   ```
   az container create \
     --resource-group azuremolchapter19 \
     --name azuremol \
     --image iainfoulds/azuremol \
     --ip-address public \
     --ports 80
   ```
3. To see what was created, look at the details of the container:

   ```
   az container show \
     --resource-group azuremolchapter19 \
     --name azuremol
   ```

   In the Events section, you can see as the image is pulled (downloaded) from Docker Hub, a container is created, and the container is then started. Some CPU and memory reservations are also assigned, which can be adjusted if needed. A public IP address is shown, along with some information on the container such as the provisioning state, OS type, and restart policy.
4. To open the basic website that runs in the container, you can query for just the assigned public IP address:

   ```
   az container show \
     --resource-group azuremolchapter19 \
     --name azuremol \
     --query ipAddress.ip \
     --output tsv
   ```
5. Open the public IP address of your container instance in a web browser. The basic pizza store should be displayed, as shown in figure 19.7.

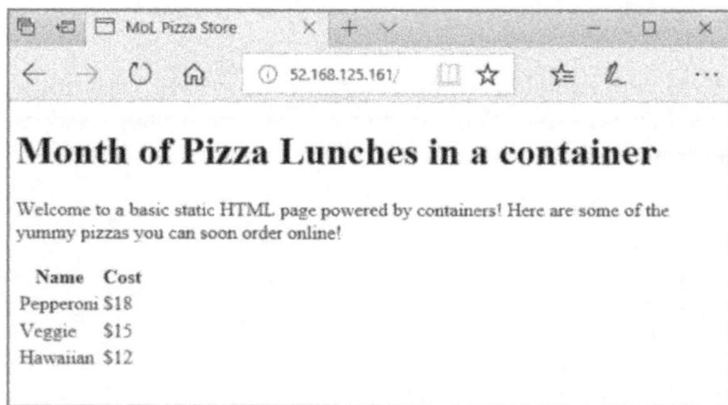

Figure 19.7 When you create a container instance, the pizza store website runs without any additional configuration. All the configuration and content are included within the container image. This quick exercise highlights the portability and power of containers—once the container image has been prepared, your app is up and running as soon as a new container instance is deployed.

Let's examine the container image. I don't want to get too far into the weeds of Docker and how to build container images, but it's important to understand where this image came from and how it runs the website without any additional configuration.

The image is built from a configuration definition called a *Dockerfile*. In a Dockerfile, you define what the base platform is, any configuration you wish to apply, and any commands to run or files to copy. Dockerfiles can be, and often are, more complex than the following example, which was used to build the azuremol sample container:

```
FROM nginx

EXPOSE 80:80

COPY index.html /usr/share/nginx/html
```

When this Dockerfile was used to build a Docker container image, NGINX was used as the source image, and the sample web page was copied into it. This container was then pushed to Docker Hub, an online, public repository that Docker provides to share and deploy containers. To deploy the container instance, you provided iainfoulds/azuremol as the container image to use. Azure looked in Docker Hub and found a repository named iainfoulds and, within it, an image named azuremol.

Let's examine each line of the Dockerfile:

- `FROM nginx`—In previous chapters, you created a basic VM, connected to it with SSH, and then manually installed the NGINX web server. In the example Dockerfile, all of that is accomplished in one line. This line says to base the container on an existing container image that's preinstalled with NGINX.
- `EXPOSE 80:80`—To allow access to your VM in previous chapters, you created an NSG rule that allowed port 80. In the Dockerfile, this line tells the container to open port 80 and map it to the internal port 80. When you created your container instance with `az container create`, you also specified that the Azure platform should permit traffic with `--ports 80`. That's all the virtual networking you have to think about!
- `COPY index.html /usr/share/nginx/html`—The final part is to get your application into the container. In previous chapters, you used Git to obtain the sample pizza store web page and then push that to your web app. With the Dockerfile, you `COPY` the index.html file to the local /usr/share/nginx/html directory in the container. That's it!

For your own scenarios, you can define a Dockerfile that uses a different base image, such as Node.js or Python. You then install any additional supporting libraries or packages required, pull your application code from source control, such as GitHub, and deploy your application. This Dockerfile would be used to build container images that are then stored in a private container registry, not a public Docker Hub repo like that in the example.

Azure Container Registry

You may think, Docker Hub sounds great: does Azure have such a wonderful thing? It does! Because you need to create a Dockerfile and build a container image, unfortunately it's not a two-minute exercise, and there's a lot to cover in this chapter. You can build your own images from a Dockerfile in the Cloud Shell, though, and I encourage you to explore this if you have time. But Azure Container Registry (ACR) is the route I'd choose to store my container images, for a couple of reasons.

First, it's a private registry for your container images, so you don't need to worry about potential unwanted access to your application files and configuration. You can apply the same RBAC mechanisms we discussed in chapter 6. RBAC helps you limit and audit who has access to your images.

Second, storing your container images in a registry in Azure means your images are right there in the same datacenters as the infrastructure used to run your container instances or clusters (which we look at next). Although container images should be relatively small, often only tens of MB in size, that can add up if you keep downloading those images from a remote registry.

ACR also provides built-in replication and redundancy options you can use to place your containers close to where you deploy and run them for users to access. This region locality is similar to how you used Cosmos DB global replication in chapter 10 to make those milliseconds count and provide your customers with the quickest possible access time to your applications.

If all this sounds exciting, check out the ACR quick starts to be up and running with your own private repository in a few minutes: http://mng.bz/04rj.

19.3 Azure Kubernetes Service

Running a single container instance is great, but that doesn't give you much redundancy or ability to scale. Remember how we spent entire chapters earlier in the book talking about how to run multiple instances of your application, load balance, and automatically scale them? Wouldn't it be great to do the same with containers? That's where you need a container orchestrator.

As the name implies, a *container orchestrator* manages your container instances, monitors their health, and can scale as needed. Orchestrators can, and often do, handle a lot more than that, but at a high level, a primary focus is handling all the moving parts involved in running a highly available, scalable, container-based application. There are a few container orchestrators, such as Docker Swarm and datacenter operating system (DC/OS), but one has risen above the rest to become the go-to orchestrator of choice—Kubernetes.

Kubernetes started as a Google-led and -sponsored open source project that grew out of the company's internal container orchestration tooling. Widely accepted by the open source community, Kubernetes is one of the largest and fastest-growing open source projects on GitHub. Many large technology companies, including Red Hat, IBM, and Microsoft, contribute to the core Kubernetes project.

In this section, let's take the same sample web app from the previous exercise with ACI to run a redundant, scalable deployment in Kubernetes. You'll end up with a few components, as shown in figure 19.8.

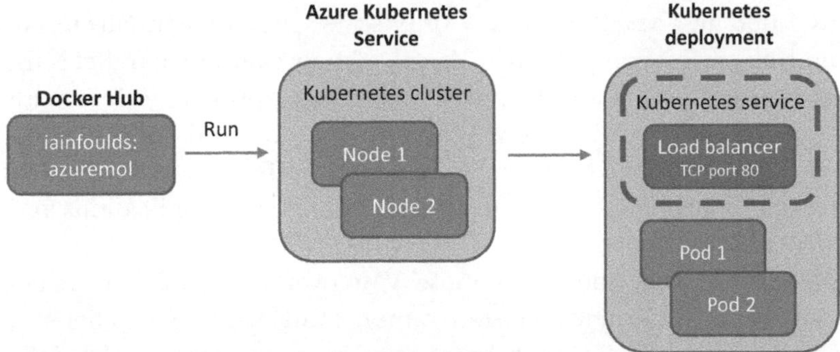

Figure 19.8 Your sample container from Docker Hub runs on a two-node Kubernetes cluster that you create in Azure Kubernetes Service. The Kubernetes deployment contains two logical pods, one on each cluster node, with a container instance running inside each pod. You then expose a public load balancer to allow your web app to be viewed online.

19.3.1 *Creating a cluster with Azure Kubernetes Services*

In chapter 9, we looked at how virtual machine scale sets reduce the complexity of deploying and configuring the underlying infrastructure. You say how many VM instances you want in a scale set, and the rest of the network, storage, and configuration is deployed for you. Azure Kubernetes Service (AKS) works in much the same way to offer a resilient, scalable Kubernetes cluster, with management handled by the Azure platform.

> **Try it now**
> To view the information on your AKS cluster, complete the following steps.

1. Open the Azure portal, and select the Cloud Shell icon from the top menu.
2. Earlier in the chapter, you created a Kubernetes cluster. The process took a few minutes, but hopefully it's ready now! Look at the status of cluster as follows:

   ```
   az aks show \
     --resource-group azuremolchapter19 \
     --name azuremol
   ```

   `provisioningState` should report `Succeeded`.

3 If your cluster is ready, obtain a credentials file that allows you to use the Kubernetes command-line tools to authenticate and manage resources:

```
az aks get-credentials \
  --resource-group azuremolchapter19 \
  --name azuremol
```

That's all it takes to get Kubernetes up and running in Azure! You may be wondering, "Can't I just build my own cluster with VMs or scale sets, and manually install the same Docker and Kubernetes components?" You absolutely can. The parallel is the IaaS and PaaS approach of VMs versus web apps. The web app approach offers many benefits: you only worry about high-level configuration options, and then you upload your application code. A managed Kubernetes cluster, as offered by AKS, reduces the level of complexity and management—your focus becomes your applications and your customers' experience.

In the same way that you may choose VMs over web apps, you may choose to deploy your own Kubernetes cluster rather than use AKS. That's fine—both approaches end up using the same Azure services components. VMs, scale sets, load balancers, and NSGs are all topics you've learned about in previous chapters, and all are still present with AKS clusters, although they're abstracted away. From a planning and troubleshooting perspective, you should have the skills to understand what's happening under the hood to make the managed Kubernetes offering work. Your comfort level, and how much time you want to spend managing the infrastructure, will help guide your decision-making process as you build a new application around containers in Azure.

19.3.2 Running a basic website in Kubernetes

You created a Kubernetes cluster in the previous section, but there's no application running. Let's change that! You now need to create the Kubernetes deployment that you saw earlier in figure 19.8; see figure 19.9.

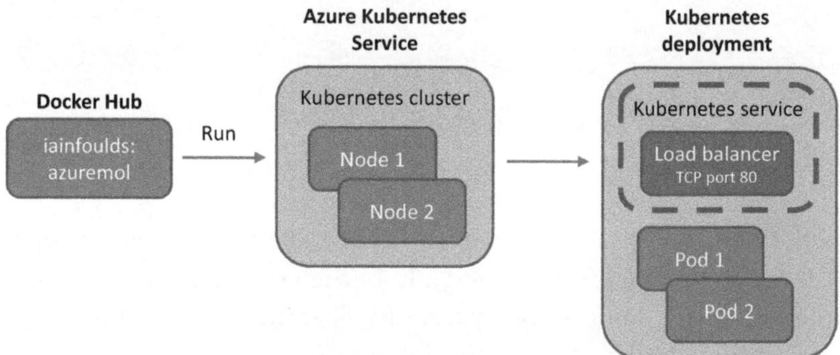

Figure 19.9 With the Kubernetes cluster created in AKS, you can now create a Kubernetes deployment and run your app. Your container runs across both nodes, with one logical pod on each node; you need to create a Kubernetes service that exposes a public load balancer to route traffic to your app.

Try it now

To deploy an application to your Kubernetes cluster, complete the following steps.

1. You interact with a Kubernetes cluster using a command-line utility called `kubectl`. Use the same iainfoulds/azuremol container image from Docker Hub that you ran as a container instance:

```
kubectl run azuremol \
  --image=docker.io/iainfoulds/azuremol:latest \
  --port=80
```

2. It may take a minute or so to download the container image from Docker Hub and start the application in Kubernetes. The application runs in a *pod*: a logical construct in Kubernetes that houses each container. Pods can contain additional helper-components, but for now, monitor the status of your container by looking at the pod:

```
kubectl get pods --watch
```

Even when the status of the pod reports as `Running`, you won't be able to access your application. The container instance you created earlier could route traffic over a public IP address directly to that one instance, but what do you think is needed for a Kubernetes cluster to route traffic to containers? If you guessed, "a load balancer," congratulations! Right now, you have only one pod—a single container instance. You scale out the number of pods in the end-of-chapter lab, and for that to work, you need a way to route traffic to multiple instances. So, let's tell Kubernetes to use a load balancer.

Here's where the integration between Kubernetes and Azure becomes cool. When you tell Kubernetes that you want to create a load balancer for your containers, under the hood, Kubernetes reaches back into the Azure platform and creates an Azure load balancer. This Azure load balancer is like the one you learned about in chapter 8. There are frontend and backend IP pools and load-balancing rules, and you can configure health probes. As your Kubernetes deployment scales up or down, the load balancer is automatically updated as needed.

3. To expose your application, tell Kubernetes that you want to use a load balancer. Add a rule to distribute traffic on port 80:

```
kubectl expose deployment/azuremol \
  --type="LoadBalancer" \
  --port 80
```

4. As before, `watch` the status of your service deployment:

```
kubectl get service azuremol --watch
```

5. Once the public IP address is assigned, that means the Azure load balancer has finished deploying, and the Kubernetes cluster and nodes are connected. Open the public IP address of your service in a web browser to see your web application running.

Application deployments in Kubernetes are often much more involved than this basic example. You typically define a service manifest, similar to a Resource Manager template, that defines all the characteristics of your application. These properties can include the number of instances of your application to run, any storage to attach, load-balancing methods and network ports to use, and so on. What's great about AKS is that you don't have to worry about the Kubernetes installation and configuration. As with other PaaS services like web apps and Cosmos DB, you bring your applications and let the Azure platform handle the underlying infrastructure and redundancy.

Keeping it clean and tidy

Remember to clean up and delete your resource groups so you don't end up consuming lots of your free Azure credits. As you start to explore containers, it becomes even more important to pay attention to what Azure resources you leave turned on. A single web app doesn't cost much, but a five-node AKS cluster and a few Container instances with georeplicated Azure Container Registry images sure can!

ACI instances are charged for by the second, and the cost quickly adds up if they're left running for days or weeks. An AKS cluster runs a VM for each node, so if you scale up and run many VMs in your cluster, you're paying for one VM for each node.

There's no charge for the number of containers each of those AKS nodes runs, but as with any VM, an AKS node gets expensive when left running. What's great about Kubernetes is that you can export your service configurations (the definition for your pods, load balancers, autoscaling, and so on) to deploy them elsewhere. As you build and test your applications, you don't need to leave an AKS cluster running—you can deploy a cluster as needed and deploy your service from a previous configuration.

This has also been a warp-speed introduction to containers and Kubernetes, so don't worry if you feel a little overwhelmed right now! Manning has several great books that can help you dive further into Docker, microservices application development, and Kubernetes. Check them out if this chapter sounds exciting and you want to explore further!

19.4 Lab: Scaling your Kubernetes deployments

The basic example in this chapter created a two-node Kubernetes cluster and a single pod that runs your website. In this lab, explore how you can scale the cluster and number of container instances:

1. You can see how many nodes are in your Kubernetes cluster with `kubectl get nodes`. Scale up your cluster to three nodes:

```
az aks scale \
  --resource-group azuremolchapter19 \
  --name azuremol \
  --node-count 3
```

2 It takes a minute or two to scale up and add the additional node. Use `kubectl` again to see the status of your nodes. Look at your current deployment with `kubectl get deployment azuremol`. Only one instance was created earlier. Scale up to five instances, or *replicas*:

```
kubectl scale deployment azuremol --replicas 5
```

3 Use `kubectl` again to examine the deployment. Look at the pods, the running container instances, with `kubectl get pods`. Within a matter of seconds, all those additional replicas were started and were connected to the load balancer.

20 Azure and the Internet of Things

For me, one of the most exciting areas of technology in the last few years is the Internet of Things (IoT). I don't quite believe that a dishwasher or fridge needs to be connected to the internet just yet, and there are valid privacy concerns over a TV or audio device that's permanently connected to the internet and always listening for the sound of your voice to issue a command. There are, however, a lot of a practical applications for IoT devices. You could have manufacturing equipment report on its health status, generate maintenance alerts, and allow operators to understand its efficiency across multiple factories around the world. A trucking company could stream telemetry from its vehicles about loads being carried and average driving times, and be able to more intelligently reroute drivers as needed. Shipping companies can track each container and help their customers better manage their supply chain by knowing where their resources are.

In Azure, you can integrate IoT devices with a range of services. Azure Web Apps can provide a frontend for your data to be visualized, Storage can be used to log data streamed from devices, and serverless features like Azure Logic Apps (discussed in the next, and final, chapter) can process the data received. In this chapter, we examine what IoT is and how to use Azure IoT Hub to centrally manage and collect data from devices. You then see how to use an Azure web app to view real-time data from an IoT device.

20.1 What is the Internet of Things?

Interest in the Internet of Things (IoT) has grown considerably the last few years, but it's a vague term and can be applied to many different scenarios. At a basic level, IoT is an approach where many interconnected devices—typically small, low-cost electronic devices—connect back to central systems and applications. The connected devices usually report information they collect from attached sensors or inputs. This information can then be processed by a central system—perhaps with AI or ML as discussed in chapter 17—and carry out appropriate actions. Figure 20.1 shows a high-level approach to IoT.

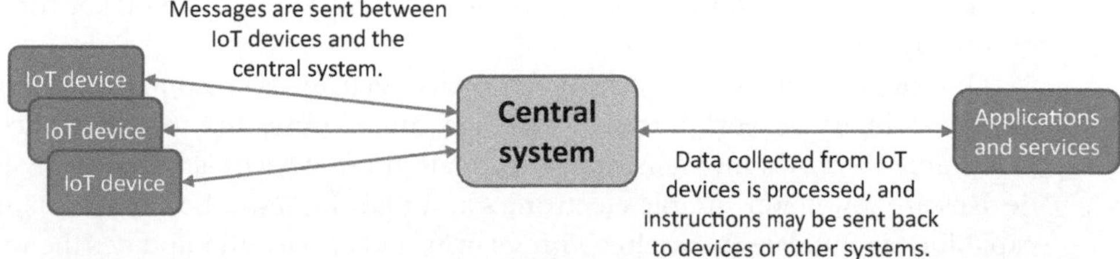

Figure 20.1 Messages are sent between many connected IoT devices and a central system. Your applications and services can then process the data received and send device instructions to perform additional actions in response to their collected data.

Some examples of IoT in action include the following:

- *Parking garage*—A small sensor above each parking bay detects whether a vehicle is parked there. A light above each bay can then illuminate green if the parking bay is empty, or red if it's occupied. Drivers entering the parking garage can see real-time information boards on each floor that let them know how many open parking spots there are. The red and green lights above each bay help drivers quickly determine the location of open spots as they drive along each aisle.
- *Factory*—Machinery on a factory floor can report back information on operating output, consumable levels, and maintenance needs. A central system can then schedule a maintenance technician to proactively repair equipment or resupply consumables, which reduces any downtime in the production line. When combined with AI and ML, maintenance schedules can be predicted, and the correct amount of supplies or raw materials can be delivered just before they're needed in production.
- *Transportation*—Public transportation buses or trains can include GPS sensors that report on location and speed. Ticketing information can also be collected to report on how many people are being transported. Passenger information boards at a train station or bus terminal can then provide real-time information about when each vehicle will arrive. When combined with AI and ML, this means waiting passengers can receive suggestions for alternate routes based on traffic conditions, delays, or heavy passenger volume.

IoT often works alongside other applications and services. The factory and transportation scenarios could use AI and ML to better inform production decision or make suggestions to passengers. Web applications can use information received from IoT devices to provide access from mobile devices or generate alerts and notifications. Data received from IoT devices could be logged to a database system like Cosmos DB that's then processed by business intelligence applications and generate reports.

More future-looking ideas around IoT include things like your refrigerator sensing food levels and generating a shopping list or even ordering food from a local grocery store. Your car could report data back to the dealership and have any required parts or consumables ready when you take the vehicle in for service. Or what if, when your alarm clock goes off to wake you up in the morning, your coffee maker turns on and gets ready for breakfast?

One big area of concern with IoT is device security. With so many devices outside of your primary network infrastructure and often connected to the public internet, being able to provision, maintain, and update those devices is a challenge. Many IoT devices are low-power, simple electronics and may not have the storage or processing capabilities to update themselves with security and application updates the way a traditional desktop or laptop does. It's not enough to deploy a bunch of IoT devices, especially consumer-level devices, without a plan to adequately secure them and provide updates and maintenance.

These security concerns shouldn't stop you from building applications and services that use IoT devices. IoT brings a new set of challenges to traditional device maintenance, but there are solutions that allow you to centrally provision and maintain devices, and secure device communication. By now, I'm sure you may have guessed that Azure has such an IoT solution! It offers a suite of IoT services; let's see how you can start to explore IoT with Azure.

Accelerating your Azure IoT deployments

This chapter focuses on Azure IoT Hub, a service that lets you provision and connect IoT devices to build your own solutions. You can define how those IoT devices connect, what users or applications can access their data, and secure connectivity. How to build and deploy the application infrastructure to connect everything together is up to you.

Azure IoT solution accelerators are prebuilt key scenarios, such as remote monitoring of devices or a connected factory. Accelerators deploy common Azure services such as IoT Hub, Web Apps, Cosmos DB, and Storage, and run a sample application that integrates all these different services.

You still need to customize the application for your own environment, IoT devices in use, and the data to be collected and monitored, but IoT solution accelerators give you a great framework to get started. Whereas IoT Hub creates a way for you to connect IoT devices to Azure and then leaves you to deploy additional services that you need, IoT solution accelerators deploy prebuilt solutions that use the most common Azure services you'd use.

> If you get hooked on IoT after this chapter and want to learn more, the Azure IoT solution accelerators are a great way to see the possibilities of what Azure can offer. As we've discussed throughout this book, Azure is way more than just one or two independent services. There are many services you can deploy together to provide the best application experience possible for your customers.

20.2 Centrally managing devices with Azure IoT Hub

Azure IoT Hub lets you centrally manage, update, and stream data from IoT devices. With this service, you can perform actions such as configuring application routes for data received from devices, provisioning and managing certificates to secure communication, and monitoring health with Azure diagnostics and metrics. You can connect your IoT devices to other Azure services and applications to let them send and receive data as part of a wider solution. As with all things in Azure, access can be controlled with RBACs, and diagnostic data can be centrally collected for troubleshooting and monitoring or alerts. Figure 20.2 outlines how an IoT hub acts as the central place for IoT devices to connect to the wider Azure services and applications.

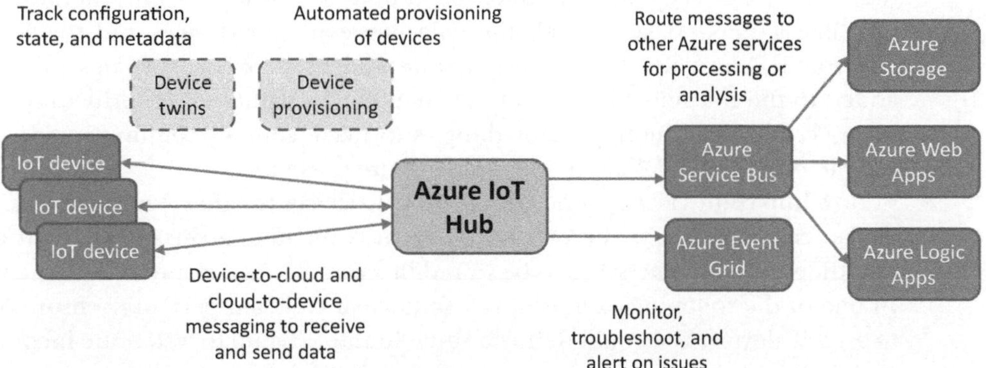

Figure 20.2 With an IoT hub, you can centrally provision and manage many IoT devices at scale. Two-way communication exists between devices and Azure to read and write data. You can process data received from devices and route it to other Azure services such as Web Apps and Storage. To monitor and troubleshoot issues, you can route information to Azure Event Grid, which we look at in the next chapter, and then link to other monitoring solutions.

You control access to an IoT hub with shared access policies. These policies are like user accounts and permissions. Default policies exist that allow devices and services to connect to the IoT hub, or to read and write information from the device registry that tracks connected IoT devices and security keys. Each policy can be assigned one or more of the following permissions:

- Registry read
- Registry write
- Service connect
- Device connect

Shared access keys are used by applications and services to connect to an IoT hub. As with Storage, discussed in chapter 4, shared access keys allow you to define connection strings to identity the host, access policy, and access key. A connection string combines the access key, access policy type, and the IoT hub hostname. Here's a sample IoT hub connection string:

```
HostName=azuremol.azure-devices.net;SharedAccessKeyName=registryRead;
➥SharedAccessKey=6be2mXBVN9B+UkoPUMuwVDtR+7NZVBq+C7A1xCmQGAb=
```

Primary and secondary keys exist, which can be rotated and updated for security purposes, just like regularly updating passwords. Solutions such as Azure Key Vault, discussed in chapter 15, are great ways to track and store these keys for applications to obtain when needed. This approach to key management means you can frequently rotate access keys without the need to also update all of your application code.

Digital certificates can be stored in an IoT hub and automatically provisioned to IoT devices. Remember, IoT devices are often outside of your core infrastructure and may connect directly over the internet without any form of secure network connection like a VPN. Make sure all the data between your devices and the IoT hub is encrypted. Azure Key Vault can generate and store SSL certificates that are then added to the IoT hub. Or you can use an existing certificate authority to request and issue certificates. The important thing is to make sure all communication between your IoT devices and Azure is encrypted where possible.

IoT hub routes let you send data from IoT devices to other Azure services. You can define criteria, such as the message content containing a certain keyword or value, and then route the messages to be stored in Azure Storage or processed by a web app. In one of the following exercises, you simulate a basic temperature sensor connected to an IoT device. You could define a route in the IoT hub to watch the incoming data and, if the recorded temperature exceeded 100°F, route the data to a logic app to send an e-mail alert. We discuss the wonderful world of serverless computing and logic apps in the next chapter!

Living on the Edge

In this chapter, we focus on Azure IoT Hub. Another service, Azure IoT Edge, lets you run some services such as Azure Functions and Stream Analytics in your local environment. Rather than all of your IoT devices streaming data to be processed centrally in Azure, you can process the data within each location.

Azure IoT Edge runs applications and services in containers, as we discussed chapter 19. The use of containers allows IoT Edge to be portable and consistent in how it works across different devices and environments. Prebuilt Azure services can be deployed, or you can write your own applications and distribute them to edge locations.

The major benefit of IoT Edge is that you offload some of the data processing and network data transfers. If you can process data locally in IoT Edge, you can batch large chunks of data and transmit that back to Azure. Central applications can then aggregate information from other Edge locations to be processed by services such as AI and ML.

Another great scenario for Azure IoT Edge is remote locations, often found in the oil and gas and transportation industries, where internet connectivity may not be reliable enough for all the IoT device data to be streamed back to Azure for central processing. IoT Edge allows those remote locations to continue to operate with some amount of autonomy, even when there's no internet connection.

As you plan an application infrastructure that involves IoT devices, examine how you handle network outages and poor internet connections. If your environment relies on the internet, plan for redundant internet connections and equipment to route the data. Or look at IoT Edge to locally process data when it can't be done centrally in Azure.

Try it now

To get started with IoT and create an IoT hub, complete the following steps.

1 Open the Azure portal, and then launch the Cloud Shell. Create a resource group, such as `azuremolchapter20`:

```
az group create --name azuremolchapter20 --location eastus
```

2 Create an IoT hub. Enter a name, such as `azuremol`. For these exercises, you can use a free-tier IoT hub, f1:

```
az iot hub create \
  --resource-group azuremolchapter20 \
  --name azuremol \
  --sku f1
```

NOTE You can create only one free-tier hub per subscription, but they're great for testing communication between devices and integrating with other Azure services. The free-tier hub is currently limited to 8,000 messages per day. This may sound like a lot, but depending on what you're doing, a single device that sends a message to the IoT hub approximately every 12 seconds would max out that 8,000-message limit!

3 You've done a lot of work with the Azure CLI in this book, because the Cloud Shell and CLI commands make it quick to create and manage resources. As mentioned in earlier chapters, the Azure CLI can also use additional modules, called *extensions.* These extensions add more functionality and often update outside the regular release cycle of the main Azure CLI. Azure IoT is rapidly

expanding and adding new features, so the main commands to interact with IoT Hub come from an Azure CLI extension.

To get the full functionality you need for later exercises, install the Azure CLI IoT extension:

```
az extension add --name azure-cli-iot-ext
```

Your IoT hub is pretty empty right now. There's not much you can do with it without one or more connected IoT devices. A common device used for IoT is the Raspberry Pi. This is a low-cost minicomputer that can connect to Wi-Fi networks and use common off-the-shelf sensors for temperature, humidity, and pressure. You can also use it to control small motors, lights, and timers. You don't need to rush out and buy a Raspberry Pi to work with an IoT hub, though—you can simulate one in your web browser!

20.2.1 Creating a simulated Raspberry Pi device

IoT devices are great, but there's a barrier to entry in that you need an actual device to use, right? Nope! There are a few different ways that you can simulate an IoT device with software. This software-based approach lets you focus on building your application quickly and then transitioning to real hardware. You still need to pay attention to how your code runs on real IoT hardware, especially low-power devices, because they may not have access to all the required libraries, or even memory resources, that your simulated application does.

Microsoft provides a free Raspberry Pi simulator through GitHub at https://azure-samples.github.io/raspberry-pi-web-simulator. A common BME280 sensor that collects temperature and humidity readings is simulated in software, along with a simulated LED to show when the device transmits data to the IoT hub. You can't customize this much, but it does let you see how a basic Node.js application can run on the Raspberry Pi, poll data from a sensor, and send that back to Azure.

NOTE If things like the Raspberry Pi, electronics and temperature sensors, and Node.js seem daunting, don't worry. As with the chapters on AI and ML, containers, and Kubernetes, we're not going to get super deep into IoT devices and programming. If you feel like you want to plug in a soldering iron and geek out with electronics by the end of this chapter, though, you're more than welcome to!

Before you can use the Raspberry Pi simulator, you need to create a device assignment in Azure IoT Hub. This process creates a unique device ID so your IoT hub understands which device it's communicating with and how to process the data. In more complex scenarios, you could provision additional settings for the device and push digital certificates. For this exercise, you just create a device identity.

Try it now

To create a simulated Raspberry Pi IoT device, complete the following steps.

1 In the Azure Cloud Shell, create a device identity in your IoT hub, such as `azuremol`. Provide a name for the device, such as `raspberrypi`:

```
az iot hub device-identity create \
  --hub-name azuremol \
  --device-id raspberrypi
```

2 Remember the shared access policies from the previous section? Each IoT device also has its own access key and connection string that are used to identify it when it communicates back to the IoT hub. To use your device with the Raspberry Pi simulator, you need the information for the device connection string. This unique identifier includes the hostname of your IoT hub, the ID of the device, and an access key:

```
az iot hub device-identity show-connection-string \
  --hub-name azuremol \
  --device-id raspberrypi \
  --output tsv
```

3 Copy the contents of your connection string—you need it in the next step. The output is similar to the following:

```
HostName=azuremol.azure-devices.net;DeviceId=raspberrypi;
➥ SharedAccessKey=oXVvK40qYYI3M4u6ZLxoyR/PUKV7A7RF/JR9WcsRYSI=
```

4 Now comes the fun part! Open the Raspberry Pi simulator in your web browser: https://azure-samples.github.io/raspberry-pi-web-simulator. Look in the code section at right in the simulator. Around line 15, there should be a `connectionString` variable, which already prompts you for *[Your IoT hub device connection string]*. Copy and paste your connection string from the previous step, as shown in figure 20.3.

5 Select the Run button just below the code window to start the simulator. Every 2 seconds, the console window displays a message that shows the data sent to the IoT hub. The red LED on the circuit diagram also flashes when this happens, to simulate how outputs connected to the Raspberry Pi can be controlled. The output message in the console window is similar to the following:

```
Sending message: {"messageId":1,"deviceId":"Raspberry Pi Web
➥Client","temperature":24.207095037347923,
➥"humidity":69.12946775681091}
```

Where did the temperature and humidity readings come from? This device is a simulated Raspberry Pi, and there's no real BME280 sensor, so the application generates these values in software. If you look at the rest of the code in the simulator window, around line 99 the application defines the sensor. The simulator then replicates how the real sensor would act, and generates data returned

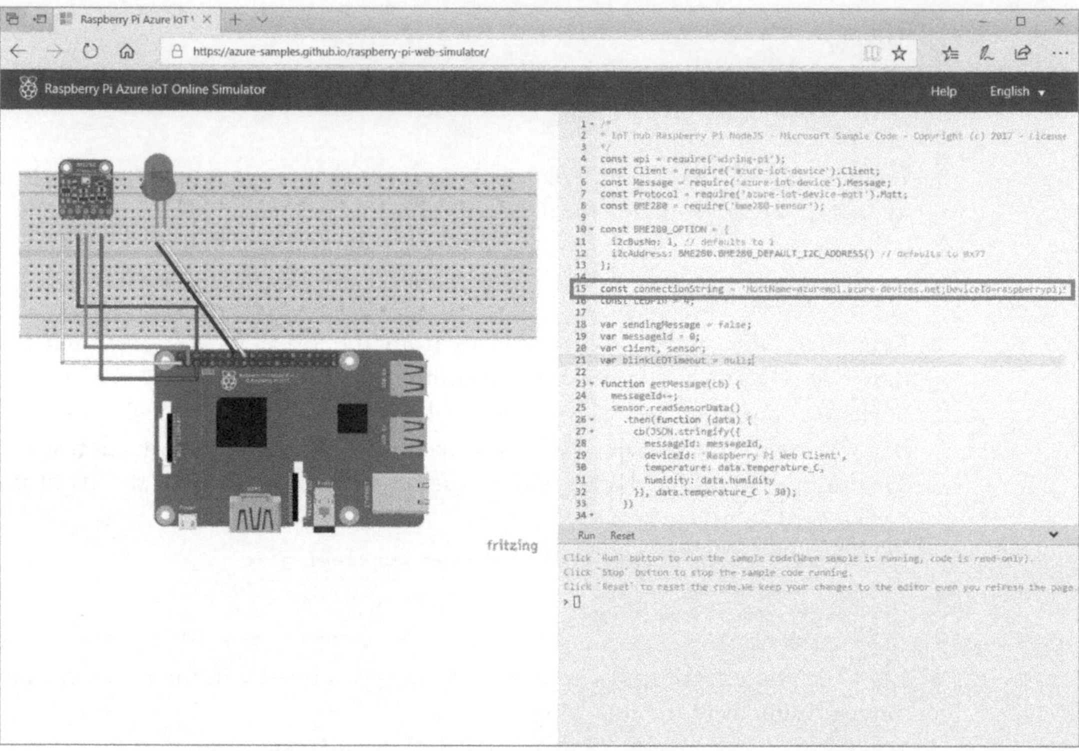

Figure 20.3 Copy and paste the connection string for your Azure IoT device into the Raspberry Pi simulator. The `connectionString` variable is used to connect to transmit the simulated sensor data to Azure.

from the sensor to the application. It's a basic example, so think what else you could read in here: revolutions per minute (RPM) of a motor or engine, or GPS coordinates of a shipping container or truck, and so on. This is where there's a balance between simulating a device in software and building a functional application with real hardware and sensor data. At some point, you need to purchase or borrow equipment if you want to get into more depth with Azure IoT.

6 To confirm that your simulated device messages are being received by the IoT hub, examine the quota status. Provide the name of your IoT hub, such as azuremol:

```
az iot hub show-quota-metrics --name azuremol
```

The output is similar to the following example, which shows that 5 messages out of the maximum 8,000 total messages per day have been received, and that there's 1 connected device from a maximum of 500 total devices. It may take a few minutes for these metrics to populate, so don't worry if you don't see any data right away:

```
[
  {
    "currentValue": 5,
    "maxValue": 8000,
    "name": "TotalMessages"
  },
  {
    "currentValue": 1,
    "maxValue": 500,
    "name": "TotalDeviceCount"
  }
]
```


You can also look in the Azure portal: choose your resource group, and then select your IoT hub. On the Overview page, the usage display reports the number of messages received and connected devices. Again, it may take a minute or two before the messages appear and are recorded against the quota. Any applications would be able to immediately use the messages received, as we look at in the next section.

Trouble in paradise

If you don't receive any messages in your IoT hub, check the output window of your simulated Raspberry Pi device. One of the first things the application does is connect to Azure IoT Hub. A connection error is shown if your connection string is wrong. Make sure you correctly copy and paste the entire connection string. The connection string starts with `HostName`, and the last character in every access key is always an equal sign (=).

If the output window reports an error, copy the error text into your favorite search engine and search for a matching result. Make sure you didn't change any of the other lines of code, which would cause a problem! The only thing you need to change in the code window is the line for your connection string.

Because the simulated Raspberry Pi device runs in a web browser, you could have a generic website problem. Try to refresh the page, or access the simulator in a different browser (https://azure-samples.github.io/raspberry-pi-web-simulator).

20.3 Streaming Azure IoT hub data into Azure web apps

A device that connects to an IoT hub isn't useful if you can't do anything with the data. This is where you can start to integrate many of the services and features you've learned about in this book. Want to stream to Azure Storage tables or queues? You can do that. Process data from IoT devices in Azure VMs or containers? Go right ahead! Use Azure Cosmos DB to replicate your data and then access it with globally redundant Azure web apps and Traffic Manager? Sure!

In the example scenario, the IoT hub is the connection mechanism and entry point for your IoT devices into Azure. The hub itself doesn't directly do anything with the data. A default endpoint exists for `events`, which is a big bucket for any messages received from the IoT device. Your simulated Raspberry Pi device sends messages to the IoT hub, which hit this `events` endpoint. The flow of messages from devices through the IoT hub to an endpoint is shown in figure 20.4.

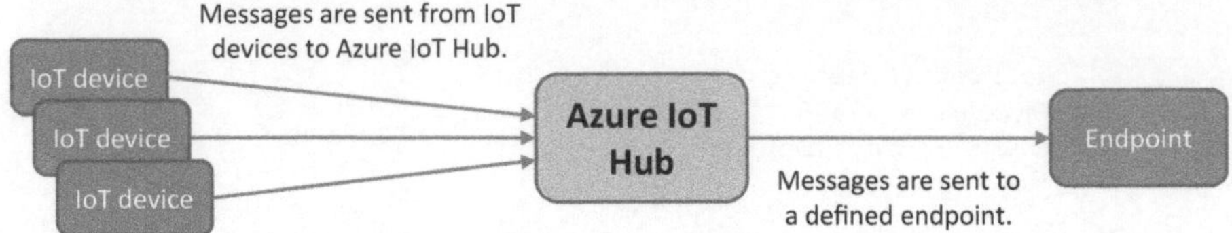

Figure 20.4 An IoT hub receives messages from connected IoT devices and sends the messages to an endpoint. These endpoints can be used by other Azure services to consume data from the IoT devices. A default endpoint for `events` exists, which services like web apps can read from.

You can create custom endpoints that route messages directly to Azure services such as Storage and Service Bus. In chapter 4, we looked at Azure Storage queues for a way to pass messages back and forth between applications. A more robust and scalable enterprise messaging platform is Azure Service Bus. Messages can be added to the service bus, such as data received from IoT devices, and other applications can then listen for these messages and respond accordingly.

If you don't need the complexity of reading messages from a message queue like a service bus, you can use consumer groups with the default `events` endpoint. A consumer group allows services like Azure Web Apps to read data from the endpoint, as shown in figure 20.5.

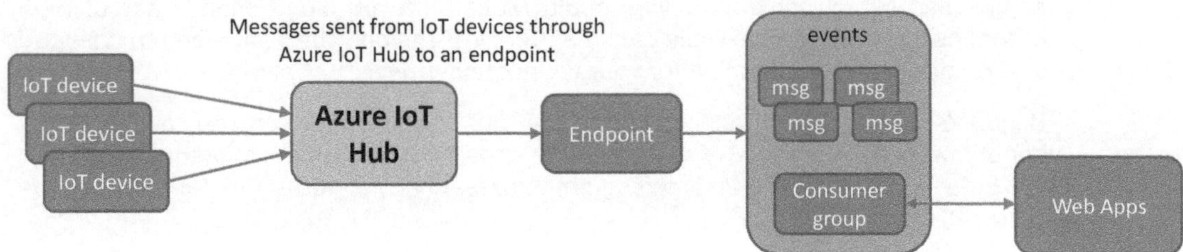

Figure 20.5 Messages are sent from IoT devices to the IoT hub, which then directs the messages to an endpoint. In each endpoint, consumer groups can be created. These consumer groups allow other Azure services to access the device messages, which they otherwise wouldn't have access to. With consumer groups, you don't have to use message queues to allow external applications to read IoT device data.

Let's create an Azure web app that uses a consumer group to read message data in real time from your simulated Raspberry Pi device. This basic example shows how you can stream data from IoT devices and access them from web applications.

> **Try it now**
> To create an Azure web app that reads data from IoT devices, complete the following steps.

1 Create an Azure App Service plan for your web app in the Azure Cloud Shell. Provide a name, such as `azuremol`. For these exercises, the free tier (f1) is good enough and keeps costs down:

```
az appservice plan create \
  --resource-group azuremolchapter20 \
  --name azuremol \
  --sku f1
```

2 Create your web app. Provide a name, such as `molwebapp`, and enable it for use with Git so that you can deploy the sample application:

```
az webapp create \
  --resource-group azuremolchapter20 \
  --plan azuremol \
  --name molwebapp \
  --deployment-local-git
```

3 You need to define the consumer group for your IoT hub, along with some web app application settings. These settings let your web app connect to the IoT hub. Figure 20.6 shows what you build in the next few steps.

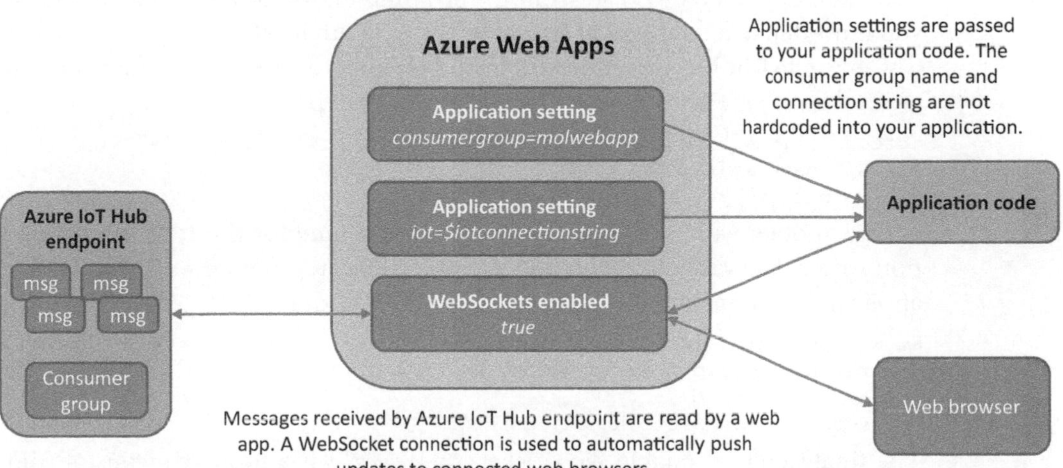

Figure 20.6 To let your web app read the data from your simulated Raspberry Pi IoT device, you create a consumer group in the IoT hub. You then define two application settings for your web app that let you connect to the consumer group. To let your web browser automatically receive the stream of data from the Raspberry Pi as new data is received, you also enable a setting for WebSockets.

4 Create a consumer group that allows your web app to access the event data streamed from your IoT device. Provide your IoT hub, such as `azuremol`, and then enter a name for your consumer group, such as `molwebapp`. Your consumer group is created in the default `events` endpoint:

```
az iot hub consumer-group create \
  --hub-name azuremol \
  --name molwebapp
```

5 You need to tell your web app what the consumer group is called. Create a web app application setting that's used by the sample application you deploy at the end of the exercise. Application settings in web apps allow you to define specific settings, such as the consumer group name and connection string, without those values being hardcoded into your application.

Provide the name of the consumer group created in the preceding step, such as `molwebapp`:

```
az webapp config appsettings set \
  --resource-group azuremolchapter20 \
  --name molwebapp \
  --settings consumergroup=molwebapp
```

6 To connect to the IoT hub, your web app needs to know the connection string for the hub. This connection string is different than the one you copied for your simulated Raspberry Pi device in the previous exercise. Remember, there's a connection string for your IoT hub, which uses shared access policies to define access permissions; and there's a connection string for each IoT device. Your web app needs to read from the IoT hub endpoint consumer group, so you must define a connection string for the IoT hub itself.

Get the IoT hub connection string, and assign it to a variable named `iotconnectionstring`. This variable is used in the next step:

```
iotconnectionstring=$(az iot hub show-connection-string \
  --hub-name azuremol \
  --output tsv)
```

7 Create another web app application setting, this time for the IoT hub connection string. The variable defined in the preceding step is used to let the sample application connect to and read data from the IoT device:

```
az webapp config appsettings set \
  --resource-group azuremolchapter20 \
  --name molwebapp \
  --settings iot=$iotconnectionstring
```

8 The final step is to enable WebSockets. A *WebSocket* is a two-way means of communication between a browser and server. The sample application automatically updates the web browser with the data received from the Raspberry Pi device. To perform this automated update, the application uses WebSockets. The server can then push data to the browser and cause it to automatically update:

```
az webapp config set \
  --resource-group azuremolchapter20 \
  --name molwebapp \
  --web-sockets-enabled
```

Let's pause here and discuss what you've done so far. You've worked with web apps in many of the previous chapters, but the web app application settings and WebSockets are new. Figure 20.7 recaps how your web app and IoT hub are connected.

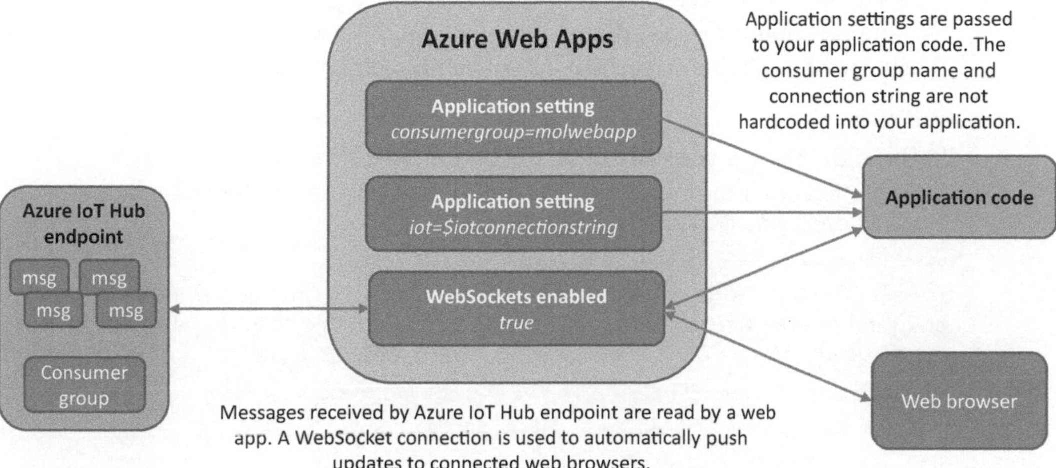

Figure 20.7 As messages are sent from IoT devices, they pass through the IoT hub to an endpoint. Your application code reads in web app application settings that define the IoT hub connection string and consumer group to use. Once connected to the IoT hub, the consumer group allows web apps to read the IoT device messages. Each time a new message is received from an IoT device, your web app uses a WebSocket connection with web browsers that access your site to automatically push updates. This connection allows you to view real-time data streamed from IoT devices, such as temperature and humidity information, from your simulated Raspberry Pi device.

Now let's finish the exercise and deploy the sample application from the GitHub repo to your web app. You can then open the web app in your browser and see the real-time data streamed from your simulated Raspberry Pi!

1 If needed, clone the GitHub samples repo in your Cloud Shell as follows:

```
git clone https://github.com/fouldsy/azure-mol-samples.git
```

2 Change into the directory for chapter 20:

```
cd azure-mol-samples/20
```

3 Initialize the Git repo, and add the basic web page:

```
git init && git add . && git commit -m "Pizza"
```

4 To upload the sample application, create a connection to your web app. The following command gets the web app repository and configures your local samples Git repo to connect to it. In previous chapters, I made you dig around for

this address; but by now I hope you've started to explore what else the Azure CLI can do and realized that much of this information can be quickly obtained:

```
git remote add molwebapp \
  $(az webapp deployment source config-local-git \
  --resource-group azuremolchapter20 \
  --name molwebapp \
  --output tsv)
```

5 Push the HTML sample site to your web app with the following command:

```
git push molwebapp master
```

6 When prompted, enter the password for the Git user you created and have used in previous chapters (the account created in chapter 3).

If you didn't write your Git password on a Post-It note

If you've forgotten the password, you can reset it. First, get the username of your local Git deployment account:

```
az webapp deployment user show --query publishingUserName
```

To reset the password, enter the name of your account from the previous command, and then answer the prompts to set a new password. The following example resets the password for the user account named azuremol:

```
az webapp deployment user set --user-name azuremol
```

7 View the hostname for your web app, and then open the address in a web browser:

```
az webapp show \
  --resource-group azuremolchapter20 \
  --name molwebapp \
  --query defaultHostName \
  --output tsv
```

It may take few seconds the first time that you open the site in your web browser, as the web app connects to the IoT hub, starts the WebSocket connection, and waits for the first device message to be received. Every 2 seconds, the web browser should automatically update with the latest simulated data from the Raspberry Pi device, as shown in figure 20.8.

Figure 20.8 The sample application uses a WebSocket connection between your web browser and web app to automatically update every 2 seconds with the latest data from your simulated Raspberry Pi device.

If your web app instance doesn't show any data, make sure the Raspberry Pi simulated device is still running. If needed, start the simulated device and make sure it connects to Azure IoT and sends messages. The data should then begin to appear in your web app instance.

20.3.1 Azure IoT component review

I hope the exercises in this chapter have given you an idea of what services are available in Azure for IoT solutions:

- *Azure IoT Hub* provides a great way to provision, connect, and manage many IoT devices and then integrate with other Azure services.
- *Azure IoT solution accelerators* provide prebuilt scenarios that automatically integrate many different Azure services to provide a complete application environment.
- *Azure IoT Edge* lets you deploy Azure services in your local environment to process data from IoT devices without the need to stream all the data centrally back to Azure.

To really dig into Azure IoT and IoT devices in general, I recommend that you purchase a basic Raspberry Pi or similar device. They're relatively cheap, often come with a few different basic sensors or electrical components to test out different ideas, and give you a great learning platform as you see what's possible when integrating hardware and software. Just remember the warnings from chapter 17 about AI and ML and building Skynet! Manning also has some excellent books, such as *Building the Web of Things* (Dominique D. Guinard and Vlad M. Trifa, 2016, www.manning.com/books/building-the-web-of-things) and *JavaScript on Things* (Lyza Danger Gardner, 2018, www.manning.com/books/javascript-on-things), that go into more depth on the Raspberry Pi, IoT best practices, and JavaScript and Node.js programming on IoT devices.

Remember how I said to always delete your resource groups?

The best practice throughout this book has been to delete your resource groups at the end of each chapter. This approach makes sure you don't leave services and applications in use that cost money when you don't need them.

Azure IoT gives you a great platform to stream data into Azure. You typically need to process that data, not just display it in a web app as you did in the exercises. Chapter 21 examines serverless computing with the Logic Apps and Functions services.

To show how these Azure services work well together, *don't* delete the resource group and services you deployed in this chapter. You use them right away at the start of the next chapter to see how you can take actions based on the data received from your IoT devices. Just make sure you go back to your simulated Raspberry Pi device and select the Stop button—otherwise, that 8,000-message limit will be used up pretty quickly!

20.4 Lab: Exploring use cases for IoT

This chapter discussed a lot of new stuff, and without a real IoT device, you're limited in what you can do. Chapter 21 builds on Azure IoT Hub and the simulated Raspberry Pi, so I don't want to configure too much more right now. Here are a couple of things you can do to think further about IoT:

1 What areas can you think of where IoT devices could benefit your business? If you don't work in a business right now, think about the fictional Azure Month of Lunches pizza store:
   - a What could you do to improve things for customers with IoT?
   - b Would you use Azure IoT Edge? Why or why not?
   - c What other Azure services would you likely integrate to run your applications?

4 If you have time left in your lunch break, try one of the Azure IoT solution accelerators from www.azureiotsolutions.com/Accelerators. There's a Device Simulation scenario that creates a VM and simulated sensors, which is like the simulated Raspberry Pi device but much bigger! It takes a few minutes to provision all the required resources, but then look around in the Azure portal to see what was created and how all the parts work together:
   - a Can you see how services from earlier chapters, such as Storage and Cosmos DB, are used?
   - b What other IoT solution accelerators are available? Do any of them align with ideas you had for your own applications?

21 Serverless computing

In this final chapter, let's gaze into the future with serverless computing. If you're a developer, the idea of containers that we examined in chapter 19 may have been appealing because there's less of a need to configure the underlying infrastructure for your applications. If so, you're going to love the Azure serverless components! And if you're an IT administrator who suddenly wonders what your job will include if there are no servers in the future, don't worry! *Serverless computing* may be more of a marketing term, and many of the server and infrastructure skills you have continue to apply!

In Azure, two main offerings provide serverless compute features: Azure Logic Apps and Azure Function Apps. In this chapter, we explore what each service offers and how they can work together. To make sure your serverless applications can communicate with each other and pass data around, we also discuss messaging services like Azure Event Grid, Service Bus, and Event Hubs.

21.1 What is serverless computing?

To say that that serverless computing is without a server is just plain wrong—a server, somewhere, runs some code for you. The difference from IaaS application workloads like Azure VMs and PaaS workloads in web apps is that serverless applications are usually broken down into smaller discrete units of an application. You don't run a single, large application; instead, you run bite-sized application components. If this sounds like the containers and microservices that we discussed in chapter 19, don't worry that you're going crazy—serverless computing has a lot of overlap with those topics in terms of how you design your applications. Figure 21.1 shows how an application is broken into small components that run on a serverless computing provider and provide small units of output.

Figure 21.1 In a serverless computing environment, each application is broken down in small, discrete units of application components. Each component runs on a serverless computing provider, such as Azure Function Apps, and output is produced that can then be consumed by other serverless application components or other Azure services such as Azure IoT or Azure Storage.

In Azure, serverless computing covers two primary services:

- *Azure Logic Apps*—To respond to certain inputs and triggers, logic apps let you visually build workflows that can process and generate additional actions in a point-and-click, no-code-required way. Logic apps can be built by users with no programming or IT infrastructure background. A simple logic app outline is shown in figure 21.2.

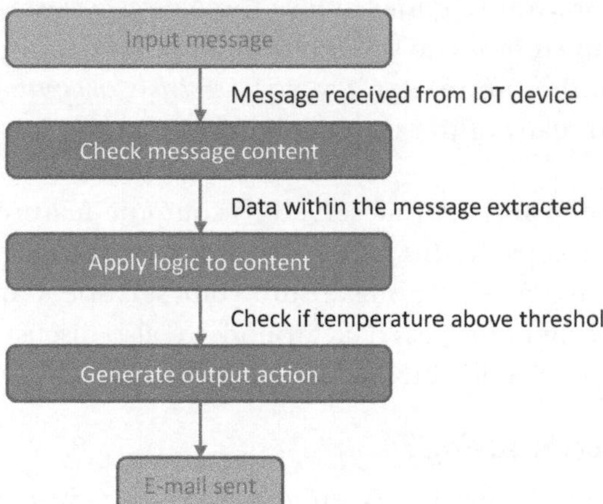

Figure 21.2 In a logic app, an input could be when a tweet is posted, a file is uploaded, or a message is received from an IoT device. The logic app applies rules and filters to the data and determines if the message meets criteria you define. Output actions, such as generating an email, are then completed. All this logic involves no programming or application infrastructure other than an Azure subscription.

There are no security updates to maintain and no design requirements around high availability or the ability to scale. The Azure platform automatically handles this. Hundreds of prebuilt connectors exist for logic apps to integrate with services such as Twitter, Office 365, SharePoint, and Outlook. You can respond to public tweets about your company or product, email an alert when a file is uploaded to SharePoint, or send a notification when a message is received from an IoT device.

- *Azure Function Apps*—To run small blocks of code, function apps let you use common programming languages such as C#, Node.js, or Python without any additional infrastructure management. Your code runs in a secure, isolated environment, and you're billed based on memory consumption per second. Figure 21.3 outlines the basic process for a function app.

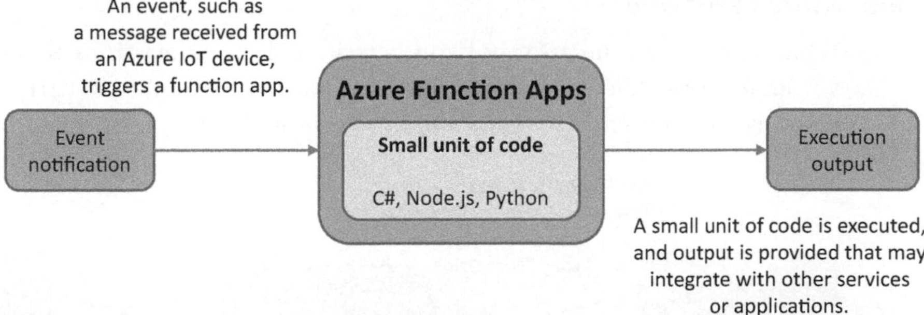

Figure 21.3 As with a logic app, an event notification or trigger usually starts an Azure function. The function app contains a small unit of code that executes a specific task. There's no infrastructure to configure or maintain. Only your small code block is required. Once the code execution is complete, the output can be integrated with another Azure service or application.

There's no VM to maintain, and no web app is required. You don't have to worry about high availability or scale, because the Azure Function Apps service handles this for you. All you provide is your code, and the Azure platform makes sure that whenever you need to run that code, resources are available to process your request.

Logic apps require no code, so they have a wider potential user base. Business application owners or finance and accounting teams, for example, can build their own logic apps without having to write code. Function apps provide more control and flexibility and let you handle events in a specific way and better integrate with other application components.

Both logic apps and function apps provide a way for you to carry out actions based on triggers without having to maintain any application environment or infrastructure. A server somewhere in Azure runs your logic app or function, but from your perspective as the IT administrator or developer, these are serverless technologies.

21.2 Azure messaging platforms

In chapter 12, we looked at how to monitor and troubleshoot Azure resources, and in chapter 16 we saw how to use Azure Security Center to detect issues and perform update management. Both features rely on streams of data, such as the Azure VM diagnostics extension, to inform the platform what's happening in the VM. The Azure diagnostics and monitoring platforms are great, and other services such as Web Apps,

Azure Container Instances, and Azure IoT Hub can also stream service diagnostics for central analysis.

With serverless applications, you often need a way to exchange messages and transmit actual application data, not just troubleshoot diagnostics or status updates. That's when you need a messaging platform.

21.2.1 Azure Event Grid

What if you just want to report on certain actions or activities being completed? In automation workflows and serverless computing, the ability to carry out an action in response to an event is useful, as shown in figure 21.4.

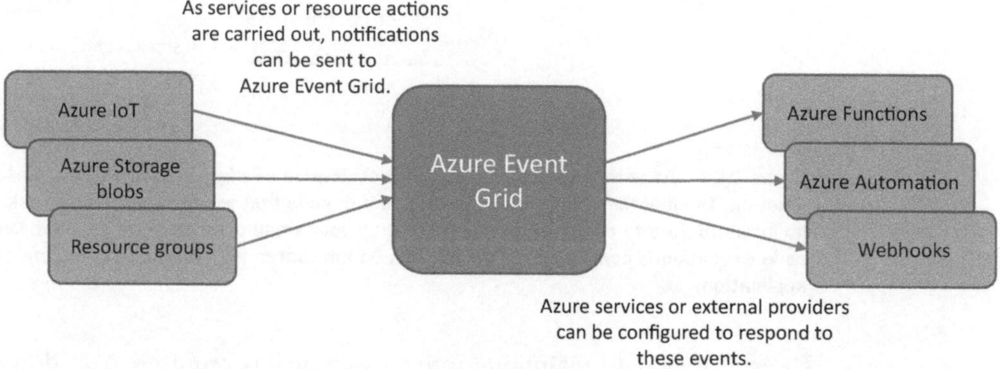

Figure 21.4 Azure services like Azure IoT and Azure Storage can send notifications to Azure Event Grid. These notifications may happen when a message is received from an IoT device or a file is uploaded to storage. Azure Event Grid allows other services and providers to subscribe to these notifications to perform additional actions in response to events.

Let's examine a couple of scenarios that you may be able to use in your pizza store:

- *Message received in an IoT hub*—An IoT device connected to the IoT hub may report a temperature reading in an oven or a delivery vehicle's location. The IoT hub is configured to forward a notification to Azure Event Grid.

  An Azure function is subscribed to the Event Grid notifications for the IoT hub and runs a small serverless application component to log the information to Cosmos DB and send an email notification. You could also use logic apps instead of Azure function apps, depending on how complex the application response needs to be.
- *File uploaded to Azure storage*—The marketing department may upload to storage a promotional coupon to save money on a pizza order. When a new file is created, a notification is sent to Event Grid.

  A webhook is subscribed to Event Grid and posts a copy of the image from storage to Twitter. This tweet lets customers know about the deal of the week or money-saving coupon.

These scenarios are for truly hands-off serverless computing scenarios, but Event Grid can also integrate with more traditional resources such as VMs and web apps. For example, a resource group can be configured to send notifications to Event Grid. There are many ways to create a VM, such as in the portal, with the Azure CLI, or with a Resource Manager template, so you want to make sure the VM is correctly configured for Update Management through Security Center. An Azure Automation runbook could be subscribed to Event Grid for notifications about VM create operations and would then on-board the VM to the Update Management service and install required security or application updates.

21.2.2 Azure Event Hubs and Service Bus

Event Grid can work with many Azure resources, and it's well-suited to serverless computing with logic apps or function apps. But logic apps and function apps can run based on other data inputs, such as event hubs or a service bus. Let's look at the differences between these various messaging services so that you can best decide when to use them:

- Azure Event Hub lets you receive a stream of data, such as from IoT devices or application telemetry. Event hubs provide a low-latency messaging platform capable of handling millions of events per second from multiple concurrent providers. The data received in the event hub can then be processed by other services, as shown in figure 21.5.

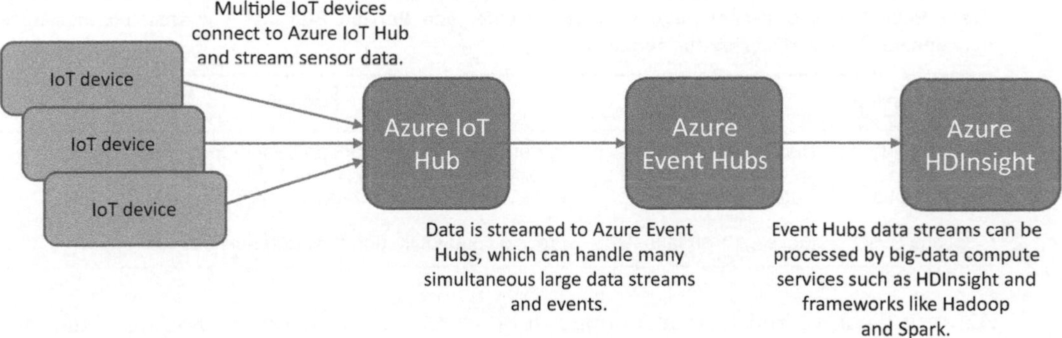

Figure 21.5 IoT devices connect to the IoT hub and can stream all their sensor data. There could be hundreds or thousands of connected IoT devices. Azure Event Hubs handles all these separate data streams and allows services such as Azure HDInsight to process the raw data in Hadoop or Spark clusters to analyze and generate reports.

Azure Service Bus allows application components to exchange message data, such as the storage queues that we examined in chapter 4. Storage queues are an earlier, more basic implementation of a messaging platform in Azure. A service bus provides more advanced features such as guaranteed ordering of messages, atomic operations, and sending messages in batches. Figure 21.6 outlines a common scenario for a service bus.

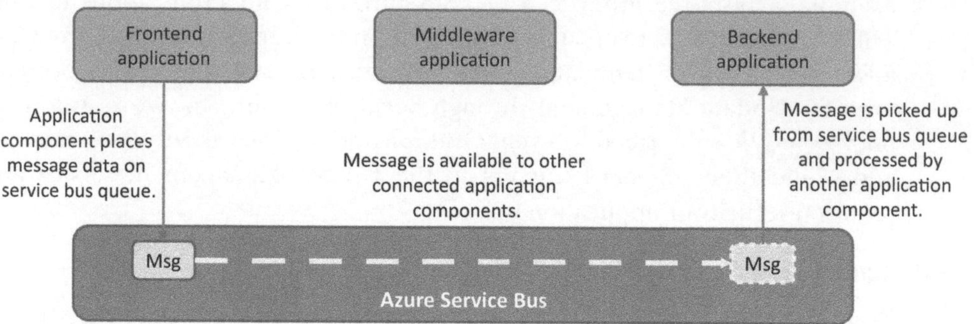

Figure 21.6 Messages are placed in a service bus queue by application components—a frontend app, in this example. Other middleware or backend applications can then pick up these messages and process them as needed. Here, a backend application picks up the message and processes it. Advanced messaging features include guaranteeing the order of messages on the queue, locking messages, timeouts, and relays.

With three services that let you transmit, receive, and process data between applications and services in Azure, which one do you use and when? Table 21.1 provides a high-level recap of the Event Grid, Event Hubs, and Service Bus services.

Table 21.1 Each service is designed to cover a different scenario. Event Grid lets you react to events, Event Hubs lets you stream large amounts of data, and Service Bus lets you transmit messages between services and application components.

Azure service	Provides	Use case
Event Grid	Distribution of events	Perform an additional action based on an event occurrence.
Event Hubs	Data streams	Receive and transmit large volumes of concurrent data.
Service Bus	Message transmission	Provide communication between services and apps.

Azure logic apps and function apps can be trigged by all three messaging platforms. Let's create a service bus that can be used to trigger a logic app.

21.2.3 *Creating a service bus and integrating it with an IoT hub*

In this scenario, you use a service bus to transmit messages received from an IoT hub. Your simulated Raspberry Pi device from the previous chapter generates temperature readings and transmits those to the IoT hub. If the temperature is higher than 30°C, another piece of data is included in the message from the IoT device: `temperatureAlert = true`. Figure 21.7 outlines how you can integrate an IoT hub with the service bus to process messages with this temperature alert.

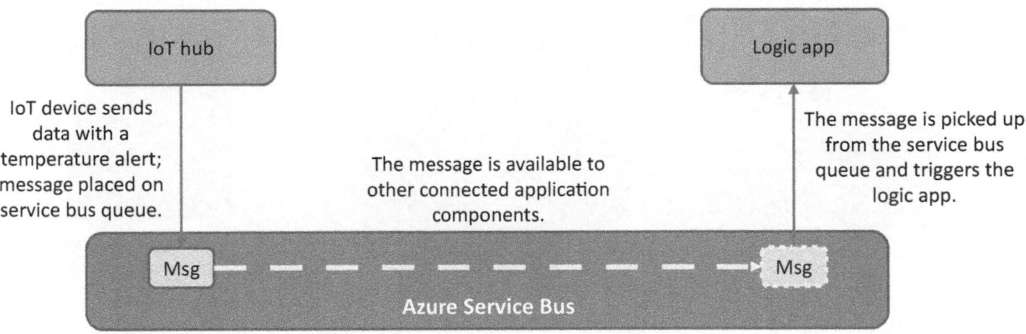

Figure 21.7 When your simulated Raspberry Pi IoT device sends message data, a temperature reading of 30°C or more generates an alert. Messages tagged with this alert are placed on a service bus. These messages can then be used to trigger logic apps.

> **Try it now**
> To create a service bus, complete the following steps.

1. Open the Azure portal, and select Create a Resource at upper left in the menu.
2. Search for and select Service Bus, and then choose Create.
3. Provide a name, such as `azuremol`, and then select the Basic pricing tier.
4. Choose Create New Resource Group, and provide a name, such as `azuremol-chapter21`. Make sure the location is the same as for the resources created in chapter 20, such as East US. The interaction between a service bus queue, a logic app, and a function app may have issues if you aren't consistent with your locations. Leave the other defaults, and choose Create.
5. Once the resource has been created, select your resource group, and then choose the service bus you created in the previous step. Select Queue, and then enter a name, such as `azuremol`. Leave all the other defaults, and choose Create.

With a service bus and a queue created, how do you configure an IoT hub to use them? In the IoT hub, you define *endpoints* as the destination for messages received from IoT devices. A default endpoint exists in the IoT hub for all messages that don't meet the defined criteria. You can configure the service bus as an endpoint to receive messages. A *route* is then defined that includes criteria for which messages should be directed to an endpoint. In this example, that route requires any message that contains `temperatureAlert = true` in the message body to be routed to the service bus endpoint, as shown in figure 21.8.

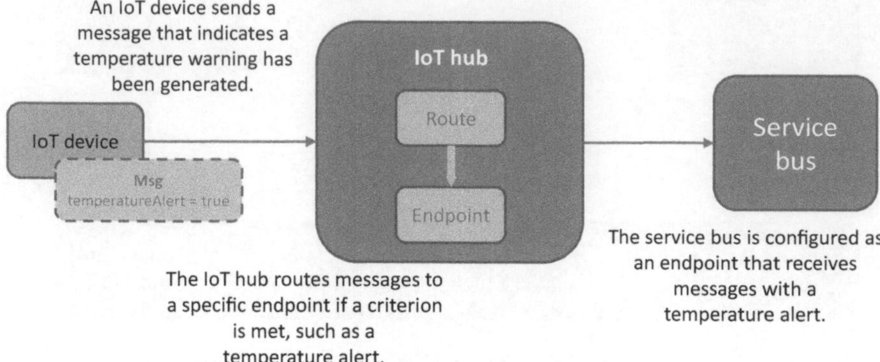
An IoT device sends a message that indicates a temperature warning has been generated.
IoT hub
Route
Endpoint
IoT device
Msg
temperatureAlert = true
Service bus
The service bus is configured as an endpoint that receives messages with a temperature alert.
The IoT hub routes messages to a specific endpoint if a criterion is met, such as a temperature alert.

Figure 21.8 As messages are transmitted from IoT devices to an IoT hub, they can be routed to specific endpoints based on criteria you define. Messages that contain a temperature alert in the message body can be routed to an endpoint that uses the service bus queue. Messages placed on the service bus queue that contain a temperature alert can then be used to trigger things like Azure logic apps or function apps.

Try it now

To configure an IoT hub to route temperature alert messages to the service bus, complete the following steps.

1. Select your resource group from the previous chapter, such as `azuremol-chapter20`, and then choose the IoT hub.
2. Under Messaging in the navigation bar on the left, select Endpoints. Choose Add an Endpoint.
3. Provide an endpoint name, such as `azuremol`, and then select Service Bus Queue from the Type drop-down menu.
4. Select your service bus queue namespace, such as `azuremol`, and then your actual queue.
5. To direct messages to this endpoint, create a route. Under Messaging in the navigation bar on the left, select Routes. Choose Add a Route.
6. Provide a name, such as `temperatureAlert`. Set Data Source to Device Messages, and then select the endpoint created in the previous step, such as `azuremol`.
7. In the Query string text box, enter the following:

   ```
   temperatureAlert = "true"
   ```
8. Your route should look like the example shown in figure 21.9. When you're finished, select Save.

You now have a simulated Raspberry Pi device that sends data to the IoT hub, and a route to place messages that contain a temperature alert on a service bus message queue. You don't really have an application yet—there's nothing you can do with the

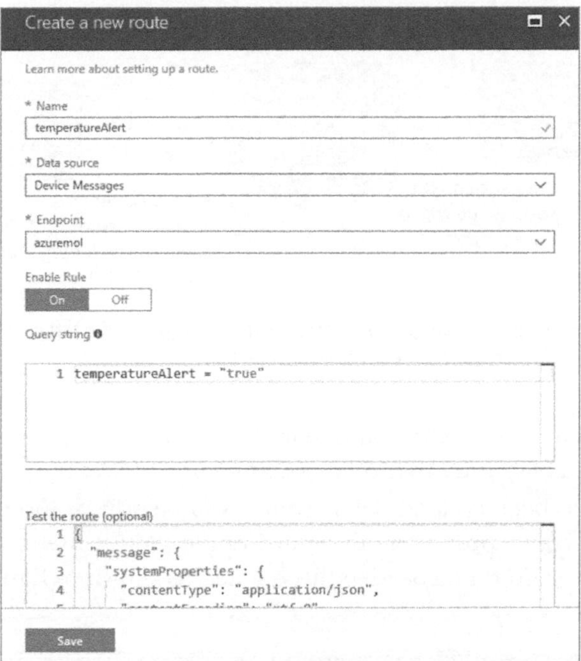

Figure 21.9 Select your service bus endpoint, and then enter the query string that gets any message received from IoT devices tagged with a temperature alert.

data on the service bus queue. What might you want to do with a temperature alert? Sending an email notification is a common example, so let's see how you can trigger a logic app each time a message is placed on the service bus queue.

21.3 Creating an Azure logic app

As you saw when we discussed logic apps earlier in the chapter, a message received from a service bus queue can be used as a trigger to start the execution process. You use the IoT hub to process the messages received from IoT devices and only route to the service bus queue endpoint messages that contain `temperatureAlert = true` in the message body. With this approach, your logic app only runs when a temperature alert is generated.

Figure 21.10 outlines what your logic app does. When a message is placed on the service bus queue, the logic app runs and sends an email alert.

> **Try it now**
> To create a logic app, complete the following steps.

1. In the Azure portal, select Create a Resource at upper left in the menu.
2. Search for and select Logic App, and then choose Create.

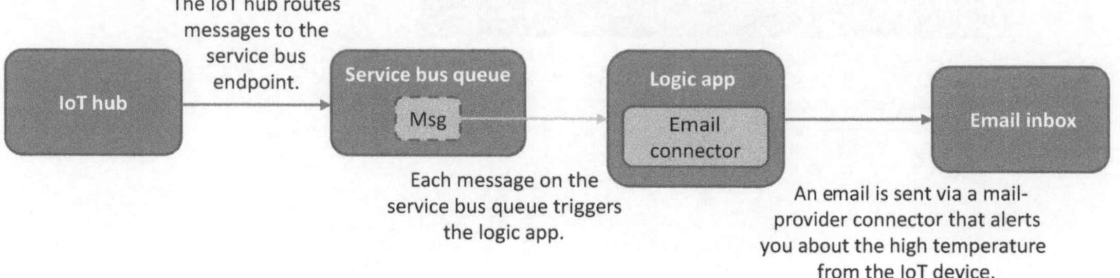

Figure 21.10 Each message received on the service bus queue from the IoT hub triggers the logic app. When the logic app runs, it sends an email notification through a defined mail provider.

3. Provide a name, such as `azuremol`, and select your resource group, such as `azuremolchapter21`. Leave the other defaults, and choose Create.
4. Once the resource has been created, select your resource group, and then open the logic app. The Logic Apps Designer wizard opens. Select the template for "When a message is received in a Service Bus queue," as shown in figure 21.11.

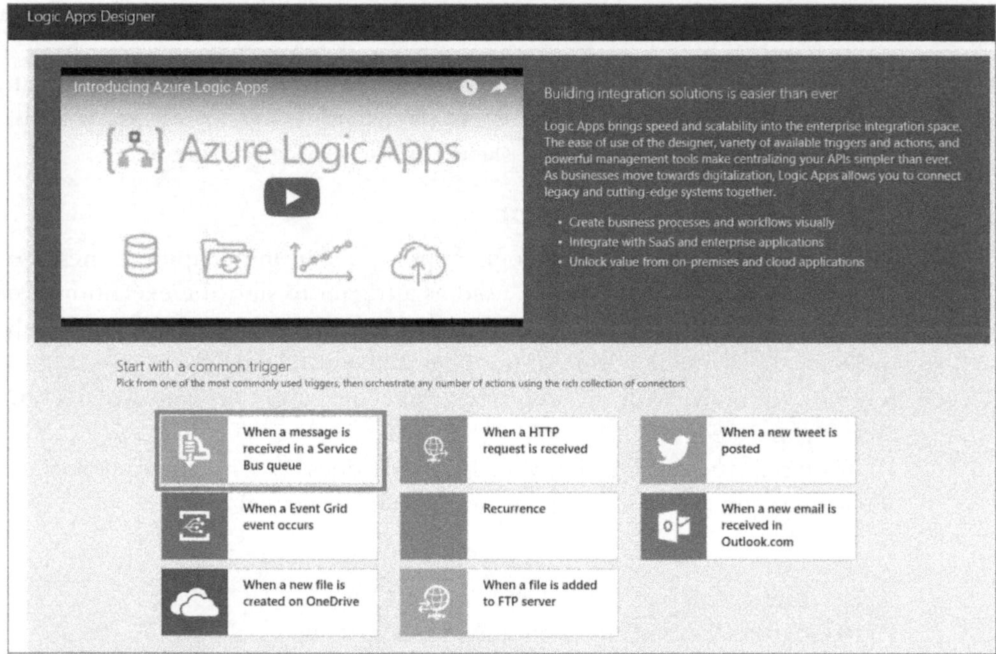

Figure 21.11 To get started with your logic app, select the template for "When a message is received in the Service Bus queue."

5 Select Create, and then provide a name, such as `azuremol`. Choose your service bus queue, such as azuremol, and then choose Create, as shown in figure 21.12.

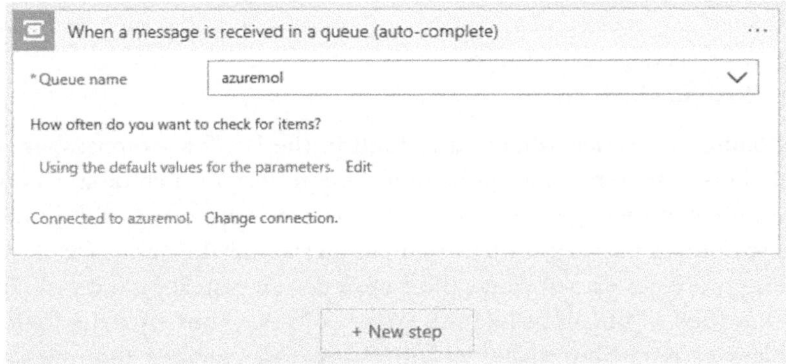

Figure 21.12 Enter a name for your service bus connection, and select your queue from the Connection Name list. Then, select the RootManageSharedAccessKey connection name, and choose Create.

6 Select Continue, and then choose your service bus queue name, such as azuremol. Choose New Step.

7 To add an action, search for *email*. Select your provider, such as Gmail - Send an Email, Outlook.com - Send an Email, or SMTP - Send an Email, as shown in figure 21.13.

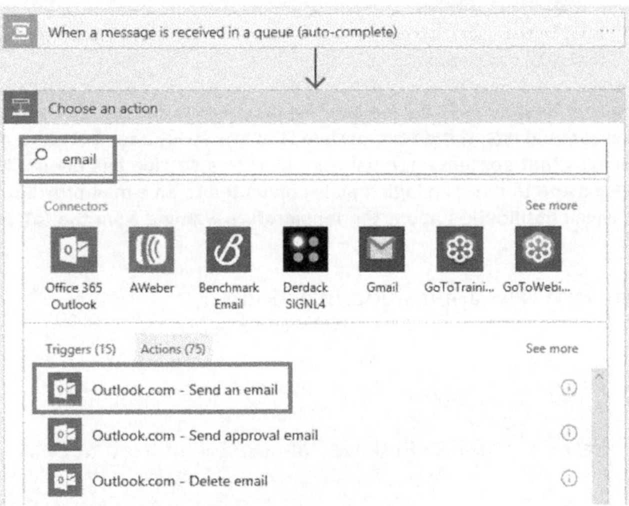

Figure 21.13 Search for and select your current email provider, such as Gmail or Outlook.com. You can also choose SMTP - Send an Email to manually configure a different provider.

8 Sign in to your email provider to authorize mail routing and confirm that you wish to grant logic apps permissions to send email.
9 Provide a recipient email address at which you receive email; an email subject, such as `Temperature alert`; and a message body, such as `High temperature detected on IoT device`.
10 Save the logic app.

Let's pause and review what you've built in the last few exercises, as shown in figure 21.14. This basic serverless application design doesn't include any controls that limit the number of messages to be sent. In the logic app, you could define that you only want to send a maximum of five e-mail alerts and then wait for 30 minutes before sending more. As part of your application design, you should consider how you want to be notified of situations like this. You could also configure the logic app to read in the message data from the service bus queue and include the timestamp of the IoT device message and the actual recorded temperature. We discuss how to do this in the next exercise.

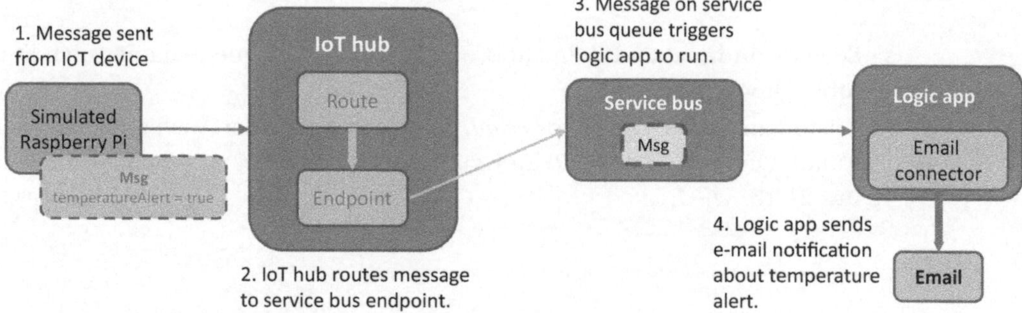

Figure 21.14 The simulated Raspberry Pi device sends a message to the IoT hub every 2 seconds that contains temperature sensor readings. If the temperature is above 30°C, a temperature alert is noted. The IoT hub routes any messages that contain a temperature alert to a service bus queue. Messages on this queue trigger an Azure logic app to run. The logic app is connected to an e-mail provider, such as Outlook or Gmail, and sends an e-mail notification about the temperature warning from the IoT device.

Let's see this basic serverless application in action.

> **Try it now**
> To run your simulated Raspberry Pi device and test your logic app, complete the following steps.

1 Open a web browser to the simulated Raspberry Pi IoT device from the previous chapter: https://azure-samples.github.io/raspberry-pi-web-simulator. Verify

that your IoT hub connection string is still added in the code window. Choose Run the App.

2. Simulated temperature and humidity sensor readings are generated every 2 seconds, and a message is sent to the IoT hub. It may take a few messages before a simulated temperature reading of 30°C is generated and shown in the output window.

   The IoT hub routes any messages that contain `temperatureAlert: true` to the service bus endpoint. As these messages are placed on the service bus queue, the logic app picks them up and sends an email through the defined provider. You then receive an email to notify you of a high temperature reading. This process should only take a few seconds, end to end.
3. The simulated Raspberry Pi device generates messages every 2 seconds, so stop the app unless you like a lot of email alerts!

When you receive email alerts, the message doesn't contain a lot of information. Your logic app doesn't extract the message contents from the service bus and format the information. It would be great if the alert email could include the IoT device name or the temperature recorded. How can you process each message and perform some analysis on it? What about the other Azure serverless component we looked at—Azure function apps?

21.4 Creating an Azure function app to analyze IoT device data

To extend your current serverless application, you can trigger an Azure function app from within your logic app. Message data from the service bus can be sent to a function app for analysis of the recorded temperature. The email notification sent by the logic app can then include information about the IoT device name and the recorded temperature. The interaction between the logic app and the function app is shown in figure 21.15.

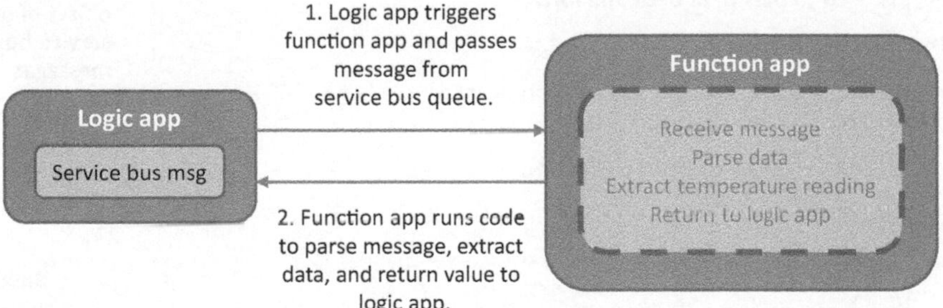

Figure 21.15 The logic app triggers the function app. The message received on the service bus queue is passed into the function. Code in the function app parses the message, extracts the temperature, and returns that value to the logic app. It takes a few milliseconds for the function app to run this code, so the cost to performing these compute tasks is fractions of a cent.

> **Try it now**
> To create a function app and trigger it from the logic app, complete the following steps.

1. In the Azure portal, select Create a Resource at upper left in the menu.
2. Search for and select Function App, and then choose Create.
3. Provide a name, such as `azuremol`, and select your resource group, such as `azuremolchapter21`. Leave the OS as Windows.
4. There are two Hosting Plan options. A Consumption Plan lets you pay per execution, and the resources you require are dynamically assigned at runtime. For more consistent, production-ready applications, you can use an App Service Plan that provides a fixed, predictable cost.

   Choose use a Consumption Plan, and then make sure you select the same region as your logic app, such as East US.
5. Leave the other defaults to create a named storage account, and then choose Create.
6. It takes a minute or two to create the function app. Once the resource has been created, select your resource group, open your logic app, and select Edit.
7. In the Logic App Designer, select New Step, and then choose to add an action.
8. Search for and select Azure Functions, and then choose the function created in the previous steps, such as `azuremol`. Choose Create New Function.
9. Provide a function name, such as `analyzeTemperature`. Delete any existing code, replace it with the code from the following listings, and then choose Create.

Listing 21.1 `analyzeTemperature` Javascript code for a function app

```
module.exports = function (context, data) {

  var buffer = new Buffer(data.ContentData, 'base64')
  var decodedString = buffer.toString();

  var objects = JSON.parse(decodedString);

  var temperature = objects["temperature"];

  context.res = {
    body: {
      analysis: "Recorded temperature was  " + temperature + "!"
    }
  };

  context.log("Recorded temperature was " + temperature);

  context.done();
};
```

- Every JavaScript function app starts with exporting a function that contains a context object. This context object is used to pass data back and forth.
- Reads in message content from the service bus
- Decodes from base64
- Creates a JSON object of decoded service bus messages
- Extracts the recorded temperature from the IoT device
- Builds a response to send back to the Logic App
- Outputs the temperature to the console log
- Every JavaScript function app must end with a call to context.done, which tells the function app that your code is finished.

10 Back in the Logic App Designer for your function step, select the Request Body text box, and then choose Service Bus Message.
11 In the Logic App Designer, drag and drop to reorder the steps so that the Send an Email action is below the analyzeTemperature function app step, as shown in figure 21.16.
12 Select the Send an Email action, and then choose the text box for the Body of the email message.
13 From the analyzeTemperature function, select the Body response, as shown in figure 21.16.

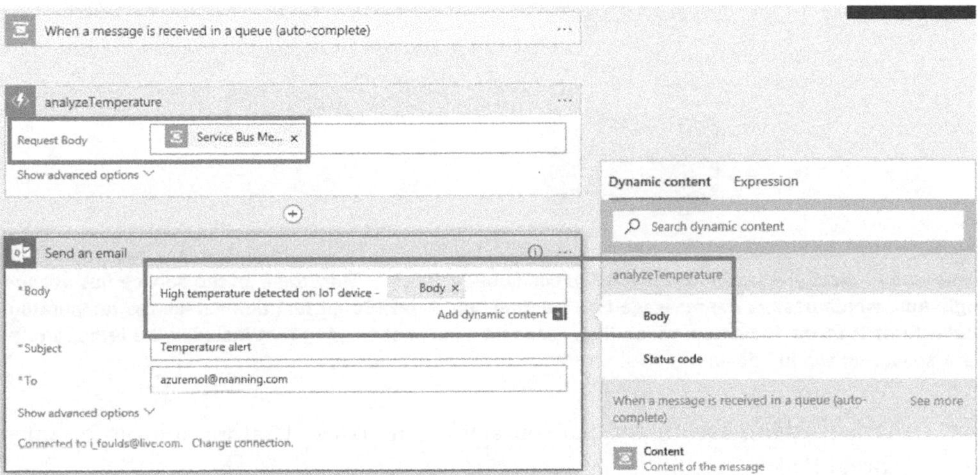

Figure 21.16 Drag the Send an Email action below the analyzeTemperature function. Select the end of the message Body, and the Dynamic content dialog appears. To insert the temperature value computed by the function app, select the message Body from the analyzeTemperature function.

14 In the Logic App Designer, select Save.

Your serverless application has a lot of moving parts. Let's examine what you've built before you run the simulated Raspberry Pi IoT device to generate email alerts that include the temperature reading as computed by the function app. Figure 21.17 provides an overview of all the components now in use in the serverless application.

15 Open your simulated Raspberry Pi device in a web browser, and run the application. Each time the temperature alert is generated, the logic app triggers the function app to extract the temperature data from the message body and include that in the email notification. It may take a few moments for a temperature reading to be higher than 30°C that then flags the message with a temperature alert. When that alert is set and the messaged is processed, you receive an email notification that reports what that temperature was.

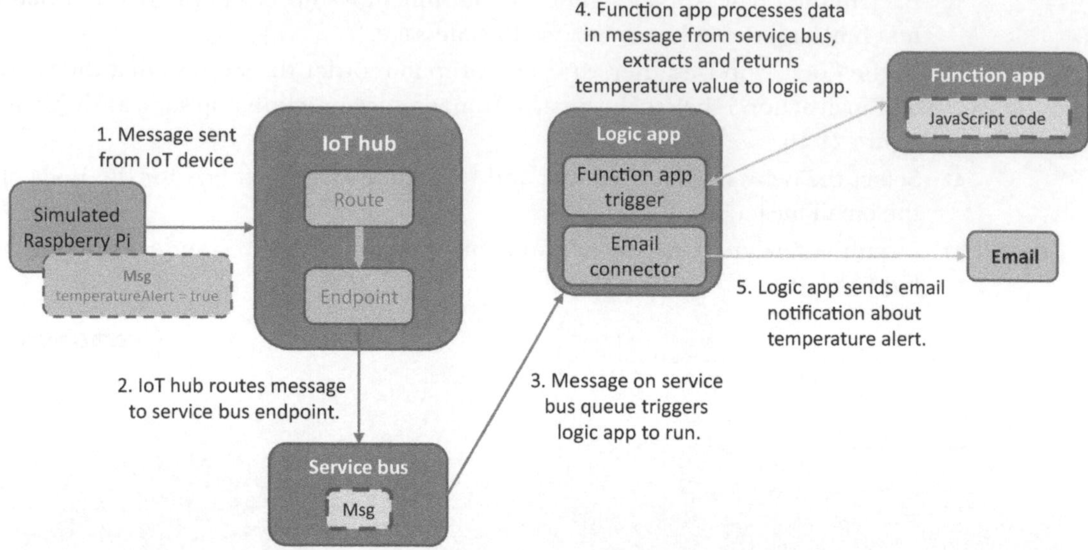

Figure 21.17 As messages are received from the simulated Raspberry Pi device, any messages that contain a temperature alert are routed to the service bus queue endpoint. Messages on the service bus queue trigger a logic app, which passes the message to a function app. A JavaScript function parses the temperature reading and returns it to the logic app, which then sends an e-mail notification that includes the temperature recorded by a sensor on the IoT device.

Take a deep breath and pat yourself on the back. That was a lot to do on your lunch break!

21.5 Don't stop learning

This chapter contained a lot of new concepts. In fact, the last few chapters have contained many new ideas and technologies! Don't worry if you're struggling to understand how you can begin to implement all these Azure services, such as containers, AI and ML, and serverless computing. These chapters were to show you what's possible in Azure and that you don't need to be limited to performing a lift and shift of legacy applications. As you start to build and run applications in Azure, take the opportunity to modernize applications and review management or deployment workflows. There are many Azure services that simplify and speed up the application lifecycle, so don't feel like you have to stick with running VMs because that's what the business is comfortable using.

Yes, Azure offers lots of new, shiny services, but they all largely build on core infrastructure components that were discussed in the main chapters earlier in this book. Developers can start to use the latest application design approaches that involve Kubernetes or serverless computing, and admins can reuse their on-premises datacenter knowledge with cloud computing fundamentals and troubleshooting techniques. As your business needs grow, Azure can support them.

In chapter 1, I was open and honest stating that I wouldn't cover every service in Azure. There are many more Azure services to learn about and more depth to get into about the services we did look at in the book. I hope you've found at least a few areas that interest you and motivate you to explore some more. My favorites include virtual machine scale sets, Cosmos DB, and Azure Kubernetes Service.

21.5.1 Additional learning materials

I'm biased, but a great place to continue learning about Azure is https://docs.microsoft .com/azure. All the core Azure service documentation, architecture guides, reference and SDK resources, and samples are there. Each Azure service has its own set of quick-starts, tutorials, and samples, along with conceptual information and individual how-to guides.

If you get serious, there are certification options for Azure. Individual exams include *Implementing Microsoft Azure Infrastructure Solutions* (70-533) and *Developing Microsoft Azure Solutions* (70-532). These exams can count toward wider certification paths such as the *Microsoft Certified Solutions Expert (MCSE) in Cloud Platform and Infrastructure*, and there are even Linux-focused certifications such as *Managing Linux Workloads on Azure* (70-539).

21.5.2 GitHub resources

Throughout this book, you've used code samples, templates, and sample applications from https://github.com/fouldsy/azure-mol-samples. These samples should stay updated as new versions of the Azure CLI are released, and the GitHub repo also includes PowerShell examples and templates for all the exercises. This book focused on the Azure CLI in the Azure Cloud Shell, but feel free to explore what each exercise looks like in PowerShell or a template.

If you notice any problems with the samples, please create an issue in GitHub at https://github.com/fouldsy/azure-mol-samples/issues. Things move fast in Azure, and I want to make sure you always have the latest, working samples to help you learn. Feel free to make suggestions, too! All the Azure docs from https://docs.microsoft .com/azure also accept feedback, issues, and edits, so as you explore the rest of what's on offer in Azure, feel free to get involved and help others learn and grow.

21.5.3 One final thought

Take a deep breath and realize that change is now normal. New features and services release almost daily. Azure, like all major cloud computing providers, may look and feel ever-so-slightly different than the last time you used it (an hour ago). If you have the core fundamental skills and understanding that you've hopefully learned in this book, you can adapt and grow with all the new opportunities Azure offers. You always have something new to learn, and I'd love to hear what you end up building and running in Azure!

index

E

F

G

H

I

J

K

L

T

U

V

W

Z

MORE TITLES FROM MANNING

Amazon Web Services in Action, Second Edition
by Michael Wittig and Andreas Wittig

ISBN: 9781617295119
528 pages
$54.99
September 2018

Learn Amazon Web Services in a Month of Lunches
by David Clinton

ISBN: 9781617294440
328 pages
$39.99
August 2017

Google Cloud Platform in Action
by JJ Geewax

ISBN: 9781617293528
632 pages
$59.99
September 2018

For ordering information go to www.manning.com